Law, Narrative and Masterplot

The book brings together a range of socio-legal and law and humanities scholars to elaborate and explore the idea of the legal 'masterplot'.

There is a class of narrative, sometimes referred to as 'masterplot' or 'metanarrative', that stands above the plethora of other stories, plots, and myths that may be found in law. This book focuses on the masterplot concept as providing a productive yet largely under-explored way of seeing, understanding, and responding to legal controversies and socio-legal problems. Masterplots may be understood as those prevalent and enduring ideas and narratives that form the basis of expectations, assumptions, stereotypes, and prejudices. In legal contexts, masterplots give shape and significance to particular experiences or issues. In aligning with them, legal arguments, judgments, and reforms gain acceptability and can be presented as authoritative, proportionate, and legitimate. Reflecting, from different legal perspectives and subdisciplines, on the masterplots at play in our current legal frameworks, this collection illuminates the often-hidden ways in which law functions.

This book will appeal to students and scholars of socio-legal studies, sociology, social policy, and humanities approaches to law.

Chris Bevan is Professor of Property Law, National University of Singapore, Singapore.

David Gurnham is Professor of Criminal Law and Interdisciplinary Legal Studies, University of Southampton, UK.

Law, Narrative and Masterplot

New Research Perspectives

Edited by Chris Bevan and
David Gurnham

Routledge
Taylor & Francis Group
a GlassHouse Book

First published 2025
by Routledge
4 Park Square, Milton Park, Abingdon, Oxon OX14 4RN

and by Routledge
605 Third Avenue, New York, NY 10158

Routledge is an imprint of the Taylor & Francis Group, an informa business

A GlassHouse book

British Library Cataloguing-in-Publication Data
A catalogue record for this book is available from the British Library

Library of Congress Cataloging-in-Publication Data
Names: Bevan, Chris, editor. | Gurnham, David, editor.
Title: Law, narrative, and masterplot: new research perspectives / edited by Chris Bevan and David Gurnham.
Description: Abingdon, Oxon [UK]; New York, NY: Routledge, 2025. | Includes bibliographical references and index.
Identifiers: LCCN 2024062008 (print) | LCCN 2024062009 (ebook)| ISBN 9781032519647 (hardback) | ISBN 9781032519661 (paperback) | ISBN 9781003404668 (ebook)
Subjects: LCSH: Forensic orations. | Law – Interpretation and construction. | Sociological jurisprudence. | Law – Philosophy.
Classification: LCC K181 .L39 2025 (print) | LCC K181 (ebook) | DDC 340/.1 – dc23/eng/20250113
LC record available at https://lccn.loc.gov/2024062008
LC ebook record available at https://lccn.loc.gov/2024062009

ISBN: 978-1-032-51964-7 (hbk)
ISBN: 978-1-032-51966-1 (pbk)
ISBN: 978-1-003-40466-8 (ebk)

DOI: 10.4324/9781003404668

Typeset in Sabon
by Apex CoVantage, LLC

Contents

Contributors

Chris Bevan, Professor in Property Law, National University of Singapore, Singapore

Steven Cammiss, Associate Professor in Law, University of Birmingham, UK

Julie Doughty, Senior Lecturer in Law, School of Law and Politics, Cardiff University, UK

David Gurnham, Professor, School of Law, University of Southampton, UK

Graeme Hayes, Reader in Political Sociology, School of Law and Social Sciences, Aston University, UK

Andy Hayward, Associate Professor in Family Law, Durham Law School, UK

Chris Hilson, Professor, School of Law, University of Reading, UK

Nina H. B. Jørgensen, Professor of Public International Law, School of Law, University of Southampton, UK

Lynsey Mitchell, Lecturer in Law, University of Strathclyde, Glasgow, UK

Luke P. Norris, Professor, School of Law, University of Richmond, USA

Rebecca Probert, Professor of Law, Law School, University of Exeter, UK

Rebecca Shaw, Lecturer in Law, School of Law, University of Leeds, UK

Allison Tait, Professor, School of Law, University of Richmond, USA

Richard Walsh, Professor of Narrative Studies, Department of English and Related Literature, University of York, UK

Ekaterina Yahyaoui Krivenko, Senior Lecturer in Human Rights, Irish Centre for Human Rights, School of Law, University of Galway, Ireland

Acknowledgements

We want to thank all those involved in the wider 'Law and Masterplot' project, including our fantastic contributors and colleagues at Southampton and Durham, who, in multiple ways, assisted thoughtfully and generously with the project's development. A massive thank-you also to the Socio-Legal Studies Association (SLSA) for providing funding for two workshops at our respective institutions, which served both to energise and shape this collection.

Chris would like to thank his family for their unwavering love and support.

David likewise.

Part 1

What are masterplots in law?

Chapter 1

Law, narrative, and masterplot

An introduction

Chris Bevan and David Gurnham

1 What are *legal masterplots*?

'Masterplot' is a term that has been oddly neglected in narrative legal studies hitherto and that is consequently now ripe for detailed consideration. H. Porter Abbott used it over two decades ago to denote 'stories that we tell over and over in myriad forms and that connect vitally with our deepest values, wishes, and fears',[1] and since that time, it has, to a limited extent, found its way into discussions of legal narratives. However, there remain significant areas of legal study in which the term has before now *never* appeared, and even in narrative studies more broadly, its existence is a matter of some doubt. There is no entry for it in the *Oxford English Dictionary* (online April 2024), or in the 2020 edition of Gerald Prince's *Dictionary of Narratology*. The former does recognise 'grand narrative' ('a story in accordance with a particular ideology'),[2] and the latter 'primary narrative' ('introduces [an]other narrating instance and is not itself introduced by any').[3] Both dictionaries additionally have 'metanarrative' ('a narrative referring to itself and to those elements by which it is constituted and communicated') and 'myth' ('a traditional narrative . . . that expresses and justifies an exemplary aspect of the way things are').[4] All these represent seeds of the concept at the heart of this book, but all are also somewhat adjacent to it in important respects.

'Masterplot' invites evaluation of two key qualities, which we will begin this introduction by exploring in the context of *legal* masterplots. The first of these is that as an apparent species of *plot*, it is likely to be closely related to

1 H. Porter Abbott, 'The Rhetoric of Narrative' in *The Cambridge Introduction to Narrative* (1st edn, CUP 2002) 42. That is not to say that Porter Abbot *coined* the term: Porter Abbott discerned 'implicit endorsement of [his] use of the term' (43) in the earlier work of Peter Brooks, specifically Brooks's 1977 essay 'Freud's Masterplot', which we discuss further in later text.

2 *'Narrative (n.)', Oxford English Dictionary* (March 2024) <www.oed.com/dictionary/narrative_n?tab=meaning_and_use#35345750> accessed 11 April 2024.

3 Gerald Prince, *A Dictionary of Narratology* (Nebraska University Press 2020) 95.

4 As described by Prince (n 3) 67, 72.

DOI: 10.4324/9781003404668-2

(if not synonymous with) *narrative*. The second is that the plot or narrative in question claims (at least some degree of) authority over other ostensibly similar plots or narratives.

1.1 Legal masterplots as legal narratives

To the extent that masterplots find their family resemblance primarily in *narrative*, they are recognisable as one species of the many ways in which relevant facts, ideas, opinions about the world may be related, accounted for, recounted, and generally *made known* (the Latin stem *narrare* literally meaning 'to make acquainted with' and traceable back to the Latin *gnarus* – 'knowing'[5]). There is thus a sense in which narrative serves as a crucial and fundamental intermediary between the world and people, and the way in which people come to know the world within social groups. Modern definitions emphasise the *ordering* quality of narrative; for example, the OED has it as an 'account of a series of events, facts, etc., given *in order and with the establishing of connections between them*'.[6] *Narrative* represents a means by which otherwise disparate or undigested information is made sense of by being brought into relation with one another and thus converted into a form that can be transmitted usefully between individuals, communities, generations. Narrat*ive* typically requires a narrat*or* and a narrat*ee* and, in this respect, arguably prioritises the 'humanness' of the relations established between elements: the particular characteristics and limitations of the narrator and the narratee; the contingent, temporal, and unfinished quality of a personal story; and its embodied and affective aspects. For Greta Olson, these are aspects of narrative that make it particularly suitable for addressing issues around marginalisation and victimisation.[7]

An initial hesitation that comes when moving across from narrative studies to *legal* narratives (and from there to an account of masterplot as a notion arising from narrative studies) is that the former credits a given text as a narrative *only* if it describes *events*. H. Porter Abbott describes this requirement as a 'bare minimum':

> 'My dog has fleas' is a description of my dog, but it is not a narrative because nothing happens. 'My dog was bitten by a flea' is a narrative. It tells

5 *'Narrative (n.)'*, *Online Etymology Dictionary* <www.etymonline.com/search?q=narrative> accessed 11 April 2024.

6 *'Narrative (n.)'* (n 2).

7 Greta Olson, 'Narration and Narrative in Legal Discourse' in Peter Hühn, Jan Christoph Meister, John Pier and Wolf Schmid (eds), *Handbook of Narratology* (de Gruyter Handbook, 2014). They were also at the centre of Nicola Lacey's critique of pre-2003 sexual offending laws' focus on abstract and disembodied notions of intention, knowledge, and consent rather than victims' embodied, affective narratives of hurt and humiliation (see Nicola Lacey, 'Unspeakable Subjects: Impossible Rights: Sexuality, Integrity and Criminal Law' (1997) 8(2) *Women: A Cultural Review* 143, 151–4ff).

> of an event. The event is a very small one – the bite of a flea – but that is enough to make it a narrative.[8]

Is law necessarily concerned with the narration of events? Certainly, legal cases are *actions* of one kind or another: trials and judgments all *involve* a recounting of events, and indeed, the word 'case' itself denotes a dynamism, the word referring to a '*cas*cading' or 'falling' (as in 'a matter that *falls* to be decided').[9] But what about legal precepts, norms, duties more broadly? These are not narratives in themselves, but they, too, emerge from narratives about events, since we can imagine that narrating 'how we do things', or 'this is how we *did* it', can, by force of habit and convention, crystalise into a narrative about 'how we *ought* to do things' or 'how *you should* do it' – the latter eventually becoming solidified in legal rules.[10] Legal narratives might in this way be thought of as prescriptions that have emerged from descriptive (narrative) historical origins. For Robert Cover, narratives are fundamentally necessary for giving meaning to any normative structure and thus are the bedrock of all legal institutions and rules: they are 'the trajectories plotted upon material reality by our imaginations', are the 'codes' that connect our sense of what the world is and what it 'might be', and are the 'common script' that allows us to live together as a community of 'sane' moral creatures.[11] Peter Brooks shares Cover's insistence on the necessary and world-forming quality of narrative: 'The imposition of narrative form on life is a necessary human activity; we could not make sense of the world without it'.[12] That necessity, Brooks argues elsewhere, exists everywhere and in all contexts that require an ordering of things.[13]

8 H. Porter Abbott, 'Defining Narrative' in *The Cambridge Introduction to Narrative* (2nd edn, CUP 2008) 13. See also the OED on narrative, that it 'represents the sequence of events, as distinguished from that dealing with dialogue, description, etc.' ('*Narrative, (n.)*' (n 2); Prince (*A Dictionary*) agrees (at 75).

9 *'Case (n.1)'*, *Online Etymology Dictionary* <www.etymonline.com/search?q=case> accessed 11 April 2024. The Latin root is *casus* (literally: 'a falling').

10 Simon Stern makes the point that this combination of a story narrated in the past tense (i.e. about what happened between the parties), and then another in the present tense (about the law itself) constitutes the 'two overlapping narratives' to be found in appeal judgments (Simon Stern, 'Narrative in the Legal Text: Judicial Opinions and Their Narratives', in Michael Hanne and Robert Weisberg (eds), *Narrative and Metaphor in the Law* (CUP 2018) 121, 132.

11 Robert M. Cover, 'Nomos and Narrative' from *The Supreme Court, 1982 Term (Foreword)*, Paper 2705 Faculty Scholarship Series (1983) 5, 10 <http://digitalcommons.law.yale.edu/fss_papers/2705> accessed 9 April 2024.

12 Peter Brooks, 'Narrative in and Out of the Law' in James Phelan and Peter J. Rabinowitz (eds), *A Companion to Narrative Theory* (Blackwell Publishing 2005) 425.

13 Peter Brooks, 'Freud's Masterplot' (1977) 55/56 *Yale French Studies: Literature and Psychoanalysis. The Question of Reading: Otherwise* 280. This assessment of the ubiquity of narratives in law is now widely considered orthodox (cf Hanne and Weisberg, *Narrative and*

Starting from the premise, therefore, that masterplots are primarily creatures of *narrative*, concepts such as *meta*narratives, *macro*narratives, *master* narratives, or *super*-narratives can be assumed to be closely related, if not entirely synonymous. Scholarship on those latter notions tends to agree that they announce the possibility that, in addition to *a number* of trajectories, codes, or scripts (to use Cover's terminology), there may arise *one* such trajectory, code, or script that, like the jealous Hebrew god of the Old Testament, demands to be set above all others.[14] Having said that, there remains some significant divergence of opinion in the scholarly literature about what this means for conceptualising the shape and size of a masterplot. For some commentators, 'masterplot' or 'metanarrative' has a decidedly local application, notwithstanding its claim to occupy a higher plane than any *mere* plot or narrative. In the context of a legal trial, argues Ralph Grunewald, everyone (crucially, jurors) will have 'his or her own narrative' about what happened, which colours their own interpretation not only of the relevant evidence but also of what the lawyers say about the case. When the verdict is finally reached, this can be called 'the master narrative', since it is the one that has survived the trial process and emerged dominant.[15]

For others, metanarrative or masterplot is much more 'global' than that. For example, Genevieve Liveley and Rebecca Shaw, in their reflections on the apparent hierarchy of narratives in law, reframe Grunewald's 'master narrative' as a more intermediate level or 'macro' narrative. They describe *masterplot* instead as a 'wider cultural narrative' (as distinguished from more local narratives) that joins an instant case (be it a verdict, an appeal judgment, a statute, or even a constitution) to firmly establish ideas and norms about how things ought to be.[16] *Masterplots* are, in this sense, those narratives that derive from very deeply and firmly embedded beliefs, conventions, and assumptions – the foundations upon which other considerations are built.

Metaphor (n 10) 2: 'Narrative . . . is central to all legal processes and the many different kinds of legal story interwoven with each other to form the grand fabric of law.'

14 Exodus 20:4, NRSV: 'You shall not bow down to them or worship them; for I the Lord your God am a jealous God, punishing children for the iniquity of parents, to the third and the fourth generation of those who reject me . . .'

15 Ralph Grunewald, 'The Narrative of Innocence, or, Lost Stories' (2013) 25(3) *Law & Literature* 366, 372. That is not to say that such dominance can be relied upon. In the context of criminal trials in periods of transitional justice that arguably purport to 'generat[e] an official memory through trial and truth commission', McAuliffe has argued that 'legal efforts to deliberately construct a single metanarrative have given way to the inevitability of a proliferation of contrasting (or complementary) mininarratives' (Pádraig McAuliffe, 'The Ambiguities of Transitional Narrative in *The Porcupine* by Julian Barnes' (2012) 24(3) *Law & Literature*, 349, 365).

16 Genevieve Liveley and Rebecca Shaw, 'Marriage Plots: A New Narratological Approach to the Augustan Marriage Laws' (2020) 14(2) *Law and Humanities* 244. The term 'wider cultural narrative' as a defining feature of 'masterplot' appears at several points in Liveley and Shaw's article, but see, especially, 245, 261, 264.

For some, this feature means that masterplots (as master *narratives*) are not themselves straightforwardly accessible for critical evaluation in the way that simple narratives are.[17] Conceived in this fashion, masterplots are arguably related at a conceptual level to 'myths' and are deeply conservative concepts; we have a little more to say about both of these points later (Sections 1.3 and 2.1, respectively).

In the trial context again, Bernard Jackson describes a successful prosecution case as a sort of narrative account which, in the minds of the jurors 'can be anchored by way of evidence to common-sense beliefs which are generally accepted as true most of the time'.[18] Common sense is the main source of knowledge – 'unarticulated', 'implicit', and which operates in any given context in a 'probabilistic' (as opposed to deductive) fashion for jurors in their assessment of the relevant evidence.[19] Peter Brooks is presumably referring to something similar when he asks, rhetorically, how it can be that, in the notorious US (Maryland) rape case of *State v Rusk* (although Brooks could have chosen any number of cases), the different courts could come to entirely opposing conclusions without there being any dispute about the facts. The answer, of course, is that the judges all brought with them to the task a whole 'set of unexamined cultural beliefs that structure our understanding of everyday happenings'. In that case, those beliefs – the relevant *masterplot* – related to 'how they believe a woman ought to behave in certain circumstances', the point being advanced a much broader one besides.

But 'common sense' is unlikely of itself to be a sufficient reason to credit any particular narrative (or plot; see 1.2 below) as a '*master*plot': something more is needed, and in this regard, a persuasive case has been made by some commentators on behalf of the narrative power of repetition. Brooks has

17 Some commentators have characterised such a concept as inherently authoritarian and, as such, anathema to the ethos of Anglo-American liberal justice (see Milner S. Ball, 'Just Stories' (2000) 12(1) *Law & Literature* 37, 41–2, and 48: 'We want no metanarrative at trials or in our national life. We need the tension, the corrective, and the promise of competing stories.'

18 Bernard Jackson, '"Anchored Narratives" and the Interface of Law, Psychology and Semiotics' (1996) 1 *Legal and Criminal Psychology* 17, 23. Jackson himself attributes this insight about the 'anchoring' of narratives in the trial context to Willem A. Wagenaar, Peter J. van Koppen and Hans F. M. Crombag, *Anchored Narratives: The Psychology of Criminal Evidence* (Harvester Wheatsheaf 1993) 10.

19 Jackson, 'Anchored' (n 18) 25. A notorious example of such 'anchoring' serving a *defence* case is the *OJ Simpson* trial in 1995, which came to a head over senior defence attorney Cochrane's application to demonstrate to the jury that the racism of one of the LAPD's leading detectives should be treated as tainting the otherwise strong DNA evidence implicating the defendant: 'African-Americans live with offensive words, offensive looks, offensive treatment every day of their lives. And yet they still believe in this country. I'm ashamed for Mr. Darden [*the prosecutor, who had urged the judge not to let Cochrane "play the race card"*] to allow himself to become an apologist for this man.' ('Issue of Racism Erupts in Simpson Trial' *New York Times* (New York, 14 January 1995)).

shown the ways in which narratives (like metaphors) can impress readers with presentations of apparent similarities between otherwise unrelated things which are conceptually and thematically linked together on the basis of perceived resemblances, the recurrence of which connotes significance and order.[20] Brooks observed that *fictional* stories, especially 'folk tale, and all formulaic literature', will often be structured around repeated returns to a salient theme: the three houses of Grimm's little pigs menaced by the wolf; the three caskets in *The Merchant of Venice*; the three times that Peter denies his association with Jesus. Similarly, the power of the 'uncanny' in Gothic literature depends upon a haunting 'return' of (or to) that which is thought to be long dead and/or forgotten and left behind and which consequently forces a protagonist to reassess and re-evaluate a formerly settled or conventional view.[21] Repeated *returns* are needed in order 'to recognize sameness within difference'[22] – a recognition (or, equally, a fabrication) that promises 'the possibility (or the illusion) of "meaning" wrested from "life"' – and hence the 'significance' and 'illumination' that readers (of fiction, but of any kind of text besides) crave.[23]

Resemblance and repetition are also clearly central to legal reasoning. This is so in the prosaic sense that the facts of a previous case must resemble those underlying an instant appeal in some crucial way if it is to be approved or applied as part of the ruling. It can also carry the kind of emotional resonance that Brooks identifies in literature. For example, in the Court of Appeal's ruling on the case of the conjoined twins, Ward LJ found it appropriate to describe Mary (the weaker of the twins, who was doomed to die no matter what) dramatically as 'killing Jodie' (the stronger twin, who would be able to live, but only if Mary were soon separated from her) and as 'a slow drip of poison' because, despite the obvious difference between an innocent baby and poisonous liquid, the one resembles the other in that both represent a mortal danger.[24] Strong tacit acknowledgement of the seductive appeal of the recurrence of an event that resembles the present can be found in the rules limiting the admissibility of evidence about a defendant's previous 'bad character'. Section 101(3) of the Criminal Justice Act 2003 requires that such evidence not be admitted if the court feels it would have a significantly 'adverse effect on the fairness of the proceedings' – in other words, that the emotional

20 Brooks, 'Freud's Masterplot' (n 13) 280.
21 Brooks, 'Freud's Masterplot' (n 13) 288.
22 Brooks, 'Freud's Masterplot' (n 13) 290.
23 Brooks, 'Freud's Masterplot' (n 13) 296.
24 'Mary uses Jodie's heart and lungs to receive and use Jodie's oxygenated blood. This will cause Jodie's heart to fail and cause Jodie's death as surely as a slow drip of poison' (*Re A (Conjoined Twins: Surgical Separation)* [2001] Fam 147, per Ward LJ).

effect of hearing the evidence would unduly prejudice the jury against the defendant.[25]

Generalising from the persuasive power of repetition and resemblance, Brooks eventually proceeds to a concept of '*master* narrative', in other words, a narrative 'into which each new narrative *episode* must be fitted'.[26] Similarly, for Tait and Norris, a 'super-narrative' is formed when a number of narratives can be shown to bear such a 'deep family resemblance' to one another that they can be understood to be single 'iterations' of one story.[27] Tait and Norris demonstrate this idea in the underlying common thread connecting various social contract theories (e.g. those of Hobbes, Rousseau, and Locke), all of which tell an 'origins' story in which a community finds itself moved by rational self-interest to come to some basic and fundamental agreement about how to organise social life in everyone's general shared interest. There can be little doubt that the social contract theories have at their heart a narrative that satisfies the narratologist's 'bare minimum', since they all depict the adoption of such a contract as an *event*, albeit an imaginary one. The essential connection between them furthermore assures their elevated or 'master' status, the appreciation of which 'helps the author to underscore the value and legitimacy of the narratives as a set' and convinces the reader that it 'has an important place in the collective cultural imagination'.[28]

1.2 Masterplots and the 'plots' of the law

On the other hand, *plot* is a term conveying the sense that, depending on the context and starting variables, events are typically expected to 'turn out' in a certain way. The distinction here between 'plots' and 'narratives' can be very fine: we already saw that existing definitions of 'narrative' already account for the ordering or sequencing of recounted events, and 'plot' chiefly concerns (as Prince has it) 'the main incidents of a narrative', including its 'outline', 'structure', and 'organization'.[29] Brooks, whose evaluation of the essential role of narrative in two publications was quoted earlier, expresses himself in the very next sentences there in terms that suggest that *narrative* and *plot* are two sides of the same coin. For example, immediately upon asserting the essential role of narrative in his 2005 chapter, he adds, 'We seek

25 For a discussion on the law on bad character evidence, see James Goudkamp, 'Bad Character Evidence and Reprehensible Behaviour' (2008) 12(2) *The International Journal of Evidence & Proof* 116.

26 Brooks, 'Narrative' (n 12) 426.

27 Allison Tait and Luke Norris, 'Narrative and the Origins of Law' (2011) 5(1) *Law and Humanities* 11.

28 Tait and Norris (n 27) 21.

29 Prince, *A Narratology Dictionary* (n 3) 90.

to understand actions as intelligible units that combine into goal-oriented plots'.[30] In his 1977 article, the initial sentence about narrative as an 'affirmation of resemblance' on p. 280 is followed up (in the same sentence) with the observation that the result of such affirmation is 'a common *plot*, which implies the rejection of merely contingent (or unassimilable) incident or action'.

A word denoting the essential elements of a story, 'plot' has a more recent etymological provenance than *narrative*; as suggested in Brooks's words quoted earlier, its main distinction here is essentially to denote a certain direction or end point. Modernist literary experiments aside, a narrative is typically expected not simply to meander endlessly before abruptly breaking off but to move towards a certain finale, climax, or denouement, in other words, to *plot a course* from one state of affairs or circumstances to another: a nautical metaphor that the *Oxford English Dictionary* traces in the literary sense to the middle of the sixteenth century.[31] Brooks affirms as much in his 1977 article, in which *plot* is characterised as the *destination* of a coherent narrative, which 'must make use of specific, perceptible repetitions in order to create plot, that is, to show us a significant interconnection of events'.[32]

If, therefore, *narrative* is what lends coherence and *plot* describes the course or direction of the elements of the narrative, then *masterplot* (as a concept emerging from both narrative *and* plot) connotes a general explanation of *what* the relevant events are, *how* they came to be, and what conclusion they are headed to. The explanatory function of plot denotes causality, and a looking back at what features of a story led to which consequences.[33] The narrative arc of a particular plot can itself be further understood by examining it in terms of *genre* and the notion that a different kind of genre has its own sets of rules for determining and explaining the broad course of events. This, again, has implications for the study of law and legal processes. In the context of the trial, Grunewald also attests to the strategy of '*emplotment*', in which plot and genre conventions are used to lead jurors to a particular view on 'how and why things happened and what the meaning of the events is'.[34] Put simply, if jurors are persuaded that a case of (say) domestic murder can be understood against the background of an archetype of tragical romance, perhaps the inevitable result of extreme passions running their

30 Brooks, 'Narrative' (n 12) 425.

31 '*Plot (v.)*' *Oxford English Dictionary* (March 2024) <www.oed.com/dictionary/plot_n?tab=meaning_and_use#29669335> accessed 11 April 2024.

32 Brooks, 'Freud's Masterplot' (n 13) 288.

33 Karin Kukkonen, 'Plot' in Hühn et al (eds), *Handbook* (n 7) 706. Plots as causal explanations of events used by appeal judges are arguably closer to those of historians than of literary authors, since the form of the legal judgment (like the historical account) is 'one of ongoing contestation' (quoting Stern, 'Judicial Opinions' (n 10) 134).

34 Grunewald, 'Lost Stories' (n 15) 373.

natural course, then they will deliver a verdict accordingly. Drawing on research in the US legal context by Bennett and Feldman, Grunewald observes:

> The stereotypical or archetypical representation of a case helps to redefine facts and makes it easier for the fact finder (i.e., the jury) to create connections that are 'satisfying, familiar, or pleasing – connections that maybe stronger than the facts, norms, or logic of the matter would suggest.' . . . Masterplots can exert an influence on how we take in new information, causing us to read narratives unconsciously in a specific way.[35]

If 'emplotment' involves determining how narrative elements should be organised in taking them forward in a certain way, then the interpretive strategies employed by judges in appeal cases can be seen to present another example. After all, the application of precedent can often be characterised as an assessment as to which of a range of somewhat similar and relevant previous cases are most *recognisable* in the instant one, and thus which legal principle is to be *repeated* and taken forward. The much-commented-upon 'homosexual sadomasochism' case of *R v Brown and others*[36] provides a handy illustration, involving as it did the infliction of bodily harm, but also consent to sexual activity. The application by the House of Lords of precedent cases on violence and assault (under the Offences Against the Person Act 1861, in which an alleged victim's consent is irrelevant) rather than those on sexual offending (and the Sexual Offences Act 1967, in which a failure to disprove consent stands in the way of prosecution) meant that the translation of the events into legal precedent followed a *crime* plot (the infliction of bodily harm for no good reason, for which Brown et al. were convicted) rather than a *sex* plot (sexual expression between consenting adults, which would have been lawful).[37]

At a rather grander level of legal thought, 'emplotment' arguably describes what Dworkin had in mind when he proposed that the rule of law, and the notion of justice as 'integrity', required judges to see law as a whole, and the

35 Grunewald, 'Lost Stories' (n 15) 373–4 (the material that Grunewald quotes is attributed to W. Lance Bennett and Martha S. Feldman, *Reconstructing Reality in the Courtroom: Justice and Judgment in American Culture* (Rutgers University Press 1981) 60).

36 [1994] 1 AC 212.

37 For analyses of how the judges 'emplotted' that case, see, especially, Leslie J. Moran, *The Homosexual(ity) of Law* (Routledge 1996). Cf Nafsika Athanassoulis, 'The Role of Consent in Sado-Masochistic Practices' (2002) 8(2) *Res Publica* 141; N. Bamforth, 'Sado-Masochism and Consent' (1994) *Criminal Law Review* (September) 661; Carl F. Stychin, *Law's Desire: Sexuality and the Limits of Justice* (Routledge 1995). Stern terms cases of this kind (i.e. cases 'that require the judges to draw on policy and analogy as their pit one doctrine against others or modify the law in some way') as 'dynamic' stories (as opposed to 'static' ones) (Stern, 'Judicial Opinions' 132).

instant case within it as 'coherent', which is to say, as part of a complex and unfolding narrative, not unlike a 'chain novel':

> [This] explains how and why the past must be allowed some special power of its own in court, contrary to the pragmatist's claim that it must not. It explains why judges must conceive the body of the law they administer as a whole rather than as a set of discrete decisions that they are free to make or amend one by one, with nothing but a strategic interest in the rest.[38]

For the appellate judge, as for the literary author, what happened previously is important when considering what is to happen now and in the future; individual elements of what went before are not to be thought of as unrelated but as part of an evolving narrative, and as such, a way should be found, if possible, to ensure they cohere satisfactorily. In neither law nor literature do we like to see too many red herrings, dead ends, or '*wrong turns*', as the UK Supreme Court in 2016 described the House of Lords ruling of *Chan Wing Sui v The Queen*[39] and the two decades of case law that followed it, during which time the courts had allowed for an unprincipled relaxation of settled common law strictures on the degree of *mens rea* to be proved in the prosecution of secondary parties to murder.[40]

Elsewhere, researchers have focused more precisely on how different sorts of genre forms might have produced certain formulations of law and legal reasoning. For example, Anthea Vogl has demonstrated how an unconscious recourse to some of the conventions typically associated with genre forms such as *bildungsroman* (the 'formation novel', depicting an individual's journey to maturity and self-realisation) provides an archetype for immigration officials to make sense of the narrative accounting of individual asylum claims. Vogl's analyses of transcripts from Australian immigration hearings have shown how conventions pertaining to narrative consistency and integrity typically demanded of *bildungsroman* protagonist narrators are unconsciously extended to impose a sometimes unrealistically critical assessment and evaluation of personal asylum testimonies.[41]

38 Ronald Dworkin, *Law's Empire* (Harvard University Press, 1986) 167.

39 [1985] AC 168.

40 *R v Jogee* [2016] UKSC 8, para [87]: 'It would not be satisfactory for this court simply to disapprove the *Chan Wing-Siu* principle. Those who are concerned with criminal justice, including members of the public, are entitled to expect from this court a clear statement of the relevant principles. We consider that the proper course for this court is to re-state, as nearly and clearly as we may, the principles which had been established over many years before the law took a wrong turn.'

41 Anthea Vogl, 'The Genres and Politics of Refugee Testimony' (2018) 30(1) *Law & Literature* 81. Cf David Gurnham, 'Stopping the Boats, Changing the Narrative: How the Migrant Refugee *Bildungsroman* Became a Ghost Story' (2025) 37(1) *Law & Literature* 29. <www.tandfonline.com/doi/full/10.1080/1535685X.2023.2221949> accessed 10 July 2024.

1.3 'Masterplots', myths, and other metaphors

It is worth returning here to the idea touched on earlier that, whether our theme concerns primarily *narratives* or *plots*, the most distinctive feature of a 'masterplot' is that it presupposes a *hierarchy* within which it occupies the top rung. A *masterplot*, in other words, is a narrative or plot about which certain claims are made regarding its authority or 'mastery' that we do not find in the case of other narratives or plots. Masterplots are (or they claim to be, or it is claimed on their behalf that they are) the most enduring, the most fundamental, and the most foundational of its relatives. Key questions arise here, therefore, as to (1) how that mastery manifests itself, (2) what such 'mastery' might say about the nature and meaning of masterplot, (3) what it is that justifies such a claim on behalf of any one narrative or plot or another, and furthermore, (4) whether the claim about that mastery is principally *descriptive* (whether it is simply the case that certain contexts are dominated by one set of assumptions or conventions), *prescriptive* (that we would like to see one particular set become so), or *critical* (the claim of mastery made as a basis for seeking to attack a given hegemony).

The final two questions posed in the preceding paragraph we shall return to in the next section, on the political and ethical dimensions of masterplots scholarship and the possibilities for critically re-evaluating or even repudiating narratives that appear to be so deeply embedded. The first two questions – as to how mastery manifests and what that says about the meaning of *masterplot* – give us an opportunity to provide a word about the scope and remit of this book. We noted at the outset that a term to have gained recognition in critical scholarship in the twentieth century was 'grand narratives' – a term characterising a tendency within Western philosophical thought to seek and privilege universalising or totalising narratives that betray certain ideological commitments, and taken to task in the critical work of Jean-Francois Lyotard, amongst other postmodern and post-structuralist thinkers.[42] Our book does not go over this ground. However, it may be useful here to say a few words about one particular strand of proto-masterplot discourse, namely, with regard to the notion of *myth*.

The various meanings that have been applied to *myth* and *the mythic* over the years are, arguably at least, highly relevant for our purposes. In the first place, accounts of the role of 'myth' in Western thought are accounts about the role of narratives and plot in our culture. Secondly, they are also attempts to explain the 'mastery' of certain of those narratives and plots as conceived here (that is, as embedded and unconsciously accepted ideas). For example, Plato strongly disapproved of myth ('*mythos*') precisely because of its

42 Jean-François Lyotard, *The Postmodern Condition: A Report on Knowledge* (Geoff Bennington and Brian Massumi tr, Manchester University Press 1984).

power to beguile and move the emotions and, consequently, to lead people to unreasoned, false, and dangerous conclusions. *Logos* was, for Plato, superior in comprising the only way to true and sound conclusions from deductive premises but was constantly vulnerable due to its need to be supplemented by *mythos* (as Plato himself demonstrated by using stories to illustrate his own arguments).[43] In the twentieth century, the distinctive deployment of the term 'myth' by, for example, Claude Levi-Strauss and Roland Barthes, respectively, accentuated the importance of deeply embedded structures of signification hidden in modern European culture. For Levi-Strauss, the continued unconscious influence of ancient rituals and kinship patterns continues to provide a mythic structures of modern mores and practices (e.g. the incest taboo, and rituals of reciprocity and hospitality).[44] In Barthes's case, it meant observing assumptions about the primacy of modern capitalist culture and consumer desire that afforded a shared meaning to everyday words and images as a system of signs.[45] Finally, 'myth' has accrued yet other meanings in legal scholarship. In his theory of modern law, Peter Fitzpatrick argued that it was law's *negation* or *denial* of its own mythic dimensions that constituted its 'modern mythology' – a way for law to maintain its own unity despite its many contradictions and 'persistent irresolutions' as both ancient and modern, transcendent and everyday, definite and flexible.[46] Additionally, certain feminist scholars have used the term to identify false or otherwise wrong beliefs about rape, sex, consent, and gender which, by virtue of being so widely held, make it less likely that instances of rape or sexual assault will be recognised as such and taken seriously by way of criminal prosecutions and jury convictions.[47]

All these approaches to the meaning of 'myth' go some way to affording explanations of the sort of 'mastery' that we have in mind when we refer to masterplots. The myths described here have all been the subject of critique as sources and means of the transmission of powerful and embedded ideas. In these respects, 'myth' has accrued a distinctly pejorative meaning, since it is charged with preventing a deeper truth from being seen properly, be it in the form of true precepts logically deduced, of the ancient roots of modern practices, of the seductive power of capitalist ideology, or of the true degree

43 Sara Brill, *Plato on the Limits of Human Life* (Indiana University Press 2013).

44 Claude Levi-Strauss, *The Elementary Structures of Kinship* (J. H. Bell, John Richard von Sturmer and R. Needham tr, Beacon Press 1969).

45 Roland Barthes, *Mythologies* (R. Howard and A. Lavers tr, Hill & Wang 2012).

46 Peter Fitzpatrick, *The Mythology of Modern Law* (Routledge 1992) x: 'Law is a sovereign imperative yet the expression of a popular spirit. Its quasi-religious transcendence stands in opposition to its mundane temporality. It incorporates the ideal yet it is a mode of present existence.'

47 Joanne Conaghan and Yvette Russell, 'Rape Myths, Law, and Feminist Research: "Myths about Myths"?' (2014) 22 *Feminist Legal Studies* 25.

of responsibility borne by men for sexual harms inflicted on women (but elsewhere in myriad other forms besides). These are all matters that lie outside the remit and scope of this book inasmuch as the present work is both narrower *and* broader than a study of the 'mythic' qualities of knowledge, beliefs, and opinion. That is to say, the notion of myth has generated separate bodies of scholarship that have moved in very different directions that would be difficult to capture here without devoting the entire book to myth(s) alone. On the other hand, our concern with masterplots has a *broader* concern than myth in that, at least in some contexts, the designation of a set of beliefs and opinions as 'myths' is arguably one way amongst others of talking critically about masterplots, that is, of attempting to account for why those beliefs or opinions may be deeply embedded, hegemonic, and ripe for exposure and critique. Gurnham has previously argued that the language of myths in feminist rape myth scholarship represents a strategic use of metaphor, that is, a way of referring to a range of different ideas – including ideas that may actually not be very widely held or that may sometimes be true, depending on context – using the terms of something else (i.e. as '*myths*') in order that they can all be 'debunked'.[48] Neil Sadler has also proposed that this limitation on the meaning of 'myth' in the context of sexual assault is a further reason to prefer 'masterplot', since the latter is arguably a more fruitful basis for contesting traditional assumptions.[49]

This brings us to the role of *metaphor* in conceptualising masterplots. We have seen already how, for Brooks, the narrative basis for masterplots works in a way akin to metaphor, namely, on the basis of resemblance. The essence of metaphor is to bring together two things, concepts, ideas which are not related in any literal terms and, indeed, that may be of entirely separate domains but which are purported nevertheless to share some salient quality or bear some resemblance that justifies describing the one *using the terms of the other*.[50] Our choice of the term 'masterplot' is already a metaphor in one sense, since the components 'master' and 'plot' can, in any case, be understood in terms of an authority ('master') figure and a planned ('plotted') course, respectively. However, the literature on masterplots is packed with various further figurative explanations based on other purported resemblances that emphasise the masterplot's salient quality as that which can support other

48 David Gurnham, 'Debating Rape: To Whom Does the Uncanny "Myth" Metaphor Belong?' (2016) 43 *Journal of Law & Society* 123. For a critical evaluation of relevant opinions as 'myths', cf David J. Hayes, 'Are Rape Myths "Myths"?' (2024) 44(1) *Oxford Journal of Legal Studies* 156; H. Reece, 'Rape Myths: Is Elite Opinion Right and Popular Opinion Wrong?' (2013) 33 *OJLS* 445.

49 Neil Sadler, 'Myths, Masterplots and Sexual Harassment in Egypt' (2019) 24(2) *The Journal of North African Studies* 247.

50 See George Lakoff and Mark Johnson, *The Metaphors We Live by* (Chicago University Press 2003).

things. For example, Sadler refers to *masterplot* as a 'crutch',[51] and Porter Abbott uses metaphors of 'glue' and 'skeleton', both conveying something of its 'receptive' quality, ready for whatever material is to be applied.[52] *Masterplot* may also be imagined variously by way of metaphors drawn from the natural environment ('horizon', the 'bedrock', 'ground', or 'atmosphere') and from the synthetic or manufactured world (e.g. the building metaphors of 'scaffolding', 'foundation', or a 'frame', which could equally refer to the initial setup for a weaver, or an artist whose 'outline' serves a similar figurative purpose[53]). In all these figurative guises, however, the explanation for its claim to mastery lies in the fact that its unfurnished quality means it can accommodate, contain, or bear whatever else should come along. The masterplot is *meta* in precisely the same linguistic sense that a metaphor is *meta*. Just as a metaphor carries (*pherin*) a freight of meaning over (*meta*) the gap between two different concepts, so is the masterplot a story that stands above and joins together smaller stories.

2 The 'politics' of legal masterplots

As this collection reveals, masterplots exist across a variety of legal domains, motivated by and possessing their own unique, individual histories, origin stories, and in some cases, endings. But what of their politics? We are speaking here not of the political cut-and-thrust of left- or right-wing politics but of the deeper policy impulses at the heart of masterplots. If, as we have argued earlier, 'masterplots' are to be understood in terms of their authority ('master') and as stories or narratives proceeding according to a planned, or charted path ('plot'), then several questions of a *political* nature follow: who created the masterplot? How was the masterplot created and sustained? What power does the masterplot enjoy, and why? Why does the masterplot endure? Who wins and who loses out under the operation of the masterplot, and does it exist to keep a certain population or interest group in power and another subjugated? These political questions are precisely those posed and addressed across the collection's 14 chapters. This introduction is not the

51 Sadler, 'Myths' (n 49) 249.

52 Porter Abbott, *Introduction* (2nd edn) (n 8) 53. See also Andreea Deciu Ritivoi, 'Explaining People: Narrative and the Study of Identity' (2009) 1 *Storyworlds: A Journal of Narrative Studies* 25, at 35 (also referring to masterplots as a skeleton), but also 36 (using the metaphor of a vessel, and masterplots as 'repositories of normativity').

53 For example, see Mary Phillips, 'On Being Green and Being Enterprising: Narrative and the Ecopreneurial Self' (2013) 20(6) *Organization* 794, 806: 'While the fabula and masterplot combine storylines in uncomfortable juxtapositions albeit that the *outline of the narrative* appears reasonably coherent, analysis of the sjuzet reveals that the narrators' *positioning within the scaffolding* of that outline has to manage the resulting contradictions' (our emphasis).

place to respond to each of these, and indeed, a close reading of the chapters contained herein offers the best opportunity to muse on these important aspects. Nevertheless, what we can say is that all these questions coalesce around an essential concern, namely, the 'political' machinations of legal masterplots.

As explored earlier in this introduction, metaphor plays a vital role in contextualising masterplots, and academic accounts unpacking the masterplot idea have routinely used metaphor to explain how masterplots are 'constructed' and how they come to be embedded as foundational or dominant discourses in a particular field. In this part of the chapter, further metaphors are engaged which, continuing the tradition of the emerging masterplot literature, seek to help elucidate how masterplots come into being and the political power they exude. In this way, this section employs the metaphor of a *frame*, of masterplot as a *lens*, a *device*, and *an agent of change*. Each is subtly distinct, but all are chosen to advance the explication of the masterplot concept. Thus, reference to masterplot as a *frame* seeks to conjure an image of a picture frame outlining, highlighting, and giving form and shape to a discourse. Similarly, the discussion of masterplot as a *lens* through which to observe different fields of law in socio-legal study and as a *device* for legal analysis is designed to invoke a sense of close inspection, searching examination of, and calling of attention to the internal workings of the masterplot. Finally, and discretely, masterplot is portrayed as an *agent of change* – here according to a far more active, positive, almost-personified characterisation that seeks to recognise and reflect the energy and dynamism of the masterplot concept. These metaphors are used to animate the central argument made in this introduction, examined and tested across the wider chapters of the collection, namely, that the political radicalism of the masterplot idea lies in its capacity, when deployed as an approach to socio-legal studies, for revealing or 'shining a light' on otherwise unconscious, under-explored, or hitherto unnoticed hegemonies. The recourse to metaphor is therefore helpful in illuminating the central mission of this collection.

In assessing the politics of legal masterplots, an important distinction can and should be drawn between, on the one hand, the politics of the masterplot *device* itself and, on the other, the politics of engaging the masterplot *frame* as an approach to socio-legal and law and humanities analysis. Both warrant further thought and consideration.

2.1 The politics of the legal masterplot: an inherently conservative device?

In addressing the politics of the masterplot *device*, an instructive starting point is to interrogate a key question, namely, are legal masterplots inherently conservative? One must caution against over-generalisation, but looking across the book, we can see that, on one view, yes, the legal masterplots identified share certain attributes or characteristics that might loosely be classified as 'conservative' in nature. It should be noted that the term 'conservative' is used here to reflect a sense of conventionalism, non-radicalism, or traditionalism. As Richard Walsh writes in Chapter 2, drawing on the work of Aristotle, 'the authority of masterplots necessarily aligns with the conservative, inertial force of narrative'[54] in that they are associated with established orthodoxies and apparent conventional wisdom. More broadly, as the wider chapters of this collection capture, legal masterplots can be seen to represent the often fixed, taken-for-granted, or accepted, long-established accounts or narratives that undergird our laws or approach and attitudes to legal problems. In most cases, the legal masterplots at play are shown to have lengthy trajectories, reaching over decades or, in some instances, hundreds of years and displaying significant tenacity and influence on legal thought and discourse. In what way, then, might we construe legal masterplots as conservative in character?

As this collection attests, once baked into the very fabric of an area of law as the orthodox, accepted, or dominant understanding of an issue or legal problem, the legal masterplot becomes settled and embedded essentially as the status quo. Masterplots come to be taken for granted as embodying common sense and logic, but they are also deliberately and consciously repeated and reinforced because they prove rhetorically coherent or effective. The result is that masterplots can be seen, in many senses, as synonymous with the preservation or maintenance of that status quo, often leading to policy stasis or reform stagnation. The word 'conservative' derives from the Latin *cōnservō* (meaning 'to preserve'). It is unsurprising, then, that as super- or dominant narratives, masterplots come to exude a character of 'preservation' of tradition, of non-radicalism and, relatedly, resistance to challenge and change. This has resonance with Gadamer's seminal work *Truth and Method*,[55] in which he explores the relationship between tradition, authority, and knowledge. Gadamer urges us to develop a consciousness of how history is at work in our understanding (*Wirkungsgeschichtliches Bewusstsein*[56]), to appreciate that preunderstanding and prejudices are conditions of knowledge, and that understanding is always a collision of traditions. In the vein of Gadamer, then, we might see masterplots, by extension, as lending stability in meaning over time. Masterplots are, consequently, status quo–biased, which, in turn, acts as a barrier to alternative approaches to reform, closes down or inhibits their dislodgement, and ensures the ongoing role and continued

54 Chapter 2 of this collection, (30).

55 Hans-George Gadamer, *Truth and Method* (2nd edn, Joel Weinsheimer and Donald G. Marshall tr, Bloomsbury 2013).

56 *The Wirkungsgeschichtliches Bewusstsein* has been variously (and at times erroneously) translated as 'effective history' and 'effective historical consciousness' but is better rendered as 'history of influence' or 'consciousness of the influence of history'.

dominance of the masterplot. How, then, do legal masterplots achieve such authoritative status and firm footing?

As noted previously, we find that masterplots derive their power (and 'mastery') from their repetition, as 'stories that we tell over and over'.[57] Thus, masterplots gain their political power through a combination of reiteration but also, crucially, association with wider social and moral values, metaphors, as well as alignment with citizens' emotional codes, beliefs, and anxieties. Abbott explains how the connection of masterplots with wider societal values ensures their standing as established and durable narratives, noting that '[t]o the extent that our values and identity are linked to a masterplot, that masterplot can have strong rhetorical impact. We tend to give credibility to narratives that are structured by it'.[58] Masterplots divorced from these wider societal values somehow cease to exude power and, arguably, lose their status as masterplots altogether. As Liveley and Shaw explain:

> [L]aws, and statutes are dependent for their authority upon their ability to reflect and represent (that is, re-present) the predominant cultural 'narratives; in which they are received. Unless a law is already attuned to the cultural character and norms of the society it aims to rule (that is, unless it already resembles, repeats, and relates to them), it will be ignored or resisted.[59]

Olson expands on this, noting that laws achieve their legitimacy and normative status through resemblances to existing, established plots and narratives.[60] Put differently, if laws align with existing narratives, they prove to be stable, long-lasting, and secure. This links neatly to the assertion from Bamberg that 'master narratives', as he terms them, 'give guidance and direction to the everyday actions of subjects; without this guidance and sense of direction, we would be lost'.[61] It is, as Sadler argues integration of masterplots within society and culture that makes them durable. This results in the masterplot taking on what Pierre Bourdieu described as a 'doxic' character[62] and forming part of what Frank Kermode has explained as 'the mythological structure of a society from which we derive comfort, and

57 Porter Abbott, *Introduction* (2nd edn) (n 8) 46.
58 Abbott, *Introduction* (2nd edn) (n 8) 46.
59 Liveley and Shaw, 'Marriage Plots' (n 16); see also Lawrence Friedman, 'Legal Culture and Social Development' (1969) 4 *Law & Society* 29.
60 Olson, 'Narration and Narrative' (n 7).
61 Michael Bamberg, 'Considering Counter Narratives' in Michael Bamberg and Molly Andrews (eds), *Considering Counter-Narratives: Narrating, Resisting, Making Sense* (John Benjamins 2004) 360.
62 Pierre Bourdieu, *Outline of a Theory of Practice* (Richard Nice tr, CUP 1977).

which it may be uncomfortable to dispute'.[63] To depart from an established masterplot is, to repurpose Kermode's words, discomforting and thus unappealing. As a consequence, this lends masterplots a 'taken-for-granted-ness' or 'accepted-ness' which further bolsters their resilience and constancy. Combined with what Abbott has explained as our human need for order, causality, and certainty,[64] it becomes clear why masterplots can appear lodged and impervious to challenge. In other words, it is the fact of their repeated rehearsal and entrenchment that cements the super-narrative as a masterplot.

Repetition and reiteration time and again, in official records, in legislation, and in policy documents, enable the masterplot to secure its place and status as rooted or fixed. This endows the masterplot with significant political influence over the shape and development of law. We might say that the masterplot becomes part of the 'psyche' of society and of the legal realm, edging close to becoming an accepted 'truth' exerting authority over current and future policymaking. In many instances, as a result, the masterplot takes on a character of orthodoxy and a taken-for-grantedness as an approved or dominant narrative in a particular area of law.

We see this repetition and reiteration play out across the various chapters of this book. By way of example, David Gurnham locates the 'punitive drive' in law and order criminal justice speech across ministerial statements and through a series of judicial sentencing remarks.[65] Rebecca Shaw highlights how residual stereotypes, biases, and characterisations of violence have become and remain entrenched within the socio-cultural domestic violence and abuse (DVA) narrative,[66] and Chris Bevan uncovers how problematic assumptions, attitudes, and representations of the homeless originate as far back as the time of the Black Death yet continue to echo today in England.[67] In the context of international criminal justice, international law, and the law of armed conflict, Nina H. B. Jørgensen, Ekaterina Yahyaoui Krivenko, and Lynsey Mitchell[68] each also locate and examine how masterplots of time, of war, and of order, peace, and justice come to assume dominance through rehearsal and re-rehearsal in the narrative landscape of the law in these fields: repeatedly deployed, reiterated, and engaged by governments, political actors, and academics, reinforcing their power and reach.

We can observe how legal masterplots come to comprise core cultural beliefs about a particular legal issue, community, or problem. They become the narrative that is told and retold, set against a welter of associated assumptions.

63 Frank Kermode, *The Genesis of Secrecy: On the Interpretation of Narrative* (Harvard University Press 1979) 113.
64 Abbott, *Introduction* (2nd edn) (n 8) 44.
65 Chapter 4 of this collection.
66 Chapter 5 of this collection.
67 Chapter 3 of this collection.
68 Chapters 8, 10, and 11, respectively, of this collection.

In turn, masterplots are used to make sense of events or developments within the legal sphere. The masterplot comes to embody a communal, cultural resource which is then summoned and marshalled to achieve particular legal ends, whether that be support for legal reforms, arguments against changing the law, or justification for (in)action. Masterplots can, moreover, be deployed as political devices by governments to favour or champion specific causes or, as Andy Hayward explores, to prioritise and incentivise certain forms of relationship norms.[69] Equally, masterplots can operate in a way that propagates national myths, such as the importance of collective action to the achievement of social and democratic progress, as explored by Steven Cammiss and Graeme Hayes,[70] or to carve out apparent, neat binaries, such as the marked-family binary identified and problematised by Luke P. Norris and Allison Tait.[71]

The force of the legal masterplot appears to be especially strong where the narrative at play is tied to or has links with religious or moral connotations – a theme that runs through many of the chapters. Here, the work of Porter Abbott[72] and Gould[73] is instructive. Porter Abbott explains that masterplots 'create an image of the world in which good and evil are clearly identifiable, and in which blame can fall squarely on one party or another',[74] and it is precisely this stereotypical, binary quality that gives masterplots their moral force.[75] Thus, masterplots routinely operate according to simplified narrative arcs which have a strong attraction and pull as a means (whether through law or by governments) of explaining or justifying difficult political decisions or complex geo-political action. The simplicity of the moral tale the good-versus-evil mentality necessarily, however, obscures more nuanced thinking around law and policymaking. Gould expands on this by locating the authority exuded by what he terms 'canonical narratives'.[76] As Gould identifies, stories linked to 'the canon' carry with them a sense of certification, of moral authority, of endorsement, affording them yet greater weight and tenacity. We can see these themes across the chapters of this book, whether that be in the echoes of quasi-biblical undertones of redemption and the 'deservingness' of the homeless;[77] around the influence of the Anglican Church on the development of marriage in England and Wales;[78] in the implication of

69 Chapter 12 of this collection.
70 Chapter 9 of this collection.
71 Chapter 6 of this collection.
72 Abbott, *Introduction* (2nd edn) (n 8).
73 Stephan Jay Gould, 'Jim Bowie's Letter and Bill Buckner's Legs' in *I Have Landed: The End of a Beginning in Natural History* (Harmony Books 2002) 54–70.
74 Abbott, *Introduction* (2nd edn) (n 8) 48.
75 Abbott, *Introduction* (2nd edn) (n 8) 44.
76 Gould, 'Jim Bowie's Letter' (n 73).
77 As explored by Bevan in Chapter 3.
78 As explored by Probert in Chapter 7.

religious arguments juxtaposed against non-formalised family forms, such as cohabitation;[79] and in the framing of armed conflict through the discourse of the righteous intervenor and the good-versus-evil discourse.[80]

Even as societies, in many parts of the world, are becoming increasingly less religious and as moral attitudes shift, still, these super-narratives, which draw on resonances of religiosity, seeking legitimacy by association with past events (such as earlier conflicts) and invoking deep moralisation, continue to wield significant influence over contemporary law and practice. We therefore find that legal masterplots secure their place and resilience through their encoding of what Nelson called society's 'shared understandings'[81] and by fixing to or being described by analogy with wider social, moral, or religious values. At the same time, their connection with the past, with tradition, with what might be regarded as accepted or 'conventional wisdom' all further contributes to the sense of masterplots' inherent conservatism. Taken together, this renders masterplots tenacious, highly durable, and resistant to change.

2.2 The politics of engaging the masterplot frame: masterplot as an agent for change

Moving beyond the politics of the masterplot *device* itself, what of the politics of engaging the masterplot *frame*? It might be contended that the deployment of the masterplot frame in a given field or discipline of law is in and of itself a political act. How so? Paul Gewirtz, writing in the 1990s, when traditional doctrinal approaches to legal study were particularly prominent, instructively argued that the turn to narrative (and, by extension, masterplot) reflected a feeling that traditional approaches to legal analysis, especially in a conservative age, had stalled. For Gewirtz, the lure of narrative sprang from a feeling that existing approaches had become linked 'to preservation of the political status quo' or are 'insufficiently responsive' to the interests and concerns of contemporary society. Gewirtz asserted that this recourse to narrative was 'politically reformist',[82] resulting from a 'frustration with the capacity of substantive legal argument to change the real world of law' or a 'loss of faith in the ability of substantive reform itself'.[83] On this view, and despite narrative approaches to legal studies now firmly established, might we nevertheless argue that the engagement of the masterplot frame is, in its

79 As explored by Hayward in Chapter 12.

80 As explored by Mitchell in Chapter 11.

81 Hilde Lindemann Nelson, *Damaged Identities, Narrative Repair* (Cornell University Press 2001) 152.

82 Paul Gewirtz, 'Narrative and Rhetoric in the Law' in Peter Brooks and Paul Gewirtz (eds), *Law's Stories: Narrative and Rhetoric in the Law* (Yale University Press 1996) 12.

83 Gewirtz (n 82).

own way, an act of political resistance or, at least, adjoinder to the more traditional modes of legal enquiry?

Connected to this is the question which, in many ways, sits at the heart of most of this collection, of whether and how established legal masterplots might be open to challenge, be dislodged, dismantled, or replaced with new masterplots or competing narratives. While the foregoing discussion, which has emphasised the concretised, rooted, and conservative nature of masterplots, might suggest that legal masterplots cannot be displaced, this book seeks to explore how these long-established (and often under-explored, hidden, or invisible) super-narratives might be challenged through engagement of the masterplot frame as an *agent for change*.[84] In so doing, the masterplot frame serves as a useful *lens* through which to observe and revisit areas of law, as well as elucidate and amplify reform failure and policy stagnation. Arguably, it is here that the masterplot frame displays its potential for radicalism and is at its politically most potent. Sadler has argued, on the issue of challenging masterplots, that 'they clearly can and do change over time, albeit slowly',[85] and offers the example, in the context of sexual violence against women in Egypt, of the emergence of new masterplots around women's lives and gender relations in the country tied to shifting social attitudes. In this collection, there are multiple accounts of authors reflecting on how the masterplot frame renders visible dominant narratives and how resistance to those narratives might be shaped. It is widely acknowledged that masterplots are rarely, if ever, univocal – just as narrative itself is not univocal. To suggest otherwise would be to misrepresent the often-profound narrative contestation that exists within particular legal spheres. Indeed, masterplots are shown across the chapters of this collection to rub up against, intersect, and even conflict with competing narratives.

Many of the authors in the collection deploy the masterplot frame, in precisely this way, as a means of exposing existing hegemonies in a bid to explore how counter or competing narratives might be embraced to shift the direction of law and policy. Julie Doughty, for example, explores the 'contradiction' between the long-standing child protection masterplot, by which the state only steps in to parent children 'as a last resort' yet, at the same time, data reveal the inexorable rise in the numbers of children being removed for their protection into state care in England and Wales.[86] Luke P. Norris and Allison Tait reflect on the shape that resistance to the masterplot of the market might take and the role of counternarrative in this endeavour.[87] Relatedly, Rebecca Shaw reflects

84 Steven Cammiss, 'Stories in Law: Providing Space for "Oppositionists"?' in M. Freeman and Fiona Smith (eds), *Law and Language: Current Legal Problems* (vol. 15, OUP 2013) ch. 14., 221.
85 Sadler, 'Myths' (n 49) 258.
86 Chapter 13 of this collection.
87 Chapter 6 of this collection.

on the pervasive masterplot of domestic violence and abuse and how a narrative shift in this space requires 'the law to recognise and articulate marginalised voices or counternarratives as discursive resistance'.[88] In the context of the so-called 'energy trilemma', Chris Hilson describes two competing masterplots of energy supply and energy demand.[89]

In short, the authors of this collection harness the masterplot frame so as to reveal existing, dominant masterplot narratives, but also to capture and nourish alternative and competing discourses within distinct areas of law, exposing fault lines and unearthing internal conflicts and competing narratives within the law. In essence, this collection recruits the masterplot lens precisely as an agent of change and engages the framework as a novel means of 'seeing' fields of law differently and thereby opening up the space to challenge existing power structures and hegemonies within them. If legal masterplots, by their inherent nature, connote authority, resilience, and conservatism, this collection seeks to shine a searching spotlight on the opportunities presented by the deployment of the masterplot frame as a vehicle for delivering progressive change by confronting and challenging established assumptions. The vibrancy and analytical potential of the masterplot frame therefore lies not just in its capacity for rendering visible hitherto under-examined or hidden masterplots in law but, furthermore, for its forward-looking potential for inspiring new thinking and new reform agendas across socio-legal research. We can see this endeavour come to life across the chapters of this collection.

3 Introducing the chapters in this book

In the first substantive chapter, **Chapter 2**, of the collection, **Richard Walsh** offers a helpful analysis of the role of narrative in the study of masterplot and of the relationship between narrative, case law, the particular, and the general. The chapter notes the growing interest in the concept of narrative and the currency it has gained across a range of disciplines and discourses, including law. The chapter scrutinises the 'relation between the particular and the general in narrative and in masterplots in order to gain some purchase upon fundamental questions of authority and change in the law'. Drawing on the works of Porter Abbott and set in the context of wider narrative theory literature, Walsh seeks to address two fundamental questions: first, whether masterplots are narratives and, secondly, what kind of authority is vested in a masterplot. In particular, the chapter 'latches onto the connotations of "master"' that make up the masterplot device by examining what kind of authority is reflected or exerted by a masterplot. The chapter then moves to offer critical reflections on the relationship between narrative and case law.

88 Chapter 5 of this collection.
89 Chapter 14 of this collection.

Part 2 of the collection explores responsibility and blame. Reflecting these themes, in **Chapter 3, Chris Bevan** deploys the masterplot frame in the field of homelessness law and policy. In so doing, this chapter locates and exposes the 'homelessness masterplot' as being a super-narrative of desert and redemption that can be traced back centuries in England to the time of the Black Death yet also survives and continues to sound in our contemporary homelessness law. The chapter isolates, elucidates, and tracks this homelessness masterplot through law, policy, and political rhetoric from the fourteenth century right to the present day to reveal the longevity, durability, and potency of this powerful narrative in the homelessness sphere. This is the first time the masterplot analytical frame has been engaged specifically in the homelessness arena and, as such, it is argued, offers new insights and a fascinating way of 'seeing' homelessness law differently at a time when the phenomenon of homelessness is more prevalent and pressing than ever and, on one view, existing homelessness policy in England has, at best, stalled and, at worst, failed. In **Chapter 4**, the second of the chapters examining responsibility and blame, **David Gurnham** engages the masterplot frame in the context of the punishment of prisoners. Gurnham reflects on 'ostensibly antagonistic' narratives on punishment which nonetheless betray a 'curious convergence' across a broad range of sources. The narrative of central interest here is the 'punitive': the angry, objectifying view that those guilty of criminal activity must be – and seen to be – humiliated, made to suffer, and thereby hurt, as they have hurt others. Analysing texts including judicial sentencing remarks, *Judge Dredd*, and prison writings from the poetry anthology *Koestler Voices: New Poetry from Prisons*, the chapter puts the punitive narrative into conversation with moral justifications for punishing and Foucault's account of the modern prison as a site of discipline and observation. Ultimately, the chapter argues that if there is a punishment 'masterplot' at all, then it must be one that acknowledges that older punitive ideas converge with these more recent ones in conceptions of the relationship between punisher and punished, including in prison poetry.

Part 3 turns to the relationship between masterplot and gender. In **Chapter 5, Rebecca Shaw** explores the masterplot operating in the context of domestic violence and abuse. As Shaw explains, the masterplot perpetuates the socio-cultural and structural forces that silence victims and survivors and thereby perpetuates domestic abuse itself. The chapter examines how the law intersects and operates within this framework of narrative contestation and focuses on the Domestic Abuse Act 2021 and the extent to which the legislation challenges or contributes to the continued existence of the 'DVA masterplot'. In so doing, and through examination of the report by the All-Party Parliamentary Group on Domestic Violence and Abuse, the chapter argues that the legislation fails to bring theory in line with practice, and that 'the masterplot continues to suffuse legislation and shape the sensemaking not only of the wider public but also of those who apply the Act in practice'.

Ultimately, the chapter argues that if there is to be a narrative shift, greater attention should be paid to survivor storytellers and the story–discourse distinction within law reform. Examining gender and the market, in **Chapter 6, Luke P. Norris and Allison Tait** identify the masterplot of the market as 'a hyper-charged, superordinating narrative put forth by political commentators, academic theorists, and other contributors to public discourse and compounded by law'. The chapter explores the long history – dating back even to ancient Greece – and nature of the masterplot founded on the binary drawn between the separate spheres of work and home. The chapter highlights what has been hitherto overlooked or under-explored in the literature, namely, how the masterplot of the market and its neat carving out of market and family life obscures functional realities of family life but also occludes individuals' true positionality and power relationships. The chapter addresses the gender implications of the masterplot, noting how legal rules cast the work done by women within marriage in the private realm of the home as a result of gift, love, or charity on the basis that women are non-market actors in this space. It closes by reflecting on how the masterplot might be resisted and the role of counternarratives.

Part 4 provides two chapters musing on history, time, and temporality. First, in **Chapter 7, Rebecca Probert** addresses the historical and contemporary definition of marriage by identifying and tracking the rise and decline of the 'Anglican marriage masterplot' as its central three elements gradually disappeared with the shift of authority over marriage from church to state. The chapter begins with the words of Lord Penzance from the 1866 case of *Hyde v Hyde and Woodmansee* and subsequently unpacks the nature of the Anglican marriage masterplot. It argues that, once one strips out the elements of 'the modern law' generally ascribed to Munby J's judgment in *Sheffield City Council v E* [2004] that no longer hold good as a matter of law, all that is left is that marriage is a contract conferring married status on the parties, along with various legal entitlements. Probert concludes by arguing that there is a need for a new masterplot that encapsulates society's twenty-first-century aspirations around marriage, but this is yet to emerge. The chapter therefore serves as a fascinating example of how a once-powerful masterplot comes, over time, to be lost. Then, in **Chapter 8**, shifting focus to the question of time in international criminal justice, **Nina H. B. Jørgensen** explores the maxim 'justice delayed is justice denied'. The chapter traces the origins of the well-known maxim from early Jewish teachings to the Magna Carta, through to its later attribution to British Prime Minister William Gladstone, and further tracks its recognition in more recent international instruments, including Article 6 of the ECHR and the International Criminal Tribunal for Rwanda (ICTR) and the 1998 Rome Statute of the permanent International Criminal Court. In so doing, the chapter seeks 'to magnify and diminish' the validity of the assertion that 'justice delayed is justice denied' and thereby explicates the two conceptions of time inherent in the maxim. The chapter argues that viewing the maxim as a masterplot takes it out of the realm of 'fancy rhetoric' and permits it to become less about time and more about the story of international criminal justice.

Part 5 explores law, peace, and order and comprises three chapters. First, in **Chapter 9, Steven Cammiss and Graeme Hayes** identify the masterplot of the criminal law in protest trials. Cammiss and Hayes place centre stage Lord Hoffmann's dicta[90] in *R v Jones* [2006] on the theme of protest identifying what the authors term 'Hoffmann's Bargain' and examine how this might be construed as a masterplot. They argue that this emplotment unfolds in two parts: first, through, at least superficially, the propagation of a national myth of the importance of collective action to the achievement of social and democratic progress and, secondly, through the imposition of artificial and arbitrary separation between the legal and the political, recognising the 'good' or deserving protester as someone who accepts legal sanction. Ultimately, Cammiss and Hayes argue that the masterplot's strategic social purpose serves to disarm the very form of collective action that it claims to protect. In **Chapter 10, Ekaterina Yahyaoui Krivenko** engages the masterplot framework to examine the proclaimed purpose of international law as establishing and maintaining order, peace, and justice. As Yahyaoui Krivenko explains, this chapter seeks to enquire as to why, after so many failures of international law exemplified by recent events in Ukraine and Gaza, the power and influence of the international law masterplot endures and retains its persuasiveness. The chapter makes use of Kafka's novel *The Castle* as an explanatory tool to address this question and argues that the persistence of the masterplot is explicable thanks, in part, to the work of international lawyers who, through their use of international law, constantly reinstate its authority and the strength of this narrative. The third chapter in this section, **Chapter 11**, is provided by **Lynsey Mitchell**, who delves into 'the architecture of the stories that underpin the deployment of UK forces abroad' to demonstrate and illuminate the overarching masterplot engaged by the UK government to justify the use of military forces overseas. The chapter explores how this masterplot of 'selling war' operates by repetition of language, and tropes presenting military intervention as benign and necessary, and influenced by rescue narratives to legitimise and rationalise military action. Mitchell draws our attention to the use of memory of past events and the framing of conflicts according to simplistic discourses of good-versus-evil to allow governments to justify recourse to war as natural and necessary.

The final part, exploring the relationship between personal choice and state intervention, comprises three chapters. In **Chapter 12, Andy Hayward**

90 As Cammiss and Hayes note, Lord Hoffmann's words were, for some time, thought to be obiter only but have since been confirmed as forming part of the ratio of *Jones*: see *R v Thacker and others* [2021] EWCA Crim 97, para [100].

locates and challenges the masterplot of choice at play in the field of family law, in particular, cohabitation, whereby cohabitants are assumed by the public, politicians, and policymakers to have actively chosen not to marry. Drawing on Barlow's examination of the concept of 'legal rationality', this chapter argues that the cohabitation masterplot takes the form, essentially, of an assumption that cohabiting couples have actively chosen the consequences of their non-formalised, interpersonal relationship based on, or guided by, the law. Hayward contends that, through operation of the masterplot of choice, 'marriage becomes synonymous with forethought, respectability, and commitment, while cohabitants, despite possessing the autonomy to choose, are painted as the reverse: disorganised, unworthy and uncommitted'. The masterplot frame is then engaged in the context of removal of children from their parents by the state and family autonomy by **Julie Doughty**. In so doing, **Chapter 13** exposes the contradiction between, on the one hand, law and policy based on the ideal of family autonomy, which champions the view that children are best brought up by their parents, and, on the other, the seemingly inexorable rise in the numbers of children being removed from their parents into state care in England and Wales. Having outlined the legal framework for the removal of children by the state, the chapter exposes the flaws in the narrative of child removal often portrayed as 'a last resort', by drawing on Fox Harding's four values perspectives on childcare policy, which, the chapter argues, are consonant with the existence of the masterplot. Rounding off our collection, **Chris Hilson** explores two competing masterplots operating in the field of energy production and in the context of the transition away from a fossil fuel–based economy. **Chapter 14** explains these two masterplots as, first, the dominant narrative of an oil and gas industry–driven demand and, secondly, the narrative of supply. Hilson argues that we are in 'a battle of competing understandings in which the masterplots of energy supply and demand feature strongly'. Unpacking these competing masterplots, the chapter explores how the demand masterplot might be regarded as the 'business as usual' approach, whereas, by contrast, the supply masterplot argues for a more proactive and direct focus on the climate crises as necessitating law's greater attention on cutting fossil fuel production.

Conclusion

In introducing this collection, we have attempted to convey our sense that the notion of 'masterplot', while not entirely unfamiliar, is still very much a creature in formation, and that this is a source of uncertainty, but also opportunity. While scholars will form their own views about its precise contours and provenance and its relationship to its nearest relatives in narratives, stories, and myths, we have proposed here that greater attention to masterplots is warranted in engaging critically with claims to authority, authenticity, and legitimacy in legal contexts. Justice Benjamin N. Cardozo's well-known suspicion of *metaphors* in law – that they 'are to be narrowly watched, for starting as devices to liberate thought, they end often by enslaving it'[91] – could equally be directed at masterplots, or purported masterplots: *what* are the plots that most urgently demand our attention, *who* made them master, and who or what, thereby, is subordinated (or even, to echo Cardozo's more dramatic term, *enslaved*)? The chapters that follow represent a wide spectrum of thought, in terms both of possible answers to these questions and of substantive legal subject matter. We present them here in the hope that they provide a useful contribution to a growing literature on legal masterplots and prompt further and deeper reflection on a provocative and intriguing aspect of narrative studies in law.

91 *Berkey v Third Avenue Railway*, 244 N.Y. 84, 94, 155 N.E. 58, 61 (N.Y. 1926). Cf Lacey's related critique of metaphor: '. . . we must attend carefully to the dangers as well as the positive potential of law's metaphors. For it is precisely through their method of carrying meaning over from one thing to another that they bear the potential to mislead: to conjure up a legitimating image which is distant from the realities of the power relations embedded in law as enforced.' (Nicola Lacey, 'The Metaphor of Proportionality' (2016) 43(1) *Journal of Law and Society* 27, 44).

Chapter 2

Narrative and case law

The reciprocity of the particular and general

Richard Walsh

Introduction

It is commonplace to observe that, in recent decades, the concept of narrative, or at least the term 'narrative', has acquired considerable currency across a broad range of discourses, both academic and non-academic. The law is one of the domains concerned, but others include medicine, politics, advertising, management, environmentalism, science communication, journalism – all broad areas of enquiry and practice well beyond the bounds of narrative's more traditional home in literary and cultural studies (as a prominent form of representation in various media), or in the social sciences (as a qualitative research method). The concept of masterplots fits within this expansive discourse on narrative, and I want to suggest that some of the key issues it raises are, in fact, issues inherent to narrative as such. In this chapter, I scrutinise the relation between the particular and the general in narrative and in masterplots in order to gain some purchase upon fundamental questions of authority and change in the law.

My approach begins by situating masterplots in the context of narrative theory and, specifically, the interplay of the particular and general in narrative, which I then elaborate in relation to the function of the common law as a basis for lawmaking. By doing so, I aim to show how the reflexive logic of narrative form is implicated, both as a symptomatic problem and as a critical corrective, in negotiating the evolving authority of the common law. Accordingly, the first business of the chapter is to clarify some theoretical premises about narrative, as a mode of discourse, but also more fundamentally as a mode of cognition, and then to formulate the double logic of the concept of 'masterplot' with respect to the particular and the general, and hence with respect to the critical issue of narrative authority. In legal terms, the reciprocity between the particular case and the general paradigm is most fundamentally inscribed in the principles of case law, for which I turn to Oliver Wendell Holmes Jr. I situate the model of case law, as Holmes presents it, between two antithetical challenges: from Frederick Schauer, who argues that the circumstantial particularity of cases tends to undermine the formal coherence of

DOI: 10.4324/9781003404668-3

the law's proper foundation in general principles, and from Meir Sternberg, for whom the pragmatics of narrative particularity subsume the law code entirely. I argue that both challenges share a misconception about the reciprocity between the particular and the general encapsulated in the concept of masterplot, and I illustrate with reference to Schauer's own examples. I then consider how this reciprocity, founded in the constitutionally reflexive logic of narrative, bears upon the strengths and limitations of the common law; I gauge the extent to which it provides for the possibility that narrative, albeit part of the problem of the law's authority, may also be part of the means to address it – and that the concept of masterplot may have a key contribution to make.

Narrative form, cognition, and masterplot

The broad currency of 'narrative' does sometimes result in significant gaps between the concept itself, understood with any distinctness, and the actual usage of the term – for reasons partly to do with the loosening of meaning that inevitably accompanies such a diversification of context, but also for reasons arising from the history of the concept's theoretical elaboration. Two common manifestations of such a gap are worth noting, by way of preliminary orientation, because they have some bearing upon relations between narrative and the law: one usage loses sight of the specificity of narrative representation as a form of sensemaking; the other loses the distinction between narrative and the experiences of which it makes sense. The first is the kind of usage involved, for example, whenever a political pundit observes that a party needs to 'change the narrative'. The term is used here to convey something like 'emphasis upon certain priorities or values'; it invokes the perspectival, hence value-laden, quality of narrative, but it has lost the concept's essential concern with temporal particularity or – more tangibly – with events. Narrative is irreducibly a way of articulating processes, occurrences, actions; it gives a specific, sequential form to what happens in time, and all its distinctive features follow from that function. It is the focus upon articulating temporality that differentiates narrative from argument, or from description, or from declarative expression in general. Conversely, the second loose use of the term 'narrative' retains a sense of temporal focus but elides the distinction between what happens and its narrative representation, as if the events in themselves possess narrative form. But narrative gives sense and meaning to what occurs by virtue of representing it, and there is always more than one way to do so; narrative is always perspectival. The inherent perspectivism of narrative representation is not merely a question of verbal expression, moreover, since narrative is also a mode of representation in visual media: at its most basic, it is a feature of mental representation, understood as a sensemaking process.

Every narrative is already committed to certain kinds of perspectival assumption just by virtue of taking narrative form, because narrative sensemaking is, at bottom, a (reflexive) mode of human cognition, in a sense intimated by David Herman, among others.[1] Herman's account actually equivocates between a view of narrative as a representational discourse upon which we draw in making sense of experience and a view in which narrative discourse is underwritten by the narrative structure of experience itself. The first of these is a less-fundamental sense of narrative than I am invoking; the second is consistent with views of narrative articulated by, for example, David Carr, Louis Mink, and Margaret Somers, for whom the structure of narrative is inherent in human experientiality.[2] Such views treat narrative representations as artifacts contingent upon the nature of their (temporal) object of representation, which is conflated with simply what happens. Cognition is relational, however, and occurs in time; the temporality of experience is itself only available upon a reflexive turn within cognition that abstracts from experiential immediacy. Narrative sensemaking is certainly grounded in cognitive embodiment and an enactive relation to environment, and for psychologists like Theodore Sarbin and Donald Polkinghorne, this makes narrative cognition continuous with cognitive embodiment.[3] However, it is not until cognition turns reflexively upon the process of experience itself that its temporal form can become the focus of attention. Polkinghorne has more recently aligned narrative with the embodied image schema SOURCE-PATH-GOAL, drawing upon Mark Johnson and Steven Winter, and I think the association is plausible.[4] Such an embodied schema is a pattern that inheres in the very basic cognitive functioning of many organisms, however, and so does not, in itself, sufficiently characterise narrative cognition. Narrative cognition can only arise when such a schema becomes available to sensemaking as a schema – that

1 David Herman, *Story Logic: Problems and Possibilities of Narrative* (University of Nebraska Press 2002) 22–3.

2 David Carr, *Time, Narrative and History* (Indiana University Press 1986); Louis Mink, 'Narrative Form as a Cognitive Instrument' in Robert H. Canary and Henry Kozicki (eds), *The Writing of History: Literary Form and Historical Understanding* (University of Wisconsin Press 1978) 129. Margaret Somers, 'The Narrative Constitution of Identity: A Relational and Network Approach' (1994) 23 *Theory and Society* 605.

3 Theodore Sarbin, 'The Narrative as a Root Metaphor for Psychology' in Theodore Sarbin (ed), *Narrative Psychology: The Storied Nature of Human Conduct* (Greenwood 1986) 3; Donald Polkinghorne, *Narrative Knowing and the Human Sciences* (State University of New York Press 1988).

4 Donald Polkinghorne, 'Possibilities for Action: Narrative Understanding' in *Proceedings of the 7th Narrative Matters Conference: Narrative Knowing/Récit et Savoir* (Archives ouvertes HAL-Diderot 2014); Mark Johnson, *Moral Imagination: Implications of Cognitive Science for Ethics* (University of Chicago Press 1993); Steven Winter, 'The Cognitive Dimension of the Agon between Legal Power and Narrative Meaning' (1989) 87(8) *Michigan Law Review* 2225.

is, reflexively. At this point, it would make sense to say that the schema acquires the function of a prototypical masterplot. Narrative form, therefore, does not manifest temporal processes in themselves, but a cognitive relation towards them that is minimally conditioned by criteria of relevance to human concerns and is always freighted with significant unexamined presuppositions. Accordingly, there are two sides to narrative's relevance across the many domains of enquiry in which it is invoked, as Peter Brooks has noted with specific reference to the law: one is that narrative's perspectival rhetorical force is always tendentious and often emotionally charged; the other is that its foundational role in human cognition makes it an inevitable part of making sense.[5] Narrative is both suspect and necessary. In the context of his own argument, Brooks invokes the place of narrative cognition in child development, which is perhaps inescapable enough, but it might be added that the narrative mode of sensemaking can also be situated within the even more foundational context of evolutionary adaptation.[6] Narrative form is integral to our cognitive inheritance and, in that sense, inescapable; but it also always entails evaluative commitments that are contingent and open to contestation.

Within the context of such a fundamental role for narrative, the specific concept of 'masterplot', along with the assortment of other terms that cluster around it, raises key issues for both narrative theory and legal studies. How do such authoritative archetypal forms arise, and can they change? This question can be referred to the tension between narrative's necessity and its contingency, which gives it pragmatic relevance. The term 'masterplot' itself is less important here than the set of narrative-theoretical concerns it encapsulates, and indeed less important than its manifest connection with the founding premises of narrative theory, which first emerged as a distinct field through the development of a series of plot-based models of narrative.[7] Porter Abbott makes a good case for the advantages of the term 'masterplot' over a number of alternatives in his general exposition of narrative theory, *The Cambridge Introduction to Narrative* – an exposition that engages specifically with the connection between narrative and the law at several points.[8] The term is also favoured by Brooks and was prominent in his work even before he first engaged directly with narrative and the law – initially, he used it with reference to psychoanalysis.[9] So there are good reasons to work with this term, quite apart from the fact that its conjunction of 'plot' and 'master'

5 Peter Brooks, 'Narrative Transactions – Does the Law Need a Narratology' (2006) 18(1) *Yale Journal of Law and Humanities* 1, 5.

6 Brian Boyd, *On the Origin of Stories: Evolution, Cognition, and Fiction* (Belknap 2009).

7 Ruth Ronen, 'Paradigm Shift in Plot Models: An Outline of the History of Narratology' (1990) 11(4) *Poetics Today* 817.

8 H. Porter Abbott, *The Cambridge Introduction to Narrative* (3rd edn, Cambridge University Press 2020) 53.

9 Peter Brooks, 'Freud's Masterplot' (1977) 55/56 *Yale French Studies* 280.

pointedly occasions two theoretical questions that frame my own enquiry here. The first, simply posed, is: 'Are masterplots narratives?' The second is: 'What kind of authority is vested in a masterplot?'

MasterPLOT: form and narrative particulars

There are good reasons for wanting a masterplot to represent the common features of certain narratives but not be itself a narrative. Most obviously, such an approach to the concept avoids a certain circularity that threatens to undermine it, or at least to erode its clarity and coherence. It is a view that draws support from the structuralist tradition of narrative theory, which founded the field on the premise that all narratives function within abstract semiotic systems that are not themselves narrative in form.[10] Other models also conceive the relation between particular narratives and general forms very broadly: Paul Ricœur's concept of 'prefiguration' expresses the prior context of cultural paradigms within which a specific narrative's configuration is situated and made possible.[11] Hayden White gives a tropological account of the relation between the form of historical narratives and a figurative, ideological, or moralising level of discourse.[12] Jerome Bruner, too, sees the particularity of narratives in relation to broader types but makes any narrative's claim upon our attention dependent upon its 'breach' of the norms of canonical scripts.[13] All these models emphasise the reciprocity between the particular and general, and though Bruner's account seems to imply that general canons are not themselves narrative, he also notes that the breach establishing a given narrative's narrativity may itself be highly conventional, implying that canonical types may, after all, themselves be narrative in form. Indeed, formulations of specific masterplots do look suspiciously like narratives, exactly to the extent that they articulate the plot concerned. It is possible to label a masterplot 'the quest', for example, just as it is possible to label a specific narrative 'the French Revolution'; but once you begin to specify what the quest masterplot is, even at a high level of abstraction, what you get is a narrative: a hero sets out in pursuit of a goal, overcomes obstacles, and arrives at a final reckoning. What is missing here is not narrative, but detail. Abbott's preference for 'masterplot' over 'master narrative', nonetheless, is explicitly a rejection of the idea that masterplots are narratives. He connects 'plot', understood as story type, with the structuralist distinction between story and discourse – that is, between the abstract structure of a narrative

10 Roland Barthes, 'Introduction to the Structural Analysis of Narrative' (1975) 6(2) *New Literary History* 237.

11 Paul Ricœur, *Time and Narrative* (3 vols, University of Chicago Press 1984–88) 1:53.

12 Hayden White, *Metahistory: The Historical Imagination in Nineteenth-Century Europe* (Johns Hopkins University Press 1973).

13 Jerome Bruner, 'The Narrative Construction of Reality' (1991) 18(1) *Critical Inquiry* 1, 11.

and its specific manifestation in an extant version, between the told and the telling.[14] In this light, he argues, it is clear that a *plot* is a skeletal structure common to many different narratives, not a narrative in itself. The problem is that you might say the same for any narrative. A narrative like 'The cat sat on the mat' is specific enough with respect to agent, action, and setting, but it is also clearly the type for any number of more precise narratives specifying kinds of cat, ways of sitting, and designs of mat. It is possible to take 'The cat sat on the mat' as a generic sentence divorced from any particular situation, in other words, and its frequent use as an example, including my own use here, encourages that view of it. That does not, however, exclude the possibility of understanding it as a narrative, which is to understand it as a particular account, however sparing of detail. Every proper narrative is particular, in its own terms; but some particulars are more particular than others, and all particulars already involve the general.

The conceptual move in the other direction, abstracting from plot to masterplot, just as clearly does not provide for a categorical difference but only a difference in granularity. Abbott quickly finds himself resorting to a distinction between 'local' and 'universal' masterplots in order to distinguish the generic Horatio Alger story from the quest more broadly.[15] But if we follow this line, the quest plot will also turn out to be one variation of a more general type, and we end up with a masterplot of a form such as 'equilibrium, disequilibrium, equilibrium', which is a plausible description of all resolved narratives, proposed as such by Tzvetan Todorov.[16] The concept of masterplot offers a basis for abstraction from narrative particulars to general forms, which helps explain the power of narratives and, in doing so, affords a certain critical detachment; but if the basis for a transition from narrative to non-narrative proves elusive, the sense of critical detachment seems illusory. It is open to question whether the concept of masterplot can provide a conceptual mediation between the syntagmatic particularity of narrative and the paradigmatic generality of law. Yet there is a manifest need for some such mediation, and there are plausible reasons for thinking that the route goes via the concept of plot. While the framework of law must, of necessity, be cast in terms general enough to encompass the range of possible instances that fall within its scope, plot aptly encapsulates some of the qualities, in the narratives of those instances, that are most needful for legal consideration: qualities of consequence and causality, intention and accountability. Brooks, in fact, considers the reciprocity of the particular and general on a narrative axis at an even higher level of jurisprudence, referring to the US Constitution as a covenant that 'is a master narrative into which each new narrative

14 Porter Abbott (n 8) 53.
15 Porter Abbott (n 8) 53.
16 Tzvetan Todorov, *The Poetics of Prose* (Cornell University Press 1977) 111.

episode must be fitted'.[17] The two-way traffic between the levels of particular and general is here mapped onto a double temporal orientation intrinsic to narrative itself: constitutional adjudication, he suggests, always appeals back to first principles that are traced through the succession of precedents, even as any given narrative – or, even more pointedly, any plot – is characterised by its teleological orientation towards the end.

MASTERplot: narrative authority

The issue of the relation between plot and narrative leads inexorably to the second of my questions, which latches onto the connotations of 'master': what kind of authority is reflected or exerted by a masterplot? This is a question of importance for all kinds of narratives, but it acquires a special pertinence in relation to the law. If the plausibility – even, to some degree, the intelligibility – of every narrative is contingent upon its relation to recognisable general forms or archetypes, the authority of those archetypes themselves is a matter of concern. How is such authority earned or acquired? Does it reflect some universal order, or is it a more pragmatic phenomenon aligned with the consensual norms of a social animal? Is it one of the conditions of possibility for a social contract? Or more contingently, does it serve to underwrite the exigencies of any given form of governance? Authority easily shades into power, and power makes its own authority. There are good reasons for suspecting the complicity of masterplots with dominant ideologies, that is, for seeing the currency – hence the authority – of certain masterplots as a product of the dominance rather than a ground for the ideology. If narratives depend upon masterplots, such an alignment between narrative authority and dominant ideology works to the exclusion of counternarratives, or of narratives that don't fit. One of the primary reasons narrative has been of interest in the law has been its association with the 'concrete particulars' of experience, the human perspective it offers as a counterweight to the impersonal logic of legal reasoning.[18] This issue of authority calls into question the efficacy of such a role for narrative, however. The particulars of every narrative still need to key into the general paradigm of recognised masterplots, on pain of failing to persuade, even of failing to achieve recognition as a coherent narrative. It should also be noted that the relative absence of a dominant masterplot in certain circumstances does not make room for the unencumbered, virtuous authenticity of the narrative particulars; what follows is a contestation between rival narratives, each seeking to ground its

17 Peter Brooks, 'The Law as Narrative and Rhetoric' in Peter Brooks and Paul Gewirtz (eds), *Law's Stories: Narrative and Rhetoric in the Law* (Yale University Press 1994) 21.

18 Peter Brooks, 'Narrative in and of the Law' in James Phelan and Peter J. Rabinowitz (eds), *A Companion to Narrative Theory* (Blackwell 2005) 401.

authority in a differently tendentious candidate for the status of the applicable masterplot. As Brooks notes, narrative is 'capable of promoting the worse as well as the better cause every bit as much as legal sophistry'.[19] The point is obvious enough but worth insisting upon, especially as a caution against a certain tendency among narrative theorists to incautiously adopt the role of advocate for narrative.

In a more abstract theoretical sense, the authority of masterplots necessarily aligns with the conservative, inertial force of narrative. In *Poetics*, Aristotle tacitly recognises this even as he defends (fictional) narrative's capacity to express general, philosophical truths. The mimetic credibility of plots, he argues, depends upon their plausibility, even where that involves a disregard for their possibility; a plausible impossibility is mimetically superior to an implausible possibility.[20] In saying so, he aligns the authority of narrative with established orthodoxy, or conventional wisdom, rather than truth. Aristotle's word for *plot*, *mythos*, connects this sense of narrative's authority with the notion of masterplot as myth, an association that is perhaps especially prominent in contemporary discourse around creative writing, especially in film, where there are strong commercial motives driving the search for a winning formula. Here, variations upon the idea of a 'monomyth' as expounded by Joseph Campbell hold considerable sway. In *The Hero with a Thousand Faces*, Campbell argued that a single universal mythic structure unifies the apparent diversity of the world's stories.[21] The claim has more circumscribed analogues in the history of narrative theory, notably Vladimir Propp's *Morphology of the Folk Tale*,[22] and popular works on story periodically make similar declarations to the effect that there are really only 4, or 7, or 12, or however many plot types.[23] The often Jungian universalist assumption underpinning these arguments is that stories necessarily gravitate towards a natural prototype, but it is salutary to juxtapose them with an antithetical view of myth, from Roland Barthes. The defining feature of *myth*, for Barthes, is its ideological function, which is precisely to present the specific values and interests of a dominant ideology as if they were natural and universal.[24]

Narrative authority and the law

With respect to the law, this perspective frames and qualifies the account of narrative authority provided by Allison Tait and Luke P. Norris, who consider the foundational role of a masterplot of social contracting in legitimating the

19 Brooks (n 17) 16.
20 Aristotle, *The Poetics of Aristotle* (Stephen Halliwell tr, Duckworth Press 1987).
21 Joseph Campbell, *The Hero with a Thousand Faces* (Pantheon Books 1949).
22 Vladimir Propp, *Morphology of the Folk Tale* (University of Texas Press 1968).
23 For example, Christopher Booker, *The Seven Basic Plots* (Continuum 2005).
24 Roland Barthes, *Mythologies* (Paladin 1972).

rule of law. They note the mythic nature of this masterplot as a retrospective legitimation of legal structures, but their emphasis falls nonetheless upon the positive value of a narrative perspective in helping us 'perceive, value and legitimate this or any "masterplot"'.[25] What seems missing is a complementary critical perspective upon the authority of masterplots, and beyond that the recognition that masterplots are not intrinsically enabling and beneficial. Such a critical perspective would be concerned with how narrative considerations inform the possibility and provision for change in the law. My supposition is that the law's evolution and reform are closely tied up with the negotiation between narrative and 'masterplot', which is ultimately the negotiation between the particular and the general that inheres in narrative as such. The values of society do shift, and reference to some such dialectic must be involved in considering how or whether the law is capable of changing in response. The centrality of narrative to this issue can be usefully brought out by considering work in the more overtly volatile domain of political rhetoric. Stefan Iversen and Mikka Lene Pers-Højholt identify a recurrent strategy in political speeches in which a personal story and a masterplot are paired with each other in order to make the speaker's point as effectively as possible.[26] The rhetorical force of such a strategy, they show, exceeds that of either the particular narrative or the general masterplot alone. Every particular narrative implicitly invokes general paradigms and, in doing so, covertly advances certain values, but while this is central to narrative's ideological power, it does not serve to advertise the values concerned, as a political speech requires; on the other hand, a masterplot pushes forward the general ideological message but lacks the instantiation in a particular experience that authenticates the speaker's stance and makes it relatable for the audience – so providing for the ethos and pathos of rhetoric. Narrative authority does not reside in either the particular or the general but in their mutual reinforcement.

To the extent that the concept of masterplot gains purchase upon the relations between the law and narrative, it does so by foregrounding the interaction between the particular and the general that is both internal to narrative and essential to the negotiation between the unitary framework of the law and the multiplicity of cases it must encompass. The question of authority that lurks within 'masterplot' is also the presiding question in this negotiation, how authority in both law and narrative arises, is maintained, and changes. To give my own discussion a little more particularity, I want to pursue these issues further by looking more closely at how they play out

25 Allison Tait and Luke Norris, 'Narrative and the Origins of Law' (2011) 5(1) *Law and Humanities* 11, 21.

26 Stefan Iversen and Mikka Lene Pers-Højholt, 'Interlocking Narratives: The Personal Story and the Masterplot in Political Rhetoric' in Cindie Aaen Maagaard, Daniel Schäbler and Marianne Wolff Lundholt (eds), *Exploring Fictionality: Conceptions, Test Cases, Discussions* (University Press of Southern Denmark 2020) 183.

in relation to the system of the common law, beginning with the legal axiom 'hard cases make bad law'. The origins of this axiom's formulation as such are obscure, but the canonical statement of it is credited to Oliver Wendell Holmes Jr. He invokes it in the course of his dissenting judgment in *Northern Securities Co. v United States*, but indirectly, by way of analogy: 'Great cases like hard cases make bad law.'[27] His point is that in both kinds of case, some particular feature 'appeals to the feelings and distorts the judgment'.[28] For hard cases, this tendency arises because the circumstances create a tension between the applicable law and an intuitive sense of natural justice; for great cases, it arises because of the undue weight of 'some accident of immediate overwhelming interest'.[29] Such unusual particulars, for Holmes, must not be allowed to exert excessive influence upon the principled integrity of legal judgment.

Nonetheless, Holmes equates making bad judgments with making bad law and, in doing so, reaffirms his broader commitment to case law, argued in his pragmatist repudiation of legal formalism in *The Common Law*. The premise of that argument is that 'the life of the law has not been logic: it has been experience'.[30] The essence of case law is that 'experience', consideration of the particulars of actual cases, is the necessary basis upon which the general principles that constitute the law are articulated and interpreted. But the axiom about hard cases raises a doubt about case law that has been pressed further, more recently, by Frederick Schauer. He poses the larger question, 'Do Cases Make Bad Law?' – making the argument that case law, as such, is an unsound methodology for lawmaking in principle and in practice.[31] While, for Holmes, the contingent particulars of a given case constitute the authority of experience, for Schauer, these same particulars – because they are, by their nature, circumstantial – are always a tendentious basis for the extrapolation of a general rule. And in practice, generalising to a rule from a particular case will tend to give the features of that case a more representative status than they merit within the class of cases to which the rule applies.

In order to bring out the tacit relation to narrative lurking in these arguments, I can invoke an antithetical view advanced by narrative theorist Meir Sternberg. In an extended essay, 'If-Plots: Narrativity and the Law-Code', Sternberg argues that even the general formulations enshrined in legislation need to be understood pragmatically and particularly; the covering rule

27 *Northern Securities Co. v United States* (1904) 193 US 197, 400 (Holmes dissenting).
28 *Northern Securities Co. v United States* (n 27).
29 *Northern Securities Co. v United States* (n 27).
30 Oliver Wendell Holmes Jr., *The Common Law* (first published 1881, The Lawbook Exchange, Ltd 2005) 1.
31 Frederick Schauer, 'Do Cases Make Bad Law?' (2006) 73(3) *University of Chicago Law Review* 883.

needs to be parsed as a bounded set of hypothetical 'if–then' plots.[32] If a certain event occurs under certain circumstances, then a certain judgment follows. The law code itself, on this view, has a fundamentally narrative form. For Sternberg, the particular is not estranged from the general, as it is for Schauer; on the contrary, the sum of particular instances entirely constitutes and exhausts the general.

Schauer's view, I want to suggest, undervalues particularity, while Sternberg's view undervalues generality. Despite the contrast between them, both positions are led astray by a strikingly similar misapprehension about the relation between the particular and the general. Schauer understands rule-making as 'prescription couched in general terms and covering a multiplicity of future instances', as if the general class were a pre-given conceptual unit, defined as the set of all the possible particular instances that fall within its scope.[33] The problem with case law is then that any particular case before the court is very likely to be atypical of the general class. What is missing here is a recognition that extrapolation from the particular, however tendentious, is the very same process of abstraction that produces the general class as such. The general is nonetheless also a qualitatively different conceptual category, not merely a cumulation of particulars. In this respect, Sternberg's view involves a reciprocal misrepresentation, at the level of the relation between law and narrative: the 'if–then' formula, through which he reads rules as in themselves tacitly narrative, effectively conflates logical and chronological implication.[34] Applying the law ceases to be a matter of interpretative negotiation between the conceptual levels of general principles and particular narratives and instead becomes a matter of reading off against an imaginary table of particular cases in order to identify the correct next step in the narrative – the judicial consequence. These two opposed views are both founded upon an inadequate conception of the qualitative difference between the particular and the general; taken together, they highlight the question not just of the hierarchy but of the reciprocity between the two – in jurisprudence and in narrative. This is, in effect, to posit a homology between the case/law relation and the narrative/masterplot relation.

The problem of the particular in case law

One of Schauer's own examples, *Kumho Tire Co v Carmichael* (1999), can help illustrate the issues. Although this is a Supreme Court judgment, it could scarcely be called either a great or a hard case (which was no doubt among

32 Meir Sternberg, 'If-Plots: Narrativity and the Law-Code' in John Pier and José Ángel García Landa (eds), *Theorizing Narrativity* (de Gruyter 2008) 29.

33 Schauer (n 31) 893.

34 Sternberg (n 32) 52–3.

Schauer's reasons for choosing it). In brief, the case concerned a road accident in which a minivan overturned as a result of a tyre blowout; it hinged upon expert testimony about the cause of the blowout. In Schauer's summary:

> [A]lthough the question of what counts as expertise is a broad and important one, the Court in *Kumho Tire* faced it in the context of an expert who, testifying in a products liability case against the manufacture of a tire that had been driven until bald and poorly repaired on multiple occasions, offered as his expert opinion that it was neither the tire's baldness nor its serial poor repair that had caused the tire failure, but rather a defect in the tire's design and manufacture.[35]

Schauer's point is that the Supreme Court decision in this case, which concerned the admissibility of expert testimony in general, was unduly influenced by consideration of a very egregious instance of such testimony.

Kumho Tire offers support for Schauer's point, but his use of it also exhibits a curious reflexiveness – a self-referential quality that pervades the whole of his argument. The reflexiveness in *Kumho Tire* arises firstly because it is the nature of expert testimony to assert a relation between the particulars of a given case and the authority of general parameters of knowledge in the field of expertise; but reflexiveness is also foregrounded because the judgment itself did not refrain from mixing a principled ruling, about the basis upon which expert testimony may be judged admissible, with a ruling about the admissibility of this particular expert's testimony. This disposition of the case was conspicuous enough to prompt the partial dissent of Justice Stevens, for whom the particular ruling was beyond the proper scope of the judgment.[36] These reflexive iterations of the problem of the interplay between particular and general proliferate throughout Schauer's article. He makes his argument against case law – that is, against generalisation from dubiously representative particular cases – by repeatedly generalising from dubiously representative particulars. So he invokes the 'availability heuristic', the psychological characterisation of a 'human tendency to make judgments based on attention to only a subset of available information', yet endorses it by offering a few hypothetical examples of its operation.[37] He proceeds immediately from this move to a critique of the prejudicial influence upon reasoning of the 'anchoring' effect, in which 'the properties of the first event [or evidence] considered . . . influence the estimation of the properties of subsequent events [or evidence]'.[38] In a later variation upon this trope of the self-subverting reflexive turn, he notes

35 Schauer (n 31) 903.

36 *Kumho Tire Co v Carmichael* (1999) 526 US 137, 159 (Stevens dissenting).

37 Schauer (n 31) 896, citing Dolly Chugh and Max H. Bazerman, 'Bounded Awareness: What You Fail to See Can Hurt You' (2007) 6(1) *Mind & Society* 1.

38 Schauer (n 31) 896–7.

that a prevailing judicial 'principle of scepticism about statistical evidence' is justified only to the extent that the case precedent, involving flawed use of statistical evidence, was 'representative of all statistical evidence cases' – that is, a statistical criterion.[39] And his entire argument against extrapolation from the particular is backed by a series of particular examples of case law judgments that set dubious precedent. Schauer resorts to these reflexive strategies with an indeterminate degree of conscious irony; the pattern is pronounced enough to suggest irony is intended, but if so, it is admirably discreet. He does eventually acknowledge, though, that, 'the very same biases I argue may exist for judges and other case-based rulemakers exist for me as I attempt to identify the very phenomenon I am discussing'.[40] This concession, nonetheless, only goes part-way towards recognising the issue. The fact that he is attempting to make a principled argument, rather than to negotiate between established principles and problematic instances, indicates that the reciprocal dependence of the particular and the general is not a problem with case law but a condition intrinsic to all conceptual abstraction and decision-making – the general domain within which the system of case law operates.

The reflexive structure of narrative and the evolution of the law

My larger point is that reflexiveness is not a belated, secondary phenomenon; indeed, it is constitutive of narrative form, from the most fundamental base level of narrative cognition upwards. Narrative cognition arises when the mind turns reflexively upon the immediacy of experience, so producing narrative's characteristic dual temporality, the time of the telling and the time of the told.[41] It is this reflexive turn that inaugurates the reciprocal relation between the particular and the general, between this experience and the formal resources that give it intelligibility; and the recursive potential of such a reflexive turn makes the reciprocity dynamic and continually feeds it. The form of the general is abstracted from particulars and itself also establishes the terms in which the particular is grasped. The circuit is dynamic, rather than a dead tautology, just so long as it is impelled by continual accommodations to the unruliness of the particular. In the same way, a masterplot is an ossification of narrative form, cognitively and culturally justified to the extent that it articulates recurrent narrative patterns, but also aligned with the negatively conservative forces of narrative – with stock narratives, clichés, stereotypes,

39 Schauer (n 31) 904.
40 Schauer (n 31) 905.
41 Abbott (n 8) 262 ('temporal structure'); Gérard Genette, *Narrative Discourse* (Basil Blackwell 1980) chs. 1–3.

with prejudicial and parochial values. The particularity of narrative can mitigate these forces just to the extent that it is rebarbative to easy generalisation or, in Bruner's terms, to the extent that its breach of canonicity is significant. This mechanism for reciprocity offers a counterbalance to Schauer's concerns about case law. Consider the dissenting opinion offered by Holmes in *Lochner v New York*, which includes the declaration 'General propositions do not decide concrete cases'.[42] On the face of it, that is exactly what you would expect an advocate of common law to say, in accordance with the principle that the common law 'decides the case first and determines the principle afterwards', which is the Holmes quote with which Schauer's discussion begins.[43] But in fact, Holmes is referring to the general proposition he has himself just formulated, the proposition that a constitution does not embody any particular economic theory but accommodates different views, and statutes are not unconstitutional merely because they conflict with any such view. He goes on, 'I think that the proposition just stated, if it is accepted, will carry us far toward the end', referring to the judgment of this particular case.[44] The opinion finely balances a presumption in favour of legislatures with an affirmation of the capacity for evolving views to occasion change in the law. It does so because it holds in dynamic equilibrium the contrary principles of abstraction from the particular and inference from the general.

The real merit of the position Holmes first advanced in *The Common Law* is not the priority it accords to the particular case but its pragmatism. The general and the particular are always reciprocally in play. Experience, in Holmes's word, is not just the raw particularity of what happens but the sense that we cumulatively make of it. That sense always involves assimilating the particular case to some general form, some paradigm, within which it can be placed, and so recognised. To the extent that any case can be grasped by a narrative account, or competing narrative accounts, of what has occurred, it is already caught up in the interplay of the particular and the general. The movement from case to law is not from particular to general but, rather, between levels of this interplay, which is recursively reflexive. It is such recursive functions of reflexive form that provide for the possibility of change in the law. The inherent tendentiousness of extrapolating from the particular has to be weighed against the power of abstraction, which creates the general and is qualitatively different from the merely cumulative inspection of particular cases within the bound of a supposedly pre-given general class. Schauer's fundamental objection to the common law as a model for the evolution of

42 *Lochner v New York* (1905) 198 US 45, 76 (Holmes dissenting).

43 Schauer (n 31) 883, citing Oliver Wendell Holmes Jr., 'Codes, and the Arrangement of the Law' in Sheldon M. Novick (ed), *The Collected Works of Justice Holmes* (vol 1, Chicago 1995) 212.

44 *Lochner* (n 42).

the law is that it is a largely blind process. It lacks oversight of the timeliness of judgments, criteria for resistance to correction, checks on the appropriateness of occasions for correction, and the capacity to address systemic problems.[45] All this accurately captures the way in which evolutionary processes work; they are bottom-up processes that occur in dynamic interaction with the determining constraints of their contexts, without the intentionality and teleological purpose that a narrative account of such processes would necessarily project upon them. Narrative is the form in which we are cognitively and culturally conditioned to understand change, not how change actually happens. The important consideration is that the change concerned is not one of gradual approximation towards an ideal legislature but circumstantial change within a changing social and cultural environment. The problem, then, is not that the law evolves but that this process is not adequately accountable to, or driven by, criteria responsive to changing social values more broadly. Social justice requires revisionary intervention in the system of the law, which is to say, the deliberative use and re-inflection of its determining constraints. This account suggests that such reformist engagement with the law might be effectively prosecuted through reflexive critical address to its masterplots.

Conclusion

As I had occasion to remark some years ago in a quite different context, the law of narrative is case law (the context was an argument about the nature of narrative creativity in fiction).[46] The process of change in the law bears comparison with the dialogic development of narrative form itself, the principles of common law echoing the relation between narrative and masterplot. But I do not think this means that advocacy for progressive legislature equates with a call for more narrative; rather, it means that more reflexive engagement with narratives in and of the law can make the reciprocity between the particular and the general, at every level, more transparent and accountable. The general authority of legislature, or of masterplots, is the foil against which a particular case or narrative is visible, thrown into relief in its distinctness, and made intelligible; but conversely, the authority of the general is also ultimately, pragmatically, accountable to the particular, just as grammar is ultimately accountable to usage. Narrative critique can offer a more conscious and reflexive attention to the dynamics involved, to the accountability of legal processes within larger contexts of value, and to the possibilities they afford for responsive change. And narrative critique itself means, reciprocally, both narrative as critique and critique of narrative.

45 Schauer (n 31) section IV, 906–11.
46 Richard Walsh, *The Rhetoric of Fictionality* (Ohio State University Press 2007) 146.

Narrative, as a mode of cognition, begins with reflexive attention to the implicit in attending to the temporality of experience, and in doing so, it generates a new implicit level, the temporality of narration, that itself becomes available for reflexive attention. The elaboration of narrative culture from such humble premises can be understood as the recursive application of every available dimension of this reflexive potential, and every reflexive turn is a form of critical scrutiny of the unexamined, bringing it within the compass of narrative sensemaking and simultaneously introducing novel complexity, discrimination, and nuance into the formal resources of narrative itself. This is the respect in which narrative functions as critique, foregrounding and holding to account both the abstraction of its masterplots and the contingency of its particulars. Narratives are also, of course, often blind to the coercive constraints of their own indebtedness to the assumptions of narrative form, which frame the possibility of making narrative sense at all. This is the respect in which critique of narrative is also needed – meaning narrative theory, certainly, and narrative criticism as the application of theory to specific instances, but more broadly meaning the cultivation of narrative literacy. The essence of narrative literacy is simply lucidity about the fact that every narrative is an instance of narrative form, or of a masterplot of some generality, and about the respects in which every narrative is, in consequence of that fact, a negotiation between the particular and the general that is fraught on both sides with evaluative commitments. Narrative literacy of this sort, I would suggest, is most needful – in society at large and, especially, among stakeholders in the law's systems and processes.

Part 2

Responsibility and blame

Chapter 3

Desert and redemption

The homelessness masterplot

Chris Bevan

Introduction

This is the first time that the 'masterplot' analytical frame has been applied to the field of homelessness law and policy. This is not, however, simply theoretical novelty for novelty's sake, because, on one view, as is advanced here, policymaking on homelessness in England has, at best, stalled and, at worst, failed. Contemporary homelessness policy in England can, it is argued, be regarded as a site of relative failure,[1] not for lack of policy itself, or for lack of statutory intervention – there has been much of both – but because despite repeated and impassioned promises to 'end homelessness',[2] of apparent cultural revolutions in the sector, of the most ambitious reforms in decades, these have all proved to be false dawns, as homelessness remains stubbornly high,[3] is estimated to cost the public sector in excess of £1 billion per year, is responsible for almost 3,000 homeless deaths in the last two years alone;[4] and this most avoidable of social phenomena remains an open canker on our national life. Described variously as 'a national crisis',[5] 'a scourge on our society',[6] 'a

1 Christopher O'Leary and Thomas Simcock, 'Policy Failure or F***up: Homelessness and Welfare Reform in England' (2022) 37(8) *Housing Studies* 1379.

2 The promise to 'eliminate homelessness' by the end of 2027 was made in the Conservative Election Manifesto 2017, 58. A promise to end rough sleeping by 2024 was made by the Department for Levelling Up, Housing & Communities in *Ending rough sleeping for good* (2 September 2022). Both targets will be missed.

3 The latest statistics at the time of writing show that there were almost 325,000 homeless households in England in 2023/24, up 10.4% on the previous year and up 3% on pre-Covid-19 levels: Department for Levelling Up, Housing & Communities, *Statutory Homelessness in England: Financial Year 2023–24* (3 October 2024).

4 The figure of annual deaths has been steadily rising year on year since data collection began in 2019.

5 Public Accounts Committee, *11th Report – Homeless Households* (HC 2017–19, 462) <https://publications.parliament.uk/pa/cm201719/cmselect/cmpubacc/462/46203.htm> accessed 25 July 2024.

6 Harriet Harman, 'Homelessness Is a Scourge on Our Society – We Can End It and We Must' *South London Press* (7 March 2018) <www.harrietharman.org/homelessness_is_a_scourge_on_society_we_can_end_it_and_we_must_sth_ldn_press_column> accessed 25 July 2024.

DOI: 10.4324/9781003404668-5

source of national shame',[7] the problem is not one of inability to diagnose the cause, for the causes of homelessness have long been readily understood. No, something in the broader landscape of policymaking in this field blocks meaningful progress. The case for 'doing better' on the homelessness issue and for new thinking is therefore easily made out. It is into this febrile context that the masterplot framework on homelessness is deployed in this chapter.

The chapter unfolds in three parts. The first part explores the value of engaging the masterplot frame on homelessness, before the second part locates and traces what is described here as 'the homelessness masterplot', by spanning hundreds of years from the Black Death right into contemporary homelessness law and policy in England. In the third and final part, the chapter adopts a more critical edge, reflecting on why the homelessness masterplot has enjoyed such traction and why it exhibits such tenacity. Ultimately, the chapter argues that if we want to dislodge the long-rooted masterplot in order to reform the law and adopt a different and more effective path towards eradicating homelessness, we must first 'see' and understand the masterplot, its origins, its potency, and what sustains it even in our contemporary legal framework on homelessness.

Part I: Why engage the masterplot lens on homelessness?

What does the masterplot lens bring to legal scholarship on homelessness? Scholars across diverse disciplines, from philosophy to psychology, have, since the 1970s, examined how the stories we tell both represent the world[8] yet also 'create knowledge about it and shape our experience of it, with storytelling functioning as a basic mechanism for the production of meaning'.[9] In the homelessness field more specifically, Schiff has illuminated how exploring understandings and meanings of homelessness reveals 'who holds power, how that power is used, how the parameters of the broader arena are shaped, how the activities of that arena are organized and determined, and finally, what the underlying conceptions of that arena are'.[10] In this chapter, it is contended that,

7 Teresa May, Prime Minister (2016–2019) 'Making Housing Fairer' (Speech to London Planning Conference, 5 March 2018) <www.gov.uk/government/speeches/pm-speech-on-making-housing-fairer-5-march> accessed 25 July 2024.

8 See, for example, Louis O. Mink, 'History and Fiction as Modes of Comprehension' (1970) 1(3) *New Literacy History* 541; Jerome Bruner, 'The Narrative Construction of Reality' (1991) 18(1) *Critical Inquiry* 1; Donald E. Polkinghorne, *Narrative Knowing and the Human Sciences* (State University of New York Press 1988); Hayden White, *The Content of the Form* (Johns Hopkins University Press 1987).

9 Neil Sadler, 'Myths, Masterplots and Sexual Harassment in Egypt' (2019) 24(2) *The Journal of North African Studies* 247, 254.

10 Lisa Schiff, 'The Power to Define: Definitions as a Site of Struggle in the Field of Homelessness' 16(4) *International Journal of Qualitative Studies in Education* 491.

viewed in the context of homelessness policy stagnation and relative strategic failure, the masterplot framework allows us to unpick these questions of power afresh and that, taking a narrative-led approach, permits a historiographical perspective which contributes to both explaining and, ultimately, reversing the failure of homelessness policy to actively and meaningfully reduce homeless and improve the lives of those experiencing homelessness. Masterplots are 'stories that we tell over and over in myriad forms and that connect vitally with our deepest values, wishes, and fears'.[11] For Porter Abbott, '[t]he rhetoric of narrative is its power' because 'narrative [is] an instrument of power'.[12] Masterplot necessarily has a close relationship to but is not directly synonymous with 'narrative'. This is best explained by uncoupling the 'master' and 'plot' elements of the masterplot device. A masterplot, as explained in the introduction to this collection,[13] is a concept that emerges from both narrative and plot. It commands an especially prominent place in the narrative hierarchy (thus reflecting its 'mastery'), which is often not seen in lesser, micro, or humbler narratives and plots. Yet masterplot is inherently a relative of *narrative*, with notions such as *meta-narrative*, *master* narrative, and *super*-narrative evidently semantically but also practically connected. What sets the masterplot apart is its 'mastery', its authority, its power, and arguably, its more 'global' nature, as explored by Liveley and Shaw.[14] As a result of the close interaction of masterplot with narrative, this chapter makes use, in places, of both terms. This is felt most appropriate, as in the context of homelessness law and policy, there is a wide range of narratives at play, at times working together, at times competing, which reflect the necessary conceptual and policy messiness and complexity of the issue. The central point being made in this chapter, however, is that overarching this hotbed of narratives is the homelessness masterplot, which occupies the top rung of the ladder of narrative hierarchy. The homelessness masterplot unearthed in this chapter has, it is argued, been fostered over centuries in England as a method of both explicit and deliberate power and 'control' over the homeless population and, even in more contemporary times, endures in 'managing' and 'governing' (used here in the Foucauldian tradition of *governmentality*)[15] those experiencing homelessness.

11 H. Porter Abbott, 'The Rhetoric of Narrative' in H. Porter Abbott (ed), *The Cambridge Introduction to Narrative* (2nd edn, CUP 2014) 46.

12 Porter Abbott (n 11) 40, 41.

13 See introduction chapter to this collection, Section 1.1, on '*Legal Masterplots as Legal Narratives*'.

14 Genevieve Liveley and Rebecca Shaw, 'Marriage Plots: A New Narratological Approach to the Augustan Marriage Laws' (2020) 14(2) *Law and Humanities* 244.

15 On which see Chris Bevan, 'Governing "The Homeless" in English Homelessness Legislation: Foucauldian Governmentality and the Homelessness Reduction Act 2017' (2021) 38(3) *Housing, Theory and Society* 259.

As this wider collection exposes, the existence of an established masterplot in a policy area allows for the maintenance of the status quo – almost always, this status quo is to the clear benefit of elites and those not targeted or implicated by that masterplot. In this case, the homelessness masterplot operates to keep the homeless 'in their place' (that place being simultaneously and ironically both on the street yet out of sight and mind of the majority) and ensures those with greater housing privilege (landowners and landlords, and the property-owning classes generally) are not threatened by the 'risky' behaviour of liberalising too far access to housing support. Narratives, and by extension, masterplots, are all about power, then. The example of homelessness is perhaps the archetype of the powerful versus the powerless, the 'haves' versus the 'have nots' (the homeless), with the all-powerful state holding the purse strings and the authority to decide who gets support and who does not. In this supercharged power dynamic, a multitude of stories and narratives play out. In identifying the homelessness masterplot in this chapter, this is not to suggest that it is the *only*, or perhaps the most important, 'story' in homelessness, nor is it to suggest that it is uncontested, but rather, it is argued that this is the central, enduring masterplot that has played out over centuries in England. So what is the *homelessness masterplot*? It is to that question that we turn in the next section.

Part 2: Locating and tracing the homelessness masterplot of desert and redemption

The homelessness masterplot exposed in this chapter is the masterplot of desert and redemption. In short, the homelessness masterplot holds that a distinction can be drawn between those homeless who are *deserving* of support and those who are *undeserving*. Only those *deserving* of help should receive it; the *undeserving* should be excluded, but for those prepared to bend to the state's will, there can be redemption from the plight of homelessness through the moral cleansing of work and, in more contemporary times, by compliance and cooperative submission to mandated steps – defined by the state – out of housing precarity. The word 'desert' entered the English language via Old French *deservir* ('to be worthy of having'), from the Latin *dēserviō* ('to gain or merit'), and instructively confirms the word's connection with notions of worth and value. The word 'redemption' derives from Latin *redemptio*, meaning 'buying back', 'rescuing', or releasing', and has historically been used in religious contexts to signify release from sin. It is argued here that these two interlocking narratives of desert and redemption have co-existed and been co-nourishing over many centuries in England. The homelessness masterplot is ancient, deeply historically rooted yet has endured and still sounds in the contemporary homelessness policy landscape today. This section explores what the homelessness masterplot actually is, how and by whom it was created, and tracks its manifestation through law and policy on homelessness as evidenced by political, legislative, and policy interventions in this sphere from the fourteenth century into the present-day legal framework.

Locating the early origins of the homelessness masterplot

The origins of the homelessness masterplot, it is argued in this chapter, can be traced back to at least the fourteenth century and the Black Death, a virulent plague that killed 30–40% of the working population in England, produced serious labour shortages, and led to significant social and economic upheaval.[16] In this feverish melting pot of post-pandemic fervour, attitudes towards work and those regarded as unwilling or unable to work[17] began to shape the early foundations of approaches towards those without a home. An image began to permeate English society, as captured by poet John Gower, that post-plague workers were 'sluggish . . . scarce, and . . . grasping. For the very little they do they demand the highest pay'.[18] In response, a raft of measures was introduced to shore up the employment market, including the Ordinance of Labourers Act 1349, which provided that all citizens under 60 years of age must work (or face prison). It became an imprisonable offence to give money or any assistance, whether 'under the colour of pity or alms', to any 'able-bodied beggar' who, in the eyes of the law, ought to be working. This period is widely recognised as the beginning of the problematic and abiding association between worklessness, poverty, disease, delinquency, and in our more modern parlance, homelessness. Building on these accounts, it is contended in this chapter that the Black Death can be viewed as the inception point of what is termed here the homelessness masterplot of desert and redemption.

The 1388 Statute of Cambridge introduced further restrictions of movement on workers and beggars. 'Beggars' (which included those without a home) could now only get help from their local area – known as their 'Hundred' – this being the area with which they had a settled connection. Relief was heavily restricted to the 'impotent poor' – in other words, those unable to work due to age or infirmity, who found themselves destitute through no fault of their own doing. The 'impotent poor' were banned from leaving their area, and the local 'Hundred' was made responsible for their housing. It is in these measures of the 1388 law that we see, remarkably, the origins of the concepts of 'local connection', 'of priority need', and of 'intentional homelessness' that remain the cornerstones of qualification for homelessness assistance in our homelessness law today. Yet beyond this, the 1388 statute

16 See generally John Aberth, *The Black Death: A New History of the Great Mortality in Europe, 1347–1500* (OUP 2020).

17 There are clear echoes of such an approach in the debate post the Covid-19 pandemic as to working from home ('WFH') and the rhetorical push from sections of the British media and members of the UK Conservative government to get people 'back into the office'. See, for example, Jim Waterson, '"Condescending": Jacob Rees-Mogg Leaves Notes for WFH Civil Servants' *The Guardian* (23 April 2022) <www.theguardian.com/politics/2022/apr/23/condescending-jacob-rees-mogg-leaves-notes-for-wfh-civil-servants> accessed 25 July 2024.

18 Cited in John Hatcher, 'England in the Aftermath of the Black Death' (1994) 144(1) *Past & Present* 3, 17.

is noteworthy for the cultural signals it projected, namely, the bifurcation it erected between, on the one hand, the 'impotent poor', who, blameless for their personal circumstances, were deemed deserving of help, and, on the other hand, the so-called 'able-bodied workers', who were compelled to work (morally, to realise a sense of citizenship) and who were undeserving of support.[19] Pinpointing a definite 'first cause' or exact starting point for the development of the homelessness masterplot is, naturally, open to debate, and opinions will surely diverge on its precise origin story; however, it is argued in this chapter that it was in the fourteenth century that the homelessness masterplot of desert and redemption – in other words, the division between deserving and undeserving citizens and the redemptive imperative of work – was born. As Timms has noted, 'the wandering poor came to be seen, at best, as immoral idlers, at worst as a threat to the very fabric of society. Punishment was the mainspring of policy'.[20]

In the subsequent 200 years or more, a plethora of legislation was introduced in England which further nourished and perpetuated the burgeoning deserving/undeserving narrative and, in so doing, continued the marginalisation and demonisation of the poor and homeless, thus contributing to the homelessness masterplot. One striking example is the Vagabonds and Beggars Act 1494, which made it a crime to be homeless or even to be suspected of being so, or of being 'idle'. The Act provided that:

> Vagabonds, idle and suspected persons shall be set in the stocks for three days and three nights and have none other sustenance but bread and water and then shall be put out of Town. Every beggar suitable to work shall resort to the Hundred where he last dwelled, is best known, or was born and there remain upon the pain aforesaid.

By the fifteenth century, a critical narrative and distinction had concretised in England both in the statute books and also in the cultural psyche of the nation – a stigma[21] fixing to those who were poor and without a home. Link and Phelan describe stigmatisation as a process of labelling, stereotyping,

19 One could argue that this approach continues to sound in contemporary attitudes underpinning the means-testing of applicants for social security benefits in the UK, including, for example, Universal Credit.

20 Phillip Timms, 'Homelessness and Mental Illness in the UK' in João M. Castaldellio-Maia, Antonio Ventriglio and Dinesh Bhugra (eds), *Homelessness and Mental Health* (CUP 1996) 12.

21 On stigma and housing, see, generally, Mervyn Horgan, 'Housing Stigmatization: A General Theory' (2020) 8(1) *Social Inclusion* 8; Loïc Wacquant, 'Territorial Stigmatization in the Age of Advanced Marginality' in Jarmo Houtsonen and Ari Antikainen (eds), *Symbolic Power in Cultural Contexts* (Brill Sense 2008) 43; Loïc Wacquant, Tom Slater and Virgilio B. Pereira, 'Territorial Stigmatization in Action' (2014) 46(6) *Environment and Planning A: Economy and Space* 1270.

separation, status loss, and discrimination.[22] These elements are explicit in the approach towards the homeless in this period in England. The deserving/undeserving distinction had taken hold in law. This latter undeserving category comprised vagrants, vagabonds, beggars, and the idle. 'The idle' were those able to work but, in the eyes of the authorities, had chosen not to do so. The undeserving were branded, imprisoned, or forced into servitude. This period, therefore, established the criminalisation and pathologisation of the homeless poor, who were depicted according to a 'plot' of fecklessness and undeservingness.

The Poor Relief Act 1601 – widely regarded as the first of many Poor Laws in England – marked a significant moment for how support was given to those who could not support themselves following Henry VIII's dissolution of the monasteries, which removed the principal source of charity in England. The Poor Laws were a response to this and sought to fill the gap. The 1601 legislation known as the 'Old Poor Law' introduced modes of 'correction' in order to cure or 'redeem' the poor of their impediments. In these early Poor Laws, the theme of redemption for the blameless poor begins to emerge most profoundly. Chief among its provisions, the 1601 Act provided for a form of hierarchy of support from the most deserving to the least deserving. At the top of the hierarchy, the most deserving were those unable to work – generally the 'lame, impotent, old, blind', as the Act records. They were to be cared for via provision of 'outdoor relief', including payments, items of food, clothing, or sometimes in almshouses or poorhouses. Next, the able-bodied poor were to be put to work in industry. Finally, at the bottom of the hierarchy, as the least-deserving group, the idle poor and vagrants were sent to 'houses of correction'[23] or imprisoned. The essence of the 1601 Act was that the 'settled' poor should be encouraged into employment to be trained, rehabilitated out of their poverty through work, while the 'wandering' or 'idle poor' should be 'corrected' and forced into work. Put differently, work became the central channel for redemption for society's supposedly most problematic groups. The Vagrancy Act of 1824, which followed later, continued in the same narrative vein by making it a criminal offence to be homeless, to sleep rough, or to beg in England. Remarkably, parts of the Act are still in force today.[24]

22 Bruce G. Link and Jo C. Phelan, 'Conceptualizing Stigma' (2001) 27 *Annual Review of Sociology* 363.

23 See Karl De Schweinitz, *England's Road to Social Security* (University of Pennsylvania Press 1943); under a 1607 amendment to the 1601 legislation, it was ordered that houses of correction be established in every county.

24 There are provisions in the Police, Crime, Sentencing, and Courts Act 2022 that will repeal the 1824 Act, but this provision is yet to be brought into force. The government has committed to reform, but only once changes to the court system are made. It argues it 'will not commence the repeal until appropriate replacement legislation is in place': Home Office, *Repeal of the Vagrancy Act 1824: Police, Crime, Sentencing and Courts Act 2022 Factsheet* (Policy Paper 20 August 2022).

Amidst growing discontent with the Old Poor Law,[25] in 1832, the government appointed a Royal Commission to prepare recommendations for reform. The findings of the Commission[26] were stark, forthright, and formed the essential framework of the legislation that followed: the Poor Law Amendment Act 1834. The Commission asserted that poverty was caused by the indigence of individuals and their choices and not by economic or social conditions.[27] As Grogan highlights, 'reformers of the poor laws protested that the poor pretended to be needier than the facts warranted'.[28] The existing system was criticised for being too soft and positively encouraging pauperism, damaging the morality of the wider country. In reforming the law, it was therefore fundamental that the undeserving be deterred from seeking poor relief in any form. In order to achieve this, the Commission put forward legislative proposals that 'all relief whatever to able-bodied persons or to their families, otherwise than in well-regulated workhouses . . . shall be declared unlawful'.[29]

The same punitivity towards the homeless endured into the new law. The new law arrived in 1834 law, referred to as the 'New Poor Law',[30] and single-handedly swept aside Poor Laws in England that reached back over half a millennium. It introduced country-wide uniformity in how the destitute and homeless were to be treated. At its heart, the core aim of the legislation was deterrence, and poor relief for the genuinely sick and destitute was governed by an abhorrent workhouse regime.[31] It was important that people be discouraged from living idly, so workhouse conditions should therefore be 'less eligible'[32] (in other words, less desirable) than the conditions an independent labourer of the lowest class would experience. Workhouses were therefore designed to be as hostile as possible. As the Commissioners noted:

> Into such a house none will enter voluntarily; work, confinement, and discipline, will deter the indolent and vicious; and nothing but extreme

25 See, generally, Sidney Webb and Beatrice Webb, *English Poor Law History. Part 1: The Old Poor Law* (Frank Cass 1963); Paul A. Fidler, *Social Welfare in Pre-Industrial England: The Old Poor Law Tradition* (Palgrave 2006).

26 Nassau Senior and Edwin Chadwick, *Poor Law Commissioners' Report of 1834* (H.M. Stationery Office 1834).

27 The Assistant to the Commissioners noted: 'The effect [of the Old Poor Law] has been to promote bastardy; to make want of chastity on the woman's part the shortest road to obtaining either a husband or a competent maintenance; and to encourage extortion and perjury': John W. Cowell quoted in 'The Amendment of the Poor Laws' *The Examiner* (20 April 1834).

28 Michael Grogan, 'Generosity and the Ghosts of Poor Laws Passed' (2004) 12(2) *Narrative* 151, 152.

29 Commission Report (n 26) Part II, Section 2 'Principle of Legislation'.

30 See Derek Fraser, *The New Poor Law in the Nineteenth Century* (Macmillan 1976).

31 See Ursula Henriques, 'How Cruel Was the Victorian Poor Law?' (1968) 11(2) *Historical Journal* 365, 368.

32 On the workhouse and 'less eligibility', see Margaret A. Crowther, *The Workhouse System 1834–1929: The History of an English Social Institution* (Routledge 2016).

> necessity will induce any to accept the comfort which must be obtained by the surrender of their free agency, and the sacrifice of their accustomed habits and gratifications.[33]

The poor and homeless could only get help if they were prepared to enter the workhouse, where they were made to wear a uniform, branded with 'P' on their shoulders, and forced to undertake pointless jobs, such as picking oakum or breaking stones.[34] The New Poor Law effectively punished and stigmatised the poor for being poor even through no personal fault. Newspapers 'never tired of telling of [the workhouse] horrors',[35] and there were multiple reports of the destitute preferring to enter prostitution, commit crime, or even starve to death rather than enter the workhouse.[36] As Dickens famously wrote:

> [W]e have come to this absurd, this dangerous, this monstrous pass, that the dishonest felon is, in respect of cleanliness, order, diet, and accommodation, better provided for, and taken care of, than the honest pauper.[37]

The Royal Commission had revived the so-called 'workhouse test', namely, that the deserving and the undeserving poor could be distinguished by a simple test: any citizen prepared to accept relief in the workhouse must, by definition, be lacking the moral determination to survive outside it. Thus, the 1834 Act re-emphasised the deeply moralistic distinction between the deserving and the undeserving poor. Dickens and Hardy stirringly described the zeal with which the 'workhouse test' was engaged and depicted how the spectre, the threat, the narrative, the 'plot' of the workhouse seeped into the collective psyche of the English working classes.[38] Dickens' *Oliver Twist* and its portrayal of the evils of the workhouse have become especially fixed as a shared reference point in the nation's cultural imagination and understanding of how the 'plotline' of

33 Commission Report (n 26) Part II, Section 2 'Principle of Legislation'.

34 On which see Ross Cranston, *Legal Foundations of the Welfare State* (Weidenfeld & Nicolson 1985).

35 David Roberts, 'How Cruel Was the Victorian Poor Law?' (1963) 6(1) *Historical Journal* 97, 98.

36 A poem, 'The Pauper's Song' (1845), famously satirised the workhouse, recounting the benefits enjoyed by criminals in prison over their workhouse compatriots: 'The Pauper's Song' *Punch* (18 January 1845) 38.

37 From Charles Dickens, 'A Walk in a Workhouse' *Household Words* (25 May 1850) full text reproduced at <https://victorianweb.org/authors/dickens/poorlaw.html> accessed 25 July 2024.

38 See, amongst others, the depictions in *Oliver Twist* (serialised in Bentley's Magazine 1837–1839); and generally on the Poor Laws and the workhouse: Crowther (n 32); Webb and Webb (n 25) Part 2; Michael E. Rose, *The English Poor Law, 1780–1930* (David and Charles 1971); Norman Longmate, *The Workhouse: A Social History* (Temple Smith 1974); Felix Driver, *Power and Pauperism: The Workhouse System* (CUP 2008).

the homeless and the destitute has historically played out in England.[39] In contrast to the pre-1834 position, under the New Poor Law, the destitute and the homeless were seen as responsible for their own precarity, as if they had elected pauperism. The poor were represented as lazy, unmotivated, and requiring of instruction. Workhouses divided the destitute 'between the innocent and the culpable Poor',[40] the latter to be subjected to 'a System . . . so repugnant to dissolute habits'[41] and repeatedly referred to '[p]ersons who through Idleness may pretend themselves sick, lame or infirm [who] shall . . . be punish'd severely'.[42] Inspired by Bentham's theory of utilitarianism and the idea of 'stigmatising' poor relief, the reforms sought to turn seeking relief into 'an object of wholesome horror'.[43] The essential 'plot' of the deserving and the undeserving homeless, and how they might be redeemed through work – what is, in this chapter, termed the masterplot of desert and redemption – was, therefore, already established in law, policy, and the psyches of the population as fundamental and foundational pillars of society and of the workhouse system more specifically.

Desert and redemption in the twentieth century

The outbreak of the Second World War in 1939 was a watershed moment, as able-bodied men were suddenly in high demand to support the war effort, and the numbers in workhouses dropped dramatically.[44] Post-war, there was a sense of optimism, pride in the nation's 'heroes', and in light of the Beveridge Report of 1942,[45] the British welfare state emerged, bringing with it a feeling in the country that vagrancy and the problems of the destitute could be eradicated. This led to the development in 1948 of the National Assistance Board (NAS), whose aim was to assist those 'in need' and 'to make provision whereby persons without a settled way of living may be influenced to lead a more settled way of life'.[46] Nevertheless, the shadow of the old workhouses loomed, and many of the practices, though rendered less explicitly punitive, remained, including 'work tasks' that those residing in newly named reception centres were obliged

39 Academics and historians have regularly referenced Dickens's portrayal, for example, Roberts (n 35); Josef L. Altholz, 'Oliver Twist's Workhouse' (2001) 97 *Dickensian* 137; Ruth Richardson, *Dickens and the Workhouse: Oliver Twist and the London Poor* (OUP 2012).

40 J. T. Belcher, 'The Anti-Pauper System' (1834) 8–19 extracted in Peter Higgenbotham, *Voices from the Workhouse* (The History Press 2012) 83.

41 Belcher (n 40).

42 Rules and Orders, 'The Workhouse of the Parish of St. John' (Hackney, London) reproduced at <www.workhouses.org.uk/Hackney/> accessed 25 July 2024.

43 John R. Poynter, *Society and Pauperism* (Routledge and Kegan Paul 1969).

44 Estimates are that numbers dropped from almost 17,000 in May 1932 to just a few thousand able-bodied men in workhouses by 1939: Timms (n 20) 14.

45 Social Insurance and Allied Services, *Report by Sir William Beveridge* (Cmd 6404, HMSO 1942); Keith Laybourn, *The Evolution of British Social Policy and the Welfare State* (Keele University Press 1995).

46 National Assistance Act 1948 ss4 and 17.

to complete.[47] The National Assistance Act 1948 declared in Section 1 that '[t]he existing poor law shall cease to have effect', and the legislation repealed more than 20 Poor Law Acts that were in force at that time. The 1948 Act stated that local authorities were required to provide a social 'security net' even to those who did not pay national insurance, including the homeless. The Act placed a duty on local authorities to provide accommodation to those with no settled residence, who were 'in need of care and attention . . . not otherwise available to them', by reason of age, infirmity, or any other circumstances, where the need could not reasonably have been foreseen, and who were ordinarily resident in the local authority area.[48] To modern eyes, these are strikingly familiar to the qualification criteria extant in the contemporary law of 'homeless', in 'priority need', intentionality, and local connection tests. Crucially, however, support was conditional. The requirements or 'tests' under the 1948 Act had to be met. The subtext was apparent – only those that could meet these criteria would be deserving of assistance. If these were not satisfied, an applicant would be excluded. In reality, 'the 1948 Act was really just an extension of the old poor law',[49] with families split up, homeless people scared to seek support, fear of having their children removed from them, and with accommodation in dormitories. Despite the repeal of the Poor Laws, as Fitzpatrick and Pawson have noted, 'nevertheless, "desert" rather than "need" remained the predominant allocation criterion for council housing' in this period.[50] As Damer[51] examined, 'desert' was most commonly demonstrated at this time through the use of 'grading systems' (whereby applicants for housing support were ranked to determine who was most deserving) and even more explicitly by openly judgmental and deeply paternalistic selection criteria, including assessment of applicants' housekeeping standards. In 1969, the influential Cullingworth Report,[52] produced by the Central Housing Advisory Committee, drew attention to the law's emphasis on desert:

> [A]pplicants are graded according to an interpretation of their desert . . . [with a] moralistic attitude towards applicants; the underlying philosophy

47 See for example the work by R. J. V. Ollendorff and A. Morgan, 'Survey of Residents in Camberwell Reception Centre' Unpublished Report to the National Assistance Board (1968).

48 National Assistance Act 1948 s21.

49 Dave Cowan, *Homelessness: The In(Appropriate) Applicant* (Routledge Revivals 2019) 24; see also John Grieve, Dilys Page and Stella Grieve, *Homelessness in London* (Scottish Academic Press 1971).

50 See also Suzanne Fitzpatrick and Mark Stephens, 'Homelessness, Need and Desert in the Allocation of Council Housing (1999) 14(4) *Housing Studies* 413.

51 Sean Damer, 'A Note on Housing Allocation' in Michael Edwards et al (eds) *Housing and Class in Britain* (Russell Press 1976).

52 Ministry of Housing and Local Government, *Ninth Report of the Housing Management Sub-Committee of the Central Housing Advisory Committee, Council Housing, Purposes and Priorities* (HMSO 1969).

> seemed to be that council tenancies were to be given only to those who 'deserved' them. Thus unmarried mothers, cohabitees, 'dirty' families and transients tended to be grouped as 'undesirable'. Moral rectitude, social conformity, clean living and a 'clean' rent book sometimes seemed to be essential qualifications for eligibility.[53]

The report underscored the continued link local authorities made between homelessness and notions of morality, of 'moral rectitude' and cleanliness, as markers of 'deservingness' for housing assistance. Despite the express repeal of the poor laws, the poor laws' spirit, if not their letter, continued to dominate.

The Housing (Homeless Persons) Act 1977: from 'overt' to 'covert' or 'disguised desert'

In 1966, Ken Loach's celebrated and impactful BBC TV play *Cathy Come Home* drew new attention to the stark realities of homelessness. A decade later, with the Housing (Homeless Persons) Act 1977,[54] the language of 'homelessness' and the 'homeless applicant' finally appeared plainly on the face of primary legislation. The 1977 Act represented the first homelessness-centred legislation in England. Yet still here, the echoes of the masterplot of desert and redemption proliferated, albeit according to a somewhat less overt and more implicit expression. As noted in the introduction to this collection, a key component of the power and politics of the masterplot device is its ability to embed as so ubiquitous as to appear often taken-for-granted, at times even hidden and invisible, and operating by stealth. Naturally, the emphasis and explicitness of a masterplot's rendering in law and policy shift across time through social and political change. Yet as exposed in this chapter, the 'plot' of deservingness and redemption of the homeless evidences its 'mastery' through its underlying coherence, through repetition, and ultimately, through its tenacity. Whereas earlier legislation had fixed on the poor, which naturally included the homeless, the 1977 Act dealt expressly with the homeless experience. The legislation provided a legal definition of homelessness, categories of 'priority need' were established, and responsibility for homelessness was accepted as 'clearly in the sphere of housing' (as opposed to social services, crime, or justice).[55] The 1977 Act laid down the foundations of the modern law. The Act can and should, however, be construed as a system chiefly of

53 Ministry of Housing and Local Government (n 52) 33.

54 Richard De Friend, 'The Housing (Homeless Persons) Act 1977' (1978) 41(2) *Modern Law Review* 173; N. J. Crowson, 'Revisiting the 1977 Housing (Homeless Persons) Act: Westminster, Whitehall and the Homelessness Lobby' (2013) 24(3) *Twentieth Century British History* 424.

55 HC Deb 18 February 1977 vol 926, col 899 per Stephen Ross MP, who introduced the Housing (Homeless Persons) Bill 1977.

exclusion, of sifting out, of rationing and gatekeeping,[56] a law driven by deep conditionality, where only certain types of homeless applicants were to get assistance while others would be rejected. Homeless people were deemed worthy of support if they, and to the extent that they could, meet the threshold laid down by Parliament. In truth, this meant that hard lines were drawn, with most single homeless people without dependents being excluded from any statutory right to assistance at all. It is in this way that the 1977 Act should, it is argued, be viewed as perpetuating the deserving/undeserving bifurcation.

Perhaps the clearest example of what we might coin 'disguised desert' were the intentionality provisions. The 1977 Act provided that a homeless person would be regarded as having made himself 'intentionally' homeless 'if he deliberately does or fails to do anything in consequence of which he ceases to occupy accommodation which is available for his occupation and which it would have been reasonable for him to continue to occupy'.[57] The intentionally homeless were owed very little by way of assistance – temporary accommodation at best. It is instructive to consider why, on what basis, and how the intentionality concept came to be inserted into the legislation. It was never part of the original scheme for the 1977 Act but was inserted at the report stage of the Bill upon the insistence of MPs, who said that local authorities would be 'flooded' by undeserving applicants, including those whose homelessness was 'self-induced' or 'self-inflicted'.[58] One striking intervention asserted that the 1977 Bill was 'a charter for scroungers and scrimshankers',[59] for the opportunistic to 'cheat' and abuse the system by falsely concocting homelessness to get housing.[60] MPs and local councils also expressed concern that the homeless would be brought to 'the front of the queue' ahead of deserving waiting list applicants.[61] The introduction of the intentionality concept was therefore entirely one premised on desert and the need to 'guard against "scroungers"'[62]

56 On gatekeeping, see Sarah Alden, 'On the Frontline: The *Gatekeeper* in Statutory Homelessness Services' (2015) 30(6) *Housing Studies* 924.

57 1977 Act s17(1), albeit that 'an act or omission in good faith on the part of a person who was unaware of any relevant fact shall not be treated as deliberate': 1977 Act s17(3). The 1977 intentionality provisions have since been adopted and further tightened under the Housing Act 1996 s196.

58 See HC Deb 18 February 1977 vol 926, col 914 per Paul Channon MP; cols 929–20 per Toby Jessel MP; cols 943–4 per Julius Silverman MP and cols 957–8 per Hugh Rossi MP.

59 HC Deb 18 February 1977 vol 926, cols 896–995, 905 per William Rees-Davies MP.

60 Interestingly, the 'intentionality' principles actually do not require any proof that an applicant 'intended' to cheat the system or become homeless for local authority support to be withheld; mere fecklessness would suffice.

61 Department of the Environment, *Local Authorities' Duties to the Homeless* (Research Paper 94/92 July 1994).

62 On the 'scrounger' narrative, see Ruth Patrick, 'Living with and Responding to the "Scrounger" Narrative in the UK: Exploring Everyday Strategies of Acceptance, Resistance and Deflection' (2016) 24(3) *Journal of Poverty and Social Justice* 245.

and "rent dodgers"'.[63] In this way, the homeless were branded, en masse and without any evidence in support of the claims, as morally blameworthy and predisposed towards mendacity, misrepresentation, and wrongdoing. At the same time, local connection principles were reaffirmed as a further way of attempting to limit the perceived 'queue-jumping' by homeless people ahead of more deserving citizens. When viewed by reference to the extraordinary political rhetoric of the day, the provisions of the 1977 Act, intentionality in particular, can only be explained as premised on the concept of desert and thus can be viewed as continuing the long history of the portrayal of the homeless as scheming, untruthful, and immoral.[64]

In a speech to the Conservative Party Conference on 7 October 1993, then minister for housing, inner cities, and construction Sir George Young announced the government's plans to reform homelessness legislation.[65] Young had infamously, in 1991, against a backdrop of decades of rising rates of homelessness in England, referred to the homeless as 'the people you step over when you come out of the opera'.[66] This statement very much signalled the mood of the political classes (certainly the Conservative Party) at that time, and it is argued, the rhetoric surrounding homelessness should be viewed as reflecting an interweaving of narratives around class that fed into the wider homelessness masterplot. Liveley and Shaw have written of the hierarchy of narratives within legal studies, arguing that masterplots exist as a 'wider cultural narrative' that connects a particular context with established notions, myths, and norms about what the state of things in that context ought to be.[67] Using their exposition, we can see how, in the homelessness context, and through the hostile rhetoric of the 1990s, the myth of the scrounging, 'queue-jumping' homeless person contributed to, harboured, and promoted the already-rooted homelessness masterplot. Meta- or master narratives routinely unfurl according to concomitant and co-nourishing codes or scripts. In precisely this way, the masterplot of homelessness operated in the 1990s in step with intense political messaging underscoring class division, undeservingness, and the moral inferiority of the homeless. The political rhetoric around reforming the law was equally provocative and framed strongly in terms of combating a now-mainstream sentiment that the homeless were 'gaming the system' and gaining an undeserved advantage over non-homeless households. This mentality must be seen as part of the Conservative government's 'back to basics' campaign in 1993–94, which sought to focus attention

63 Patrick (n 62) 3.
64 These intentional and local connection provisions continue to operate today: s196 Housing Act 1996.
65 By then, the 1977 Act had been tightened up and consolidated in Part III of the Housing Act 1985.
66 Sir George Young, 'BBC Radio 4' *Today* (June 1991).
67 Liveley and Shaw (n 14).

on support for traditional moral values.[68] According to Young, 'the homelessness route [had] become increasingly attractive', and 'it [was] now virtually impossible for anyone other than statutorily homeless households to obtain a council or housing association tenancy'.[69] This view, shared by many fellow MPs, underscored a common sentiment that the fears expressed during the 1977 Act's passage through Parliament as to potential abuse by homeless applicants were justified. The government repeated its rallying cry of homeless 'queue-jumping' and 'widespread abuse' of the system, stressing that 'the main flaw in the current legislation . . . [was] that those who apply for assistance as homeless gain priority in the queue for local authority tenancies at the expense of others who have comparable underlying housing needs'.[70]

As Fitzpatrick and Pawson noted, 'the rhetoric adopted by ministers suggested that the key underlying motivation in seeking to change the legislation was . . . the desire to reduce assistance to "undeserving" groups, particularly never-married lone parents'.[71] In fact, there was never any evidence base to support the claims made against the lone parent homeless, but the significance of the discourse should not be understated, for it dominated the narrative – the narrative of desert that pervaded the reform agenda. On the ground, research showed that local authorities were still allocating inferior houses to 'less deserving' homeless people on the basis of apparent 'respectable' and 'disreputable' categories of applicants.[72] This contributed to an ongoing sense of stigma ascribed to those who were homeless.

The role of the media in reinforcing the myths and narratives surrounding the deserving and the undeserving homeless at this time can hardly be overstated and must not be ignored. The media expressly perpetuated the masterplot of desert. From the 1980s into the 1990s, resuscitated by the New Right, there was an explosion in reports and depictions of social housing, homelessness, and the welfare state more broadly as being the realm of 'scroungers' and 'queue-jumpers', with repeated references to a welfare 'dependency culture' bolstered by the government's assertion that 'a secure tenancy is a valuable asset . . . [that] has to be earned'.[73] Again, particular opprobrium was reserved, in frequent newspaper columns, for the apparent scores of teenage

68 On which, see Suzanne Fitzpatrick and Mark Stephens, *Housing the Homeless: Policy and Legal Issues – Centre for Housing Research and Urban Studies Occasional Paper No. 2* (CHRUS 1994).

69 HC Deb 20 January 1994 col 842–4W.

70 HC Deb 18 July 1994, cols 21–23 per Sir George Young MP.

71 Suzanne Fitzpatrick and Hal Pawson (2007) 'Welfare Safety Net or Tenure of Choice? The Dilemma Facing Social Housing Policy in England' (2007) 22(2) *Housing Studies* 163, 168.

72 Jeff Henderson and Valerie Karn, *Race, Class and State Housing: Inequality and the Allocation of Public Housing in Britain* (Gower 1987).

73 Department of Environment, *Anti-Social Behaviour on Council Estates: A Consultation Paper on Probationary Tenancies* (HMSO 1995) at [3.1].

girls who were reportedly getting pregnant simply to secure council housing.[74] This 'single mother myth'[75] was propagated by government ministers,[76] given air time and credence on BBC *Panorama*,[77] and rehearsed in frequent articles in the *Daily Mail* referencing how 'unmarried mothers can leap-frog married couples on council housing waiting lists',[78] with other outlets citing George Young's reform agenda as intended to 'stop single mothers jumping the housing queue'.[79]

In the end, the reforms, in fact, pursued a far less vindictive path than the unsubstantiated rhetoric presaged. When the Housing Act 1996 was subsequently enacted, despite the strength of the rhetoric and earlier radical reform proposals,[80] it retained much of the essential framework of the 1977 law but did restrict access to homelessness services, not just for lone parents or single mothers, but for all homeless households, to a two-year period, which could subsequently be renewed.[81] Adults with dependent children as a category were given particular priority under the 1996 Act – over and above single homeless people. One might ask why. As with much of the homelessness legislation, the most 'convincing explanation is that people with children fall into the somewhat nebulous category of greater "desert"'.[82] This special

74 See Dave Cowan, 'Reforming the Homelessness Legislation' (1998) 18(57) *Critical Social Policy* 435; Karen Atkinson, Sarah Oerton and Diane Burns, '"Happy Families?": Single Mothers, the Press and the Politicians' (1998) 22(1) *Capital and Class* 1; Pat Thane and Tanya Evans, *Sinners? Scroungers? Saints? Unmarried Motherhood in Twentieth Century England* (OUP 2012).

75 On which see Cowan (n 49) 174.

76 John Redwood MP, 'Speech to the Conservative Political Summer School, Trevithick Building, The Parade, Cardiff' (2 July 1993) as reported by Rosie Waterhouse and Jason Bennetto, 'Tories Clash over Single Mothers: Lilley Rejects Demand to Axe Benefits' *The Independent* (3 July 1993) <www.independent.co.uk/news/tories-clash-over-single-mothers-lilley-rejects-demand-to-axe-benefits–1482903.html> accessed 25 July 2024.

77 BBC *Panorama* focused on single motherhood variously in July 1993 and most notably hosted a programme, 'Babies on Benefit', in the autumn of 1993 (13 September 1993).

78 'Editorial' *Daily Mail* (8 October 1993).

79 Peter Hennessy, 'Minister: We'll Stop the Queue Jump Mums' *Daily Express* (19 January 1994); John Murphy, 'Ban on Single Mums Jumping Housing Queue' *The Sun* (21 January 1994).

80 Including redefining homelessness so that it covered 'rooflessness' only, that is, assistance would only extend to those with 'no accommodation of any sort available for occupation': Department of the Environment *Access to Local Authority and Housing Association Tenancies* (HMSO 1994). at [5.1], [8.4]–[8.5]. But on the wider proposals and generally, see Ian Loveland, 'Cathy Sod Off! The End of Homelessness Legislation' (1994) 16(4) *Journal of Social Welfare and Family Law* 367.

81 1977 Act ss193(3) and 194. Homeless households were also removed from the list of people given 'reasonable preference': S167(2)); and a 'single housing register' was introduced: s161, 162.

82 Fitzpatrick and Stephens (n 50) 427.

treatment was explained by Young again by re-asserting the myth of the morally deficient teenage mother:

> How do we explain to the young couple . . . you want to wait for a home before they start a family . . . that they cannot be rehoused ahead of the unmarried teenager expecting her first probably unplanned child?[83]

Desert, in this manifestation, is strongly allied to notions of moral fibre, of social conformity, of standards of decency and respectability. To be a single parent is to be feckless and morally inferior. To be a teenage, 'unplanned' mother rendered you undeserving.[84] A clear hierarchy of desert was being restated.

One of the surest expressions of desert from the 1977 Act – the intentional homelessness provisions – not only survived but were also further extended and rendered more robust under the 1996 Act, apparently to deter queue-jumping and abuse of the system by people masquerading as homeless. It was moreover suggested that homeless families would engage in 'collusion'[85] to feign homelessness and abuse the system (though again no tangible evidence of this other than anecdote was offered). As such, intentional homelessness was expanded to include a person who 'enters into an arrangement under which he is required to cease to occupy accommodation which it would have been reasonable for him to continue to occupy' with the purpose of enabling him to claim assistance under the Act and 'where there is no other good reason why he is homeless'.[86] The Homelessness Code of Guidance itself supported this myth of collusion by warning that '[h]ousing authorities need to be alert to the possibility of collusion'.[87] The image of the scheming, conspiratorial homeless trickster taps into long-established tropes of the homeless as delinquent and felonious.

83 George Young, Speech to the Conservative Party Conference (7 October 1993).

84 There never was any evidence to support George Young and others' claims against teenage mothers; see, for example, the survey conducted by the Institute of Housing: *One Parent Families – Are They Jumping the Housing Queue?* (IoH 1993); Wendy Wilson, *Lone Parents and Housing* (House of Commons Library Research Paper 11 January 1994).

85 Department of the Environment (n 61) at 44.

86 Housing Act s191(3); see also s191(4), which provides that if he is 'given advice or assistance under s197 (duty where other suitable alternative accommodation available) but fails to secure suitable accommodation in circumstances in which it was reasonably to be expected that he would do so, shall, if he makes a further application under this Part, be treated as having become homeless intentionally'.

87 Ministry of Housing, Communities and Local Government, *Homelessness Code of Guidance* (2018) [6.16].

Desert and redemption in an era of alleged homelessness prevention

Law and policy towards the homeless in the 2000s can be characterised as unfolding according to a more pronounced 'preventative turn', as legislatively there has been a shift towards a greater focus on homelessness reduction and prevention. However, in spite of this, the essential coherence and status of the homelessness masterplot remain, and it is argued, the masterplot continues to undergird homelessness law and praxis in our contemporary law. The Homelessness Act 2002[88] and, most prominently, the more recent Homelessness Reduction Act 2017 ('HRA17') have seen the law transition from its hitherto more punitive stance to promoting measures aimed at earlier intervention and prevention. Space does not permit discussion of the finer aspects of the 2002 or 2017 Acts,[89] but these reforms have made big strides towards broadening the categories of people given homelessness support,[90] to increasing homelessness prevention activity,[91] and to giving local authorities new discretion in how they frame their housing allocation schemes.[92] The HRA17, styled as 'the most ambitious reform in decades',[93] expanded existing and 'bolted on' to local authorities new legal duties to provide advice to anyone threatened with homelessness,[94] to assess eligible applicants and work with them to agree on a 'personalised housing plan',[95] to intervene to prevent homelessness,[96] to relieve homelessness,[97] and to refer those homeless or threatened with homelessness to a local authority housing department.[98]

88 Introduced during the Labour years of government, the language on housing shifted towards seeing housing applicants as 'consumers' with 'choice' over their housing circumstances; see, generally, David Mullins and Hal Pawson, 'The Land That Time Forgot: Reforming Access to Social Housing in England' (2005) 33 *Policy & Politics* 135; Fitzpatrick and Pawson (n 71).

89 For a discussion of the 2017 Act, see David Cowan, 'Reducing Homelessness or Re-Ordering the Deckchairs?' (2019) 82(1) *Modern Law Review* 105; Bevan (n 15); Chris Bevan, 'The Homelessness Reduction Act 2017: Furthering Not Fracturing Marginalisation of Those Experiencing Homelessness' (2022) 18(1) *International Journal of Law in Context* 41.

90 Abolition of minimum period for which an authority is subject to main homelessness duty: s6 Homelessness Act 2002.

91 Every local authority is required to devise a homelessness strategy (including prevention activity): ss1, 3 Homelessness Act 2002.

92 See, for example, Chris Bevan, 'The Localism Act 2011: The Hollow Housing Law Revolution' (2014) 77(6) *Modern Law Review* 964.

93 Sajid Javid, Secretary of State for Communities & Local Government (2018–2021) Press Release, 'New Government Initiative to Reduce Rough Sleeping' (30 March 2018) <www.gov.uk/government/news/new-government-initiative-to-reduce-rough-sleeping> accessed 25 July 2024.

94 Homelessness Reduction Act 2017 ss1, 2, including widening of the definition of 'threatened with homelessness' from widened definition of 'threatened with homelessness' from 28 days to 56 days.

95 Homelessness Reduction Act 2017 s3.

96 This has become known as the 'prevention duty': Homelessness Reduction Act 2017 s4.

97 This has become known as the 'relief duty': Homelessness Reduction Act 2017 s5.

98 This has become known as the 'referral duty': Homelessness Reduction Act 2017 s10.

Despite these important, prevention-focused reforms, however, the law's approach remains ultimately 'minimalist'[99] in mentality, continuing a long history of homelessness legislation in England founded on gatekeeping of resources, conditionality, and marginalisation. Crucially, then, the reforms did not dislodge the 1996 Housing Act as the major source of our homelessness law, and the problematic and deeply conditional technologies of intentionality and local connection remain central to qualifying for support. In short, despite the law's preventative turn, the concepts of desert and redemption survive into the contemporary homelessness regime.[100] Two central examples from the HRA17 exemplify this: first, local authority 'personalised housing plans' and, secondly, the sanction provisions. Under the former, local authorities are to agree on a personalised plan, laying down mandated steps that a homeless person must follow (to avoid penalty), and if these are not followed, the homeless person's support is withdrawn. These plans consist chiefly of measures of compliance – steps that, if not obeyed, terminate the authority's duties to that individual. The plans are essentially behaviour-centric, 'implicat[ing] homeless applicants as the cause of their own homelessness through their own personal pathology, choices or (in)actions'.[101] These plans come with the threat of 'comply or lose your support'[102] and reflect the worst instincts of the desert and redemption masterplot, namely, that only the homeless who are malleable, are compliant, and submit to the authority's 'tutelage'[103] are deserving of help. This advanced liberalist ideology[104] is made all the starker by the second example: the sanctions provisions. If, in the view of a local authority, there has been a 'deliberate and unreasonable failure to co-operate' (including in failing to follow the housing plan), the authority's housing duties come to an end.[105] These distinctly punitive provisions have clear echoes of the intentionality test and are another means by which the behaviour of applicants is creeping into assessments supposedly based on objective determinations of housing 'need'.[106] Palpably, these sanctions

99 Keith Jacobs, Jim Kemeny and Tony Manzi, 'The Struggle to Define Homelessness: A Constructivist Approach' in Susan Hutson and David Clapham (eds), *Homelessness: Public Policies and Private Troubles* (Cassell 1999) 11.
100 See Bevan (n 89); Chris Bevan, 'Reconceptualising Homelessness Legislation in England' (2021) 84(5) *Modern Law Review* 953.
101 Bevan (n 15) 44.
102 There are reports that authorities are using these plans to exclude applicants not making progress: Shelter, Consultation Response: Department for Communities and Local Government Consultation on Draft Homelessness Code of Guidance for Local Authorities: Executive Summary (2017).
103 Cowan (n 89).
104 See Bevan (n 15); Nikolas Rose, *Powers of Freedom: Reframing Political Thought* (CUP 1999).
105 Homelessness Reduction Act 2017 s7.
106 On the role of 'need': see Bevan (n 100) and Fitzpatrick and Stephens (n 50).

are about weeding out undesirable, undeserving homeless applicants from those deemed more worthy of support, who are given the opportunity for what we may term 'housing redemption'. In different ways, both personal housing plans and the sanctions provisions leave the homeless as 'othered, constructed as marginalised, ethically incomplete, pathologized'.[107] Only certain kinds of homeless people get support – or put differently, we might say that only certain types of homeless people are 'redeemable'. The homeless are only deserving and considered 'redeemable' if they are prepared to submit to mandated steps, to engage in self-work, to behave themselves and conform. These are the contemporary iterations of the worst reflexes of the Poor Laws writ large and still biting almost 200 years later. In November 2023, then home secretary Suella Bravermann MP described homelessness as 'a lifestyle choice', re-enforcing the centuries-old and long-peddled apparent association between homelessness, criminality, and moral decline. Ms Braverman wrote:

> We will always support those who are genuinely homeless. But we cannot allow our streets to be taken over by people . . . living on the streets as a lifestyle choice. Unless we step in now to stop this, British cities will go the way of places in the US . . . where weak policies have led to an explosion of crime, drug-taking, and squalor. [W]hat the law-abiding majority wants us to stop, is those who cause nuisance and distress to other people by pitching tents in public spaces, aggressively begging, stealing, taking drugs, littering, and blighting our communities.[108]

These words – remarkably redolent of the overtly punitive, marginalising, and demonising language used towards the poor and the homeless as long ago as the fourteenth century – serve as a contemporary reminder that the construction of and policy responses to the homeless remain as hostile and as rooted in notions of desert and redemption as they ever have been. Put simply, even in this ostensibly new culture and 'era of prevention',[109] the ideologies of desert and redemption are alive and well both in our current homelessness legal framework and also in our contemporary political discourse.

107 Bevan (n 89) 50.

108 S. Braverman MP, *X* (formerly Twitter) (4th November 2023) reported in Jedidajah Otte, 'Suella Braverman Says Rough Sleeping Is "Lifestyle Choice"' *The Guardian* (4 November2023)<www.theguardian.com/society/2023/nov/04/suella-braverman-says-rough-sleeping-is-lifestyle-choice> accessed 25 July 2024. Braverman previously suggested her wish to introduce a ban on homeless people living in tents and on charities providing homeless people with tents, in a clear echo of the early vagrancy legislation which criminalised giving assistance to the poor and homeless.

109 A phrase used by Peter K. Mackie, 'Homelessness Prevention and the Welsh Legal Duty: Lessons for International Policies' (2015) 30(1) *Housing Studies* 40.

Part 3: Why does the homelessness masterplot have such enduring influence and traction?

The homelessness masterplot has demonstrated exceptional staying power and resilience, enduring through centuries of social, economic, and political upheaval, persisting through changes in government of all stripes, through pandemics, revolts, and revolutions.[110] But why? Why has the homelessness masterplot proved so tenacious and had such traction? This section explains the masterplot's durability. It contends that there are four interconnected reasons.

First, we cannot ignore the moralising and organising power of the homelessness masterplot. The masterplot exhibits intense moral and ordering force. It erroneously suggests that we live in a world in which good and evil, deserving and undeserving, are easily delineated, and that ascribing blame to one group or another is possible and straightforward. Moreover, as Porter Abbott explains, 'narratives draw their power from what we want to be the case'.[111] Most people want to live in a world where those who deserve help get it, ahead of those who do not deserve it; that the undeserving are not first in the queue; but that there is scope for redemption. This gives the homelessness masterplot crucial societal and moral 'buy-in' and may explain its resistance to challenges and its fixed, assiduous status. Just like rhyme, narrative 'gratifies our need for order',[112] our need to make sense of difficult histories, to help us 'weather the storm' through social change with a clear sense of direction, a set of beliefs which appear to have an internal logic. In this way, the homelessness masterplot continues in the ancient tradition 'of storytelling as a meaning-making process'.[113] As Austrian novelist Robert Musil explained, '[m]ost people . . . love the orderly sequence of facts because it has the look of necessity, and the impression that their life has a "course" is somehow their refuge from chaos'.[114] One way of securing that order is to believe that some

110 In considering the enduring power and influence of the masterplot in contemporary law, one might draw a useful parallel with the concept of 'path dependence' developed in the social sciences discipline. Path dependence refers to the idea that past events and history more generally constrain subsequent events or outcomes – often captured by the shorthand 'history matters'. It might be thought that masterplot is a keen example of path dependence. For more, see James Mahoney and Daniel Schensul, 'Historical Context and Path Dependence' in Robert Goodin and Charles Tilly (eds), *The Oxford of Handbook of Contextual Political Analysis* (OUP 2006) 454–71.

111 Porter Abbott (n 11) 43.

112 Porter Abbott (n 11) 42.

113 Sadler (n 9) 254; see also Mink (n 8); Louis O. Mink, 'Narrative Form as a Cognitive Instrument' in Geoffrey Roberts (ed), *The History and Narrative Reader* (Routledge 2001) 221.

114 Robert Musil, *The Man without Qualities* (Sophie Wilkins and Burton Pike tr, Basic Books 1995) 709.

homeless people are the masters of their own misfortune and are undeserving, while others are 'genuinely' deserving.

Secondly, the masterplot, through repetition over centuries, re-enforced by policy and rhetoric, has become imbued with an almost-canonical, authoritative quality largely going uncontested.[115] It is not too far removed from the universal masterplots of 'good versus evil' or of 'death and regeneration'. The masterplot of desert and redemption sets up a quasi-religious invocation of the 'sinner' and 'the forgiven', as the deserving homeless are offered redemption through self-work, to become rehabilitated as respectable citizens engaged in the housing market. This canonical, almost-biblical character gives the masterplot power and ensures its longevity. Allied with this, the roots of the masterplot run so deep in England that it has become an established part of our social history – representations such as Dickens' portrayal of the workhouse have become so lodged in our collective mindset as to have been elevated almost to a cultural glue,[116] or collective memory, running like an artery through our national story.

Thirdly, in every narrative and masterplot, there are threads or even fragments of truth that chime with and tap into, even in small ways, the belief systems (or more likely fears) of citizens. Masterplots become embedded because something in their fabric rings true or resonates even faintly with our human experience. News reports of wrongdoing by homeless people[117] – however infrequent – fortify and sustain the existing narrative surrounding homelessness. Homeless people can, to many, appear 'risky'[118] and, at times, even threatening. And yes, some homeless people do lead chaotic lives. Some commit crimes. Some use illicit substances. Equally, many do none of these. Yet however uncommon, these grains of truth and resonances with citizens' own lives and fears give the masterplot a credibility, solidifying its place as ostensibly true. Porter Abbott notes, '[t]o the extent that our values and identity are linked to a masterplot, that masterplot can have strong rhetorical impact'.[119] Research by housing charity Evolve[120] into public perceptions confirms the masterplot's continued force. Almost a quarter of those surveyed believed

115 See Gould, who used the term 'canonical story' to reflect stories with official sanction: Stephen J. Gould, 'Jim Bowie's Letter and Bill Buckner's Legs' in *I Have Landed: The End of a Beginning in Natural History* (Harmony Books 2002) 54.

116 A phrase Porter Abbott and others deploy: see Porter Abbott (n 11) 47.

117 See, for example, the tragic case of a woman and her son who had offered support to a homeless man who went on to murder them: Steven Morris, 'Homeless Man Who Murdered Woman and Her Son Jailed for Life' *The Guardian* (4 October 2017) <www.theguardian.com/uk-news/2017/oct/04/aaron-barley-homeless-man-who-murdered-woman-who-helped-him> accessed 25 July 2024.

118 Bevan (n 100).

119 Porter Abbott (n 11) 46.

120 Research Carried Out on Behalf of Evolve <www.evolvehousing.org.uk/campaign/perceptions-of-homelessness/> accessed 25 July 2024.

homeless people were 'themselves to blame for ending up on the streets', with 72% of the view that 'homeless people could get themselves off the street if they wanted to'. These misconceptions and misperceptions of homelessness and desert are a clear by-product of the 'master-plotted' legal and media environment in which citizens' lives play out. The masterplot, therefore, both feeds and is fed by society's fears of the homeless 'other', which, in turn, leads to the greater 'othering' of that homeless population. This makes the masterplot self-fulfilling and compelling, infusing the emplotment[121] with supposed common sense, a taken-for-grantedness which, in turn, elevates and secures its mastery and inherent power.

Fourthly, as humans, we are predisposed to seek out causation to impose a logic on otherwise seemingly random and possibly unsettling events. The homelessness masterplot creates a (false) sense of logic and clarity, that blame can be readily ascribed to the undeserving but not to the deserving. To accept the fact that homelessness could happen to any one of us at any time (we are all just one lost job, one lost tenancy, or one illness away from losing our homes) is too confronting, and so we look for justification to explain away others' homelessness – as self-inflicted or somehow intentional – in order to becalm us. The homelessness masterplot of desert and redemption is, on one level, therefore reassuring to a fearful society. As we explored, early accounts presented the idle poor as dangerous, criminal, and not worthy of support. Far easier for us to blame the poor for their own homelessness and later give them a way out of homelessness – redemption through work – than to accept the essential randomness of events. The masterplot appears to present citizens with a pacifying bargain: if we accept that the homeless are homeless because of their own choices and (in)actions, then, provided *you* behave differently, this fate will not befall you. Of course, however, this is wrong thinking. But to 'other' and imagine that the homeless are 'not like us' in this way offers a comforting if flawed logic. The Latin phrase *post hoc ergo propter hoc* ('after this, therefore, before of this') encapsulates this fallacy, suggesting that things that follow other things are caused by those things. This is what Barthes calls 'the mainspring of narrative . . . the confusion of consecution and consequence'.[122] The fact that some poor people are idle does not mean that poverty causes idleness. This is the essential falsehood at the heart of the homelessness masterplot that perpetuates the view that certain kinds of homeless people are to blame for their circumstances and are therefore less deserving.

These four factors outlined here, when taken together, and combined with centuries of continuity, repetition, and reiteration of the deserving/

121 On employment, see, amongst others, Ralph Grunewald, 'The Narrative of Innocence, or, Lost Stories' (2013) 25(3) *Law and Literature* 366.

122 Roland Barthes, 'Structural Analysis of Narratives' in Stephen Heath (trans), *Image, Music, Text* (Fontana 1982 [Original work published 1966]) 79, 94.

undeserving binary, produce a masterplot that possesses an intoxicating narrative coherence. This has the result of overriding both reason and evidence.[123] Scaffolded through legislation, sustained by political rhetoric and media replication, the status quo (and power balance between the haves and have-nots) is maintained, and the masterplot becomes accepted as hanging together, of producing order over disorder, of 'just how things are done', and with that, so the masterplot endures.

Conclusion

Homelessness law in England has been on quite the journey from the times of the Black Death, but as this chapter has explored, by deploying the masterplot framework of desert and redemption, perhaps not quite so great a distance has been travelled as we might have hoped. While much of our law today speaks of 'housing need', it rests, it is argued, ultimately on the age-old conceptions of the deserving and the undeserving homeless applicant. As Cowan wrote over 25 years ago:

> [H]omeless legislation never concerned need. . . . [It] has always required us to oppress the homeless by making *moral judgments*, not about their housing need, but about why the homeless became homeless in the first place. . . . [T]he successful homeless applicant is defined by reference to our perceptions of their deservingness.[124]

As this chapter has demonstrated, the tentacles of the homelessness masterplot of desert and redemption do not simply reach back to the influential BBC television film *Cathy Come Home* (often credited as the pivotal moment in the development of modern homelessness law)[125] but have their roots in the Black Death and the fear the state felt at the burgeoning power of the labouring classes. This masterplot of desert and redemption is persistent, stubborn, rooted in the nation's history, its literature, its psyche, feeding on our worst fears and essential desires to protect our own positions and the status quo, nourished and buoyed by our inherently conservative predispositions and suspicions of outsiders and others. At the macro-level in legislation and at

123 See the widespread support for the New Poor Law and the workhouse regime at the time and the extensive media coverage of 'scroungers' and 'single mothers' in the 1990s despite no evidence to substantiate such targeted discrimination.

124 Cowan (n 49) 21.

125 Ian Loveland, 'Legal Rights and Political Realities: Governmental Responses to Homelessness in Britain' (1991) 16(2) *Law & Social Inquiry* 249; see also Laura Smith interviewing Ken Loach, 'It's Probably the Most Influential Hour and a Half of Television There Has Ever Been' *The Guardian* (15 February 2006) <www.theguardian.com/society/2006/feb/15/2> accessed 25 July 2024.

the meso-level in political rhetoric and the media, the masterplot has developed and become so firmly rooted in the thinking around homelessness that it has, to a degree, fooled us as a society into believing that the homeless are, in various ways and in varying degrees, to blame for or at least implicated in their own circumstances of precarity, and that they can and should be 'normalised' or 'redeemed' into '"a settled way of life" or in effort to "treat" or "reform" them'.[126]

For those interested in pursuing a new and more person-centred approach to homelessness law and policy, the power, place, and influence of the homelessness masterplot of desert and redemption must be challenged. If we want to dislodge or unseat the masterplot and adopt a different and more effective path towards eradicating homelessness, we must first look the masterplot clean in the face to understand its origins, its potency, and what sustains it even today. This chapter has sought to do just that.

126 Joanne Neale, 'Homelessness and Theory Reconsidered' (1997) 12(1) *Housing Studies* 47, 53.

Chapter 4

Punitive rhetoric and prison poems

A curious narrative convergence

David Gurnham

Introduction

It is generally regarded as untenable in legal studies now to try to claim that any one agenda can provide an overarching (or underpinning) account of things, against which all else is secondary. In the context of punishment, as in other legal contexts, the perennial difficulty is that any such claim is necessarily compromised by the multiplicity of competing perspectives, all of which meet with objections and counterclaims from various others and which, in combination, undermine the idea of a single organising framework or 'masterplot'. This would seem to be especially true when it comes to the main theme discussed in this chapter, namely, the punitive narrative. To take a punitive view on punishment is to place a high value on seeing a guilty person suffer for the pain they inflicted on others and on satisfying feelings of anger and loathing directed at that offender.[1] But while it may explain why offenders are punished, or, rather, why a society might *want* to punish them, the punitive narrative does not account for the wider social function or purpose of punishment in a modern state. In the UK, the Ministry of Justice recognises that imprisonment has a number of different aims, and in one of her first speeches as the incoming Labour lord chancellor, Shabana Mahmood affirmed that she is 'unapologetic in [her] belief that criminals must be punished', but also that this must be balanced by a strategy for 'driving down reoffending'.[2]

1 See Alan W. Norrie, 'Restoration, Abolition and the Loving Prison: Jimmy Boyle and Barlinnie Special Unit' (2022) 61(1) *The Howard Journal of Crime and Justice* 104: 'prisons . . . are generally seen as punitive and persecutory environments [with] harsh and persecutory conditions'.

2 Shabana Mahmood, 'Lord Chancellor Sets Out Immediate Action to Defuse Ticking Prison "Time-Bomb"' *HMP Five Wells* (Northamptonshire, 12 July 2024) <www.gov.uk/government/news/lord-chancellor-sets-out-immediate-action-to-defuse-ticking-prison-time-bomb> accessed 24 July 2024.

DOI: 10.4324/9781003404668-6

It may be added, further, that reasons to punish and the aims of doing so are not a *justification* for hard treatment in any normative or moral sense, nor do they help us understand its historical development or future direction. Philosophers of punishment have therefore sought to explain what moral or social value punishment might have for the prisoner (as a human being and a person who bears responsibility for their actions and who comes from a particular community and wider context) or for society more broadly (as the means necessary to reform and rehabilitate prisoners).[3] Scholarship on the historical and sociological dimensions of punishment, meanwhile, have been dominated in large part by Foucault's account of the 'birth of the prison' and his argument that the pre-eminence of punitive thinking in the early modern period (and its 'ritual, costly, violent forms of power') has been replaced by new penal techniques for the disciplining of the offender through a 'subtle, calculated technology of subjection'.[4] The Foucauldian story of the prison is thus a further reason to put into question the symbolic value of punitive anger as the main driver of modern punishment and of the offender's defeat and suffering as its aim.

There is yet one further potential challenge to the significance of the punitive narrative to take into account, namely, the growth of interest in creative arts produced from prisons. An expanding body of prison arts, facilitated by organisations such as *Koestler Arts*, is often assumed to counter the objectifying and abjecting tenor of the punitive narrative. The logic underpinning that assumption is clear: a society that recognises and makes room for creative arts from prisons surely recognises a shared humanity and countenances the eventual re-integration of offenders back into communities. Scholars have previously described and discussed prison arts (1) in terms of the textual, visual, and other techniques and strategies involved in the translation of the experience of punishment into creative forms;[5] (2) as a source information about prisons themselves;[6] (3) as a resource for understanding the construction and negation of imprisoned identities (the prisoners' 'cast' self and their 'authentic' self);[7] (4) as an expression of solidarity and resistance to state

3 See R. A. Duff, *Punishment, Communication and Community* (OUP 2001).

4 Michel Foucault, *Discipline and Punish: The Birth of the Prison* (Alan Sheridan tr, 2nd edn, Vintage Books (Random House) 1995) 220.

5 See Monika Fludernik, *The Confinement Metaphor: The Prison in Fact, Fiction, and Fantasy* (OUP, 2019) for a detailed analysis of the metaphorics of imprisonment.

6 Visitors to Ai Wei Wei's *Freedom* exhibition at the Southbank in 2022 learned from the size of the tiny niches in which the artworks were displayed about the size of the cells in which prisoners lived. Similarly, Gary Mansfield's 2021 exhibition *Domestic Waste* displayed floor plans of typical British cells within standard skip (1.8 m × 3.6 m) to draw attention to the cramped living conditions of cells shared by two prisoners <https://artplugged.co.uk/gary-mansfield-domestic-waste/> accessed 8 July 2024.

7 Georgina DeValiant, Laura McGrath and Zetta Kougiali, 'Through the Prison Walls: Using Published Poetry to Explore Current UK Prisoners' Narratives of Past, Present and Future Selves' (2020) 17(2) *Qualitative Research in Psychology* 240.

power;[8] and (5) as a route to rehabilitation and atonement.[9] As a record of the perspectives and interior lives of imprisoned people and the prisoner's own perspective on the extent to which imprisonment does cause suffering, it is not obvious that prison arts could be anything except antagonistic to the punitive narrative (for which, to repeat, the very point is to ensure that the prisoner does suffer).

Against this context of multiple narratives, then, it would appear unlikely that anything more could plausibly be claimed on behalf of the punitive as a framework for understanding punishment than that it has very partial and limited application. However, taking 'masterplot' in the sense of a story that recurs and repeats itself in different forms and in sometimes surprising places, this chapter shows how the punitive narrative has a broader and deeper significance than is typically supposed. The chapter locates it first across a range of sources where its presence may be anticipated, including ministerial statements, sentencing remarks, victim impact statements, and in a wider popular culture. The more surprising move the chapter then makes is to identify it as recurring also in poems written by people serving prison sentences. For present purposes, we focus on one particular collection of such poems, namely, *Koestler Voices: New Poetry from Prisons*, an anthology comprising (at time of writing) four volumes, the first of which was published in 2017 and the fourth in 2023.[10] Our focus here on the punitive narrative as a potential punishment masterplot does go against the grain of more common readings of prison arts and is offered here as a corrective to the assumption that art from prisons is necessarily or fundamentally antithetical to it. Making space for these different readings together offers a richer, more nuanced, and dialectical understanding of the work than is otherwise possible.

This chapter proceeds as follows: section 1 outlines some of the key qualities of the punitive narrative as an angry reaction to crime, harnessed by the state and levelled against the guilty person. Punishment as the infliction of suffering by the state on an individual is here set in the context of modern criminal justice and the broader history of Western thought and culture. Illustrating the operation of the punitive as an important narrative amongst a broader context in the analysis of punishment 'discourse', Section 2 offers a reading of a short scene from a popular culture text, namely, the comic *Judge Dredd*. Section 3 finally then turns to a more detailed analysis of prisoners'

8 M. Eve Hanan, 'Invisible Prisons' (2020) 54 *UC Davis Law Review* 1185, 1233.

9 Stephen John Hartnett, Jennifer K. Wood and Bryan J. McCann, 'From Silence to Speech and Action, Prison Activism and the Pedagogy of Empowered Citizenship' (2011) 8(4) *Communication and Critical/Cultural Studies* 331.

10 Kate Potts (ed), *Koestler Voices: New Poetry from Prisons: Volume 1* (The Koestler Trust 2017); Kate Potts (ed), *Koestler Voices: New Poetry from Prisons: Volume 2* (The Koestler Trust 2019); Martha Sprackland (ed), *Koestler Voices: New Poetry from Prisons: Volume 3* (The Koestler Trust 2021); Beth Aydon and Esther Sorooshian (eds), *Koestler Voices: New Poetry from Prisons: Volume 4* (The Koestler Trust 2023).

own words as collected by empirical researchers and by the editors of the *Koestler Voices* prison poetry anthologies. Like Section 2, this final section recognises more familiar Foucauldian and moral philosophical readings of the poems, but it also goes beyond these by finding less-obvious but nonetheless significant convergences between the themes of the prison poems and the punitive narrative described in Section 1. To be clear, the argument here is *not* that prison poems express punitive attitudes to crime directly (they patently do not), but rather that, in their framing of relevant themes, poems from prisons can be shown to draw on punitive notions: of an angry, fearful, muscular punisher and a prisoner who is objectified as a defeated, suffering, and isolated foe. The chapter thus proposes that, despite all its apparent narrowness and negativity, the punitive narrative might be thought of as a kind of 'masterplot' for punishment discourse.

The punitive narrative of anger and persecution

The punitive narrative of punishment is one in which a wrongdoer is made to suffer and in which that suffering continues until the 'requirements of pure punishment' are satisfied.[11] The punitive occupies an emotional register, and although it does deal in 'retribution' and presupposes the moral 'responsibility' of the offender, it is to be distinguished from *normative* accounts of punishment as retribution, the latter grounded in the necessity to recognise the offender as part of a community and, as such, part of a two-way moral dialogue in which punishment serves to communicate censure and to impress the need for reform.[12] The punitive sensibility as a desire to see offenders suffer may be identified in ministerial commentary. During the anti-immigration riots in British cities in August 2024, for example, Prime Minister Kier Starmer promised that rioters would 'feel the full force of the law'.[13] Similarly, in 2023, the then home secretary Suella Braverman wrote in an open letter to police that '[c]riminals must have *no place to hide*'.[14] In such rhetoric, the

11 In sentencing in England and Wales, this is typically expressed in the form of the minimum term that must be served before a prisoner may be considered for parole, when the assessment switches to one of safety.

12 See R. A. Duff, 'Penal Communications: Recent Work in the Philosophy of Punishment' (1996) 20 *Crime and Justice* 1; R. A. Duff, *Punishment, Communication and Community* (n 3); A. Duff and A. von Hirsch, 'Responsibility, Retribution and the "Voluntary": A Response to Williams' (1997) 56(1) *Cambridge Law Journal* 103.

13 Ido Vock and Jeremy Culley, 'PM Says Communities "Will Be Safe" in Face of Riots' *BBC News* (6 August 2024) <www.bbc.co.uk/news/articles/cx2nnj8301yo> accessed 13 August 2024.

14 Matthew Weaver, 'Braverman "Interfering with Police Independence" after Crime Pledge' *The Guardian* (London, 29 August 2023) (my emphasis) <www.theguardian.com/uk-news/2023/aug/29/braverman-interfering-with-police-independence-after-pledge> accessed 9 July 2024. Arguably more explicitly still, in 2019 the former Home Secretary Priti Patel asserted: 'I want [criminals] to *literally feel terror at the thought* of committing offences.' Damien

offender is made a radical 'other' for society, and commentors have observed that this can produce punitive fantasies that are violent in nature and can be traced psychoanalytically to childhood aggression: of 'purifying the good' by 'destroying, getting rid of or controlling the bad'.[15]

A normative basis for punitive emotions?

Attempts periodically made to justify punitive hatred have argued, for example, that natural feelings of guilt are an implicit acceptance that suffering is warranted,[16] and that the desire to do something that is permissible (i.e. make offenders suffer by punishing them) should itself be a permissible response.[17] These arguments have, in turn, been criticised from moral and philosophical perspectives. Alan Norrie has suggested that the vindictiveness reflected in state punishment performs an important (albeit limited) role in that it 'accesses an "atavistic", "primitive impulse" to hit back, taking that impulse away from the "lynch mob" and locating it in a state institution'.[18] Similarly, and from a sociological perspective, Carvalho and Chamberlen have argued that the state's demonstration of its power and prerogative to punish produces a collective sense of 'reassurance' for a community and a crucial 'emotional release together with a sense of belonging' that unifies people against a common enemy.[19]

It is arguably evidence of moral approval of a sort that when punitive feelings are expressed by families of victims, these are generally not considered wrong or misplaced. For example, at the sentencing of Lucy Letby in 2023 for the murder and attempted murder of 13 babies at the hospital where she worked as a nurse, statements from some of the parents of the victims underlined the necessity in their view of seeing Letby serve a whole life sentence (i.e. a life sentence with no minimum term): 'We hope you live a very

---

Gayle, 'Home Secretary Priti Patel Criticised over Wish for Criminals "to Feel Terror"' *The Guardian* (London, 3 August 2019) <www.theguardian.com/politics/2019/aug/03/priti-patel-home-secretary-wants-criminals-to-literally-feel-terror> accessed 23 June 2023.

15 Quoting Craig Reeves, 'What Punishment Expresses' (2019) 28 *Social and Legal Studies* 31, 39, 40. Cf Carvalho and Chamberlen, 'Why Punishment Pleases: Punitive Feelings in a World of Hostile Solidarity' (2018) 20(2) *Punishment & Society* 217, 226; Alan Norrie, 'Crime and the Metaphysical Animal' (2023) 22(5) *Journal of Critical Realism* 904, 916.

16 M. S. Moore, 'The Moral Worth of Retribution' in *Responsibility, Character and the Emotions* (F. Schoeman ed, Cambridge University Press 1987) ch 8, 213, 215. On criticisms of these attempts to justify punitive hatred, see Duff, 'Penal Communications' (n 12) 28–31; cf Norrie, *Punishment, Responsibility, and Justice: A Relational Critique* (OUP 2000) ch 5, 93–116.

17 Jeffrey G. Murphy and Jean Hampton, *Forgiveness and Mercy* (Cambridge University Press 1988) ch 3, 94–5.

18 Norrie, 'Crime and the Metaphysical Animal' (n 15) 6.

19 Carvalho and Chamberlen, 'Why Punishment Pleases' (n 15) 227, 228.

long life and *spend every day suffering* for what you've done.'[20] When Wayne Couzens was handed his whole life order in 2021 for the kidnap, rape, and murder of Sarah Everard, the family's impact statement spoke of the reassurance they derived from knowing that the strongest penalty possible under the law had been used, albeit without explicitly separating punitive sentiments from the question of incapacitation: 'Nothing can make things better, nothing can bring Sarah back, but *knowing he will be imprisoned forever brings some relief*.'[21]

Contrastingly, when in March 2024 prosecutors accepted paranoid schizophrenic Valdo Calocane's plea of manslaughter by diminished responsibility, leading to an indefinite hospital order rather than a life sentence, the families of his victims were understandably angry that the seriousness of the crime and Calocane's responsibility for it was not being properly recognised, going so far as to say that it shows that 'murderers will get away with murder'.[22] The family's public and vociferous condemnation of Calocane's treatment as a hospitalised patient and not a punished murderer was met everywhere with sympathy and understanding. This arguably suggests that punitive emotions form an important normative role in criminal justice, at least in the popular consciousness.

The punitive separation of punisher and punished

Sentencing remarks in criminal cases serve in part to vindicate the victim's and their family's hurt and injury, but they also serve a more symbolic purpose that further draws from a punitive narrative – that is, they reinforce the authority of the punishing state itself and separate it (at least rhetorically) from the punished offender. For example, the reasons that Fulford LJ gave for finding a whole life order to be warranted in Wayne Couzens's case spoke to the question of law's special status as *legitimate* inflictor of suffering, as opposed to a mere torturer dressed up in a smart uniform. The crucial fact was that Couzens had used his authority *as an agent of the law* in order to achieve his aim. Beyond the obvious horror of the abduction, rape, and

20 Judith Moritz, Daniel O'Donoghue, Lauren Hirst and Monica Rimmer, 'Mother of Lucy Letby Victim Says It Was Like a Horror Film' *BBC News* (21 August 2023) (my emphasis) <www.bbc.co.uk/news/uk-england-merseyside-66569303> accessed 24 July 2024.

21 Vikram Dodd and Haroon Siddique, 'Sarah Everard Murder: Wayne Couzens Given Whole-Life Sentence' *The Guardian* (London, 30 September 2021) (my emphasis) <www.theguardian.com/uk-news/2021/sep/30/sarah-everard-murder-wayne-couzens-whole-life-sentence> accessed 24 July 2024.

22 Quoting the words of Emma Webber, mother of 19-year-old victim Barnaby Webber, in Alex Smith and Greig Watson, 'Nottingham Attacks: Families Call for Law Change after CPS Review' *BBC News* (25 March 2024) <www.bbc.co.uk/news/uk-england-nottinghamshire-68643143> accessed 24 July 2024.

murder of a young woman, therefore, Couzens had unforgivably undermined the public legitimacy of law's violence (as retaliation against crime) with his own depraved private motives:

> In my judgment, the misuse of a police officer's role such as occurred in this case in order to kidnap, rape and murder a lone victim is of equal seriousness as a murder carried out for the purpose of advancing a political, religious, racial or ideological cause. All of these situations attack different aspects of the fundamental underpinnings of our democratic way of life.[23]

Fulford LJ's sentencing of Couzens then underlines a crucial aspect of punitivity: that the legitimation of law's righteous anger requires a rhetoric of clear demarcation and separation between the two relevant 'wills', namely, the punisher and the punished. Law reserves for itself the authority to inflict suffering against those it deems to be guilty on the basis that punisher and punished are separate figures and not to be confused. Any attempt to harness that authority for criminal purposes is particularly dangerous, since, as Lord Coleridge darkly warned in the notorious cannibal seafarers murder case *R v Dudley and Stephens*, it threatens to reduce law and the legal process to the role of a 'legal cloke for unbridled passion and atrocious crime'.[24] It also explains why serious crimes committed by police officers against vulnerable people (such as victims or suspects in custody) in the course of their duties are considered an especially grievous abuse of authority.[25]

The idea that senior officials charged with upholding and applying the law should be anxious to detach law's 'righteous' violence from the moral turpitude of those it punishes is entirely understandable, although achieving this by *isolating* the offender as so malign an element that they must be forcefully separated and excised from the rest of society is a move more particular to the punitive narrative. This is not to suggest that such a move is either empirically true or normatively right, however, and the punitive *rhetoric* that asserts its necessity is strenuously rejected by those who see the offender as necessarily a part of a wider, or even a universal, community. For moral communicative retributivism, for example, R. A. Duff insists that responsibility for crime is always 'relational' in the sense that it necessarily requires a dialogue between someone called to 'answer for' his actions to one with 'standing' to

23 L. J. Fulford, 'Wayne Couzens Sentencing Remarks' (30 September 2021) [19] <www.judiciary.uk/wp-content/uploads/2022/07/Wayne-Couzens-Sentencing-Remarks-1.pdf> accessed 19 August 2024; Couzens' appeal against his sentence was dismissed by the Court of Appeal in *R v Couzens (and Others)* [2022] EWCA Crim 1063.

24 (1884) 14 QBD 273.

25 cf Dara E. Purvis and Melissa Blanco, 'Police Sexual Violence: Police Brutality, #MeToo, and Masculinities' (2020) 108(5) *California Law Review* 1487–1529.

hold him responsible.[26] Alan Norrie has also strongly rejected the idea that punishment represents the separation of offender and society. Going further than Duff, Norrie argues:

> Responsibility is contemporaneously shared between the individual and the 'significant others' in her community or communities, and, indeed, with those communities themselves [and that] [a] fully moral account of the wrongdoing in such cases would have to recognize both that the social and structural factors operating behind the back of the criminal were effective in causing crime, and that the criminal was also its causal agent.[27]

It is arguable that the criminal justice system in England and Wales does tacitly recognise lines of unbroken continuity between offender and the wider society in that sentencing typically makes space for a route back to society even though this may be a long way off and liable to be delayed.[28] The need and the possibility that the perpetrator of such a serious offence may yet be assisted to repair and rebuild connections to the community he or she injured, and that imprisonment has a role to play in communicating that need and facilitating that possibility, have been the subject of sentencing remarks, of scholarly texts, and also of remarkable and moving personal stories of redemption, reform, and forgiveness.[29] Apart from those (like Letby or Couzens) sentenced to a whole life order, prisoners who are *un*able to navigate a route back to society are most often blocked not by punitive considerations but by the denial of parole after the punishment part of the sentence is complete, owing to a perceived need to guard against risk.[30]

26 See Duff, 'Penal Communications' (n 12) 74; R. A. Duff, *Answering for Crime: Responsibility and Liability in the Criminal Law* (Bloomsbury Publishing 2009) 34, 36, and ch 1 generally.

27 Norrie, *Punishment, Responsibility, and Justice* (n 16) 201, 218.

28 *Re Thompson and Venables (Tariff Recommendations)* [2000] All ER (D) 1534, per Lord Woolf CJ [8], [19]; Cf 'The Parole Journey: For Parole Practitioners 2012/13' *Parole Board of England and Wales* (2014) <www.gov.uk/government/publications/the-parole-journey-for-parole-practitioners> accessed 9 July 2024.

29 See Katie Barnfield, "I Feel Compassion for Killers' Families', Says Brianna Ghey's Mum' *BBC News* (2 February 2024) <www.bbc.co.uk/news/uk-england-manchester-68147985> accessed 24 July 2024.

30 Prisoners serving IPP (imprisonment for public protection) sentences (abolished prospectively but not retrospectively in March 2012) may be held in prison well beyond the term stipulated by the sentencing judge. The period between release from prison on licence and the expiry of the sentence (during which time the prisoner may be recalled to prison) has been reduced from ten years to three (Victims and Prisoners Act 2024, s.66). See Dary Makoona and Nicola Maynard, 'Light at the End of the Tunnel – Major IPP Changes' *Inside Time* (1 July 2024) <https://insidetime.org/legal/light-at-the-end-of-the-tunnel-major-ipp-changes/>.

Remorse and guilty conscience: emotional impacts of punitive treatment

Establishing and affirming the separation of punished and punisher may well be the ultimate goal of the punitive narrative at its most extreme, but this does not mean that the thoughts and feelings of the offender are irrelevant. To the contrary, these play an important (albeit negative) role. According to the punitive narrative, it is necessary for the offender to anticipate their punishment with feelings including abjection, dismay, fear, despair, and even terror. When such feelings are produced, these tend to validate and further inflame punitive anger, since they can be (and often are) understood as signs of self-pity (i.e. self-serving[31]) rather than true remorse or desire to atone and make amends. It is not unusual to hear sentencing judges drawing such a distinction and deciding that the guilty party falls on the wrong side of the equation, often because the latter tried to offer some alternative account of events with the aim either of denying responsibility altogether or else of putting it in a more favourable light. After a guilty verdict, such unsuccessful attempts are typically treated at the sentencing stage as signs of a *guilty conscience* (in the negative Freudian sense of fear of authority) and *not* of true remorse or desire for atonement. Sentencing a young father for the murder of his baby daughter, Mrs Justice Ellenbogen spelled this out:

> I consider that such remorse as you have manifested during your trial is for the fact that you find yourself facing the inevitable consequences of the brutal, deliberate actions by which you deprived your baby daughter of her life, from which it follows that I do not consider it to be an additional mitigating factor.[32]

Fulford LJ makes the same distinction when sentencing Couzens: 'I have seen no evidence of genuine contrition on your part as *opposed to evident self-pity and attempts by you to avoid or minimise the proper consequences of what you have done*.'[33] The relevant sort of 'evidence' that Fulford LJ finds lacking in Couzens is any sign that the latter was prepared to take 'responsibility', to offer a 'full explanation';[34] that he suffered any 'trauma' at the realisation of what he had done, or even simply that he had 'second thoughts'.[35]

31 The archaic root of 'regret' in the Old French *regreter* connoting a sense of self-pity (literally: after + weeping). See Robert K. Barnhart (ed), *Chamber Dictionary of Etymology* (Chambers 2010) 904.

32 Courts and Tribunals Judiciary, 'Sentencing Remarks by the Hon Mrs Justice Ellenbogen DBE: *R -v- Ali Zain*' (Manchester Crown Court, May 18, 2022) <www.judiciary.uk/judgments/sentencing-remarks-by-the-hon-mrs-justice-ellenbogen-dbe-r-v-ali-zain/> accessed 9 July 2024.

33 Fulford (n 23) [23], emphasis added.

34 Fulford (n 23) [13].

35 Fulford (n 23) [23].

In the modern criminal justice context, however, the idea that the prisoner's despair or terror is an important component of a punishment masterplot runs up against a further objection, namely, Foucault's history of the emergence of modern penal institutions as places of more subtle discipline than the terrorising infliction of physical pain and suffering. Even if we accept, however, that the modern penal institution is so designed to encourage the prisoner, cognisant of his visibility to the eye of the law, to 'become the principle of his *own* subjection' (as opposed to merely being subdued by the prospect of punitive retaliation),[36] it should not be imagined that this excludes a starring role for punitive anger and the desire to hurt and humiliate the offender. Echoes of the sadistic excesses of pre-Enlightenment accoutrements of punishment – the scaffold, dungeon, irons, and chains – are not entirely absent from modern punishment, albeit they are much less overt. The next sections explore these echoes in the context of the imaginative reconstruction of punishment in a comic strip (Section 2) and then, in more detail, in poetry from prisons (Section 3), but they are discernible also in *law*. It is there, for example, in the principle underpinning sentencing for murder that the public demand for 'repayment' can sometimes be so great as to outlive the offender's natural lifespan.[37]

The *excessiveness* of that demand – the logical *impossibility* of repaying such a debt in full – marks a very different understanding of the commercial metaphor to that offered by Foucault. In *Discipline and Punish*, Foucault writes that the familiarity of the expression 'to pay one's debt' was evidence that prison (and the extraction of the prisoner's time as its currency) is understood to be a 'natural' extension of the logic of equivalences.[38] But guilt as an *unpayable* debt (further metaphorised in culture as an indelible *stain* of guilt[39]) has survived in the modern English law on sentencing for the most serious murders. The technology of suffering without end represented by the whole life order is *pre*-modern, and it finds its apotheosis in Dante's medieval vision of souls punished in Hell in his *Divine Comedy*, who 'figuratively (and, sometimes, even literally) carry the burden of their pasts, destined to remember their sins for the rest of eternity'.[40] That the sentencing of a prisoner to a 'whole life' term is incompatible with the subtler norms of *modern* penalty is

36 Foucault, *Discipline and the Punish* (n 4) 203, emphasis added.

37 As stated by Lord Steyn in *R v Secretary of State for the Home Department, exp Hindley* [2001] AC 410. cf David Gurnham, 'The Moral Narrative of Criminal Responsibility and the Principled Justification of Tariffs for Murder: Myra Hindley and Thompson and Venables' (2003) 23(4) *Legal Studies* 605.

38 Foucault, *Discipline and Punish* (n 4) 232–233.

39 For example, the telltale bloody key of Perrault's *Bluebeard*, which cannot be washed clean after it is accidentally dropped in the blood of that murderer's victims; the bloodstain that the dreaming and distracted Lady Macbeth cannot wash out of her hands; or Cain's facial mark that lets others know he is the original murderer.

40 Patrick O'Callaghan, 'Enlightened Remembering and the Paradox of Forgetting: From Dante to Data Privacy' (2023) 17(2) *Law and Humanities* 210, 223.

suggested by recent jurisprudence of the European Court of Human Rights.[41] However, such a suggestion has so far been resisted by the English courts.[42]

The punitive narrative in popular culture: a case study

We have now identified some key aspects of the punitive attitude in modern legal and criminal justice discourses on punishment: the desire to inflict pain and to establish a clear separation, divide, or gulf between the punished person and the community from which his or her crime has necessitated his or her removal, ideally resulting in the prisoner feeling isolated, reduced, demoralised. As we have seen, the punitive is far from the *only* narrative at play in this space, but it remains a strong voice within this multiplicity of narratives. This can be illustrated with reference to a range of familiar pop cultural 'justice fantasies' in the twentieth and twenty-first centuries, across formats including films, TV serials, and comic strips. The central figure of authority in the comic strips *2000AD* and *Judge Dredd* is a well-known example, on which we will pause briefly here by way of illustration. The creators of the dystopian future world of *Judge Dredd* imagined the threat of crime as constituted by an entire urban population, and the state as a muscular and brutally repressive group of officials who combine the roles of police, judge, and juror.

In one intriguing scene from a *Judge Dredd* story ('The Graveyard Shift' – one night in the life of the city), the titular official and his colleague Judge Hershey go house to house on a nocturnal 'crime swoop', kicking in citizens' doors at random – acts which would be outrageous violations but for the judges' vindicated belief that crime is practically *everywhere*. In answer to one unfortunate resident's protest that he and his partner are 'innocent', Dredd replies, brusquely: '*Nobody's* innocent, citizen. We're just here to determine the *level* of your guilt.' With nefarious activity duly uncovered there in the form of possession of illegal items (87 g of sugar, seven prohibited 'vid-slugs', and an unlicensed antique firearm), the couple is summarily sentenced to 11 years in gaol and herded outside to join a growing parade

41 In *Vinter v United Kingdom (Applications nos. 66069/09, 130/10 and 3896/10)* [2013], the Grand Chamber of the ECtHR considered the very restrictive conditions for considering the release of a 'whole life' prisoner in the English Lifers Manual, ruling that 'where domestic law does not provide any mechanism or possibility for review of a whole life sentence, the incompatibility with Article 3 on this ground already arises at the moment of the imposition of the whole life sentence' [122].

42 Lord Thomas CJ later held in *Attorney General's Reference No. 69 of 2013; R v McLoughlin; R v Newell* [2014] EWCA Crim 188: 'We do not read the judgment of the Grand Chamber in *Vinter* as in any way casting doubt on the fact that there are crimes that are so heinous that just punishment may require imprisonment for life' [17] and considered that the matter of the Lifer Manual that concerned the Grand Chamber was 'of no consequence' as a matter of law [30].

of other similarly convicted people, in view of the surrounding apartments. The narrator observes, philosophically, that such operations are, admittedly, 'harsh' but also 'effective' in that they 'act as a positive deterrent to other potential lawbreakers'.[43]

Reflecting on this scene helps illustrate the different kinds of readings that depictions of punishment make possible, and how the different available narratives help frame what we think is going on. The scene is itself an instructive one for our purposes, since in its presentation of the roles of judge, offender, and omniscient narrator, it speaks to three key relevant experiences of criminal justice and the relationships between them. First, the scene arguably critiques the privileged role of the punisher against the punished and calls into question the justifiability of punitive treatment that isolates the offender.[44] If we take Judge Dredd's words '*Nobody*'s innocent' at face value, then presumably this evaluation of the offenders' responsibility also applies to the judges themselves. After all, they represent a justice system that has allowed crime to become endemic (so translated: 'everyone's *responsible*'). Following such a relational framing of criminal responsibility, the narrator's defensive apology for the judges' 'harsh' treatment would seem to admit to a legitimacy gap in law's claim to be a justified user of violence rather than a mere 'torturer in a smart uniform', which we referred to previously in connection with Couzens's use of his authority as a police officer to facilitate his own crime.

A second, different reading takes a Foucauldian perspective and notices especially the unhesitating, almost breezy way in which the judges go about rounding up offenders in their own homes and which conveys a remarkable degree of confidence on their part that the intrusion would prove warranted. The judges take it for granted that no matter which door they kicked in, their crime swoop was *always* going to uncover incriminating evidence. Such a reader might suggest that the reason for this is that the futuristic state depicted has perfected and generalised its panoptic technologies of surveillance to such a degree that the citizens have been 'set up' to be caught. Hence, '*nobody's* innocent' here emphasises the penetration of that surveillance into every corner of society (i.e. 'nobody can *escape* us') – a future that Foucault himself envisaged.[45]

43 John Wagner, Alan Grant and Rob Smith, 'The Graveyard Shift, Part 4' in *Judge Dredd 10: The Chronicles of Judge Dredd* (Titan Books 1988) 23–4, original emphasis.

44 Recall, for example, Norrie's argument that individuals are always 'embedded within structures of social relations' (Norrie, *Punishment, Responsibility and Justice* (n 16) 212), and Duff's that 'we might do better and more justly to look instead at the context from which her action flowed' (Duff, 'Penal Communications' (n 12) 74).

45 Foucault, *Discipline and Punish* (n 4) 207: 'The panoptic schema, without disappearing as such or losing any of its properties, was destined to spread throughout the social body; its vocation was to become a generalized function.' 106: 'The punishment must proceed from the crime; the law must appear to be a necessity of things.'

However, those two readings are unsatisfying on their own in that they fail to capture the *theatricality* of the display of justice in action. The scene admits a third reading, therefore, that speaks to the narrative of punitivity, which I propose makes good that deficit. This reading emphasises the humiliating violence of the scene – the sudden violation of the citizens' home in the middle of the night, the parading of the couple in the street to shame them in front of their neighbours, and the narrator's reflection that the process is a 'positive deterrent' – replaying the sort of persecutory fantasy we referred to above (see n 15). Following this interpretive approach, '*nobody*'s innocent' is very much an expression of the state's readiness to use brutal force ('nobody can *resist*') that promises a display that is angry, unfocused, but *dreadful* in its reach and power. Indeed, Dredd's remark to his colleague as they leave – 'That'll do for tonight, Hershey. Reckon the rest of the block'll get the message' – affirms that the whole episode is intended to terrorise and admonish, which was precisely the aim of the early modern scaffold. It is a nice example of the fantastical double-think of punitive logic, as Reeves puts it: '[T]he persecutors are indeed everywhere, but the state will omnipotently destroy them.'[46]

All these readings are 'valid' in that they each bring out something about the scene and the themes that has a place in the broader question about what punishment is and what it is for. Our aim here has not been to try to claim that punitive reading should replace moral, critical, or Foucauldian readings but merely that there are good reasons to believe that the punitive, with all its excess and performance, remains an important part of the picture. The next stage is to show how it also finds its way into creative arts from prisons, which might be expected to revile it entirely.

The punitive and prison poems: narrative convergences

We can now get to the main contention of this chapter: that the punitive narrative can also be found in modern poems from prisons, and thus that its significance for understanding punishment is much broader and deeper than ordinarily assumed. The poems included in the *Koestler Voices* anthologies explored here represent a small fraction of a much larger body of work produced inside British prisons, secure hospitals, and migrant detention centres, selected for commendation by Koestler's awards committee.[47] It goes without saying that the poems as a whole convey a very broad variety of themes and

46 Reeves, 'What Punishment Expresses' (n 15) 41.

47 In 2019, Koestler Arts stated that the 50 or so poems chosen each year for the anthology of prisoner poetry are drawn from nearly 1,000 entries from across the country <https://koestlerarts.org.uk/shop/books/koestler-voices-new-poetry-from-prisons-vol-2/> accessed 27 July 2023.

topics. The 'carceral topography'[48] of creative writing from prisons is a figurative landscape full of imagery that assists readers 'outside' to understand what imprisonment might be like for those who endure it, and how prisoners find ways to deal with the limitations and confines of prison.

Figuring key elements of that experience in metaphor, prison writings have depicted imprisonment in terms of, for example, live burial[49] or drowning,[50] or the caging of animals.[51] There are numerous different ways in which the poems of the *Koestler Voices* collections may be analysed, and the approach taken here follows from the discussion of the previous section, that is, that in addition to the more dominant moral philosophical and Foucauldian framings, it is possible to find in the prison poems a surprising recurrence of some of the notions transmitted in punitive rhetoric (i.e. punishment as objectifying, isolating, and terrifying). This section discusses three themes that recur in the poems and considers what an attention to *punitive* notions therein adds to our understanding of them. It examines first, then, the impact of punishment on a prisoner's identity and sense of themself as subject or object; second, the constraints placed on a prisoner's ability to determine their own physical movement; and third, punishment's impact on the prisoner's sense of time.

Punishment and the prisoner's identity: 'subjected' or 'objectified'?

Many of the poems collected in the *Koestler Voices* anthologies address the problem of imprisoned subjectivity and the fragility of an imprisoned person's sense of self. In their analysis of poems published in *Inside Time*, DeValiant and Kougiali observe examples of a fragile sense of self dictated and negotiated through awareness of the dangers and deprivations of prison. They claim to find in the poems evidence that the prison environment 'moulds' the prisoner, 'making and remaking' them, 'ingraining' and 'inscribing' them with prisoner subjectivity.[52] This notion of the imprisoned self as a *plastic*

48 Monika Fludernik, 'Carceral Topography: Spatiality, Liminality and Corporality in the Literary Prison' (1999) 13(1) *Textual Practice* 43; cf Fludernik, *The Carceral Metaphor* (n 5) 24.

49 Fludernik, 'The Metaphorics and Metonymics of Carcerality: Reflections on Imprisonment as Source and Target Domain in Literary Texts' (2005) 86(3) *English Studies* 226, 230; Fludernik, *The Confinement Metaphor* (n 5) 27.

50 Robert Johnson and Nina Chernoff, '"Opening a Vein": Inmate Poetry and the Prison Experience' (2002) 82(2) *The Prison Journal* 141, 156–8.

51 'No Bird sings sweeter then the Bird in Cage,/And Satyrists (like Dogs) ty'd, fiercest rage.' – Eighteenth century verse quoted by Molly Murray, 'Measured Sentences: Forming Literature in the Early Modern Prison' (2009) 72(2) *Huntington Library Quarterly* 147, 147.

52 DeValiant, McGrath and Kougiali, 'Through the Prison Walls' (n 7) 247–8.

form and liable to change (and being changed) is very much in keeping with Foucauldian ideas of the production of the subject by exposure to the prison regime, and as we will see, there are a number of examples of *Koestler* poems that may be understood in this way. For example, in the anonymous poem 'Kindness, Hope and Compassion', the imprisoned poet's sense of self is presented as compromised and pushed to the limits of endurance:

> Misery surrounds you and seeps into your soul
> Programmed to break you, so you'll never feel whole[53]

This poem highlights the role of the prison's exercise of power that effectively reshapes the prisoner's identity, here depicted as exposed to a sense of a 'seeping' of unwanted liquid into a container (the prisoner's 'soul') which ought to be able to resist such an intrusion but is now struggling to do so. The quoted text arguably describes the disciplinary techniques of the modern prison, designed to mould the prisoner in certain ways that suit the state, and, in so describing them, simultaneously resists their power, as Larson writes of prison writing more broadly:

> The prison cell is remapped as a position of privileged insight. The space isolating the lawbreaker from common citizenry assumes an axial position as a historically honored seat of judgment; he speaks with the authority of the body whose pain the state and its complacent citizens prefer not to hear.[54]

Alongside that insight, however, it is also important to notice how some of the reflections on identity and selfhood in the *Koestler* collection speak to an experience of self as not merely reinscribed or remoulded by prison but more radically objectified, even lost altogether. The anonymous 'A Prisoner' provides an example:

nothing depends
upon

a prisoner

and that's what
hurts

so much
I think[55]

53 Anon, 'Kindness, Hope and Compassion' in Sprackland (ed), *Koestler Voices: 3* (n 10) 89.
54 Doran Larson, 'Toward a Prison Poetics' (2010) 37(3) *College Literature* 143, 149.
55 Anon, 'A Prisoner' in Aydon and Sorooshian (eds), *Koestler Voices: 4* (n 10) 54.

I don't mean to suggest that such abnegation of self necessarily represents a more authentic identity, but rather that it indicates that ideas germane to the punitive narrative of punishment (here, of the victory over crime symbolised in the purported objectification of the offender) have impact in this context as well.

In this light, an alternative reading of 'Kindness, Hope and Compassion' also emerges, namely, about the poet's awareness of the punitive rhetoric that identifies them (the imprisoned poet) as the object or target of an angry, resentful, and capricious punisher: *who* is trying to break me, and *why*? That there are no answers to these questions is really the point of the punitive narrative: the point is simply to inflict pain and humiliation on a hated and reviled 'other'. The seething dread in those two lines from 'Kindness, Hope and Compassion' is what connects that poem to more prosaic complaints about the deprivations and strictures of prison. Consider '12 Books' and 'Networked Gym-fit Recidivist', quoted in the following, respectively:

> 'Your visit has been cancelled as you are not available' . . .
> 'Your clothing parcel will not be authorised as you
> Recently received a pair of socks'[56]

> a Joint Enterprise robbing you blind . . .
> a broken-legged Vietnamese was untreated for sixteen days . . .
> It's just a scam, the wrapper's off.[57]

Here, the absurdist humour of '12 Books' and the explicit accusation of institutional wrongdoing on the part of the criminal justice system in 'Networked Gym-Fit Recidivist' call attention to the irrationalist violence underpinning punitive rhetoric and the 'retributive hatred' of the offender that Jeffrey Murphy referred to (see first section earlier).[58]

In a similar vein, a poem by a prisoner writing in the style of Kipling's 'If –' is susceptible to the same revision of the dominant Foucauldian reading. 'IF: a prisoner's perspective with apologies to Rudyard Kipling' sardonically tells the reader that 'this is your cell and everything that's in it', provided he or she can put up with myriad indignities, including interrupted sleep ('bed while tannoys beckon'), insecurity ('clothing going missing'), and lack of agency ('no say in decisions').[59] On the one hand, the poet is describing the struggle to find one's own sense of self despite the all-consuming subjection to penal routine and regime; the use of the second person ('you', 'your' – a direct style

56 Richard, '12 Books' in Sprackland (ed), *Koestler Voices: 3* (n 10) 82.
57 Neil, 'Networked Gym-Fit Recidivist' in Potts (ed), *Koestler Voices: 1* (n 10) 23–4.
58 Murphy and Hampton (n 19).
59 Michelle, 'IF: A Prisoner's Perspective with Apologies to Rudyard Kipling' in Potts (ed), *Koestler Voices: 1* (n 10) 25.

adopted in a number of the *Koestler* poems) ambiguously denotes the prisoner herself but also addresses the reader of the poem and, in that way, brings the imprisoned author and the reader 'outside' into closer contact. This is a technique that calls to mind both Foucault's arguments that disciplining panoptic techniques impact on everyone, not only prisoners, and also the *relational* theories of responsibility proposed by Norrie and by Duff. On the other hand, the poem is also remarkable for the way it harnesses the emotive power of the punitive, albeit turning it around to reflect its impact back to the reader to show them what punitivity produces. In this way, the poem is saying, 'Look, here is the box you have put me in – this is what your anger has led to'.

Another common theme relating to the prisoner's compromised identity and sense of self is the identification with the lowliest of creatures: injured or trapped birds and animals, whose own sorry state the narrator finds analogous to their own. Hence, Solomon (in 'Meep-Meep and Jesus on the Roof') notices a 'little wood pigeon', a 'poor' creature with 'pin-prick eyes', who appears at the scene when a prisoner is on the roof, threatening to hang himself:

I send her violet light
And all my love and protection.
How hard to be in the circle
Of brute survival: bullied
and blasted by life
yet still so trusting and so sweet.[60]

This strategy of using a lowly and downtrodden creature as a metaphor for the offender's own place in the prison system is taken up also by Kharhak, in the poem 'Wandsworth', who reports on his reaction upon discovering a mouse in his cell trying to steal '[his] last half ounce'. At first responding to the discovery with punitive, angry violence ('Grabbed him in a vice like grip and hurled him against the door'), the narrator then experiences a shift in identification. Sympathy for the creature is stirred, first, by signs of the its vulnerability ('I noticed these tiny tear drops appearing around his eyes') and then by its sad life story, leading to and including imprisonment, which it relates to the narrator:

I was born and raised in Brixton, my father was a rat,
He used to beat me badly but I won't go into that.
I jumped a dust cart heading east and wound up stuck in here,
They put me in a fraggle's cell to live in constant fear.[61]

The narrator's identifying sympathy is won on account of the creature proving itself, like the narrator, to have been reduced by external forces to crime for

60 Solomon, 'Meep-Meep and Jesus on the Roof' in Potts (ed), *Koestler Voices: 2* (n 10) 21.
61 Kharhak, 'Wandsworth' in Potts (ed), *Koestler Voices: 2* (n 10) 22–3.

basic survival. Again, there are several different things going on here in terms of how we might read these lines. In the first place, the imprisoned poets are finding routes to reflect upon, reclaim, and reconstruct their own identities under the constraining and examining gaze of the prison. Subjected to the prison regime and the many uncertainties and perils it may bring, positive qualities of love, protectiveness, and trust come through as humanising counterweights to 'brute survival'. Listening, identification, and empathy are routes to breaking down the dichotomy of punisher against punished and puts into question the retributive justification for a violent response to wrongdoing.

At the same time, though, the resort to such lowly identifications raises the further issue of the prisoner as *object* of a punitive determination to cause suffering. The creatures in question – the pigeon, the mouse – are themselves typically objectified in human culture as pests, pilferers, and vermin, against which measures are taken to keep them out of human life (the vicious spikes atop roofs and eaves to prevent pigeons from landing, the traps and cats deployed to destroy mice). Even if we accept that the *identification* with lowly animals is itself part of a negotiation and affirmation of identity – and an act of resistance to the reductive discourse of prison routine – the violence of the relation of punisher to punished is also, at the same time, affirmed and dramatised. To the extent that these different readings of the poems are in tension with one another is not itself reason to reject one in favour of the other. We propose, instead, that this sense of the prisoner as both subject and object is itself held in tension together in a dialectical relation.

Prison as a place of enforced stillness

Perhaps the most familiar visual symbol of the state's domination of the prisoner is provided in the image of the confining prison cell itself, with its oppressive iron bars, thick walls, and solid clanging doors calling to mind a tomb or a morgue. These features allow the cell to serve as a metaphorical device for articulating imprisonment, and characterised by forcing the prisoner to endure prolonged stasis, stuckedness, waiting, and suspension of time. Sarah Armstrong, although herself resolved to challenge the conceptual dominance of the prison cell, concedes that it is

> deeply embedded in collective memory as the crucial space of incarceration . . . allied to, and descended from, other 'coercive spaces of segregation' (Matthews, 2009: 25) – monasteries, barracks and asylums . . . where prison's purpose, and purposelessness, can be found: in penitence, boredom, suicide.[62]

62 Sarah Armstrong, 'The Cell and the Corridor: Imprisonment as Waiting, and Waiting as Mobile' (2018) 27(2) *Time and Society* 133, 136. All these are examples given by Foucault (in *Discipline and Punish* (n 4)) as *disciplinary* spaces, and this participates in the production of 'docile' and compliant subjects.

Ben Crewe reports interview material that offers support to the idea of the cell as characterising imprisonment as such, with the confined box-space into which the prisoner is squeezed symbolic of live burial:

> Dirk explained that 'You start to feel that you're suffocated – there's no exit route'; Yiannis commented that 'Time's just stood still for me at the moment. I'm just stuck in a cave, without a ladder'; Christophe conveyed an almost total lack of hope and agency: 'You can be buried and lost in the system.'[63]

The imagery of being 'stuck in a cave' and 'buried and lost in the system' engages an aesthetic more generally associated with the dark and dank of the 'old' *dungeon*, into which offenders are 'thrown' and 'loaded' with chains, rather than the 'new' prison and its panoptic technologies producing disciplined, docile prisoners.[64] A number of the *Koestler Voices* poems reflect this prison of the Gothic imagination in drawing on the metaphor of the tomb or grave as a means for articulating the arrest of movement by containment in the cell. For example, Matthew's account of the experience of being in the cell at night ('Prison-somnia') uses imagery of death and burial to figure the distinctive sensory qualities of prison that combine to extinguish memories of freedom:

> As I lie here on this rock-hard slab
> the cold dark walls come closing in.
> I can't remember how it was
> before this silent din. . . .
>
> I wonder if I'll ever get used to it?
> As days and nights go out and in.
> And I try to remember how it was
> before this silent din.[65]

Daniel's 'The Ghost Inside' similarly presents the narrator's imprisonment as a living death: the cell 'a shroud of stone and steel', and the prisoner made '[t]o suffer, damned, forever bound'. The final verse spells out the sheer and utter evisceration of the soul of the prisoner narrator, and the latter's conviction that any significant change of circumstances – by any movement in time or space – is surely impossible:

> Within that prison chamber tomb
> Where life was ended far too soon,
> Where hope had left and sorrow stayed

63 Ben Crewe, 'The Depth of Imprisonment' (2021) 23(3) *Punishment & Society* 335, 348.
64 Fludernik, 'Carceral Topography' (n 48) 62.
65 Matthew, 'Prison-Somnia' in Sprackland (ed), *Koestler Voices: 3* (n 10) 28–9.

And to a soul the price was paid,
There's no escape – there cannot be
For I am dead – that Ghost is me.[66]

Having in mind the foregoing discussion, it is important to clarify here that our reading of these references to oneself as 'dead' and entombed is not to deny that these imprisoned poets are engaging in a process of negotiating notions of identity and that, in part, this involves resisting the disciplinary impositions of the institution. The imprisoned poet who reduces themself (or their narrator) to the level of disembodied consciousness lingering on after ordinary (bodily) life is over is the ideal Cartesian subject (the naked 'ego') produced by the isolation of prison. But it also takes to a logical conclusion the punitive desire to see the prisoner extinguished, removed as far as is possible short of there being nothing left to experience anything at all. A fuller understanding of the poems thus comes from noticing and appreciating how *pre*-modern aesthetic qualities, deriving from punitive rhetoric, are part of the picture. Taking these readings together produces useful dialectical tension between the narrators of Matthew's and Daniel's poems as both subject (i.e. subjectivity created by penal incarceration) *and* object (the target of angry, vengeful emotion).

Prison time as torture time

As well as being captured in three-dimensional space, prisoners are likewise captured in time, and this is clear from existing interview data in which prisoners describe the experience of the repetitious. There is no doubt that Foucault was correct to identify the timetable as a key part of the apparatus of the new prison in gaining and retaining control over its subject.[67] However, a close reading of what prisoners actually say about their experience of time reveals more than the routinised docility that Foucault had in mind. Note the metaphors of physical pain, torture, and death (italicised) in this research data reported by Medlicott:

> 'Minutes, hours, days slip away with *terrifying* insubstantiality. Months will *pass away* like this, and years. *Life*! The problem of time is everything. Nothing distinguishes one hour from the next: the minutes and hours *fall* slowly, *torturously*. Once past, they *vanish into near nothingness*'[68] –

66 Daniel, 'The Ghost Inside' in Potts (ed), *Koestler Voices: 2* (n 10) 28–9.

67 Foucault, *Discipline and Punish* (n 4): 'The *time-table* is an old inheritance. The strict model was no doubt suggested by the monastic communities. It soon spread. It [has] three great methods – establish rhythms, impose particular occupations, regulate the cycles of repetition' (149).

68 Diana Medlicott, 'Surviving in the Time Machine: Suicidal Prisoners and the Pains of Prison Time' (1999) 8(2) *Time & Society* 211, 212 (my emphasis).

[Jimmy]: 'It's just like a matter of waiting *for the end of waiting*, you know. *Killing* time before *time kills you*.'[69]

Sekulak identifies that conceptual metaphors for speaking about time can be broadly divided into imageries of 'lines' (in which the prisoner may feel they are still while time moves past) and 'circles' (accounting for repetition): both metaphors that 'endow [time] with a physical dimension' and that arguably 'explain why the passage of imprisonment time may be associated with pain, boredom, and stagnation'.[70] The central question for this discussion, though, is whether that 'pain, boredom, and stagnation' is merely a disciplinary technique or, beyond that, a sign of the punitive drive to see prisoners suffer being internalised and reflected back in the prisoner's voice. As we found earlier, the poems themselves do not admit of any single answer to such a question. In Joanne's poem 'Sentenced', we find a sobering daily schedule of sleeping, eating, working, watching TV, showering, taking meds: stretching in its numbing repetitiveness over an eight-week period that fills a single page:

MONDAY	work	food	work	food	meds	bed		
TUESDAY	work	shower	food	work	food	meds	bed	
WEDNESDAY	work	food	work	food	meds	bed		
THURSDAY	work	food	phone credit	work	food	meds	bed	
FRIDAY	work	food	canteen	work	shower	food	meds	bed
SATURDAY	watch TV	shower	food	watch TV	food	meds	bed	
SUNDAY	watch TV	laundry	food	watch TV	food	meds	bed	

[*and so on . . .*][71]

A poem that invites 'viewing' rather than 'reading', where one is struck by the fact that the routine is so numbingly mundane that any little variation can seem interesting or notable, such as there being one more 'activity' on Friday than on other days, or that watching TV replaces work at weekends, or even that phone credit and the canteen become available once a week. It might be imagined that Joanne should continue to exist on that loop indefinitely, the predictability and repetition of it all keeping her going and keeping her from being disruptive. This suggests that the provision of meds is part of a broader disciplinary strategy: the routinised provision of medication, alongside all the other timetabled activities, disabling the prisoner's own agency and capacity for action. That is only hinted at in Joanne's poem; there is no 'final verse' in

69 Medlicott (n 68) 220 (my emphasis).

70 Martyna Sekulak, Kaja Głomb, Kinga Tucholska, Bożena Gull, Małgorzata Wysocka-Pleczyk, Przemysław Piotrowski and Stefan Florek, 'Spatial Metaphors of Psychological Time: The Study of Imprisoned Men' (2022) 67 *New Ideas in Psychology* 100963 [*no page numbers*].

71 Joanne, 'Sentenced' in Potts (ed), *Koestler Voices: 2* (n 10) 20.

which the narrator comes to reject, or challenge, let alone break free of the prison routine altogether. However, I would like to suggest that by reading 'Sentenced' alongside other work that engages with the role of medication, we can see that there is more going on than a carceral conditioning of the self. In the poem 'Lit', the anonymous author figures the institutional medication routine as a casting and setting within a mould that incites at least the awareness of coercive constraint:

> Agents, no agency; Concrete, my feet poured
> Into blocks of meds.[72]

'Lit' articulates the medicated prisoner's loss of agency through the enforced stillness of drying concrete: a metaphor that encapsulates both the containment (in the cell) and the stopping of time. It is an important verse in that it speaks to an experience of prison routine not merely as dull but as an effect of the punitive desire to prevent the individual from enjoying the experiences that normally come with temporal changes: the turning of the seasons and the weather, the milestones of personal development in the world and those of loved ones, the possibility of changing one's surroundings, or the people one sees every day. Following this approach, another poem, 'Therapy', conveys the experience of time lost to imprisonment in terms of *death* and a *separation* between the imprisoned self and that which he or she holds dear (which, again, are both key aspects of the punitive):

> Men walk backwards through time
> In search of yesterday
> Yet, to no avail, find
> *Yesterday has fallen*
> Like the leaves of autumn.[73]

Conclusion

Scholars have long been concerned with the ways in which prisoner subjectivities are produced by the negotiation between discipline and resistance, as well as by the potential for the prisoner voice to serve as a source of critical commentary on the penal state and its practices.[74] Alongside those concerns, though, the poems also betray the framing devices germane to the punitive narrative of punishment. They express complex emotions that include fear

72 Anon, 'Lit' in Potts (ed), *Koestler Voices: 2* (n 10) 32–3.
73 Moses, 'Therapy' in Potts (ed), *Koestler Voices: 1* (n 10) 29.
74 See Mary Bosworth, *Engendering Resistance: Agency and Power in Women's Prisons* (Routledge 1999).

and resentment at being made to suffer at the hands of an objectifying and oppressive punisher and, in this respect, are also inheritors of pre-modern ideas about the retaliatory persecution. Our proposal, then, is that reading *Koestler Voices* and other creative responses to punishment must be a dialectical process – in other words, that it can and should accommodate ostensibly antagonistic interpretations in getting to a more sophisticated, rounded understanding. Yes, 'the modern prisoner' is constructed in the discursive space between the disciplining state and the variously docile or resistant individual. And yes, observations in the poems about the treatment of prisoners, the behaviour of officers, and the overall impressions of 'the system' all connect with critical scholarship on punishment and responsibility. But the writings of imprisoned people are also important sources that compel us to continue to take seriously notions of punishment as the spectacular infliction of pain, and the sound of the prisoner's voice as (to quote the words Foucault used when describing the bygone age of the scaffold) 'the very ceremonial of justice being expressed in all its force'.[75]

For this reason, the chapter here has argued that poems from prisons may be thought of, at least in part, as texts that affirm the punitive narrative's framing of crime and punishment and its actors. This is not a normative judgment about the appropriateness of the punitive urge in criminal justice and, for this reason, is to be distinguished from the moral accounts of punishment also referred to earlier. The aim here has instead been to identify and to describe evidence for its salience within both punishment rhetoric and poetry from prisons. This curious narrative convergence warrants further consideration of the punitive as a criminal justice 'masterplot', or perhaps some similar label that connotes a significance greater than one narrative among many. Whatever we call it, we hope to have shown here, at least, that it is a narrative that is not quite so narrow or obscure, as it is often assumed to be.

75 Foucault, *Discipline and Punish* (n 4) 34.

Part 3

Legal masterplot and gender

Chapter 5

Dismantling the masterplot of domestic violence and abuse

Rebecca Shaw

In 2016, Robin Wharton and Derek Miller set out to assess the state of scholarship on law and narrative and demonstrate how 'narrative suffuses all of legal practice'.[1] They established three major intertwining strands which thread throughout law and narrative: 'storytelling in witness testimony . . . , how legal opinions narrativize their own logic and tidy the narratives presented as evidence . . . , [and] narratives of the law that constrain and define the possibilities of legal practice'.[2] Such strands are underpinned by several decades of study of the concept of narrative in legal scholarship, which has demonstrated the power that stories can have: '[L]aw ultimately is the product of commonly shared narratives and other cultural frames that form the soil from which all legal principles grow.'[3] Thus, as Brooks argues, 'narrativity belongs to our cognitive toolkit, it constitutes one of the large categories in which we understand and construct the world' and, by extension, the laws of our world.[4] The ubiquity and applicability of narrative, thus, lies in the fact that stories give human experiences shape and meaning, providing a means by which we can account for the new or even the self-evident. It is fundamental to our understanding of the world.[5]

However, within these strands outlined by Wharton and Miller, there is arguably a fourth strand for law and narrative that should be considered: how narratives, and specifically the analytical study of the nature of narrative and narration, can effect law reform. The deployment of legal storytelling as an integral part of law reform has been explored, most notably through the perspective of oppositional storytelling or counternarratives. Work by scholars

1 Robin Wharton and Derek Miller, 'New Directions in Law and Narrative' (2019) 15(2) *Law, Culture and the Humanities* 294, 297.
2 Wharton and Miller (n 1) 297–8.
3 Linda H. Edwards, 'Speaking of Stories and Law' (2016) 13 *Scholarly Works* 157, 160.
4 Peter Brooks, 'Narrative in and Out of the Law' in James Phelan and Peter J. Rabinowitz (eds), *A Companion to Narrative Theory* (Blackwell 2005) 415.
5 Bernard S. Jackson, *Law, Fact and Narrative Coherence* (Deborah Charles Publications 1988) 3.

DOI: 10.4324/9781003404668-8

such as Delgado has examined the integration of powerful human stories in law reform efforts, how stories told by members of 'out-groups' can subvert the conventional legal position, and how, in legal discourse, narratives which embody preconceptions or myths shape mindsets and supply the background against which formal laws are not only interpreted and applied but also created.[6] Yet this appreciation of storytelling, particularly those stories from the margins, has been criticised (*inter alia*) for its omission of any analytic study of the nature of narrative, what it is and how it works.[7] If storytelling, therefore, is to be a successful tool in law reform and effect a 'narrative shift' within legislation, do we need to re-think this perspective and consider the narrative templates and devices adopted to persuade lawmakers to take action?

This chapter, then, investigates the use of storytelling within law reform efforts and how an appreciation of the narrative devices deployed in these stories might offer fresh insights into their ability to effect successful legislative changes and, in turn, dismantle socio-cultural masterplots. Taking as a case study the Domestic Abuse Bill and evidence submitted by experts and interest groups prior to, and during, the Bill's passage through Parliament, it analyses the narratives presented in these reports and their attempts to persuade lawmakers to dismantle the 'masterplot' of domestic violence and abuse (DVA).[8] Comprising of prominent socio-cultural beliefs, in this case about DVA, the masterplot is a narrative that gets told against a background of assumptions which people believe to be true and which they use to make sense of events and of each other. It is a shared cultural resource, one which individual tellers and the law are able to invoke, mobilise, or work to dismantle.[9] Residual stereotypes, myths, biases, and characterisations of domestic violence and abuse

6 Richard Delgado, 'Storytelling for Oppositionists and Others: A Plea for Narrative' (1989) 87 *Michigan Law Review* 2411. See also Jane B. Baron, 'The Many Promises of Storytelling in Law: An Essay Review of Narrative and the Legal Discourse: A Reader in Storytelling and the Law' (1991) 23 *Rutgers Law Journal* 79; Jane C. Murphy, 'Lawyering for Social Change: The Power of the Narrative in Domestic Violence Law Reform' (1993) 21(4) *Hofstra Law Review* 1243; Robert S. Chang, 'Toward an Asian American Legal Scholarship: Critical Race Theory, Post-Structuralism, and Narrative Space' (1993) 81(5) *California Law Review* 1241; Richard Delgado and Jean Stefancic, 'Critical Race Theory: An Annotated Bibliography' (1993) 79 *Virginia Law Review* 461; Michael Bamberg and Molly Andrews (eds), *Considering Counter Narratives: Narrating, Resisting, Making Sense* (J. Benjamins 2004); Narelle Bedford, 'Storytelling in Our Legal System: Healing for the Stolen Generations' (2019) 45(2) *Australian Feminist Law Journal* 321.

7 Brooks (n 4) 416.

8 Throughout this article, *domestic violence and abuse* (DVA) is the term that will be used. While 'domestic abuse' is the language adopted by the Domestic Abuse Act 2021, it is recognised that this shift is problematic. See J. Aldridge, '"Not an Either/or Situation": The Minimization of Violence against Women in United Kingdom "Domestic Abuse" Policy' (2021) 27(11) *Violence against Women* 1823.

9 Matti Hyvärinen, Mari Hatavara, and Hanna Rautajoki, 'Positioning with Master and Counter-Narratives' (2021) 31(1) *Narrative Inquiry* 97, 103. See also Anthony Amsterdam

remain embedded within the socio-cultural narrative and thus still serve as the blueprint for DVA's masterplot.[10] Although invisible and only identifiable because of competing counternarratives, the masterplot 'perpetuates socio-cultural and structural forces that silence victim/survivors and perpetuate' domestic violence and abuse.[11]

The law, then, can be positioned as intersecting and operating within this framework of narrative contestation. Theorised in this way, the masterplot thus forms part of the groundwork of the law, infusing and shaping how the law is made, debated, upheld, or repealed. The important consequence being that we must also recognise the inherent limitations of legislation in challenging the masterplot, as well as its power. A single piece of legislation, or indeed, the law more broadly, cannot disrupt such entrenched socio-cultural narratives alone. Indeed, as Bishop recognises with the Domestic Abuse Bill and its final enactment as the Domestic Abuse Act, it was never going to provide a 'panacea' for protecting lives and providing justice for victims.[12] Nonetheless, given the ubiquity of narrative in legal practice, we shouldn't resist what narrative can mean for law reform efforts. If we are going to effectively maximise this relationship between law reform and narrative, bringing the entire narrative transaction into this fourth strand of law and narrative is imperative: focusing on the combination of both story (the 'what') *and* discourse (the 'how').

This chapter is divided into three parts. It will begin by considering the role of storytelling in law reform and the theoretical framework of narrative transactions, namely, the story–discourse distinction, which underpins this chapter. I then discuss the key provisions of the Domestic Abuse Bill (and the subsequent Act) and situate this within the broader context of the masterplot of domestic violence and abuse. Drawing on structural and feminist narratologies, I then move to a close textual analysis of two survivor narratives, analysing the need to pay attention to narrative voice. I argue that there is a correlation between the erasure of voice in organisational narratives and the legal reproduction of the masterplot of DVA, offering a narrative explication as to why policy influencers failed to persuade lawmakers to make the changes they desire. The chapter closes with the proposal for greater consideration of the 'communal' voice – a conscious investment of narrative

and Jerome Bruner, *Minding the Law* (Harvard University Press 2000), who suggest that narrative structures are ways of sharing culturally shared human experiences.

10 For a discussion on masterplots and their counternarratives, see Molly Andrews, 'Introduction: Counter-Narratives and the Power to Oppose' (2002) 12(1) *Narrative Inquiry* 1; Danielle Corple, Jasmine R. Linabary and Cheryl Cooky, '"He Never Hit Me #WhyIStayed": Countering the U.S. Domestic Violence Master Narrative (2021) 49(5) *Journal of Applied Communication Research* 532; Hyvärinen et al. (n 9).

11 Corple et al. (n 10) 536. See also Hyvärinen et al. (n 9).

12 Charlotte Bishop, 'Prevention and Protection: Will the Domestic Abuse Act Transform the Response to Domestic Abuse in England and Wales?' (2021) 33(2) *Child and Family Law Quarterly* 163, 164.

authority in a definable community of survivors – in order to help negotiate the tensions faced by employing legal storytelling in law reform efforts. If a shift in the narrative is going to occur, if a masterplot is going to continue to be dismantled through further reform, then we need to turn to a narrative solution and consider how storytelling within law reform can be used more effectively.

Legal storytelling and narrative transaction

That vivid stories play out in the arena of law is a well-accepted tenet. As Gerwitz points out, there has been a 'striking convergence' between the law and its stories, with both academics and the general public as each 'absorbing the ways law brings together story, form and power'.[13] Narrative is ubiquitous in the law because it allows us to account for the self-evident: to tell a story about an experience is to give it shape and meaning, allowing us to relate and compare it to other similar or contesting stories. Indeed, as Liveley points out, narrative not only 'represents but [also] re-presents events that have already happened'.[14] This idea endures when we consider the role that storytelling can play in law reform. The recounting of past events can focus, or rather refocus, the attention of legal decision-makers to the human dimension of the problem before them.[15] This is particularly congruous in the area of domestic violence and abuse. However, in this context, there are certain types of discourses which are 'most likely to shape the implementation of legislation'.[16] Not only, as Hunter goes on to argue, discourses from legal culture but also the wider socio-cultural resource of the masterplot. In order to course-correct legislative efforts away from the masterplot, a simple solution often argued for is to include the narratives of the excluded, of the marginalised.[17]

Indeed, while the majority of the reports submitted during the parliamentary debates on the Domestic Abuse Bill did not include any stories from the human dimension, there are a few examples which included 'case studies' of people directly affected by domestic violence and abuse. A joint written

13 Paul Gerwitz, 'Narrative and Rhetoric in the Law' in Peter Brooks and Paul Gerwitz (eds), *Law's Stories: Narrative and Rhetoric in the Law* (Yale University 1996) 2.

14 Genevieve Liveley, 'Fables for Tomorrow: Narrating Net Zero' in Paul Dawson and Maria Mäkelä (eds), *The Routledge Companion to Narrative Theory* (Routledge 2023), 530.

15 Murphy (n 6) 1253.

16 Rosemary Hunter, 'Narratives of Domestic Violence' (2006) 28 *Sydney Law Review* 733, 750.

17 See the work of Chang (n 6). For further work on applied legal storytelling, see Christopher Rideout, 'Storytelling, Narrative Rationality and Legal Persuasion' (2008) 14 *Legal Writing: The Journal of the Legal Writing Institute* 53; and Christopher Rideout, 'Applied Legal Storytelling: A Bibliography' (2015) 12 *Legal Communication and Rhetoric: JALWD* 247 and bibliography there cited.

submission from 29 different VAWG (violence against women and girls) sector organisations included one case study highlighting the barriers to access justice for deaf and disabled survivors, narrated by the organisation Stay Safe East.[18] Additionally, we can see in the individual submission from Women's Aid Federation England a selection of brief quotes from survivors of DVA.[19] However, this experiment of incorporating narrative into evidence reports, as noted earlier, is somewhat lacking: these self-revelation narratives, which are superficial and supplementary additions, are placed in the category of anecdotal evidence and do not occupy a privileged place within written submissions. Thus, there appears to be a resistance to narrative: storytelling, perhaps, is viewed as a risky endeavour, and rhetors are desirous to conform, instead, to objective modes of discourse.[20] How, then, can stories be used to 'persuade legal decision-makers'[21] and 'create a bridge across gaps in experience and . . . elicit empathic understanding'[22] if there is such a resistance to narrative? Chang argues that this resistance to narrative emerges as people do not want to believe in these personal counter-stories. Although, discussing this in the context of racism towards Asian Americans, he argues that people do not want to see it because 'it is ugly [and] they have learned or convinced themselves that such ugliness does not exist'.[23] The same could be said about domestic violence and abuse.

Scholars have been arguing for decades about the power of storytelling for transforming legal thinking. As a leading proponent of legal storytelling, Delgado maintains the attraction of storytelling within what he terms out-groups (groups whose marginality defines the boundaries of the mainstream) should come as no surprise, 'for stories create their own bonds, represent cohesion, shared understandings, and meanings. The cohesiveness that stories bring is part of the strength of the outgroup'.[24] Legal storytelling has been championed 'on the basis that it will result in a legal system that is more encompassing and fairer'.[25] As Olson contends in the context of Harvey Weinstein's trial, in the best-case scenario, there will be a triumphant narrative of recognising marginalised voices, with more real stories of rape, sexual coercion, and sexual harassment addressable, which, in turn, will lead to a

18 See Domestic Abuse Bill Deb Written Evidence Submission DAB32 (2020) <https://publications.parliament.uk/pa/cm5801/cmpublic/DomesticAbuse/memo/DAB32.pdf> accessed 17 June 2024.
19 Domestic Abuse Bill Deb Written Evidence Submission DAB65 (2020) <https://publications.parliament.uk/pa/cm5801/cmpublic/DomesticAbuse/memo/DAB65.pdf> accessed 17 June 2024.
20 See Chang (n 6) 1273, discussing this 'resistance to narrative' in the context of Asian American legal scholarship.
21 Murphy (n 6) 1246.
22 Martha Minow, 'Words and the Door to the Land of Change: Law, Language and Family Violence' (1990) 43 *Vanderbilt Law Review* 1665, 1688.
23 Chang (n 6) 1274.
24 Delgado (n 6) 2412.
25 Bedford (n 6) 324.

change in those problematic cultural-legal norms.[26] Yet that is a best-case scenario. With the written submissions in the parliamentary debates for the Domestic Abuse Bill, 'messy, individual stories'[27] were rarely used. Bedford states that it is uncontroversial that there is an ongoing role for storytelling.[28] Yet if written evidence, designed with the ostensible aim to convince legislators to make changes, is resistant to narrative and to including such stories, then the unanimity of legal storytelling's power and role is somewhat moot. Even acknowledging Brook's caution about legal storytelling's flaw(s) as a 'moral chameleon'[29] still leaves the question of how we can effectively harness the power of storytelling (of minoritarian voices, of counternarratives, of 'others') to effect successful law reform and dismantle masterplots. To help negotiate this tension, if we want narratives to have power and persuasion in law reform, greater consideration needs to be given to the story–discourse distinction in legal storytelling.

The juxtaposition of story and discourse, and the way their relationship operates, is the cornerstone to comprehending how narratives are received and judged. The 'what' of the story – the content, the basic story stuff, the narrated, the existent and events – is all too familiar to readers of legal stories. We are focused on bringing to life the experiences of victims, of survivors, so that these marginalised voices can tell their story. Undoubtedly, these stories hold significant power. Feminist work to date has (rightly) focused on the transformative potential of these stories: they are concerned with the figure of the survivor-storyteller 'speaking out' to produce social change, with 'women's narrative experiences . . . told to shatter the taboo, mythologies and silences' that surround violence and abuse.[30] The priority, therefore, has been on recounting and disseminating survivor narratives, signalling a commitment to using such stories to dismantle masterplots. However, the transformative potential of these stories is equally reliant on how they are transmitted – the narrating, the rearrangement and treatment of the events and existents, the emplotment of the basic story stuff. If we want these narratives to have power and persuasion, to have that impact that justifies and brings about change, then we need to consider form as well as content.

Certainly, this reflection should come as no surprise. Scholars of narrative theory have continued to explore and reassess this distinction since it

26 Great Olson, 'Legal Facts, Affective Truths, and Changing Narratives in Trials Involving Sexual Assault: Harvey Weinstein and #MeToo' in Paul Dawson and Maria Mäkelä (eds), *The Routledge Companion to Narrative Theory* (Routledge 2023) 182.

27 Olson (n 26) 183.

28 Bedford (n 6) 330.

29 Peter Brooks, 'The Law as Narrative and Rhetoric' in Peter Brooks and Paul Gewirtz (eds), *Law's Stories: Narrative and Rhetoric in the Law* (Yale University Press 1996) 16.

30 Tanya Serisier, 'What Does It Mean to #BelieveWomen?' in Paul Dawson and Maria Mäkelä (eds), *The Routledge Companion to Narrative Theory* (Routledge 2023) 342–3.

was first put forth by French narratologist Todorov in 1966.[31] In 1999, Herman argued that narrative grammar is inseparable from questions about the contexts in which narratives are designed and interpreted.[32] More recently, Lanser sets out that 'the story *won't* tell unless we study narrative form as narrative content'.[33] Likewise, when considering what it means to #BelieveWomen, Serisier refocuses her attention to consider the 'narrative transaction as a whole', recognising that narrative theory offers a useful lens for understanding these cultural and political contestations.[34] Yet a brief analepsis back to the use of narrative as the Domestic Abuse Bill passed through Parliament shows that this appreciation of form, of its significance for imbuing meaning into stories, does not extend into the written evidence of policy influencers. Not only is there a resistance to using narrative and embedding stories within written reports (a disjunction between theory and practice), but on the occasions when stories are told, there is a lack of consideration as to *how* that story is told. Content and form have to be viewed integratively; otherwise, at best, legal storytelling will only be 'read' rather than granted authority and validation. This seems apodictic when considering the survivor narratives of domestic violence and abuse. Indeed, as will be examined later, the institutional act of disregarding form and re-organising the lived experience of survivors into an admissible and agreeable story, in order to enable reform, involves the erasure of precisely the voices that ought to be central to that reform. Any meaningful commitment to the use of legal storytelling in law reform, so that the latter does not sustain erasure, needs, therefore, to think about the narrative transaction as a whole.

The Domestic Abuse Bill and the masterplot of DVA

The Domestic Abuse Bill, which was announced in the Queen's Speech in 2017,[35] received royal assent and became the Domestic Abuse Act in April 2021. As noted by both Bettinson and Ormerod, the huge response to the consultation[36] and the evidence presented by so many experts, campaign

31 Tzvetan Todorov, 'Les catégories du récit littéraire' (1966) 8 *Communications* 125.

32 David Herman, 'Introduction' in David Herman (ed), *Narratologies: New Perspectives on Narrative Analysis* (The Ohio State University Press 1999) 11.

33 Susan S. Lanser, 'Toward (a Queerer and) More (Feminist) Narratology' in Robyn Warhol and Susan S. Lanser (eds), *Narrative Theory Unbound* (The Ohio State University Press 2015) 24–5.

34 Serisier (n 30) 343.

35 Queen Elizabeth II, *Queen's Speech 2017* (21 June 2017) <www.gov.uk/government/speeches/queens-speech-2017> accessed 17 June 2024. It is worth noting that this was PM Theresa May's only Queen's Speech during her three years as prime minister.

36 HM Government, 'Transforming the Response to Domestic Abuse' (2018) <https://consult.justice.gov.uk/homeoffice-moj/domestic-abuse-consultation/> accessed 17 June 2024.

groups, and criminal justice professionals in evidence on the Bill illustrated the scale of the problem and the wider public desire to see legal reform in this area.[37] Crucially, the Bill (and the subsequent Act) provided a highly anticipated statutory definition of 'domestic abuse', which stated that *domestic abuse* encompasses behaviour between 'personally connected' people that can include physical or sexual abuse; violent or threatening behaviour; controlling or coercive behaviours; economic abuse; and psychological, emotional, or other abuse.[38] The definition also provided that it is irrelevant whether the behaviour is a single incident or a course of conduct, and that children can also be victims if they see, hear, or experience the effects of domestic abuse and are related to the abused or the abuser.[39] The recognition of non-physical forms of abuse and that children who live with domestic abuse are victims, in particular, was welcomed for addressing some of the inadequacies surrounding the previous laws on domestic violence and abuse.[40] The Bill also included the establishment of an independent Domestic Abuse Commissioner, a role which involves raising public awareness, speaking on behalf of victims and survivors, and using its statutory powers to hold government and agencies to account in their provision of domestic abuse services in England and Wales.[41] Other substantive criminal measures included the extension of the offence of controlling or coercive behaviour under the Serious Crime Act 2015, the extension of the scope of offences dealing with revenge porn, and the introduction of a new offence of non-fatal strangulation.[42] However, the breadth of the Bill extended beyond solely criminal law, with the legislation introducing a new domestic abuse protection order (DAPO) with a wider scope than the existing occupation orders or domestic violence protection orders (DVPOs).[43] Undoubtedly, the legislation's commitment to addressing this social issue and

37 Victoria Bettinson, 'Adding to the Domestic Abuse Criminal Law Framework: The Domestic Abuse Act 2021' (2022) 2 *Criminal Law Review* 88; David Ormerod, 'The Domestic Abuse Bill 2021' (2021) 6 *Criminal Law Review* 423.

38 Domestic Abuse Bill, HC Bill, (2019–2021), cl. 1; Domestic Abuse Act 2021, s1.

39 Domestic Abuse Bill, HC Bill, (2019–2021), cls. 1 and 3; Domestic Abuse Act 2021, ss.1 and 3.

40 Bishop (n 12) 163.

41 Domestic Abuse Commissioner's Office <https://domesticabusecommissioner.uk/about/> accessed 17 June 2024.

42 For analysis of the strangulation and suffocation offence introduced in s.70 of the Act, see Rory Kelly and David Ormerod, 'Non-Fatal Strangulation and Suffocation' (2021) 7 *Criminal Law Review* 532.

43 This article will not discuss the nature of DAPOs, and their place within the existing framework of legal remedies for victims of DVA. For further discussion on this topic, see Ana Speed and Kayleigh Richardson, '"Should I Stay or Should I Go Now? If I Go There Will Be Trouble and If I Stay There Will Be Double": An Examination into the Present and Future of Protective Orders Regulating the Family Home in England and Wales' (2022) 86(3) *Journal of Criminal Law* 179.

providing far-reaching provisions is why it has been hailed as a 'landmark moment' for the prevention of domestic violence and abuse.[44]

However, despite these legislative changes, the inherent limitations of the law in disrupting the masterplot, in its inability to counter the different elements of a systemic cultural narrative, account for the view that the masterplot of DVA remains prevalent today. Given that the masterplot can be viewed as an 'abstraction of routinised stories',[45] of stereotyped scripts stored in memory rather than a tellable story or reference to an individual narrative, it can be difficult to define. Yet in a 2022 Women's Aid survey of UK attitudes to domestic violence and abuse, we encounter many still resilient narrative elements and patterns that perpetuate the masterplot of domestic violence and abuse.[46] Within public perception, there persists a culture of victim-blaming towards survivors, with a significant proportion of UK adults still placing responsibility on the victim for the perpetrator's actions.[47] Likewise, 'the idea that if a woman does not present a certain way, she is culpable in the behaviour of the abuser' is prevalent in the study's findings, with 'bad behaviour' actions such as infidelity seen as justification for abuse.[48] A further issue identified by the study was the prevalence of attitudinal drivers on perceptions of DVA, and that those with 'stereotypical views of gender roles and underlying misogynistic views' were simultaneously more tolerant, and also less aware, of domestic violence and abuse.[49] Even a 'modern' conception and approach to DVA, therefore, is still fostered by a climate of misogyny and has roots in broader social and cultural narratives of gender inequality.

Other recurring scripts and stereotypical characterisations identified include the belief that 'it won't happen to me, as this is something that happens to other people'; the concept of coercive control is still not widely understood, with some types of abuse viewed as more tolerable than others; responsibility is placed on survivors for the abuse they experience; and there is a lack of collective societal responsibility for domestic violence and abuse.[50] The stereotyped script of equating domestic *abuse* with violent behaviour is one that remains prevalent today, along with a lingering tension between the characterisation of victims as legitimate and deserving on the one hand, and underserving and blameworthy on the other. Victims, therefore, are still expected to conform to the series of norms and expectations which are imposed

44 Bishop (n 12) 163.
45 Hyvärinen et al. (n 9) 102.
46 Women's Aid, 'Come Together to End Domestic Abuse: A Survey of UK Attitudes to Domestic Abuse 2022' <www.womensaid.org.uk/wp-content/uploads/2022/10/Come-Together-to-End-Domestic-Abuse-a-survey-of-UK-attitudes-to-domestic-abuse-2022.pdf> accessed 17 June 2024.
47 Women's Aid (n 46) 26.
48 Women's Aid (n 46) 30.
49 Women's Aid (n 46) 30.
50 Women's Aid (n 46) 30.

by this masterplot.[51] We, as a society, therefore, are still cueing into these prevalent myths and stereotypes regarding DVA, subsequently perpetuating its powerful but invisible masterplot. And as the study concluded, 'we need to change the stories that influence the way that we think about [domestic violence and] abuse'.[52]

Indeed, the Domestic Abuse Bill set out with the stated aim to change the masterplot of domestic violence and abuse. Its goals were to raise awareness, to improve understanding of its impact on victims and families, and to further improve the effectiveness of the justice system in providing protection for victims and bringing perpetrators to justice.[53] However, as a dynamic, interactive process, law reform efforts inevitably involve a range of myriad, multifaceted narratives aimed at countering different aspects and elements of the masterplot. These counternarratives are not 'uniform, monolithic or pure, but rather . . . plagued by inconsistencies and contradictions',[54] and as such, each submits different attempts to disrupt the canonical course of events and the corresponding masterplot. As a result, there is a fallacy in the notion that a single piece of legislation, as a tool for social change, can possibly respond to, and dismantle, all the recurring scripts and characterisations identified. This can explain the numerous criticisms levied against the Act, including, *inter alia*, simply adding to the existing piecemeal approach to legislation and failing to specifically address migrant women, with no recourse to public funds, as victims of DVA.[55] Indeed, nowhere is this more evident than with the criticism of the legislation for failing to consider the gendered dynamics and harm of domestic violence and abuse.[56] Despite extensive evidence submitted during the Bill's progression through Parliament, including

51 For more on the 'ideal victim', see N. Christie, 'The Ideal Victim' in E. A. Fattah (ed), *From Crime Policy to Victim Policy: Reorienting the Justice System* (Palgrave Macmillan 1986); M. Duggan (ed), *Revisiting the Ideal Victim* (Policy Press 2018); L. J. Long, 'The Ideal Victim: A Critical Race Theory (CRT) Approach' (2021) 27 *International Review of Victimology* 344; L. Goodmark, *Imperfect Victims: Criminalised Survivors and the Promise of Abolition Feminism* (University of California Press 2023); Hannah Bows, Paige Bromley and Sandra Walklate, 'Practitioner Understandings of Older Victims of Abuse and their Perpetrators: Not *Ideal Enough*?' (2023) 20 *The British Journal of Criminology* 1.

52 Women's Aid (n 46) 31.

53 Home Office, 'Domestic Abuse Act 2021: Overarching Factsheet' <www.gov.uk/government/publications/domestic-abuse-bill-2020-factsheets/domestic-abuse-bill-2020-overarching-factsheet#:~:text=Raise%20awareness%20and%20understanding%20about,and%20bringing%20perpetrators%20to%20justice> accessed 12 December 2023.

54 Michael Bamberg and Zachary Wipff, 'Reconsidering Counter-Narratives' in Klarissa Lueg and Marianne Wolff Lundholt (eds), *Routledge Handbook of Counter-Narratives* (Routledge 2020) 77.

55 Bishop (n 12); Vanessa Bettinson, 'Adding to the Domestic Abuse Criminal Law Framework: The Domestic Abuse Act 2021' (2022) 2 *Criminal Law Review* 88; Koho Boboye, 'A Gender-Neutral Law for Gender-Based Violence?' (2023) <https://blog.lselawreview.com/2024/01/15/a-gender-neutral-law-for-gender-based-violence/> accessed 17 June 2024.

56 For more on this, see Bishop (n 12) and Boboye (n 55).

both oral evidence and written reports submitted by various organisations during the committee stage, the final statutory definition was gender-neutral, with the gendered nature of the crime recognised in the statutory guidance. Organisations such as Women's Aid, Southall Black Sisters, Refuge, Against Violence & Abuse, Respect, Standing Together Against Domestic Abuse, to name a few, fiercely advocated for an accurate definition of 'domestic abuse', one which reflected its gendered nature.[57] Additionally, the Joint Committee of the House of Commons and Lords, in responding to the Bill, recommended that the gendered context of DVA should be recognised, and that in doing so, they sought to 'embed a nuanced approach to the most effective response to domestic abuse for all individuals who suffer such violence'.[58] However, by taking this gender-neutral approach, it is argued that the legislation failed to bring theory in line with practice.[59]

This raises the question as to why these calls for a gendered definition of DVA were unsuccessful. In the government's response to the Joint Committee of the House of Commons and Lords, it stated that a gender-neutral statutory definition was critical 'so that all types abuse are identified and that no victim is inadvertently excluded from support or protection'.[60] Positioning these reports – of policy influencers, practitioners, and academics – as counternarratives which have attempted to utilise the law as a tool to disrupt the masterplot, I suggest, offers a *narrative* explication as to why they failed to persuade lawmakers to make the changes they desired. Countering the masterplot is not just a question of organisation, of organising the various scripts, characterisations, and the content of DVA into a palatable story. Otherwise, as we shall see in the following case study, any legal storytelling proceeds via erasure. Rather, countering the masterplot is also a question of narration, of recognising the value of narrating, the narrative voice, and the form that the story takes. There is, thus, a correlation between the institutional act of organisation and the final act of reform which simply perpetuates that erasure. If the story of DVA cannot be located in 'pre-designed categories that were created for [its] erasure',[61] then the observations lack authority and validation.

57 Domestic Abuse Bill Deb Written Evidence Submission DAB32 (2020) <https://publications.parliament.uk/pa/cm5801/cmpublic/DomesticAbuse/memo/DAB32.pdf> accessed 17 June 2024.

58 Joint Committee on the Draft Domestic Abuse Bill, *Draft Domestic Abuse Bill* (2017–19, HL 378, HC 2075), [71]–[72] <https://publications.parliament.uk/pa/jt201719/jtselect/jtddab/2075/2075.pdf> accessed 17 June 2024.

59 Boboye (n 55).

60 The Government Response to the Report from the Joint Committee on the Draft Domestic Abuse Bill, *Draft Domestic Abuse Bill* (2017–19, HL 378, HC 2075) [62] <https://assets.publishing.service.gov.uk/media/5d2db85be5274a14f7889981/CCS0619467038-001_Domestic_Abuse_Bill_Print_WEb_Accessible.pdf> accessed 17 June 2024.

61 Ana Gómez Parga, 'Dis(missing) Voices: A Persistent Battle against Erasure' (2021) 42(3) *Frontiers: A Journal of Women Studies* 33, 34.

Before embarking on a close reading of one particular case study to highlight this dis(missing) of narrative form, it bears discussing the theory underpinning this reading. Specifically, it will draw on both structuralist and contextual (feminist) narratologies. The way we examine a literary text necessarily requires this dual emphasis, with the former providing a vocabulary for the latter. Certainly, each has their limitations, yet as Shen argues, there is nonetheless a mutually benefitting relationship between the two that, when acknowledged, can preserve and enrich our interpretative tools.[62] Genette has famously observed that there are three aspects in the analysis of narrative discourse: tense (including order, duration, and frequency), mood, and voice.[63] Given that the purpose of these narratives in legal reform attempts is to foreground the lived experience of victim-survivors, for that experience to be recognised and validated, the question as to 'who speaks' seems an especially pertinent one to ask. Yet severing texts entirely from their context – particularly when that context is a problematic, wider socio-cultural masterplot – is now recognised as a defective approach. We can see this from the work, *inter alia,* of feminist narratology, which has productively focused on the 'gendered and gendering impact of particular narrative strategies upon flesh-and-blood readers'.[64] Narratives can be critical to exposing and dismantling the masterplot of DVA; however, the gendered construction of the voice of these narratives can have real implications in keeping that dominant narrative in place.[65] With the Domestic Abuse Act's gender-neutral approach, specifically to the definition of 'domestic abuse', the centrality of gender in these narratives is complicit in perpetuating the gender normativity of DVA and impacting lawmakers, the 'flesh-and-blood readers' of these narratives. Deconstructing this case study through a feminist lens will, therefore, play a role in understanding the necessary preconditions for these narratives and the role discourse should take in their construction.

Case study: 'a survivor's experience'

The following narrative is taken from the All-Party Parliamentary Group (APPG) on Domestic Violence and Abuse recommendations for 'Creating a Truly Transformative Domestic Abuse Bill'.[66] This informal cross-party group,

62 See Dan Shen, 'Why Contextual and Formal Narratologies Need Each Other' (2005) 35(2) *Journal of Narrative Theory* 141.

63 Gérard Genette, *Narrative Discourse: An Essay in Method* (Cornell University Press 1980).

64 Robyn Warhol and Susan S. Lanser, 'Introduction' in Robyn Warhol and Susan S. Lanser (eds), *Narrative Theory Unbound* (The Ohio State University Press 2015) 6.

65 Warhol and Lanser (n 64) 7–8.

66 All-Party Parliamentary Group on Domestic Violence and Abuse, 'Creating a Truly Transformative Domestic Abuse Bill' (2017–18) <www.womensaid.org.uk/wp-content/uploads/2019/12/APPG-Report-2018.pdf> accessed 17 June 2024.

working alongside Women's Aid, is a highly influential non-partisan group, and their recommendations set the tone and reflected the core issues that many other organisations campaigned for during the parliamentary debates. Not only is it an effective way of bringing together parliamentarians and interested stakeholders; it also provides an important platform for survivors of DVA to share their experiences. In their 2017–18 report, submitted ahead of the Domestic Abuse Bill, we encounter a 'survivor's experience', which is not the dramatic centrepiece of the report. The 'story' is as follows:

> *The APPG heard evidence from a survivor who faced huge barriers in accessing support after she came to England with two of her sons to live with her husband, a British national. Her husband became progressively more controlling and violent and threatened to get her deported. This made her feel extremely anxious and frightened to tell the police or other statutory agencies about the abuse she has suffered. Organisations reported to the APPG that this is a common tactic of coercion and control by a perpetrator who has a wife on a spousal visa. Despite contacting both the police and local housing services, neither provided her with quality advice or support despite local authorities having statutory duties under Section 17 of the Children Act to support women and children. She contacted the National Domestic Violence Helpline (run in partnership with Women's Aid and Refuge) but struggled to access any refuge due to having no recourse to public funds; many refuges are unable to cover the costs of rent for a woman if she has no access to welfare benefits or other means of paying. She applied for the destitute domestic violence (DDV) concession under the domestic violence rule. Once the DDV concession was in place, and she was able to claim welfare benefits for a limited period, she secured a place for herself and her youngest son in a refuge. Sadly her other son had to 'sofa surf'.*[67]

Returning to Genette's aspects of discourse, the temporal ordering of the raw story material has been emplotted and arranged in a certain, formulaic fashion in this discourse. Indeed, this is indicative of the style of 'stories' used in other written submissions during the parliamentary debates. There are no anachronies or deviations from the chronology of the story, no disarrangements so to speak. The discourse follows the same chronological pattern of the events as they occurred. The narrator sets out the survivor's history, how she experienced abuse, the (lack of) resources available to her, the eventual (and limited) help she received, and a resolution leading to an unsatisfactory ending that aims to showcase the need for legal reform. The priority here, it seems, is to stick to generic conventions of narrative creation, with little to no embellishment or

67 All-Party Parliamentary Group on Domestic Violence and Abuse (n 66) 15–16.

experimentation in the discourse. This brings attention to a lacuna with the use of storytelling in effecting law reform. If the personal testimony does not cohere or conform to a standard model, if a woman's experience of domestic violence and abuse is not (re)told in a chronological sequence and in an accepted way, then it has no place within formal reports attending debates on law. However, emplotting personal testimony in such a way undermines its power as a vehicle to challenge the legal status quo and the masterplot of DVA. Such personal, individual testimonies are necessarily messy, fuzzy, and complicated, yet the narrative 'smoothing' on the part of the narrator, to make the experience more agreeable and comprehensible to the reader, dilutes its power for action and social change: not simply the kind of incremental change that can be achieved by legislation but rather radical, wholesale alteration of the masculine foundations of parliamentary principles and processes.

The 'voice', namely, who does and does not speak within this narrative, also looms large throughout the testimony: what is the narrator's identity and position vis-à-vis the events as they are narrated? We are invited into the survivor's 'story' by a heterodiegetic narrator, with the narrative authority invested in the APPG committee who has heard this woman's experience and is going to share her 'story'. The narrator, the committee's voice, does not amount to a 'communal voice' as articulated by Lanser.[68] Here, Lanser refers to a practice in which the narrative authority is invested in a 'definable community and textually inscribed either through multiple, mutually authorising voices or through the voice of a single individual who is manifestly authorised by a community'.[69] In this context, the narrator is not a collective of DVA survivors, whether speaking in a singular, simultaneous, or sequential form;[70] rather, the APPG committee is an outsider to this wider collective of marginal or suppressed voices, speaking in a paternalistic manner on their behalf. This narrator, therefore, is focused on providing an edited and revised version of the raw story, with the discourse told by an implicitly gender-neutral or even masculine narrator. This makes sense when we consider the context within which this narrator operates. Politically and legally constructed, this narrator is a product of the gendered history of Parliament, and the law, where women were historically excluded from lawmaking. Their utterances, then, are shaped by this gendered public sphere, and in this context, the sense of what constitutes a 'well-formed narrative' is conditioned by the authoritative, masculine voice and a male way of telling.[71] In accepting that the 'story' must be retold within this normative, masculine framework, the narrator

68 Susan S. Lanser, *Fictions of Authority* (Cornell University Press 1992).
69 Lanser (n 68) 21.
70 Lanser (n 68) 21.
71 See Ruth E. Page, 'Feminist Narratology? Literary and Linguistic Perspectives on Gender and Narrativity' (2003) 12(1) *Language and Literature* 43.

aims to position themselves as reliable in constructing a discourse that will hopefully be labelled believable. Yet this reliance on a politically and legally constructed masculine narrator is inherently problematic for a gendered crime and continues to mythologise a masterplot that fails to recognise the gendered harm and dynamics of domestic violence and abuse. That is not to doubt the sincerity of the narrator and their efforts to compel belief: they are simply cognisant of the criteria by which these narratives will be assessed and know that to doubt the narrator is to then doubt the 'story' they are telling. However, the refusal to branch out of heterodiegetic narration in this political-legal context makes the discourse inherently flawed: the call to believe this 'story' is undermined by the fact that the narrator is not the voice of the survivor, or even a communal voice authorised by the community. If narratives within legal reform efforts continue to follow the norm, then they will continue to contribute to the epistemic perpetuation and reconstitution of the very masterplot they are trying to dismantle.

What is further significant in this 'story' is that the third-person, heterodiegetic narrator has the effect of distancing the narratee from the object of their narration. By operating within these formulaic narrative boundaries, the victim-survivor has not been granted subjectivity and the right to speak. While quotes of victim-survivor narratives are intermittently incorporated into written evidence submissions, there is a sense of reluctance here to foreground the voice of survivors and their raw story material. This raises the question of precisely why narratees, the real and ideal audience to whom the narrative is directed and who are not part of the story world, need to be distanced from the voice of the survivor.[72] That is a question that can only be adequately answered when considering the wider socio-cultural masterplot of DVA (and, indeed, violence against women and girls more broadly): it draws attention to the fact that even in a post-#MeToo era, which 'signalled the ongoing feminist priority of recounting and disseminating survivor narratives', there still remains a fear of the power of women's stories of domestic (and sexual) abuse which challenge that masterplot.[73] While the narratee may be sympathetic to the survivor's experience, distancing them from the narration allows for a passivity which lessens the burden on the narratee to imagine themselves in the 'story'. Indeed, this uncomfortableness with survivor narratives is part of the wider narrative politics of survivor discourse, the believability of survivor-storytellers, and the fear that women's stories of harm have been granted excessive (punitive) power.[74] It is easier, then, and perhaps more strategic, to distance the narratee through heterodiegetic

72 See Shlomith Rimmon-Kenan, *Narrative Fiction: Contemporary Poetics* (Methuen 1983).
73 Serisier (n 30) 342, who discusses the politics of survivor-storytellers speaking out and the controversies that surround it in the context of #BelieveWomen and stories of sexual harm.
74 Serisier (n 30).

narration rather than to demand they actively engage with uncomfortable 'stories'. Shifting the focus of narration from the individual, intradiegetic survivor-storyteller to a third person, therefore, would undoubtedly mitigate the complications of having the speaking survivor tell her story. However, even if there is recognition on the part of the authors of the narrative politics surrounding survivor discourse, where reports choose to avoid being marked by the doubt and suspicion attached to survivor narratives, there are two key consequences of this. First, the fact remains that the status quo of heterodiegetic narration, however reliable that may be, has failed to fully effect law reform. Rather, in eschewing the voice of the survivor and any narrative strategies that will amplify that voice, we are left with an unconvincing discourse that is unpreferable to the alternative. Second, there is a correlation which emerges between the APPG report and the perpetuation of the cultural production of DVA and keeping the masterplot in place.

This eschewing of the survivor voice continues into the parliamentary debates themselves, most notably during the Committee stage debates. Over the course of 12 sittings of the Bill's Committee, only two survivors of domestic violence and abuse were called as witnesses during the second sitting of the Committee: Saliha Rashid and Somiya Basar.[75] Saliha Rashid, a survivor of DVA, gave evidence in her capacity as a campaigner representing a group of survivors that were part of Women's Aid's 'Law in the Making' project. She was invited to tell the Committee about her experiences as a disabled survivor of domestic violence and abuse, and the focus of her evidence was on the barriers faced by disabled women experiencing gender-based violence and the need for adequately funded services for not only disabled survivors but also survivors from other minority groups as well.[76] Somiya Basar, an immigrant woman, set out more fully her own experience as a survivor of domestic violence and abuse:

> *When I got married, it was based on cultural customs in India. I was living in Bombay, and I was 19 when I was married to a British citizen whom I did not know. I wanted to further my studies, but my parents thought differently and according to our custom. I did not want to disappoint them, so I agreed. My idea of marriage was quickly shattered, because it was not long before I began to feel that I was married to be a slave. I was the housemaid; I was there for him to use as an object to have babies. I was the nanny, and I was the nurse.*
>
> *The situation soon developed into physical, emotional and financial abuse – verbal belittling at every opportunity. My husband had total*

75 Domestic Abuse Bill Deb Second Sitting 4 June 2020, cols 30–37 <https://hansard.parliament.uk/commons/2020-06-04/debates/53d6764e-24e5-4287-8e40-fc3690d696b1/DomesticAbuseBill(SecondSitting)> accessed 17 June 2024.

76 Domestic Abuse Bill Deb Second Sitting 4 June 2020 (n 75), cols 30–31.

financial control over me. He controlled every aspect of my life. I was strongly disallowed from making contact with my own family, which has left me isolated and alienated from my family. I was not allowed to have friends or to work outside the house, except for at the family business. I remained in the marriage because of the constant threats that if I would not conform or do as they said, my children would be taken away from me. Because of the fear of losing my children, I remained in the marriage, which lasted for 12 years.[77]

While both the organisational narrative of the APPG and Somiya's narrative set out to challenge and denaturalise the official masterplot, there is a striking contrast between the two voices. On the one hand, there is the institutional organisation voice which offers that 'gender neutral mask or distancing "third person" . . . a generic voice that may pass as masculine'.[78] On the other hand, Somiya is self-consciously telling her own history. As a narrator who is also the story's protagonist,[79] Somiya invites the narratees into her own experience and demands that they actively engage with her story, however uncomfortable that may be. The distance between narration and narratee that was evident in the APPG's narrative is thus diminished. However, this is just one individual's experience given as oral evidence. While other witnesses from various domestic violence and abuse organisations also drew on their own experiences with DVA as part of their evidence, crucially they were present at the Committee stage debates in their capacity as a member of an organisation, not 'simply' as a survivor like Somiya.

The apparent tendency to oppose this mode of narration speaks to the tension between foregrounding the raw story of the survivor and addressing DVA as the wider, systemic social issue that it is. This tension is one which the domestic violence movement has had to negotiate since its inception in the early 1970s, when it attempted to 're-frame the cultural understanding of domestic violence from an apolitical, individual problem to a profoundly social problem rooted in structural systems of patriarchy and ideologies of gender equality'.[80] As Lehrner and Allen continue, if we are to take seriously the fundamental need for cultural change, then we must investigate the 'status of the narratives or action frames currently being voiced by those who most visibly represent the [domestic violence] movement'.[81] Yet as we've seen, attempts to transmit

77 Domestic Abuse Bill Deb Second Sitting 4 June 2020 (n 75), col 32.

78 Lanser (n 68) 19.

79 This is what Genette calls 'autodiegetic', in which the 'I' who tells the story is also the story's protagonist: Genette (n 63) 227–47.

80 Amy Lehrner and Nicole E. Allen, 'Social Change Movements and the Struggle Over Meaning-Making: A Case Study of Domestic Violence Narratives' (2008) 42 *American Journal of Community Psychology* 220, 220.

81 Lehrner and Allen (n 80) 222.

narratives voiced by institutions that work in, and represent, the domestic violence and abuse field lack authority and proceed via erasure. Here, Lanser's communal voice as a narrative practice offers possibility. Lanser notes that this is 'a category of underdeveloped possibilities' in fictional literature[82] and, I suggest, in legal storytelling as well. Whether this is a singular form (one narrator speaks for a collective), a simultaneous form (plural 'we' narrates), or a sequential form (individual members of a group narrate in turn),[83] a conscious investment of authority in a definable community of survivors would help negotiate the tension between the erasure of experience and the permeation of the masterplot on the one hand and the individualisation of a social problem on the other. Recognising the whole narrative transaction and the operation of narratological devices such as voice is therefore fundamental to the rhetorical, political, and legal power of policy influencers, practitioners, activists, *and* survivors to effect the legislature.

Conclusion

The All-Party Parliamentary Group on Domestic Violence and Abuse report 'Creating a Truly Transformative Domestic Abuse Bill', along with other written submissions in the parliamentary debates of the Domestic Abuse Bill, draws our attention to the status of legal storytelling within law reform efforts and attempts to dismantle the masterplot of DVA. Any engagement with such narratives in this context has been limited at best, casting doubt on the true transformational power of legal storytelling. Examining these reports raises questions about how legal storytelling can be used more effectively if it is to be a successful tool in law reform and effect a 'narrative shift' in the masterplot of domestic violence and abuse. What has been less understood is the way in which particular narrative devices, such as narration, also play a part in legal storytelling. Proper attention to form as well as content, I suggest, is therefore the necessary starting point for the integration of narrative in law reform efforts. It is both of these elements that play a role in the creation of a narrative and its reception, and any meaningful commitment to the use of legal storytelling needs to think about the narrative transaction as a whole. And as Brooks has rightly noted, now more than ever, we need the 'reflective knowledge that the humanities can provide, very much including analysis of the dominant stories' along with the 'means to dismantle the noxious myths of our time'.[84]

It is in this sense that the report of the All-Party Parliamentary Group on Domestic Violence and Abuse offers an interesting case study, highlighting particularly the impact that the choice of voice and narration can have

82 Lanser (n 68) 21.
83 Lanser (n 68) 21.
84 Peter Brooks, *Seduced by Story: The Use and Abuse of Narrative* (The New York Review of Books 2022) 152.

on the authority of the narrative and its ability to dismantle the masterplot of DVA. The choice to eschew the raw story of the survivor in favour of a heterodiegetic narration reflects an orientation to narratives that have been 'smoothed out' by the narrator and that distance the narratee from the subject of the narration. To call for legislators to believe these 'stories' and utilise them as powerful tools of persuasion to justify legal and social change is to accept, then, that the status quo of legal storytelling is not working. Not least because the legislative output notably failed to counter and dismantle pervasive and problematic aspects of the masterplot of DVA. However, as this chapter has demonstrated, the apparent tendency to oppose autodiegetic narration (in both the APPG report and the committee stage debates) speaks to the inherent tension with legal storytelling more broadly: foregrounding the voice of the survivor to avoid erasure on the one hand and, conversely, submitting an accepted, valid story that negotiates the narrative politics of survivor discourse and the individualisation of a social problem on the other. However, despite the flaws, the messiness, the lack of neutrality, and the vulnerability of survivor narratives, their role in resolving epistemic injustices and dismantling the masterplot of domestic violence and abuse is nonetheless fundamental. By considering the use of a communal voice in legal storytelling, and thus the narrative transaction as a whole, we can crucially explore how we tell these narratives effectively alongside the survivor's experience itself. In this way, we can turn to a narrative solution to realise the full potential of storytelling in law reform and continue to dismantle the masterplot of domestic violence and abuse.

Note

My thanks to Robin Warhol for feedback and insightful discussion on early ideas for this chapter.

Chapter 6

The masterplot of the market

Constructing exchange, family, and work

Luke P. Norris and Allison Tait

Stories about the family, work, and the market circulate in law, legal discourse, and beyond. The family, we are told by numerous authorities, is a non-market site, centred on emotional attachment rather than economic transaction. It is a site of interpersonal care, growth, and nurturance that acts as a counter to the excesses of an unbridled marketplace. The market, in contrast, is a site where autonomous beings contract, pursuing their interests efficiently and maximising wealth. This is one masterplot of the market, which, as it operates in the United States, constructs certain household members outside of the market and constructs the market as a sphere of rational exchange and value creation. And while one might think of it as two masterplots – one about home and the other about the marketplace – we understand it as one plot that both delineates and separates the spheres and the kinds of value and exchange within them. The masterplot of the market is a hyper-charged, superordinating narrative put forth by political commentators, academic theorists, and other contributors to public discourse and compounded by law. The masterplot of the market – the sum of a thousand political and cultural stories – structures the ways in which we collectively and culturally think and talk about various kinds of exchange and also leads to a legal system that organises itself around reifying that masterplot, serving the idealised market, and enriching those certain legal actors to the detriment of others.

What is also important about the masterplot of the market is its flexibility and plasticity. The masterplot of the market is supple and, as we will show, can shift according to the needs of those whose interests it serves. In particular, the masterplot of the market works to support the interests of those parties who hold market resources and power by centring their rights and needs over the rights of others. In the case of the family, the standard legal masterplot of the market characterises feminised actors as non-market by framing their contributions as non-economic and produced for affection rather than profit. This characterisation not only strips them of wealth and bargaining power but also casts them as peripheral legal and cultural beings in the great theatre of market matters. Nevertheless, what is overlooked in this story is that when market interests would be better served by characterising domestic

DOI: 10.4324/9781003404668-9

matters as market-based, then the narrative shifts and previously marginalised actors are suddenly endowed with bargaining capacity, autonomous rights, and economic motives. Accordingly, the family version of the masterplot of the market is deeply foundational, not just for the binaries it creates, but also for the ways in which it morphs in order to accommodate new cultural developments as well as new legal questions. What the masterplot of the market, and the way it operates in the family, helps us understand, then, is not just how legal parties are either included or excluded from market participation but how the masterplot of the market is sensitive to circumstance and easily moulded to address other social and economic relationships of labour and exchange in American law. The masterplot is, in this way, perhaps best defined by its malleability, but also its capacity for deliberate misprision.

For example, beyond the home, the masterplot of the market also operates in the workplace. At first glance, the workplace is highly and easily differentiated from the family. In most instances, work is paid. Workplace relationships, too, are said, in one prominent version of the story, to not be defined by connections of care and emotion. If anything, the workplace is a site of market prevalence and primacy, where, the story goes, supposedly rational actors bargain strategically and successfully. Law integrates this view of the workplace into legal doctrines, which privilege ideals of contract and bargained-for exchange. This story, however, turns out to be just one more variant of the market masterplot, an example of the pliancy of the masterplot and also its core strategy: misrepresenting the actual power and positionality of those subject to the needs of capital. So while in the family context the masterplot constructs most household workers as outside the market (not counting paid domestic labour, which is significantly underpaid in most cases), the masterplot of the market imbues the vast majority of workers outside of the home with a surcharge of market power (deflecting from the fact that they do not have the market capacities that employers and other economically powerful actors do). In both cases, the masterplot of the market misstates the powers and the precarities of the individuals who are seeking rights in order to occlude the overwhelming power of the resourced market actor and the gains flowing to such actors. The masterplot of the market both overstates and understates, as needed, in order to embed the power of the market masters.

Based on this concept of the market masterplot, this chapter explores how the masterplot does extensive work within an aggressively capitalist political economy to extract wealth and work from individuals by occluding their true positionality and power relationships. We begin with a brief discussion of masterplots, detailing how we use the term and understand the concept. We then explore through property rules at divorce the ways in which the masterplot within the family operates in multiple ways to paper over the exploitation of under- and unpaid labour of gendered subjects, demonstrating a consistent commitment to the maintenance of masculinised interests.

Finally, we explain how the market–family masterplot, with its ability both to adapt and to misstate, provides the skeletal outline of a transferable technology that can be mapped on to other dynamics, such as the workplace relationship, in order to help explain power asymmetries and hidden profits. In each case – with the market–family as well as the market–workplace narrative – the false narration and stipulation of market positionalities define the masterplot, as these fallacious framings obscure patterns and practices of economic oppression that works along axes of gender, race, and other forms of minoritisation.

Narrating the masterplot

From the outset, it is useful to press on the notion of masterplot, both as it is used in this chapter and more generally, because it forms the organising principle of this volume. On the one hand, a masterplot can be thought of as a particular narrative that has been supercharged through repetition and constant cultural reference. In this sense, a masterplot is one of those 'stories that we tell over and over in myriad forms and that connect[s] vitally with our deepest values, wishes, and fears'.[1] Similarly, we might describe masterplots as 'easily recognised, oft-repeated story templates that frame understandings, interpretations, and retellings of events'.[2] Masterplots are bound up with types – stereotypes, archetypes – and genres, and they follow predictable routes to predetermined ends. Some critics have elaborated how basic plots undergird the vast majority of stories we tell, dealing with injustice, rebirth, reward, and other pivotal moments of human development and expression.[3] Examples include rags-to-riches stories, voyage-and-return stories, tragedies, and rebirth stories. From this psychoanalytically informed perspective, masterplots are mechanisms of connection because they narrate purportedly universal stories and depend on the deployment of tropes that have become recognisable to a large group of people over time.

In Peter Brooks's foundational article in which he analyses the masterplot through a reading of Freud, he explores the masterplot as a totalising device that trades in repetition and inheres in all narratives. Brooks states that '[r]epetition in all its literary manifestations may in fact work as a 'binding,' a binding of textual energies that allows them to be mastered by putting them

1 H. Porter Abbott, *The Cambridge Introduction to Narrative* (CUP 2002) 42.

2 Gerald Roche, 'Introduction: Contexts of Efflorescence' in Gerald Roche, Åsa Virdi Kroik and Hiroshi Maruyama (eds), *Indigenous Efflorescence: Beyond Revitalisation in Sapmi and Ainu Mosir* (ANU Press 2018) 24. <https://library.oapen.org/bitstream/handle/20.500.12657/27366/indigenous.pdf?sequence=1#page=57> accessed 4 September 2024.

3 Christopher Booker, *The Seven Basic Plots: Why We Tell Stories* (Bloomsbury Continuum 2004).

into serviceable form within the energetic economy of the narrative'.[4] He goes further, however, explaining that the masterplot is a

> dynamic model which effectively structures ends (death, quiescence, non-narratability) against beginnings (Eros, stimulation into tension, the desire of narrative) in a manner that necessitates the middle as detour, as struggle toward the end under the compulsion of imposed delay, as arabesque in the dilatory space of the text.[5]

The masterplot is, then, a story, parts repeated and end known, that 'seek[s] illumination in its own death . . . the correct end' after the detours and deviations of the middle, replete with obstacles and subplots. Brooks recognises that the middle of the masterplot may look any number of ways, may take the shape of any number of arabesque lines, and in this he underscores not only the energy of the masterplot but also the idea that the vital energy of the masterplot lies in the plasticity of its middle rather than the predetermined death of its ending. This is an important claim in that it helps explain why and how masterplots can look exceedingly different and yet tell the same story, have the same end – because the life-giving component of the masterplot is not the predetermined end but, rather, the endlessly malleable middle.

Brooks complicates the definition of the masterplot by highlighting its unity. Other critics and writers have, however, complicated Brooks's thesis by pointing out what masterplots may overlook, intentionally or not, by assuming the universality of one particular experience or point of view. And the particular point of view that the masterplot supports is perhaps predictable; it 'supports elite forms of power, strengthens the illusion of the autonomous individual, and idolizes an economic rationalism that ingrains masculinity and invisibilizes the agency of nonhumans and subordinated groups'.[6] In this way, the masterplot is less about narrative structure alone and more about what narrative structures and substance reveal when pressure is applied. In this way, 'the concept of a masterplot, can function as a means to expose that which may not be explicit, but assumed, in a discourse'.[7] For example, feminist critics, responding to Brooks and the masculinist bias of the masterplot, have suggested that '[i]t is time to start again, to see what comes of unstringing the Masterplot that wants to have told us in advance where it is that we should take our pleasures and what must inevitably come of them'.[8]

4 Peter Brooks, 'Freuds Masterplot' (1977) 55/56 *Yale French Studies* 280.
5 Brooks (n 4).
6 Arturo Escobar, *Designing for the Pluriverse* (Duke University Press 2017).
7 Roche, Kroik and Maruyama (n 2) 30.
8 Susan Winnett, 'Coming Unstrung: Women, Men, Narrative, and Principles of Pleasure' (1990) 105 *PMLA* 505.

And as we discuss in the conclusion, there is also space for competing narratives that deconstruct masterplots by telling the fuller stories of existences that masterplots seek to tidy up.

More broadly, literary critics have similarly worked to excavate the hidden (or sometimes hiding-in-plain-sight) political nature of masterplots and the work that they do to prop up certain political systems and economies. In this mode of analysis, '[d]iscourses, or discursive formations, are always linked to the exercise of power',[9] and masterplots may be more properly defined as 'modes of utterances or systems of meaning which are both constituted by, and committed to, the perpetuation of dominant social systems'.[10] As Achille Mbembe wrote, the controlling narratives produced by the politically powerful are 'officially invested with a surplus of meanings which are not negotiable and which one is officially forbidden to depart from or challenge'.[11] The masterplot is thus an exercise of power, a prescriptive rather than descriptive mode of narrative, and even sometimes a form of discursive gaslighting in which 'champions of state power invent entire constellations of ideas'. And in so doing, agents of political and judicial power 'adopt a distinct set of cultural repertoires and powerfully evocative concepts'[12] that further the financial interests of certain individuals and groups at the expense of others.

Staging the masterplot

To lay the groundwork for what follows, it is important to understand both how the masterplot of the market is embedded throughout legal discourse in US law and the historical moments in which the embedding flourished. The market masterplot has deep roots in US law, politics, and culture, but any understanding of it would be incomplete without acknowledging the rise of the modern neoliberal political and legal order (in jurisdictions including but not limited to the United States). In the policy space, American historians speak of a neoliberal 'rollback' of New Deal and Great Society regulatory programmes protecting workers and consumers and taming market excesses and a 'roll-out' of policies that inure to the benefit of the wealthy and powerful corporations.[13] The masterplot of the market, deployed ably in the hands of leaders, such as Reagan and Clinton, provided a tidy organising frame justifying these policies – that the market was an

9 Leel Gandhi, *Postcolonial Theory: A Critical Introduction* (Columbia University Press 1998).

10 Gandhi (n 9).

11 Achille Mbembe, 'Provisional Notes on the Postcolony' (1992) 62 *Africa: Journal of the International African Institute* 3.

12 Mbembe (n 11).

13 Samuel Aber, 'Neoliberalism Primer' *LPE Blog* (10 August 2020) <https://lpeproject.org/primers/neoliberalism-an-lpe-reading-list-and-introduction/> accessed 4 September 2024.

exciting space generating outsize returns and wealth flowing to entrepreneurial Americans.[14] The masterplot of the market, through repetition and resonance, shaped the polity as much as policy during the ascendancy of the neoliberal state. In this way, one can appreciate, as historian Gary Gerstle has documented in his chronicle of neoliberalism in the country, the resonance of Ronald Reagan's economic message with working people.[15] Reagan promised acolytes an ecstatic version of economic freedom, being unshackled from cumbersome governmental policies and obligations and released into a free market, where they could experience freedom, create, innovate, and flourish.[16] The idealised market was the site of the American dream, the city on the hill shining because it was gilded. Of course, Reagan did not make up this message out of whole cloth. He was repeating an old tune – one that Democrats would repeat in their own way, particularly as the Democratic Party came to embrace the business community – but its repetition is the point and the power.

What was also important about the market masterplot as crafted by politicians and other market radicals was that the masterplot permitted ordinary people to imagine themselves as flourishing agents in policy frameworks that quietly increased their inequality and precarity. This phenomenon helps resolve a puzzle that sometimes befuddles scholars and commentators: how political parties that consistently favour the interests of the economically powerful can mobilise broad coalitions and secure electoral victories. There are a variety of explanations, including the obstacles people face in voting, campaign finance laws that permit powerful actors to flood the market with outsized spending, undemocratic structures such as the American electoral college, the absence of a strong political Left in the United States, and the use of cultural issues to motivate voters and obscure economic agendas.[17] But the masterplot of the market belongs in the mix because it assures people facing conditions of economic precarity that they, too, might be the lead player in a story of economic success and flourishing, all the while subjecting them to dynamics that have been described both as 'cruel optimism'[18] and 'letting die'.[19] From this perspective, the roster of legal privileges available to the wealthy and the policies favouring corporations are bounties that even the m.ost dispossessed individual may someday yet secure. And in this way, the masterplot

14 Gary Gerstle, *The Rise and Fall of the Neoliberal Order: America and the World in the Free Market Era* (OUP 2022).
15 Gerstle (n 14).
16 Gerstle (n 14).
17 Jacob S. Hacker and Paul Pierson *Let them Eat Tweets: How the Right Rules in an Age of Extreme Inequality* (LiverLight 2020).
18 Lauren Berlant, *Cruel Optimism* (Duke University Press 2011).
19 Giorgio Agamben, *Homo Sacer: Sovereign Power and Bare Life* (Daniel Heller-Roazen tr, Stanford University Press 1998).

of the market is a kind of disciplinary technology that finds success through the cover of capitalism's enchanting possibilities.

Successful in cultural and political circuits, the masterplot also moved into law and became the coin of the realm in judicial thought. Looking more closely at the US legal system, the masterplot of the market clearly undergirds a great deal of doctrine as well as judicial decision-making. And just as lawyers can be coders of capital, judges can also be expositors of the masterplot of the market – repeaters and adopters, and ones with particular power and institutional authority.[20] One can find numerous examples of the masterplot in legal discourse, but consider as just one initial example the field of civil procedure, a class that every first-year law student in the United States takes and a doctrinal area that has significant trans-substantive effects. In US civil procedure, at the motion to dismiss for failure to state a claim stage in *Bell Atlantic Corp. v Twombly*, the Supreme Court dismissed antitrust claims because they were 'economically implausible' in light of their deviation from the premises about rational, efficient behaviour that forms the backbone of the masterplot of the market.[21] In *Twombly*, the alleged conspiracy could have just as easily been, the Court reasoned, 'routine market conduct' by competitors seeking to augment their own power.[22] The masterplot emerges in other major doctrinal areas as well, including in contract law in discussions about efficient breach, and in tort law when judges and scholars discuss the least cost avoider. The examples are numerous, but even these cursory ones give a flavour of how ingrained the market masterplot is in legal doctrine and decision-making.

One can see, then, how the masterplot of the market in the hands of judges can revise existing motivations, desires, and aims and reinscribe them with the familiar script of the masterplot. Markets are creations of law, policy, culture, and products of human relationships, and they differ based on their structures, time, and context. The masterplot of the market removes that functional complexity and permits state power to operate without reference to it. And for this reason, scholars organizing under a law and political economy (LPE) framework have begun and (in our estimation) should continue to pay renewed attention to questions of political economy, how law is implicated in the struggles between democratic imperatives and market ordering, and how that struggle is narrated through the masterplot of the market.[23] Indeed, law and humanities approaches have not been central in LPE work,

20 Katharina Pistor, *The Code of Capital: How the Law Creates Wealth and Inequality* (Princeton University Press 2019).

21 550 US 544, 555 (2007); 475 US 574 (1986).

22 550 US at 566.

23 Jedediah Britton-Purdy, David Singh Grewal, Amy Kapczynski and K. Sabeel Rahman, 'Building a Law-and-Political-Economy Framework: Beyond the Twentieth-Century Synthesis' (2020) 129 *Yale Law Journal* 1784.

and we hope this chapter helps show how they can illuminate the study of political economy issues.

The masterplot we know: markets and families

The masterplot of the market in the context of the family is an oft-told tale in Western thought, one that gained favour way before the onset of neoliberal politics and one that fell on fertile ground at numerous historical points because of its gender implications. We find the masterplot of the market and that of home as separate spheres circulating as far back as ancient Greece. As Amanda Vickery writes, '[t]he dialectical polarity between home and world is an ancient trope of western writing; the notion that women were uniquely fashioned for the private realm is at least as old as Aristotle'.[24] The notion of separate spheres gained real traction, however, during the European Enlightenment and into the nineteenth century, when industrialisation reinvented the market and workplaces and relatedly reimagined, revitalised, and re-entrenched the notion of a divide between home and marketplace, public and private. Jean-Jacques Rousseau was a leading proponent of the idea of separate spheres, and his ideas were foundational for the deluge of prescriptive texts about gender roles that appeared in the following century, exemplified by Coventry Patmore's famous eloge of *The Angel in the House*.[25]

Above and beyond these household texts, the idea of separate spheres was reiterated by philosophers of many different perspectives. Friedrich Engels, with singular oversight regarding the extractive nature of the home, 'gave classic expression to the concept of a public/private split, a split in which the most important psychic locus was the home, understood to be a woman's place, but ultimately controlled by man'.[26] And to bring the story back to the American context, Alexis de Tocqueville stated:

> In no country has such constant care been taken as in America to trace two clearly distinct lines of action for the two sexes and to make them keep pace one with the other, but in two pathways that are always different.[27]

In reality, as feminist historians demonstrated, 'the negotiation of sphere boundaries . . . was full of fissures that resulted not only from the uneven relationship

24 Amanda Vickery, 'Golden Age to Separate Spheres? A Review of the Categories and Chronology of English Women's History' (1993) 36 *The Historical Journal* 383.

25 Coventry Patmore, *The Angel in the House* (first published 1854, Kessinger Publishing 2010).

26 Linda Kerber, *Separate Spheres, Female Worlds, Woman's Place: The Rhetoric of Women's History* (OUP 1988).

27 Alexis de Tocqueville, *Democracy in America* (first published 1835, University of Chicago Press 2002).

between discourse and institutional practice, but also from the historical indebtedness of spheres to older ones from which they emerged'.[28] Nevertheless, the masterplot of separate spheres persisted into the twentieth century and beyond, proliferated even sometimes by feminists historians studying it.[29]

The US legal system, in both the nineteenth and twentieth centuries, upheld this 'separate spheres' narrative in a number of ways, but family law and marriage regulation were a central site of the separate spheres ideology. American law inherited the legal framework of coverture from the English common law, under which a married woman was unable to own property while married, with limited exceptions, and her husband controlled all her non-trust property.[30] There was no market, only the co-opting of property, personhood, and legal rights. After the series of Married Women's Property Acts (both in England and the United States) that granted married women the right to own and control property, the 'reformed' common law approach identified 'two distinct interests, the husband's separate property and the wife's separate property'. This distinction was important during the marriage in terms of what creditors could attach and what a woman could keep from her husband to make her own purchases. The real test to property interests, however, came once divorce became available starting at the end of the nineteenth century, around the same time as the Married Women's Property Acts.

And what happened at divorce was a true outcome of the market masterplot: all property remained with the title-holder, placing the emphasis squarely on the notion of legal earning, ownership, and investment and typically benefitting husbands and their work or wealth creation in the 'market' outside the home. The work of a wife in the home was not subject to valuation or compensation, and the husband was able to secure his 'earned' property and market gains. American women in the twentieth century were largely subject to these property rules, such that, as one legal scholar has described,

> [e]ssentially, the court made its property division as if no marriage had taken place. If a couple compiled vast wealth during the marriage and placed it all in the husband's name, the wife would be totally dependent

28 Anat Rosenberg, 'Separate Spheres Revisited: On the Frameworks of Interdisciplinarity and Constructions of the Market' (2012) 24 *Law and Literature* 393.

29 The separate spheres masterplot was even reinforced by feminist historians who framed histories around this concept. Vickery states: 'The assumption that capitalist man needed a hostage in the home was endorsed by subsequent historians who linked the cult of true womanhood to a shrinkage of political, professional and business opportunities for women in the years 1800–40. In this way, the glorification of domestic womanhood became associated with the deterioration of women's public power, which was itself presented as a function of industrialization. Consequently, the early nineteenth century assumed its present status as one of the key, constitutive periods in the history of gender'.

30 Allison Tait, 'The Beginning of the End of Coverture: A Reappraisal of the Married Woman's Separate Estate' (2014) 26 *Yale Journal of Law & Feminism* 165.

> on alimony after the divorce. Unless she could prove some concrete ownership interest in the property, her efforts in amassing the assets would go totally unrecognized and uncompensated.[31]

These rules not only disadvantaged women in very practical terms, leading to financial dispossession and widening the gender wealth gap, but also bolstered the masterplot of the market. Legal rules cast the work done by women within marriage and the supposedly private realm of the home as gift, love, and charitable contribution. And because married women were labelled as non-market actors, their work was disallowed monetary value or economic worth. Moreover, this legal story of the home defined in opposition to the external world of market forces, paid labour, and rational exchange silently centred the rights, opportunities, and legal privileges of the earner or owner in the family. The continuing result (if not the actual aim) of the masterplot and the legal rules that supported it was the enrichment of husbands, to the detriment of their spouses, through the deliberate misapprehension of the market nature of household labour.

That this masterplot has always, at its core, facilitated a highly gendered imbalance of power with ramifications far beyond the walls of the home has not gone unnoticed. Feminist scholars have ably and accurately deconstructed the market masterplot as it pertains to the home in order to shine light on the ways in which the market/family masterplot works to both advantage certain parties and disadvantage others, in particular feminised subjects and women working within the home, through the process of what Maria Mies has called 'housewifization'.[32] Feminist economists and others who work on the problem of social reproduction have offered comprehensive analyses of the ways in which the masterplot constructs a false dichotomy between domestic space and marketplace, a dichotomy that prioritises (and overestimates) the needs and desires of men and masculinised subjects while marginalising the rights and opportunities of female-identified subjects within the home. Silvia Federici, a leading voice in social reproduction theory, has explained that the feminist intervention into Marxist analysis was both 'discovering that unpaid labour is not extracted by the capitalist class only from the waged workday, but that it is also extracted from the workday of millions of unwaged house-workers' and 'unmasking the socio-economic function of the creation of a fictional private sphere, and thereby re-politicising family life, sexuality, procreation'.[33] As Federici has stated:

> We must admit that capital has been very successful in hiding our work. It has created a true masterpiece at the expense of women. By denying

31 Elizabeth Cheadle, 'The Development of Sharing Principles in Common Law Marital Property States' (1981) 28 *UCLA Law Review* 1269.

32 Maria Mies, *Patriarchy and Accumulation on a World Scale: Women in the International Division of Labor* (Zed Books Ltd 1986).

33 Silvia Federici, 'Social Reproduction Theory: History, Issues and Present Challenges' (2019) 204 *Radical Philosophy* 55.

> housework a wage and transforming it into an act of love, capital has killed many birds with one stone.[34]

Progressive lawyers and feminist groups, from the 1960s onward, advocated for reform to the common law property system at divorce and pushed for the adoption of equitable distribution statutes that would give married women rights to marital property based on their contributions to the household and regardless of who held title or who had earned the money. Accordingly, states across America began to adopt equitable distribution statutes in the 1970s and 1980s, just as neoliberal market logic was also beginning to take hold across the country in political discourse. Reform spread such that, in the space of a little more than two decades, equitable distribution statutes were the new normal. Moreover, there was a new language that came with equitable distribution, that of marriage as a partnership. This trope surfaced in a high percentage of judicial opinions from that time, as did a new market logic and corporatist language. In 1974, in an early case concerning New Jersey's equitable distribution statute, *Rothman v Rothman*, the state supreme court observed: 'Thus the division of property upon divorce is responsive to the concept that marriage is a shared enterprise, a joint undertaking, that in many ways it is akin to a partnership.'[35] A decade later, in Mississippi, the state supreme court reiterated this notion of partnership in justifying the move to equitable distribution of marital assets:

> If the breadwinner happens to be the husband and has all property in his name, this serves to relegate the non-breadwinner wife to the equivalent of a maid – and upon division of the marital estate entitled to a minimum wage credit for her homemaking service. We abandon such an approach. We, today, recognize that marital partners can be equal contributors whether or not they both are at work in the marketplace.[36]

These modifications of the property rules at divorce represented an important improvement, giving property rights to married women based on their non-economic contributions to the household and marriage. Nevertheless, as the language in these judicial opinions underscored through its emphasis on partnership, the narrative was still driven by the masterplot of the market. The market masterplot appeared in these opinions in that they reinforced the distinction between home and the workplace. In fact, the language used by the Mississippi Supreme Court – 'marital partners can be equal contributors *whether or not they both are at work in the marketplace*' – strongly

34 Silvia Federici, *Wages against Housework* (Falling Wall Press 1975) 3.
35 *Rothman v Rothman* 65 NJ 219 (1974).
36 *Hankins v Hankinson* 729 So 2d 1283 (Miss 1999).

reiterated the idea of a separation between the home and market, private family and public worker. Laura Rosenbury writes:

> The partnership theory itself does nothing to challenge the assignment of wives to care work and husbands to wage work. . . . Indeed, the partnership theory of marriage does nothing to challenge the 'genderization' of care work and may even provide incentives to perpetuate it in those situations where women are married to wealthy men.[37]

What is more, these statutes did not place a value on the work done in the household until the time of divorce, when property division became an issue, nor did these statutes necessarily compensate married women who worked outside of the home, in the paid labour market, for their 'second shift' work.[38]

Perhaps more importantly, however, the market masterplot was also there, hiding, beneath the partnership language in that divorcing women were compensated – but they were generally not adequately or fairly compensated for their substantial contributions, especially over the span of a long-term marriage. Courts still resisted equal division of marital assets, such as pensions, business goodwill, and family business shares – all assets that were generally owned by the husbands in a divorcing couple. Using vocabulary about special skills, individual talent, and personal labour, courts managed to resist the call to economic equality between spouses and gave special status to market workers as well as special status to assets acquired through market means.[39] Despite the equality rhetoric, the adoption of equitable distribution rules did not 'live up to their promise of providing a fair apportionment of assets between the parties'.[40] In fact, as some scholars pointed out, equitable distribution statutes actually produced a '[s]harp decline in single women's standards of living following divorce'[41] and exacerbated the 'feminization of poverty'.[42] The market masterplot, then, continued to support the interests of the masculine earners, the market players, and the male dollar.

37 Laura Rosenbury, 'Two Ways to End a Marriage: Divorce or Death' (2005) 2005 *Utah Law Review* 1227.

38 Arlie Hochschild and Anne Machung, *The Second Shift: Working Families and the Revolution at Home* (2nd edn, Penguin Publishing Group 2012).

39 Allison Tait, 'Divorce Equality' (2015) 90 *Washington Law Review* 1245.

40 Herma Hill Kay, 'Beyond No-Fault: New Directions in Divorce Reform' in Stephen Sugarman and Herma Hill Kay (eds), *Divorce Reform at the Crossroads* (Yale University Press 1990) 31.

41 Marsha Garrison, 'Equitable Distribution in New York: Results and Reform: Good Intentions Gone Awry: The Impact of New York's Equitable Distribution Law on Divorce Outcomes' (1991) 57 *Brooklyn Law Review* 621.

42 Deborah Rhode and Martha Minow, 'Reforming the Questions, Questioning the Reforms: Feminist Perspectives on Divorce Law' in Sugarman and Kay (n 40) 191, 197.

Making matters worse, since stay-at-home spouses (again, usually women) were receiving what was supposed to be a 'fair' distribution of marital property, alimony awards took a sharp nosedive in most courts. Courts became more reticent to award alimony, particularly permanent alimony, on the theory that women were already being compensated and alimony overtaxed the husbands, who needed to keep their own earnings. Therefore, in a spectacle of reverse logic and revising the masterplot script at lightning speed, the same judicial actors who insisted on maintaining the divide between home and marketplace remarked that divorcing women did not need much spousal support because they were capable market actors. As early as 1957, a New York judge wrote:

> The married woman has come a long way since the days of Blackstone. . . . [S]he is no longer the Victorian creature, 'something better than her husband's dog, a little dearer than his horse.' She is now the equal of man, socially, politically and economically. It is time that consonant with this new approach to woman's status we develop a modern basis for fixing alimony and support which will have its roots in reality.[43]

Along the same lines, another judge, in 1970, wrote:

> Alimony has the effect of hindering a woman from putting herself in a position where she would be induced to reorganize her life on a new and better basis. She does not work and develops no talents. She can neither reject the past, accept the present, nor anticipate the future – 'wandering between two worlds one already dead the other powerless to be born.'[44]

From this marketised perspective, proper compensation for work done within marriage would 'hinder' a woman from developing her market skills and becoming the actualised market actor she could never have become within the household. And if there were any questions about whose interest was truly at stake, the court added:

> At the same time that the wife is in this netherworld, the former husband is unable to make feasible plans for his financial or social future as the obligations to his former wife sway above him like a sword of Damocles.[45]

With the masterplot's adaptability in high evidence, married women went from non-market actors to capable market participants depending on the

43 Doyle v Doyle, 5 Misc 2d 4, 6 (NY Sup Ct 1957).
44 Dulber v Dulber, 63 Misc 2d 259, 261–62 (NY Sup Ct 1970).
45 Dulber v Dulber, 63 Misc 2d 259, 261–62 (NY Sup Ct 1970).

financial resources at stake and the ultimate enrichment of law's most important household member, the market earner.

The masterplot of the market, then, in the context of family, home, and gender, misidentifies the market capacity of those who provide unpaid labour, historically and primarily women, by either understating or overstating their market positionality as necessary to protect the vested economic interests of men. With evolving property rules in marriage, the market masterplot required that stay-at-home spouses be characterised as market outliers in the property distribution stage and market players in the alimony stage. And in both cases, the masterplot – and its misprision of market participation – adapted as needed to discount gendered work and to centre the contributions and rights of the masculinised subject, earner, and owner. A key takeaway, then, is that the market masterplot demonstrates flexibility in service of dominant interests, with a key strategy being misprision. And given the story of dominant interests, one might expect to see the masculine subject thrive in the market – at work or in business. But as we explore next, the real descriptive story there has more similarities with the real story of homework and builds on the capacity of the masterplot to change in service of capital.

Transposing the market–family model onto the workplace

The masterplot of the market–family relationship reveals a particular framing strategy that depends on the misstatement of one party's market capacities. In the context of work, the misstatement flows in the opposite direction in that the masterplot of the market strategically creates parties who acquire skills or knowledge and put them to use through a series of bargains or exchanges in which their aim, and end, is to efficiently compete, innovate, and maximise wealth. In doing so, it misstates the actual agency and power of so many marketplace workers. At times, the masterplot has had a nostalgic and agrarian bent – with atomistic individuals learning a trade or profession in a local context, perhaps as an apprentice, forming their own enterprises and contracting in various ways to become an economically flourishing and independent business owner.[46] At other times, it takes on a more modern and corporate hue, with individuals making alliances and forming large enterprises – a corporation that is fictively corporeal but more accurately composed of a nexus of contacts, those entered into by owners, managers, employees, vendors, customers, or by competitors who merge or acquire, each seeking to make

46 Gordon Wood, *The Creation of the American Republic, 1776–1787* (2nd edn, The University of North Carolina Press 1998).

pareto-optimal bargains.[47] On the one hand, then, corporate tales posit an entrepreneur or budding employee, and on the other hand, there are tales of economic independence and flourishing, large-scale organisation, and the evolution of a machine of capitalism that seeks more wealth, innovation, and efficiency. The form of the masterplot can bend to accommodate the Randian John Gault and the roguish Elon Musk, as well as the ambitious juniors who cleverly scale their way from the mailroom to the boardroom. In the masterplot of the market, existing power distributions, inequality, and concepts like race and gender only matter insofar as they are examples that this person, with these hurdles, has made it. Structural inequality and marginalisation are merely bit parts in a larger story of individual and organisational skyrocketing.

Within this landscape of rational bargaining and agentic workers, consent is the cornerstone of US work law – or at least its fiction is. At times expressing neoclassical or neo-Lockean views, a variety of legal actors put forth the image of a worker who, with rationality and intent, enters into a series of bargains with their employer and maximises their preferences. In this idealised notion of the labour market, a worker's power and market forces collide to set the appropriate terms of the bargain. The workplace, for these reasons, plays a central role in the masterplot of the market. But here, in reality, the positionality of many workers places them more squarely in the subplot identified in our discussion of the market–family binary. The same things are being occluded in homes and workplaces – in particular, the actual market positionality of non-dominant parties – with the masterplot covering up that which would allow us to see more clearly the forms of extraction, dispossession, and disempowerment happening. But there is a twist: in the sphere of work, the weaker party is not construed as non-market but, rather, hyper-market. So where domestic actors are positioned as having no market authority, workers are positioned as having either a surplus of market power or more market power than they actually possess. In both cases, the true extent, and nature, of the economic circumstances of the weaker party is obscured.

One can find both the masterplot and its occlusion in the political and judicial treatment of various aspects of the workplace. Indeed, it goes to the core of who gets to be an employee and access the bundle of benefits associated with the designation. Consider the treatment of independent contractors, many of whom are so-called 'gig workers', in the United States. Reflecting the increasingly removed premises of the New Deal order, the Supreme Court once held that newspaper sellers, though nominally independent contractors, were employees within the meaning of the National Labor Relations

47 William Bratton, Jr, 'The "Nexus of Contracts" Corporation: A Critical Apprasial' (1989) 74 *Cornell Law Review* 407.

Act (NLRA), providing them the right to engage in concerted activity for mutual aid and protection and to unionise.[48] However, after an employer campaign, Congress soon clarified in the Taft–Hartley Act that the NLRA did not protect independent contractors, and along the way, it reframed joining *or refraining to join* a union as a matter of free contractual choice.[49] Across a patchwork of US labour and employment laws today, independent contracts receive far fewer protections than do employees. And the rationale for this reality accords with the masterplot of the market – independent contractors, courts and other legal actors tell us, are entrepreneurial actors who bring their own talent and skill to their enterprise and are free agents performing work across multiple settings. To be sure, this notion captures some workers – one only need to think of a successful painter or comic book artist selling their talents, albeit temporarily, to the highest and best bidder.

But the masterplot of the market and its hyper-marketised ideal of independent contractors occludes more than it clarifies. Here, Veena Dubal's discussion of 'essentially dispossessed' gig workers during the Covid-19 pandemic is instructive.[50] Dubal explains:

> As the Covid-19 pandemic ravaged human bodies and economies across the world, millions of app-deployed drivers in the United States – primarily immigrants and subordinated racial minorities – faced a dangerous and perplexing paradox created by law. This paradox – their simultaneous treatment as independent contractors, excluded from economic security, and their newly anointed legal status as 'essential workers' – rhetorically celebrated their labour while disproportionately exposing them not just to poverty, but to disease and death.

These app-deployed works were hailed as embodying the promise of techno-modernism, having the entrepreneurial freedom to make their own schedules and flexibly perform their work.[51] Yet the companies they worked for waged long campaigns to ensure that they were not characterised as employees – entitled to the minimum wage, union organising rights, health insurance, certain forms of unemployment pay, and more.

Dubal tells the story of one such worker, Hope, who worked for Lyft for 40–60 hours a week, with mounting medical debt, and her winding struggle along with other drivers to receive both pandemic-era aid. Through Hope's stories and others, Dubal reveals how the masterplot obscures the

48 NLRB v Hearst Publications, Inc. 322 US 111 (1944).
49 Labor-Management Relations (Taft-Hartley) Act 1947 (US); see also Cynthia L. Estlund, 'The Ossification of American Labor Law' (2002) 102 *Columbia Law Review* 1527, 1534.
50 Veena Dubal, 'Essentially Dispossessed' (2022) 121 *South Atlantic Quarterly* 285.
51 Dubal (n 50).

true tale of capitalist dispossession. *Dispossession* is 'a combined political and economic phenomenon, in which capitalists . . . attempt to appropriate, co-opt, confront, and/or supersede the manifold achievements of the working classes'.[52] Companies like Uber and Lyft both exercised substantial control over ride-hail drivers – including setting their fees and managing how they worked – and sought to keep their labour costs and obligations low, excising them from the patchwork of labour and employment law. The material consequences for drivers in the pandemic were dire: the 'cruel contradiction of the law' for workers like Hope was that:

> [If] her unemployment insurance check did not arrive, as an essential worker, she had the option to risk her life and earn. This fictive possibility of self-sufficiency enabled both by the independent contractor status and by her purported ability to labour as an essential worker was a central feature of her dispossession.[53]

Even for those who earn the moniker 'employee' and all that goes with it, the masterplot of the market once again fails to capture much of what functionally and sociologically constitutes the employment relationship. One can find this in various aspects of the relationship. The prominence of 'at-will' employment – a unique US doctrine permitting the employee to leave or the employer to terminate the relationship at any point, for most any reason – is justified in contractarian terms. The notion is that employees and employers are rational, powerful, atomistic bargaining agents, heroes in the masterplot of the market. But the reality is that at-will employment both removes from employees promises of job security, introducing precarity, and, in reality, functions asymmetrically. Employers increasingly make use of 'non-competes', which deny employees the ability to work for competitor companies for a certain duration and in a certain geographical stretch. With the FTC seeking to curb these agreements (currently subject to legal challenges), employers are now turning towards aptly named 'TRAP' agreements, or training repayment agreement provisions, which once again reveal dispossession where the masterplot fashions consent. Jonathan Harris describes one recent example:

> In February 2021, BreAnn Scally decided to take a job as a groomer at her local PetSmart. The job, which pays on average $14.80 per hour, advertised its 'Grooming Academy' as an added perk: 'FREE Paid Training' that is valued 'at $6,000.' BreAnn had always loved dogs and was excited to

52 Sharryn Kasmir and August Carbonella, 'Dispossession and the Anthropology of Labor' (2008) 28(1) *Critique of Anthropology* 5.
53 Dubal (n 50).

> begin her course of instruction. In reality, however, the so-called 'training' that PetSmart required of all inexperienced groomers was minimal, and the manager quickly assigned BreAnn to groom pets for paying customers. The job itself proved to be similarly disappointing. Due to unsustainable working conditions, including short staffing that led to an overwhelming workday, BreAnn quit. Yet, as she would discover, BreAnn was not yet free of her employer: PetSmart soon sent a debt collector after her for $5,000 for her training plus another $500 for tools that PetSmart required groomers to purchase.[54]

Saddled with student debt, BreAnn's credit was ultimately ruined by her inability to pay PetSmart. The use of these agreements is growing, and indeed, nearly half of nurses in the United States are bound by TRAPs.

Examples of asymmetric power and take-it-or-leave-it contracting by employers abound in the modern workplace, blessed by courts who hew to the masterplot's contractarian terms even in the face of evidence to the contrary. And the ability of workers to leave or to remedy employer misconduct is winnowing, closing workers into systems of privatised governance. With regard to shrinking employee ability to remedy employer misconduct, consider the rise of private arbitration. When Congress was considering passing the Federal Arbitration Act of 1925, generally directing federal courts to enforce arbitration agreements (with merchant-to-merchant arbitration in mind), labour leaders raised the spectre that employers would start moving towards arbitration, mandating arbitration in adhesive contracts and minimising the legal power of employees to turn to public courts to correct employer wrongdoing.[55] Congress thus included Section 1 in the law, asserting that it would not apply 'to contracts of employment of seamen, railroad employees, or any other class of workers engaged in foreign or interstate commerce'.[56] However, several decades later, a divided Supreme Court – in interpretive acrobatics that have confounded many a legal scholar – read the statute only to apply to transportation workers, opening the door to employee arbitration.[57] The result has been the somewhat-meteoric rise of employment arbitration – meaning, that the same employees who are constrained in their ability to leave employment relationships are also constrained in their ability

54 Jonathan Harris, 'Can Consumer Law Protect Workers?' *LPE Blog* (27 February 2023) <https://lpeproject.org/blog/can-consumer-law-protect-workers/> accessed 4 September 2024.

55 Luke Norris, 'The Parity Principle' (2018) 93 *NYU Law Review* 249.

56 United States Arbitration Act, 1925 (US).

57 Norris (n 55); Matthew W. Finkin, 'Workers' Contracts' under the United States Arbitration Act: An Essay in Historical Clarification' (1996) *Berkeley Journal of Employment & Labour Law* 282; Margaret Moses, 'Statutory Misconstruction: How the Supreme Court Created a Federal Arbitration Law Never Enacted by Congress' (2006) 34 *Florida State University Law Review* 99, 106–8.

to turn to courts as public fora to remedy workplace wrongdoing.[58] And the fiction of consent runs deep. As one scholar puts it:

> In the arbitration cases, the Court treats both workers and employers as free choosers. If they each sign onto an arbitration agreement, that is a choice that both sides freely made – even if the employer drafted the agreement and imposed it on the worker as a take-it-or-leave it condition of keeping a job.[59]

The fiction of consent permeates these areas and others, reflecting, for some, a return to *Lochner*-era roots, where the court's decisions 'rest on a principle of employee consent that ignores many of the forces that actually impose limits on an employee's choice'.[60] The employment relationship, especially under declining union density rates, widening economic inequality, and concentrating corporate power, is thus one of asymmetric vulnerability, with employees 'need[ing] their employer more than their employer needs them', a reality that augments employer power.[61] Indeed, it is no surprise that today scholars are returning to the *Lochner* era and the legal realists who challenged it to explain and resist patterns in work law.[62] Where the masterplot of the market sees freedom, choice, and independence, realists then and scholars today instead paint a picture of subordination, coercion and constraint, and dependence. In this way, the stories of family and work life share striking similarities. And they raise the question: if the masterplot of the market describes less and less of the world of human experience and exchange, carving off and carving in ways that defy those experiences, where does that leave us, and how can we challenge it?

Conclusion: masterplots and counternarratives

The masterplot of the market, as deployed in the family and work settings, is not only prescriptive but also occlusive, as it manipulates the positionality of those seeking rights and resources from market masters in order to set the stage for legal victory for already-resourced market players. As feminist scholars might remind us, this ordering and outcome should come as no surprise, given nothing other than the root term *master*plot. From this perspective, masterplots are 'socially and culturally informed master narratives (about, for example, gender, sexuality, ethnicity, and profession), which

58 EPI Report on rise of private sector employment arbitration provisions.

59 Samuel R. Bagenstos, 'Consent, Coercion, and Employment Law' (2002) 55 *Harvard Civil Rights-Civil Liberties Law Review* 409, 414.

60 Bagenstos (n 59) 410.

61 Samuel R. Bagenstos, 'Employment Law and Social Equality' (2013) 112 *Michigan Law Review* 225, 238.

62 Bagenstos (n 61).

are often normative or oppressive, or exclude perspectives or experiences that diverge from those conveyed through master narratives'.[63] Put differently, '[t]he dominant group creates its own stories . . . [that] remind it of its identity in relation to outgroups and provide it with a form of shared reality in which its own superior position is seen as natural'.[64] Masterplots, in all their changeability and plasticity, are primarily a tool of the resourced, a mechanism of state power, majority voice, corporate expression, constituted by cognisable characters, predetermined beginnings and endings. The repertoire of stories is limited, and the asymmetries of power are construed as inevitable, natural, and even compelling – obstacles to be overcome in pursuit of gain and growth.

A question then arises as to what shape resistance might take to these masterplots and the ways in which they narrate the propriety of home, work, gender, and power. Is it possible to have countervailing masterplots? Do feminist, decolonial, or otherwise critical masterplots exist? Certainly not, scholars have suggested, if masterplots are discursive cover for legal privilege, economic wealth, and political power. Speaking to this dilemma, Maria Mies has written:

> [I]n a contradictory and exploitative relationship, the privileges of the exploiters can never become the privileges of all. . . . If the emancipation of men is based on the subordination of women, then women cannot achieve 'equal rights' with men, which would necessarily include the right to exploit others.[65]

Accordingly, any controlling narrative of resistance cannot legitimately aspire to be masterplots until masterplots themselves are divested of their status and power as mechanisms for control, exploitation, and extraction. As another option, rejecting the masterplot absolutely as a tool of privilege, we might consider the role and use of counternarratives, more contextualised narratives that are built to resist. As scholars have explained, counternarratives have 'been seen as a means of opposing or resisting socially and culturally informed master narratives', and '[i]n this sense, counternarratives play a role in storytellers positioning themselves against, or critiquing, the themes and ideologies of master narratives'.[66]

63 Marianne Lundholt, Cindie Maagaard and Anke Piekut, 'Counternarratives' (2018) *The International Encyclopedia of Strategic Communication*. <https://doi.org/10.1002/9781119010722.iesc0201> accessed 1 July 2024.

64 Richard Delgado, 'Storytelling for Oppositionists and Others' in Richard Delgado and Jean Stefancic (eds), *Critical Race Theory: The Cutting Edge* (2nd edn, Temple University Press 2000) 259.

65 Mies (n 32).

66 Lundholt, Maagaard and Piekut (n 63); see also Michael Bamberg and Molly Andrews (eds), *Considering Counter-Narratives: Narrating, Resisting, Making Sense* (John Benjamins Publishing Company 2004).

Counternarratives, as opposed to masterplots, are not totalising narratives that assume universality, outcome, or characters; they are highly context-dependent, deeply personal, and essentially deconstructive. As scholars have noted, '[a] counternarrative is morally defined and developed for the purpose of resisting or countering one or more master narrative. Accordingly, the narrative is not an exhaustive account, but a representation of selected experiences and elements as interpreted by the narrator'.[67] Countering the market-family-work masterplot, then, becomes an exercise in finding and telling counternarratives that uncover corners of the curtain and reveal the inequities and inconsistencies wrought by the masterplot – just as Veenda Dubal did with Hope and Jonathan Harris did with telling BreAnn's story. These counternarratives can also help resist the false binaries and salient dualisms that undergird the market-family-work masterplot and help us imagine what it would look like to decentre the market and market masters, attenuating their legal privilege and power. And ultimately, at each turn and with each telling of the masterplot, a counternarrative might help us imagine the toppling of hierarchies, the strengthening of collectives, and the possibility of proliferative, diverse economies.

67 Lundholt, Maagaard and Piekut (n 63).

Part 4

History, time, and temporality

Chapter 7

Defining marriage

Losing the masterplot

Rebecca Probert

Who gets to define marriage, and how they do so, has always been a contested issue. But the stories that are told about what marriage 'is' do not always acknowledge the contingencies and power relationships that have shaped and continue to shape such definitions. Instead, they appeal to a higher authority or claim a broader or even universal application. In other words, they seek to invoke – or imply that there is – a masterplot.

In England and Wales, explanations of the law's concept of marriage still tend to begin with the 1866 case of *Hyde v Hyde and Woodmansee*, if only to explain how much has changed since Lord Penzance asserted that marriage 'as understood in Christendom' was 'the voluntary union for life of one man and one woman to the exclusion of all others'.[1] But while *Hyde* has been described as providing 'the' definition of marriage,[2] there are many reasons that Penzance's words cannot be accorded the status of a masterplot in the sense of an overarching narrative governing attitudes, expectations, and developments across the legal spectrum. His 'definition' of marriage reflected a particular view as to what marriage should be, rather than its legal reality, and its impact was only ever partial.[3]

Penzance's words in *Hyde* should instead be seen as the residual trace of an earlier, more comprehensive masterplot, in which legal recognition was accorded only to Anglican marriages and where the Anglican Church not only defined the rules governing entry into marriage but also established expectations of marriage. In the first section, I outline the key elements of that masterplot.

1 (1866) LR 1 P&D 130, 133.

2 See, for example, *Re Bethell* (1888) 38 Ch D 220; *Brinkley v Attorney-General* (1890) 15 P D 76; *Nachimson v Nachimson* [1930] P 217; *Apt v Apt* [1948] P 83; *Baxter v Baxter* [1948] AC 274; *Way v Way* [1950] P 71; *Risk v Risk* [1951] P 50; *Isaac Penhas v Tan Soo Eng* [1953] AC 304; *Corbett v Corbett (otherwise Ashley)* [1971] P 83; *J v S-T (Formerly J) (Transsexual: Ancillary Relief)* [1997] 1 FLR 402; *Bibi v Chief Adjudication Officer* [1998] 1 FLR 375; *Re E (An Alleged Patient); Sheffield City Council v E and S* [2004] EWHC 2808 (Fam), [2005] 1 FLR 965.

3 See further below.

DOI: 10.4324/9781003404668-11

I then go on, in the next section, to trace how the power to define the law's concept and expectations of marriage gradually shifted from the church to the state, and the equally gradual decline in the influence accorded to the principles of the church courts, the narrative of 'Christian' marriage, and the Anglican Book of Common Prayer. The modern implications of this are explored in the final section, where I examine recent case law which limits any claims about marriage to what can be discerned from the legal remedies available to the parties and which makes no bolder claims as to its meaning.

I should emphasise at the outset that my subtitle is not intended to convey disapproval of these developments. My point is rather that they have occurred so gradually that the displacement of one masterplot has not been accompanied by the creation of a new one.

The key elements of the Anglican marriage masterplot

There were three key elements to the Anglican marriage masterplot. First, the Church of England set the rules governing entry into marriage, both in terms of the capacity of the parties to marry and the form with which they needed to comply. Second, its official marriage service – set out in a new *Book of Common Prayer* in 1549 – contained a set of expectations about marriage that were repeated through subsequent iterations.[4] Couples vowed that they would be faithful to each other, 'love and cherish' each other, and remain together 'for better, for worse', until parted by death. And third, the church was also responsible for adjudicating upon whether its rules had been met and providing various remedies to the parties in the event of either of them failing to adhere to the standards expected of them, through its own courts.

That summary is, of necessity, an oversimplification. In particular, identifying those elements is easier than pinpointing a particular moment in time when all of them applied and a clear consensus had been achieved as to what the church's expectations were. The Anglican marriage masterplot was, in many respects, little different from that of the Catholic Church, whose rules had governed marriage prior to the Reformation.[5] Such continuities in practice were reassuring to some but problematic for those who wanted a more decisive break. One particularly controversial issue – which went to the heart of what was expected of married couples and what remedies should be available – was whether England and Wales should follow other Protestant

4 For discussion of these later iterations, see Sarah Farrimond, 'Church of England Weddings and Ritual Symbolism' in Joanna Miles, Perveez Mody and Rebecca Probert (eds), *Marriage Rites and Rights* (Hart 2015). On the way in which the Anglican liturgy evolved from the pre-Reformation Catholic marriage service, see Kenneth W. Stevenson, *To Join Together: The Rite of Marriage* (Pueblo Publishing Company 1987); Mark Searle and Kenneth W. Stevenson, *Documents of the Marriage Liturgy* (The Liturgical Press 1992).

5 John Witte Jr, *From Sacrament to Contract: Marriage, Religion, and Law in the Western Tradition* (Westminster John Knox Press 2012).

countries in making divorce available. While the Church of England had dropped matrimony from the list of sacraments,[6] there were differing views on what this meant in practice. Under Edward VI, a committee was appointed to consider the possibility of a wholesale reform of ecclesiastical law.[7] Amongst the recommendations of the resulting *Reformatio Legum Ecclesiasticarum* was that divorce with the possibility of remarriage be made available on the basis of the other spouse's adultery, desertion, prolonged absence, 'deadly hostility', or ill-treatment. Nor did the failure to implement these proposals end the debate. Even at the start of the seventeenth century, we find Hercules Foljambe arguing that he had been advised that a divorce *a mensa et thoro* – the forerunner of the modern judicial separation – entitled him to remarry legally.[8] The view of the court – with the support of the Archbishop of Canterbury and 'les pluis sage Divines & Civilians' – was that it did not. But by this time the exclusive jurisdiction of the church over matters matrimonial was already coming under challenge – first by the common law courts, holding that certain marriages were void without the need for any sentence from the church courts, and second by Parliament, which, in 1604, passed legislation making it a felony to go through a ceremony of marriage during the lifetime of an existing spouse,[9] thereby removing the church courts' power to punish those who remarried.

Yet despite such continuities, contestations, and challenges, there was still a remarkable degree of cohesion to the Anglican marriage masterplot. It provided an overarching narrative governing attitudes, expectations, and – perhaps most importantly – practices, across England and Wales. The reach of the Anglican Church meant that its influence was pervasive and inescapable.

In terms of the influence of the church on how couples married, there was no real alternative to getting married according to Anglican rites.[10] The claims that have been made about supposed informal marriage practices in the seventeenth and eighteenth centuries are simply unfounded, both in terms of the underpinning law and as a matter of practice.[11] That is not to suggest that

6 Eric Josef Carlson, *Marriage and the English Reformation* (Blackwell 1994) 42.

7 James C. Spalding, 'The *Reformatio Legum Ecclesiasticarum* of 1552 and the Furthering of Discipline in England' (1970) 39 *Church History* 162.

8 *Rye v Foljambe* (1602) Moore (KB) 684, 72 ER 838; Noy 100, 74 ER 1066. The case and its implications are discussed by K. J. Kesselring and Tim Stretton, *Marriage, Separation and Divorce in England, 1500–1700* (OUP 2022).

9 Bigamy Act 1604. The Act contained a number of important exceptions, for example, if there had been a divorce *a mensa et thoro* or a lengthy absence: see Rebecca Probert, *Double Trouble: Bigamy and the Law in England and Wales, 1604–2023* (in preparation).

10 By 'real' alternative I mean an alternative that was recognised by the law. For the legal treatment of non-Anglican marriages – and their rarity – see Rebecca Probert, *Marriage Law and Practice in the Long Eighteenth Century: A Reassessment* (CUP 2009).

11 For examples of such claims see, for example, John Gillis, *For Better, for Worse: British Marriages 1600 to the Present Day* (OUP 1985); Stephen Parker, *Informal Marriage, Cohabitation and the Law, 1754–1989* (Macmillan 1990); Lawrence Stone, *Road to Divorce:*

every couple who married did so in strict conformity with the requirements of the canon law. The seventeenth century saw various churches marrying couples without banns or licence, outside the canonical hours, or without too scrupulous a regard as to whether either of the parties was resident in the parish.[12] And during the first half of the eighteenth century, many marriages were not celebrated in a church at all.[13] Yet even such 'clandestine marriages' were still conducted by Anglican clergy and according to the service set out in the *Book of Common Prayer*. In literature, too, there was a very clear idea of how couples *should* marry. Clandestine marriages are generally confined to minor characters and anti-heroes; the good generally marry in church.[14] The clear correlation between the mode of marriage chosen and the moral standing of the characters indicates that there was a standard set of assumptions about the proper way to marry. And even the most private and secret of marriages are celebrated (validly, if clandestinely) by clergymen.[15] If the services of a priest cannot be obtained, the parties do not marry.[16]

So virtually everyone who got married in England and Wales did so according to Anglican rites, and everyone who did so heard and said the same words. In assessing the impact of the marriage service set out in the *Book of Common Prayer*, neither the continuities with Catholic liturgy nor the subsequent contestations that resulted in a revised version in 1662 mattered so much as the fact of uniformity at any given point. With these words now being in English, rather than the Latin of the Catholic service, they were understandable by all. Over the years, the language of the Anglican vows provided an easily

A History of the Making and Breaking of Marriage in England (OUP 1990). For a rebuttal of such claims see Probert (n 10).

12 See, for example, Edward M. Tomlinson, *A History of the Minories, London* (London: Smith, Elder & Co, 1907); Jeremy Boulton, 'Clandestine Marriages in London: An Examination of a Neglected Urban Variable' (1993) 2 *Urban History* 191 and 'Itching after Private Marryings? Marriage Customs in Seventeenth Century London' (1991) 16 *The London Journal* 15.

13 The most famous centre for 'non-church' clandestine weddings was the Fleet prison in London: on which, see Roger Lee Brown, 'The Rise and Fall of the Fleet Marriages' in R. B. Outhwaite (eds), *Marriage and Society* (Europa Publications Ltd 1981); Gill Newton, 'Clandestine Marriage in Early Modern London: When, Where and Why?' (2014) 29 *Continuity and Change* 151; Jacob F. Field, 'Clandestine Weddings at the Fleet Prison, c.1710–1750: Who Married There?' (2017) 32 *Continuity and Change* 349.

14 See, for example, Henry Fielding, *Joseph Andrews* (1742): when the eponymous hero proposes to, and is accepted by, Fanny Goodwill, he demands an instant wedding from their travelling companion, Parson Adams. This is indignantly denied by the good parson, and the mere suggestion of a marriage without banns, witnesses, or a church brings a blush to the cheeks of the modest Fanny.

15 See, for example, Tobias Smollett, *The Adventures of Roderick Random* (1740); *The Adventures of Peregrine Pickle* (175).

16 In John Gay's *The Beggar's Opera* (1728) the marriage of the highwayman Macheath to the jailor's daughter Lucy Lockit is postponed when they fail to find the chaplain of the prison where Macheath is imprisoned.

recognisable lexicon of marriage. In Defoe's *Moll Flanders*, Moll's then future husband tries to persuade his family that he is sincere in his avowed wish to marry her, declaring that if she would agree, '[he'd] have her to morrow Morning fasting, and say, *To have, and to hold*, instead of eating [his] Breakfast'.[17]

The expectation that married couples would not only remain married but would also live together was reflected in the remedy of 'restitution of conjugal rights'. By this means, one spouse could ask the church courts to order the return of an absent or recalcitrant partner. Even if both parties wished to live apart, this was not a matter for them to decide: the church courts could still order them to reunite. In either case, a refusal brought the risk of being ordered to do penance and the threat of excommunication if they did not comply. Only if there had been a formal divorce *a mensa et thoro* would couples be exempt from the duty to live together.[18] Again, to point out such expectations is not to suggest that every couple conformed to them. Nor indeed, did those whose marriages had broken down necessarily avail themselves of the formal remedies provided by the church courts. There were always some who resorted to extra-legal alternatives. At the same time, it needs to be borne in mind that marital breakdown and separation were relatively rare; the vast majority of couples remained together, if not necessarily happily, until parted by death.

So even if there was never a point when the Anglican marriage masterplot was absolute and uncontested, there was a relatively lengthy period during which it held considerable sway in terms of shaping how couples married, ideas (and ideals) about what marriage entailed, and the remedies available to those whose spouses did not live up to those ideals. Yet from its very inception, it depended on the assertion of political power rather than religious authority. The Church of England was established by – and subject to – law. And as the next section will discuss, all three elements of the Anglican marriage masterplot gradually disappeared as authority over marriage shifted from church to state.

The shift of authority from church to state

The shift of authority from church to state was a slow and gradual one. Yet even by the start of the eighteenth century, the influence of the church courts was declining,[19] their jurisdiction was increasingly subject to prohibitions granted by the common law courts, while Parliament had undermined the idea that a marriage, once validly entered into, was for life, by allowing divorce by private Act of Parliament.[20]

17 Daniel Defoe, *Moll Flanders* (1722; Penguin Classics 1989) 87.

18 For the details of these remedies see Richard H. Helmholz, *The Oxford History of the Laws of England: Vol 1: The Canon Law and Ecclesiastical Jurisdiction from 597 to the 1640s* (OUP 2004) ch 10.

19 R. B. Outhwaite, *The Rise and Fall of the English Ecclesiastical Courts, 1500–1860* (CUP 2006).

20 For details of the first parliamentary divorce, see Rebecca Probert, 'The Roos Case and Modern Family Law' in Stephen Gilmore, Jonathan Herring and Rebecca Probert (eds),

The passage of the Clandestine Marriages Act 1753 marked a new approach to the regulation of marriage. That said, in setting out the formalities required for a legally recognised marriage, it did not change the substance of what was required. A ceremony conducted according to the rites of the Church of England remained the only means of marrying specified under the Act. Quakers and Jews were exempted, without any mode of marrying being specified for them. But although the formalities prescribed by the Act were essentially the same as those directed by the 1604 canons of the Church of England, the Act did change the consequences of not complying with those requirements.[21] Moreover, the fact that these requirements were now set out in legislation made it clear that it was the state that was the ultimate arbiter and guarantor of validity.[22] It was no longer the church that set the rules.

Following the 1753 Act, Blackstone commented that:

> Our law considers marriage in no other light than a civil contract. The *holiness* of the matrimonial state is left entirely to the ecclesiastical law. . . . And, taking it in this civil light, the law treats it as it does all other contracts; allowing it to be good and valid in all cases, where the parties at the time of making it were, in the first place, *willing* to contract; secondly, *able* to contract; and, lastly, *did* contract, in the proper forms and solemnities required by law.[23]

But this rather overstated the case. The church courts retained jurisdiction to determine the validity of a marriage, even if they were now obliged to refer to the terms of the 1753 Act to determine whether it was void on account of a failure to comply with the formal requirements. And as historian Jeremy Gregory has noted, the marriage service set out in the *Book of Common Prayer* continued to shape 'much eighteenth-century thinking on marriage and on relations between husbands and wives'.[24] In *Mortimer v Mortimer*,[25] Sir William Scott, presiding over the London Consistory Court, referred to the obligations that spouses 'have contracted in the sight of God and man, to live together "till death them do part"'.[26] While marriage was now, as Scott explained elsewhere, a 'civil

Landmark Cases in Family Law (Hart Publishing 2011). For their subsequent history, see Stuart Anderson, 'Legislative Divorce – Law for the Aristocracy?' in G. R. Rubin and David Sugarman (eds), *Law, Economy and Society* (Professional Books Ltd 1984); Sybil Wolfram, 'Divorce in England 1700–1857' (1985) 5 *OJLS* 155; D. James, 'Parliamentary Divorce, 1700–1857' (2012) 31 *Parliamentary History* 169.

21 See Probert (n 10).

22 See, for example, Lisa O'Connell, *The Origins of the English Marriage Plot: Literature, Politics and Religion in the Eighteenth Century* (CUP 2019) 7.

23 William Blackstone, *Commentaries on the Laws of England: Vol 1* (1765) 421.

24 Jeremy Gregory, '"For All Sorts and Conditions of Men": The Social Life of the Book of Common Prayer during the Long Eighteenth Century: Or, Bringing the History of Religion and Social History Together' (2009) 34 *Social History* 29, 46.

25 (1820) 2 Hag Con 310; 161 ER 753.

26 (1820) 2 Hag Con 318.

contract' in the sense of being regulated by law, that did not mean that it was *purely* civil. As he noted in *Lindo v Belisario*, although the jurisdiction of the ecclesiastical courts had been founded on the idea that marriage was a 'sacred, religious, and spiritual contract',[27] it was incorrect to insist upon it as being purely religious or, indeed, purely civil.[28] Later, in *Dalrymple v Dalrymple*, he suggested that, within civil society, marriage became 'a civil contract regulated and prescribed by law and endowed with civil consequences', but added that

> [i]n most civilized countries acting under a sense of the force of sacred obligations, it has had the sanctions of religion superadded: it then becomes a religious as well as a natural and civil contract; for it is a great mistake to suppose that because it is the one therefore it may not likewise be the other.[29]

This acknowledged the importance of religion while subtly downplaying it as something additional to state-made law.

Yet once it had been accepted that religion played a supporting role, rather than a central one, it became more difficult to justify the requirement that marriages could only be conducted according to Anglican rites. As Catholics and Protestant Dissenters pointed out, the principle of allowing exemptions had already been accepted, in that Quakers and Jews were not required to marry according to Anglican rites. They pressed for an alternative to be provided for themselves too. The Marriage Act 1836 eventually introduced two alternatives: those of marrying in a registered place of worship or in the office of one of the newly appointed superintendent registrars. In contrast to the 1753 Act, which had exempted Quakers and Jews by the simple expedient of stating that its provisions did not apply to them without clarifying what their status would be, the 1836 Act explicitly recognised Jewish and Quaker weddings, requiring them to be preceded by notice and followed by registration in the same way as the new forms of marriage it had introduced.[30] In addition, the initial limitation that only Christian places of worship could be registered for weddings was lifted in 1856,[31] although it was some time before any non-Judeo-Christian places of worship availed themselves of this option.

27 (1795) 1 Hag Con 215, 230.

28 See also *Turner v Meyers* (1808) 1 Hag Con 414, 416–17, in which he described the view that marriage was primarily a religious contract as a notion that prevailed in the dark ages, noting that '[i]n more modern times it has been considered, in its proper light, as a civil contract, as well as a religious vow'.

29 (1811) 2 Hag Con 54, 63.

30 For a discussion of the 1836 Act and the factors that led to its passage, see Rebecca Probert, *Tying the Knot: The Formation of Marriage, 1836–2020* (CUP 2021) ch 2.

31 As a result of the Places of Worship Registration Act 1855, which removed the previous restriction that only Christian places of worship could be certified as such (the prerequisite for registration for weddings).

In practice, most couples continued to marry in the Church of England.[32] Even so, once an Anglican wedding was no longer the only legally prescribed route to a valid marriage, it could no longer be assumed that everyone who had married had made the same vows. Although the words prescribed by statute for inclusion in every wedding in a registered place of worship or register office were clearly modelled on the Anglican service,[33] they simply consisted of each party confirming that they were free to marry to and agreed to marry the other. There was no requirement to say anything else. Questions were therefore raised by contemporaries as to whether couples who had married in one of the new forms introduced by the 1836 Act with only this simple exchange of vows would, or should, be able to avail themselves of remedies in the ecclesiastical courts. The lack of any religious ceremony was highlighted as a reason why an ecclesiastical court was no longer the appropriate venue to hear disputes.[34] It was also questioned whether a deserted spouse would be able to sue for restitution of conjugal rights 'on the strength of such an engagement as the civil-contract law demands', drawing attention to the fact that the words prescribed for use contained no pledge to love and cherish or to live together forever.[35] The answer, of course, was that the legal consequences of a marriage did not depend on how it had been contracted, as long as it was in one of the forms recognised by the law. But it illustrated how there could no longer be a cohesive masterplot based on the ideals of Anglican marriage.

And with the passage of the Matrimonial Causes Act 1857, the church courts ceased to have any role in deciding on the validity of marriages or their consequences. Parliament not only legislated for judicial divorce, thereby confirming that marriage did not have to be for life, but also transferred jurisdiction over marriage (and its breakdown) to a new civil court, the Court for Divorce and Matrimonial Causes.

At one level, then, none of the three key elements of the Anglican marriage masterplot remained in place. The Church of England no longer set or adjudicated upon the rules governing entry into marriage or its consequences, and it could no longer be assumed that those marrying would all make the same vows. Nonetheless, as the next section will discuss, the Anglican marriage masterplot has had a long legacy in terms of the principles applied by the courts, judicial references to 'Christian' marriage, and the linguistic footprint of the Anglican marriage service.

32 Probert (n 30).

33 For an analysis of the structural similarity between the *Book of Common Prayer* and the new prescribed words, see Rebecca Probert, 'Secular or Sacred? The Ambiguity of "Civil" Weddings in England and Wales, 1836–56' (2022) 43 *Journal of Legal History* 136.

34 *Cheltenham Chronicle*, 5 January 1843.

35 *Yorkshire Gazette*, 1 July 1837.

The long legacy of the Anglican marriage masterplot

The 1857 Act directed the new court to give relief on the basis of principles that were as 'nearly as may be' those previously applied by the church courts.[36] This had particular relevance in the context of nullity, since the grounds on which a marriage might be deemed void or voidable were nowhere set out in statute.[37] For some time, judges continued to refer back to the earlier case law of the church courts in determining their approach.[38] However, it was recognised that the principles applied by the church courts could only be of limited assistance in deciding divorce cases.[39]

Moreover, the direction in the 1857 Act did not constrain the practice of *other* courts. As early as 1862, in *Hunt v Hunt*,[40] the Lord Chancellor held that the existence of a separation agreement precluded either of the parties from bringing a suit for restitution of conjugal rights in the Divorce Court. He explicitly cautioned against confounding the 'religious view of the question' with 'that view which alone ought to be taken in Courts sitting to administer justice according to civil law'.[41] Lest it be thought that this was some radical new approach, he sought justification in the changing status of ecclesiastical law at the Reformation, arguing that post-Reformation ecclesiastical law was subordinated to the common law, which 'regards a deed of separation as any other legal contract'.[42]

Even where the jurisdiction of the church courts had not been explicitly curtailed, their activities might be restricted by decisions in the secular courts. In 1876, for example, it was confirmed that the church courts no longer had the power to punish individuals for false statements as to their place of residence prior to the marriage, with Lord Penzance stating emphatically:

> [I]t cannot, I think, be doubted that a recurrence to the punishment of the laity for the good of their souls by ecclesiastical Courts, would not be in harmony with modern ideas, or the position which ecclesiastical authority now occupies in the country.[43]

36 Divorce and Matrimonial Causes Act 1857, s2.

37 Stephen Cretney, *Family Law in the Twentieth Century: A History* (OUP 2003). The only exceptions to this were the Marriage Act 1835, which had stated that subsequent marriages within the prohibited degrees were to be regarded as void rather than voidable, and the provisions of the Marriage Acts 1823 and 1836, providing that a 'knowing and wilful' failure to comply with certain of the formalities required for a marriage rendered it void.

38 Cretney (n 37) 77, 163.

39 See, for example, *Baker v Baker* (1880) 5 PD 142.

40 *Hunt v Hunt* (1862) 4 De Gex, Fisher & Jones; 45 ER 1168.

41 *Hunt v Hunt* (1862) 4 De Gex, Fisher & Jones; 45 ER 1170.

42 *Hunt v Hunt* (1862) 4 De Gex, Fisher & Jones; 45 ER 1175.

43 *The Office of the Judge Promoted by Phillimore v Machon* (1976) LR 1 PD 481, 487.

The direction to have reference to the principles applied by the ecclesiastical courts was repeated in Section 32 of the Supreme Court of Judicature (Consolidation) Act 1925, but not in Section 26 of the Senior Courts Act 1981. In *Akhter v Khan* in 2018, Williams J took the view that this omission had been a deliberate one, adding that it was 'hardly a surprise given the intervention of 134 years in which it might reasonably be thought that the principles and rules of the Ecclesiastical Courts had become embedded in the High Court family division *in so far as they remained relevant*'.[44] It was an important qualification. Remedies once available had been abolished – restitution of conjugal rights in 1970,[45] and jactitation in 1986.[46] The significance of a marriage being voidable had been altered by the Nullity of Marriage Act 1971. Even the grounds on which a judicial separation could be granted were radically different from those on which a divorce *a mensa et thoro* could have been granted before 1857, having been expanded to include separation when divorce law was reformed in 1969.

The narrative of English marriage as 'Christian' marriage persisted for longer, and this brings us back to *Hyde v Hyde and Woodmansee* and Lord Penzance framing his 'definition' of *marriage* 'as understood in Christendom'.[47] That 'definition', as I've argued elsewhere, is better understood as a *defence* of a particular vision of marriage.[48] Its very vehemence is an indication that this particular vision of marriage was perceived to be under threat. That is one reason that it should not, in my view, be accorded the status of a 'masterplot': there is a difference between a narrative that shapes a particular area of law and one crafted as an attempt to hold back developments.

Admittedly, over the years, Penzance's words were to prove influential, being relied upon to justify the recognition of certain types of marriages and the non-recognition of others.[49] Even in relatively recent decades, *Hyde* was cited as justification for refusing to allow those who had undergone gender reassignment to marry in their reassigned sex[50] and for the non-recognition

44 [2018] EWFC 54, para 51 (emphasis added). While his decision on the status of the marriage in that case was subsequently overturned, the Court of Appeal did not take issue with his comments on the status of ecclesiastical law.

45 Matrimonial Proceedings and Property Act 1970, s20. The remedy had, in any case, lost much of its force when the sanction of imprisonment was abolished by the Matrimonial Causes Act 1884.

46 Family Law Act 1986, s61.

47 For criticisms of it as a definition of marriage, see Sebastian Poulter, '*Hyde v Hyde* – A Reappraisal' (1976) 25 *ICLQ* 475 and 'The Definition of Marriage in English Law' (1979) 42 *MLR* 409.

48 Rebecca Probert, '*Hyde v Hyde*: Defining or Defending Marriage?' (2007) *Child and Family Law Quarterly* 322.

49 Probert (n 48).

50 *J v S-T (Formerly J) (Transsexual: Ancillary Relief)* (1997) 1 FLR 402; *Bellinger v Bellinger* (2001) EWCA Civ 1140.

of a same-sex marriage entered into overseas.[51] But when the House of Lords, in *Bellinger v Bellinger*,[52] affirmed the decision of the Court of Appeal that a male-to-female transsexual could not be regarded as female under the law as it then stood, they pointedly avoided citing *Hyde*, and legal reform eventually followed in 2004.[53] The Court of Appeal's decision in *Bellinger* also appears to be the last occasion on which Penzance's reference to 'marriage as understood in Christendom' was cited without any qualification.[54] When *Hyde* was invoked in *Wilkinson v Kitzinger*, it was framed as 'the common law definition of marriage' rather than as 'marriage as understood in Christendom'.[55]

But even at the time, Penzance's words reflected a particular view as to what marriage should be, rather than its legal reality, and were not always applied so literally. The recognition of a marriage by the English courts did not depend on that marriage being 'for life'.[56] Nor did it have to be Christian. In *Brinkley v Attorney General*,[57] the marriage had taken place in Japan, between an Englishman and a Japanese woman. The marriage was upheld, the court citing *Hyde* but glossing Penzance's references to 'Christian' marriage by deciding that what he had meant was 'exclusive marriage'.[58] Moreover, ideas about 'Christian' marriage were only accepted insofar as they did not conflict with the general law. Following the passage of the Deceased Wife's Sister's Marriage Act 1907, one Anglican clergyman refused to recognise a by-then legally valid marriage between a man and his deceased wife's sister and denied them Holy Communion on the basis that they were 'open and notorious evil livers'.[59] In the resulting litigation, it was held that while clergy could not be compelled to conduct such a marriage, they could not refuse to recognise it as a marriage. For present purposes, its significance lies in the fact that the court was affirming that 'the law of the land' had priority over individual Christian – even Anglican – views of marriage.[60]

In other words, subsequent courts did not treat Penzance's words as a masterplot; instead, they selectively chose to give weight to certain elements of his 'definition', but not others. Legal writers were similarly slow to accord significance to his words. Writing in 1885, William Pinder Eversley devoted several pages to different definitions of marriage from a variety of cases but

51 *Wilkinson v Kitzinger (No 2)* [2006] EWHC 2022 (Fam), [2007] 1 FLR 295, [11].
52 [2003] UKHL 21.
53 Gender Recognition Act 2004.
54 [2001] EWCA Civ 1140, [6].
55 *Wilkinson v Kitzinger (No 2)* [2006] EWHC 2022 (Fam), [2007] 1 FLR 295, [11].
56 See, for example, *Nachimson v Nachimson* [1930] P 217.
57 (1890) 15 PD 76.
58 (1890) 15 PD 80.
59 This graphic phrase appeared in the rubric to the 1662 *Book of Common Prayer*: A clergyman was entitled to refuse communion to any 'open and notorious evil liver'.
60 *Banister v Thompson* [1908] P 362, 391–2.

significantly failed to quote Penzance's words from *Hyde*.[61] James Hammick's textbook on marriage, published two years later, made no mention of *Hyde* at all.[62] Only with Charles Crawley's *The Law of Husband and Wife*, published in 1892, was *Hyde* quoted as offering a definition of marriage, and even then it was not the only one cited.[63] All this puts into context the once-regular citation of *Hyde* to justify the exclusion of same-sex couples, or the non-recognition of even potentially polygamous marriages. Penzance's words simply reflected, and were later cited to reflect, certain existing ideas about marriage.

Moreover, in thinking about the use of terms such as 'Christian', there is an important distinction between using it normatively, to justify interpreting the law by reference to Christian ideas, and adjectivally, to describe what the law is or was and to reflect its Christian origins. That same distinction can be seen in the changing status accorded to the words of the Anglican marriage service. Examples can be found of judges invoking the ideas in the Anglican marriage service to determine the rights and obligations that followed from marriage.[64] The idea that marriage was ordained 'for the procreation of children' was relied on by Sir Samuel Evans P in *Dickinson v Dickinson*, for example, to justify granting a decree of nullity on the basis of the wife's wilful refusal to consummate the marriage, over two decades before this became a statutory ground.[65]

There were even proposals that the language used in register office weddings should be revised to echo the vows made in the Anglican marriage service. The post-war Committee on Procedure in Matrimonial Causes was set up in response to an increase in the number of marriages ending in divorce. In its view, register office weddings were sadly lacking when compared to church weddings in terms of the guidance offered to those embarking on married life together. It therefore advocated that the ceremony could be used to try to send a message to couples about marriage and prevent matrimonial problems from arising, proposing that it should 'express the principle that marriage is the personal union, for better or for worse, of one man with one woman, exclusive of all others on either side so long as both shall live'.[66] The echoes of the *Book of Common Prayer* – in which couples vow to take each other 'for better, for worse' and are asked whether they are willing to promise to 'forsake all others . . . as long as [they] both shall live' – could not have been clearer.

61 William Pinder Eversley, *The Law of the Domestic Relations* (Stevens & Haynes 1885) ch 1.

62 James T. Hammick, *The Marriage Law of England: A Practical Treatise on the Legal Incidents Connected with the Constitution of the Matrimonial Contract* (2nd edn, Shaw & Sons 1887).

63 Charles Crawley, *The Law of Husband and Wife* (William Clowes & Son Ltd 1892), also quoting *Lindo v Bellisario* (1795) 1 Hag Con 216.

64 Or indeed, the perceived immorality of relationships outside marriage: see, for example, the comments of Darling J in *Upfill v Wright* [1911] 1 KB 506, 510.

65 *Dickinson v Dickinson* [1913] P 198, 205.

66 *Final Report of the Committee in Procedure in Matrimonial Causes*, Cm 7024 (London: HMSO, 1947) 17. See also its specific recommendation to this effect (at 33).

Yet in the same year that the Committee published these recommendations, the House of Lords made it clear that the Anglican marriage service was not an appropriate reference point by which to assess the legal meaning and consequences of a marriage. The specific legal question in *Weatherley v Weatherley*[67] was whether a wife's refusal to engage in sexual relations constituted desertion so as to entitle the husband to a divorce. A majority of the Court of Appeal had held that it did not, but Scott LJ, in his dissenting judgment, had invoked the *Book of Common Prayer* to justify his different interpretation. The House of Lords unanimously affirmed the decision of the Court of Appeal. The passage in which the Lord Chancellor, Viscount Jowitt, explicitly rejected the approach adopted by Scott LJ is worth quoting at length:

> I think this a dangerous and fallacious line of argument. It proceeds upon the basis that any fundamental breach of the obligations contracted in Holy Matrimony, as laid down in the Book of Common Prayer, constitutes desertion within the meaning of the Act of 1937. It could not be contended that a marriage which had been duly consummated could be dissolved, because one of the spouses was unable, by reason of some physical infirmity, to procreate children. Yet the consideration which prevailed with the learned lord justice would appear in such a case to be equally valid. The marriage which is contemplated in the Book of Common Prayer is a lifelong union which imposes an obligation on the one spouse towards the other 'to love and to cherish till death us do part.' The fact is that the law of the land cannot be co-extensive with the law of morals; nor can the civil consequences of marriage be identical with its religious consequences. What marriage means to different persons will depend upon their upbringing, their outlook and their religious belief. We must remember, as Scott L.J. rightly says that marriage, whether solemnized in a church or a register office, whether contracted between Christians or between those who have different or no religious beliefs, must in each case have the same legal consequences: and remembering those things, we shall, I think, find the solution to the question which arises for determination in this case, and in similar cases, not upon a consideration of the Christian doctrine of marriage, as laid down in the Book of Common Prayer, but on the true construction of the relevant Acts of Parliament.[68]

The following year, the idea of marriage being 'for' the procreation of children was also rejected by the House of Lords, with Viscount Jowitt similarly eschewing resort to the *Book of Common Prayer*.[69]

67 [1947] AC 628.
68 [1947] AC 633.
69 *Baxter v Baxter* [1948] AC 274.

Similarly, following a run of cases in which counsel or judges had made reference to the promises in the Anglican marriage service for each spouse to take the other 'for better, for worse' when deciding what actions constituted 'cruelty' or 'constructive desertion',[70] Lord Pearce, in *Gollins v Gollins*, noted that these words carried 'religious associations knit up with the indissolubility of marriage and are of little help in estimating whether a spouse is legally entitled to the relief provided by Parliament'.[71]

It is true that linguistic echoes of the *Book of Common Prayer* can still be found in judgments throughout the second half of the twentieth century, and even into the twenty-first, but they can no longer be seen as part of a cohesive Anglican marriage masterplot. Somewhat ironically, it is in the context of cases involving cohabitants that judges are now most likely to invoke the language of the *Book of Common Prayer*, generally to hold that they do not meet the threshold of living together 'as if' they are married. In *Nutting v Southern Housing Group*, for example, Evans-Lombe J confirmed that the defendant 'had failed to demonstrate that his relationship with [the deceased] displayed a sufficient commitment to permanence'.[72] One of the indicia used by the Recorder at first instance to determine whether the parties were living together as if married had been whether the relationship was 'one which has been presented to the outside world openly and unequivocally so that society considers it to be of permanent intent – the words "till death us do part" being apposite'.[73] Similarly, in *Amicus Horizon Ltd v Mabbott's Estate*, Ward LJ noted:

> One does not have to spend too much time in the Family Division to realise that husbands and wives live their married lives in many and various ways, yet always at its heart marriage is a serious but public commitment to have and to hold the other as one's husband or one's wife and in whatever religious or civil form the promises are made, in essence always to love and to cherish until death us do part.[74]

In the context of marriage, with the number of suits for nullity having dwindled and divorces rarely coming to court, judicial pronouncements as to the 'essence' of marriage are now primarily found in the context of assessments of capacity to marry, in setting out what an individual needs to understand in order to be able to marry. And it is here that we see most clearly the loss of any masterplot, as the final section will show.

70 *Walker v Walker* [1962] P 42; *Hall v Hall* [1962] 1 WLR 478.
71 *Gollins v Gollins* [1964] AC 644.
72 [2005] 2 P & CR 14; [2005] EWHC 2982 (Ch), [17].
73 [2005] 2 P & CR 14; [2005] EWHC 2982 (Ch), [9].
74 [2012] EWCA Civ 895, [16].

The 'essence' of marriage in the twenty-first century

The starting point for discussion of the modern law is *Sheffield City Council v E*.[75] Two elements of Munby J's judgment are of particular significance. The first is his statement that marriage is now 'a civil institution whose duties and obligations are regulated by the secular courts of an increasingly secular society'.[76] The second is his attempt to summarise the 'duties and responsibilities that normally attach to marriage':

> Marriage, whether civil or religious, is a contract, formally entered into. It confers on the parties the status of husband and wife, the essence of the contract being an agreement between a man and a woman to live together and to love one another as husband and wife, to the exclusion of all others. It creates a relationship of mutual and reciprocal obligations, typically involving the sharing of a common home and a common domestic life and the right to enjoy each other's society, comfort and assistance.[77]

If marriage is regarded *only* as a legal institution, then any claims as to its duties and responsibilities must similarly be rooted in the law. At the time that Munby delivered his judgment, it was still possible to infer that it was of 'the essence of the contract' for a couple to 'live together . . . as husband and wife, to the exclusion of all others' from the remedies that were available to either party if the other failed to do so. A persistent refusal by one spouse to live with the other would enable a divorce to be granted on the basis of desertion.[78] A divorce could also be granted on the basis of separation if the parties were living apart,[79] or on the basis of adultery,[80] if the marriage had not been 'to the exclusion of all others'. Any of these factors also enabled the courts to grant a decree of judicial separation authorising the parties to live apart.[81] Moreover, if 'lov[ing] one another as husband and wife' is to be construed as a coy reference to the parties' sexual relationship, then that, too, was backed up by remedies: a spouse could seek an annulment on the basis that they or their spouse was incapable of consummating the marriage or that the other

75 [2004] EWHC 2808 (Fam).
76 [2004] EWHC 2808 (Fam), [116].
77 [2004] EWHC 2808 (Fam), [132].
78 Matrimonial Causes Act 1973, s1(2)(c), which provided that the irretrievable breakdown of the marriage could be inferred from the fact that the respondent spouse had deserted the other for a period of at least two years.
79 Matrimonial Causes Act 1973, s1(2)(d) and (e), providing for irretrievable breakdown to be inferred from a period of separation for two years if the other spouse consented to the divorce, or a period of five years if they did not.
80 Matrimonial Causes Act 1973, s1(2)(a).
81 Matrimonial Causes Act 1973, s17.

had wilfully refused to do so.[82] Save in that narrow sense, however, 'love' was not a justiciable issue.

Even at that time, however, commentators pointed out that the language of 'duties and responsibilities' was inapposite, given the lack of any means of enforcement, such enforcement methods as had once existed having been consigned to history.[83] And since *Sheffield* was decided, it has become more difficult to describe marriage in terms of these particular duties and responsibilities. With the implementation of the Divorce, Dissolution, and Separation Act 2020 in April 2022, it is no longer necessary for those seeking a divorce to establish irretrievable breakdown by proving adultery, 'unreasonable' behaviour,[84] desertion, or separation. As a result, even this residual basis for implying an obligation of fidelity or cohabitation disappears. Moreover, while it is still possible for the parties to an *opposite*-sex marriage to seek an annulment on the basis of incapacity or wilful refusal to consummate, this option has not been extended to the parties to a *same*-sex marriage. And the idea that this remedy connoted any 'duty' or 'responsibility' to engage in a sexual relationship was quickly repudiated. Munby J himself emphasised that this was not what he had meant, noting in *X City Council v MB, NM and MAB* that 'the sexual component of marriage (where it arises) cannot properly be described as either a duty or a responsibility'.[85] In the later case of *In the matter of X (A Child)*,[86] he went out of his way to stress that the fact that a marriage has not been consummated does not, by itself, affect its validity, noting that '[t]he fact that it is platonic, and without a sexual component, is, as a matter of long-established law, neither here nor there and in truth no concern of the judges or of the State'.[87]

In addition, the evolving law on capacity has forced a disjuncture between marriage, living together, and love. Since capacity is decision-specific, having capacity to marry does not necessarily mean having the capacity to decide whether to live with one's spouse.[88] The position as regards capacity

82 Matrimonial Causes Act 1973, s12(a) and (b).

83 Ruth Gaffney-Rhys, '*Sheffield City Council v E and Another* – Capacity to Marry and the Rights and Responsibilities of Married Couples' (2006) *Child and Family Law Quarterly* 139.

84 To use the convenient and commonly used, if inaccurate, phrase. As Lord Wilson has pointed out, s1(2)(b) of the MCA 1973 did not require that the *behaviour* should have been unreasonable but, rather, 'that the expectation of continued life together should be unreasonable': *Owens v Owens* [2018] UKSC 41, [37].

85 [2006] EWHC 168 (Fam).

86 [2018] EWFC 15.

87 At [7]. The validity of the marriage was not directly in point in that case, but it provided a useful reminder of the difference between incapacity or a wilful refusal to consummate, rendering a marriage voidable and consummation being necessary for a valid marriage.

88 *PC & Anor v City of York Council* [2013] EWCA Civ 478; *Sandwell Metropolitan Borough Council v RG, GG, SK, SKG* [2013] EWHC 2373 (COP).

to engage in sexual relations is less clear. Certainly, having the capacity to engage in sexual relations does not necessarily mean having the capacity to marry.[89] It has, however, been suggested that, for an individual to have capacity to marry, they must also have capacity to engage in sexual relations.[90] This was questioned by Mostyn J in *NB v MI*, who noted that while they will 'normally function at an equivalent level, they do not stand and fall together; the one is not conditional on the other'.[91] Moreover, it is clear from the cases on capacity that love – in the broader sense of an emotional relationship – is not enough. In *AMDC v AG*,[92] AG wished to marry a fellow resident of her care home 'because they loved each other', but it was held that she did not have the mental capacity to do so, although she was held to have capacity to consent to sexual relations.[93] As was emphasised in *YLA v PM, MZ*, understanding the concepts of 'love, sex, living together, companionship and mutual parentage' is not enough without an understanding of 'status, rights, responsibilities, obligations, exclusivity, or agreement'.[94]

All this makes it much harder for courts to maintain that the 'essence' of marriage is an agreement to 'live together and love one another as husband and wife'. There is, quite simply, no longer any underpinning law from which that can be inferred. Indeed, in *Mundell v Name I*,[95] Mostyn J stated that he did 'not believe that it is of the essence of a marriage contract that the parties should live together, let alone that they should love one another'.[96] As he noted, while it was 'empirically the norm' for spouses to do so, that could not make these elements 'essential features of the marriage contract'.[97]

Yet once we strip out the elements of *Sheffield* that no longer hold good as a matter of law, little is left except that marriage is a contract which 'confers on the parties the status of husband and wife' and which generates certain mutual (largely financial) rights and responsibilities. Understandably, then, the emphasis in more recent cases is on the concept of marriage as a status that may entail financial obligations.[98] Equally understandably, judges have

89 See, for example, *EJ (as attorney for DMM) v SD* [2017] EWCOP 32; *AMDC v AG* [2021] EWCOP 5.

90 See, for example, *X City Council v MB, NM and MAB* [2006] 2 FLR 968; *London Borough of Southwark v KA* [2016] EWCOP 20, [37] ('P must not lack capacity to enter into sexual relations'). See also *AMDC v AG* [2021] EWCOP 5, [19], where this proposition was described as 'well established'.

91 [2021] EWHC 224 (Fam), [26].

92 [2021] EWCOP 5.

93 [2021] EWCOP 5, [22].

94 [2013] EWHC 4020 (COP), [150].

95 [2019] EWCOP 50.

96 At [14].

97 At [27].

98 See, for example, *London Borough of Southwark v KA* [2016] EWCOP 20, in which Parker J held that an individual must have at least a rudimentary understanding that a marriage may

not wished to make capacity to marry depend on a detailed grasp of what those obligations are.[99] Moreover, given that these obligations largely only arise on divorce, individuals need to demonstrate an understanding that a marriage may end in divorce.[100] Any attempt to say what marriage 'is' has been lost.

Conclusion

While the decline of the Anglican marriage masterplot was slow, its key elements have now been dismantled. Courts no longer make explicit reference to the principles applied by the church courts, unless it is to emphasise how far the modern law departs from those principles. As Mostyn J concluded in *NB v MI*, '[m]odern marriage has moved on a long way from the days when canon law ruled the legal roost'.[101] Marriage is no longer explicitly defined as 'Christian', and the expectations set out in the *Book of Common Prayer* have been rejected as a source of guidance.

It might, of course, be quite validly objected that English marriage law is still *implicitly* Christian. After all, the Anglican Church still retains a privileged position in the making of marriages; the words prescribed for use in weddings in register offices, approved premises, and registered places of worship still bear echoes of the Anglican marriage service; and even if English law now recognises the validity of polygamous marriages in certain circumstances, there is no possibility of entering into a valid marriage involving multiple spouses in England and Wales. Yet it seems unlikely that any future challenge to any of these elements would be successfully defended solely on the basis of the 'Christian' nature of marriage.

Does marriage need a new masterplot? Twenty years ago, the pared-down definition offered by Thorpe LJ in his dissenting judgment in *Bellinger v Bellinger* seemed attractively simple – and, from one perspective, aspirational,

entail financial consequences 'and that spouses have a particular status and connection with regard to each other'; *AMDC v AG* [2021] EWCOP 5, [22], in which the court noted that AG had 'no real understanding of the financial and other implications of her entering into marriage'.

99 See, for example, the comments of Mostyn J in *Mundell v Name I* [2019] EWCOP 50, [31] and *NB v MI* [2021] EWHC 224 (Fam), [20], [26], although note that, in *EJ (as attorney for DMM) v SD* [2017] EWCOP 32, it was held that an individual needed to understand that a marriage would revoke a will.

100 See, for example, *X v A*, in which the judge primarily focused on the issue of status. Against the evidence that the respondent had seemed happy to be going through a ceremony of marriage, she noted that the respondent 'demonstrates little or no real understanding that marriage confers a status on the parties to it' ([71]) or of the implications of that status 'such as the financial effect following divorce' ([75]).

101 [2021] EWHC 224 (Fam), [28].

since it envisaged a time in which the gender of the parties did not matter. His suggestion was that marriage should be defined as

> a contract for which the parties elect but which is regulated by the state, both in its formation and in its termination by divorce, because it affects status upon which depend a variety of entitlements, benefits and obligations.[102]

Yet without some idea of what marriage is for, it is difficult to decide what entitlements, benefits, and obligations it should bring. We do, then, need a new masterplot that reflects society's aspirations for marriage for the twenty-first century rather than shadows of the past.

102 *Bellinger v Bellinger* [2002] EWCA Civ 1140, [128].

Chapter 8

The maxim 'justice delayed is justice denied' as a masterplot in international criminal justice

Nina H. B. Jørgensen

Introduction

In a video produced some years after the Rwandan genocide of 1994, Tharcisse Karugarama, then minister of justice of Rwanda, commented on the state of the country following the 100 days of fighting, during which up to 800,000 people perished, noting that there was no infrastructure, no public services, and just the smell of death and destruction and a prevailing sense of hopelessness.[1] At the same time, prisons were quickly filling up and overflowing with those suspected of involvement in the genocide in their distinctive pink prison garb, estimated to be around 100,000 by 1996. The former minister referred to the competing interests of various actors, including the new government, which needed to establish control and authority and prove its worth; alleged perpetrators of the genocide who could not be kept in prison awaiting trial indefinitely; survivors who were calling for justice or even vengeance; and the international community, with its maxim 'justice delayed is justice denied'.[2]

This maxim features prominently in the rhetoric associated with the trial and punishment of the perpetrators of core international crimes, such as genocide, crimes against humanity, and war crimes. It was invoked by former chief prosecutor of the International Criminal Court (ICC) Fatou Bensouda, who lamented in relation to the situation concerning Libya that 'unexecuted warrants of arrest for alleged crimes against humanity or war crimes, delay the process of justice, undermine accountability and ultimately prevent closure for victims'.[3] Indeed, the maxim is so entrenched that one commentator described it as 'an old adage, almost a cliché, in international

1 'Gacaca – The Heart of the Matter' *Rwandapedia* (18 June 2012) <www.youtube.com/watch?v=5PkIZ814nS8> accessed 2 September 2024.

2 'Gacaca – The Heart of the Matter' (n 1).

3 'Libya: "Justice Delayed Is Justice Denied", ICC Chief Prosecutor Tells Security Council' *UN News* (17 May 2021) <https://news.un.org/en/story/2021/05/1092132> accessed 2 September 2024.

DOI: 10.4324/9781003404668-12

law circles'.[4] Understandings of the maxim in the post-conflict context are, however, becoming more nuanced, even to the point of rejecting it as 'misguided'.[5] Picking up the Libya baton following his appointment as ICC Prosecutor in 2021, Karim Khan told the UN Security Council, which had referred the situation to the court, that 'it may be the case that the old adage "justice delayed is justice denied" is not correct. Maybe justice delayed still can be arrived at.'[6] This was as long as the situation did not become a 'never-ending story'.[7]

There exists an undeniable, indeed fundamental, relationship between time and justice, although it has been noted that 'the connection between temporalities and fact construction in law has scarcely been discussed'.[8] Empirical studies have tended to focus on the link between time, measured in terms of speed and efficiency, and the quality of justice.[9] In cases concerning international crimes, fact construction most commonly occurs years, even decades, after the events and plays an important role in historical as well as judicial truth-finding while aiming to fulfil other aims, such as healing for victims of what have often been protracted armed conflicts. Fact construction may even be deemed to be forward-looking in the sense that the ICC carries out its work 'for the sake of present *and future* generations'.[10] Thus, combating impunity spans considerations connected to the past, present, and future. Once criminal proceedings are initiated, efficiency becomes a paramount concern, and it has been suggested in this domain that '[a]ccelerating international justice is a condition for its credibility'.[11]

4 Mark Kersten, 'Justice for War Crimes in Ukraine Must Not Be Delayed' *Al Jazeera* (3 October 2022) <www.aljazeera.com/opinions/2022/10/3/justice-for-war-crimes-in-ukraine-must-not-be-delayed> accessed 2 September 2024. See also Amnesty International, 'Open Letter to the Chief Prosecutor of the International Criminal Court: Comments on the Concept of the Interests of Justice' (17 June 2005) 1, urging the ICC chief prosecutor to bear in mind the maxim 'justice delayed is justice denied' when considering any suspension of investigations.

5 See Padraig McAuliffe, 'Justice Delayed Is Justice Developed, Questioning the Rush to Judgment in Post-Conflict Prosecutions' (2014) 6 *Human Rights and International Legal Discourse* 293, 298.

6 'ICC Prosecutor, Karim A.A. Khan QC, Outlines Renewed Approach to Investigations in the Situation in Libya to the United Nations Security Council' (29 April 2022) <www.icc-cpi.int/news/icc-prosecutor-karim-aa-khan-qc-outlines-renewed-approach-investigations-situation-libya> accessed 2 September 2024.

7 'ICC Prosecutor, Karim A.A. Khan QC, Outlines Renewed Approach to Investigations in the Situation in Libya to the United Nations Security Council' (n 6).

8 Tanzil Chowdhury, *Time, Temporality and Legal Judgment* (Routledge 2020) 3.

9 See, for example, Tania Sourdin and Naomi Burstyner, 'Justice Delayed Is Justice Denied' (2014) 4 *Victoria University Law and Justice Journal* 49.

10 Rome Statute of the International Criminal Court (17 July 1998), (ICC Statute), Preamble (emphasis added). See also Antoon De Baets, 'The View of the Past in International Humanitarian Law (1860–2020)' (2022) 104(920–921) *International Review of the Red Cross* 1586, 1596.

11 Nicolas Guillou, 'Le temps et la justice pénale internationale' ('Time and International Criminal Justice') in 'Time, Memory and Criminal Law' *A Quarterly Review for Criminal Justice* (vol 4, Bologna 2018) 286, 296.

In this chapter, the lens of a masterplot is employed both to magnify and diminish the validity of the assertion that justice delayed is justice denied in the context of international criminal justice.[12] A *masterplot* is defined as a story told over and over in different guises that connects with the identities and values of a culture, affording it strong rhetorical impact.[13] Viewed as a masterplot, the maxim 'justice delayed is justice denied' is seen to undergird two narratives that run parallel with each other, the first being concerned with procedural efficiency and the second focusing on the timing of justice. Both aspects have been addressed in the literature, with emphasis placed on what is perceived as the snail-like pace of proceedings.[14] However, the general tendency to 'overread or underread narratives in an often-unconscious effort to bring them into conformity with a masterplot' has been noted.[15] The analytical framework of a masterplot permits a more profound appreciation of the temporal forces at play. It assists in highlighting the degree to which the two coexisting narratives are overread or underread to abide by the principle of timely justice, in turn helping to sketch the mutable boundaries of delayed justice that may credibly be deemed 'justice delivered'.[16] The chapter concludes that while the maxim 'justice delayed is justice denied' appropriately governs the narrative of procedural efficiency, it should be minimised as a masterplot when evaluating the timing of post-atrocity justice due to the myriad characters, locations, and subplots within each story.

'Justice delayed is justice denied' and the narrative of time

The origins of the well-known maxim 'justice delayed is justice denied' have been traced to early Jewish teachings according to which '[t]he sword comes into the world, because of justice delayed and justice denied'.[17] The *sword* in

12 Although this chapter is primarily concerned with criminal proceedings before international or specially established international-domestic ('hybrid') institutions, the relevance of the maxim to purely domestic proceedings concerning international crimes has been noted. See, for example, Kelsey Guthrie-Jones, 'Justice Delayed, Justice Denied?' (2019) *Civitas Maxima Annual Report* 30; Robert Roth, 'How to Accelerate National Proceedings' (2019) *Civitas Maxima Annual Report* 34.

13 H. Porter Abbott, *The Cambridge Introduction to Narrative* (3rd edn, CUP 2020) 52–3.

14 See, for example, Report by Friedrich-Alexander-Universität Erlangen-Nürnberg and International Nuremberg Principles Academy, 'Length of the Proceedings at the International Criminal Court' (2022) (Nuremberg Report); A. Whiting, 'In International Criminal Prosecutions, Justice Delayed Can Be Justice Delivered' (2009) 50 *Harvard International Law Journal* 323.

15 Abbott, *Cambridge Introduction to Narrative* (n 13), 254–5.

16 Whiting, 'International Criminal Prosecutions' (n 14).

17 Quoted text taken from Sourdin and Burstyner, 'Justice Delayed Is Justice Denied' (n 9) 49, footnote 1. See Pirkei Avot (Chapters of the Fathers) 5:8, a section of the Mishnah, (c. 190-c. 230CE). English translation: <www.sefaria.org/Pirkei_Avot?tab=contents> accessed

this understanding is representative of war, which results from delay and the perversion of justice.[18] The parable of the widow and the judge told by Jesus has also been interpreted to refer to the injustice of failing to make judicial decisions sufficiently quickly.[19] The Magna Carta formally set the framework for viewing timely justice as a human right, stating that '[t]o no one will we sell, to no one deny or delay right or justice'.[20]

In the 1600s, authors such as John Musgrave, John Godolphin, and Charles Molloy expressed the idea that to delay justice is an injustice. John Musgrave aired various grievances against what he deemed to be his illegal imprisonment in his pamphlet 'Another Word to the Wise, shewing that the Delay of Justice is great injustice'.[21] The publisher's introduction proclaims that '[a]s time (that precious jewel) bringeth forth the truth of all things, so have we gained more knowledge of your just cause, and unjust sufferings'.[22] This acknowledgement recognises that delay may be beneficial for the discovery of truth even where procedural justice has been lacking.[23] The same introduction contains an ominous reflection on the circularity of injustice as it concerns upholding human rights in their then nascent form, noting that 'though persecutors and oppressors be changed, yet both persecution and oppression remain'.[24] Thus, justice – without delay – functioned to break the cycle of injustice.

Molloy's treatise on maritime law discusses instances where 'the Party injur'd has Justice deny'd him, or the same illegally delay'd', in the complex field of reprisals, where treaties and the law of nations complemented

2 September 2024. 'The sword comes to the world for the delay of judgment, and for the perversion of judgment.'

18 See Dr Joshua Kulp, English Explanation of Pirkei Avot 5:8, §6: 'Because the System of Justice Was Not Implemented Properly, Society Will Decay into the Anarchy of War Which Is an Inherently Unjust Situation' <www.sefaria.org/English_Explanation_of_Pirkei_Avot.5.8.6?lang=bi&with=all&lang2=en> accessed 2 September 2024.

19 *The Bible*, Luke 18: 1–8. See Paul Sciberras, 'Jethro and Moses in Dialogue (Exodus 18: 8–26): Ethics of Communitarian Responsibility' (2023) 14(5) 587 *Religions* 6.

20 Magna Carta 1215, cl 40. Translation by the British Library, The National Archives <www.nationalarchives.gov.uk/education/resources/magna-carta/british-library-magna-carta-1215-runnymede/> accessed 2 September 2024.

21 Pamphlet titled 'Another Word to the Wise, Shewing that the Delay of Justice Is Great Injustice' (London 1646). Full text available at University of Michigan Digital Library <https://quod.lib.umich.edu/e/eebo/A25494.0001.001?rgn=main;view=fulltext> accessed 2 September 2024.

22 'To Our Worthy and Much Respected Friend, Mr. John Musgrave' Pamphlet titled (n 21).

23 In the 'Coppie of a Letter sent by Mr. John Musgrave, to Sir Arthur Hasilrigge, Knight, A Member of the House of Commons', Musgrave sets out a detailed account of the denial of his rights in the proceedings against him, making reference to the Magna Carta, including cl 40.

24 'To Our Worthy and Much Respected Friend, Mr. John Musgrave' (n 22).

domestic practice.[25] At that time, a denial of justice was a prerequisite for international private reprisals arising from an alleged crime, such as a failure to pay a debt or robbery on land or at sea, committed by a subject of one state against a subject of another.[26] A denial of justice was frequently grounded in undue delay, a concept which took account of relevant steps to obtain justice initiated by the injured citizen and his ruler.[27] Thus, Molloy elaborates, '[t]o deny or delay Justice, is injustice; Justice is every Mans right, who hath not forfeited what he might claim by the *Jus Gentium*'.[28] Godolphin had previously stated the same principle in the introduction to his book *A View of the Admiral Jurisdiction*,[29] suggesting broader acceptance of the idea. Molloy goes on to say:

> If therefore the Party cannot obtain his Definitive Sentence or Judgement, within a fit time against the Person of whom he complains, or if here be a Judgement given against apparent right and Law; yet if no relief can be had, the Bodies or movables of his Subjects, who renders not right, may be taken.[30]

Undue delay and manifest unfairness or illegality were seen to constitute twin bases for reprisals.[31] Both authors stray beyond emerging procedural requirements in relation to private reprisals into wider questions of justice under the *jus gentium*, hinting that military action may be used as a last resort if justice is persistently denied. Indeed, affording timely justice was seen by Molloy as helping to prevent war.[32] Writing during the same period, but from a more general perspective, William Penn included among his 'reflections and max-

25 Charles Molloy, *De jure maritimo et navali, or, a Treatise of Affairs Maritime and of Commerce in Three Books* (London 1676). Full text available at University of Michigan Digital Library <https://quod.lib.umich.edu/e/eebo/A51124.0001.001?rgn=main;view=fulltext#backDLPS87> accessed 2 September 2024.

26 See Evelyn S. Colbert, *Retaliation in International Law* (New York 1948) 15, 18.

27 Colbert (n 26) 19–21.

28 Molloy, *De jure maritimo et navali* (n 25), CHAP. II. Of Letters of Marque, and Reprizal, 16, section V.

29 John Godolphin, *Synēgoros thalassios, a View of the Admiral Jurisdiction* (London 1661). Full text available at University of Michigan Digital Library <https://quod.lib.umich.edu/e/eebo/A42930.0001.001?rgn=main;view=fulltext> accessed 2 September 2024.

30 Molloy, *De jure maritimo et navali* (n 25), CHAP. II. Of Letters of Marque, and Reprizal, 16, section V.

31 See also Godolphin, *A View of the Admiral Jurisdiction* (n. 29), Introduction, who states, 'This Right of Reprizals . . . is not only admissible in cases of denyal, or protelation of Justice, as when Judgement may not be had within the time prescribed by Law, but also when Judgement is given plainly against the Law, and no Remedy to be had against such wrong Judgement'.

32 Molloy, *De jure maritimo et navali* (n 25), CHAP. II. Of Letters of Marque, and Reprizal, 16, section IV.

ims relating to the conduct of human life' the maxim that '[o]ur law says well, "To delay justice, is injustice"'.[33]

Despite its much earlier origins, the maxim is often attributed to the former British prime minister William E. Gladstone, who used it in a parliamentary debate concerning the situation of Ireland in 1868. In his speech, Gladstone advocates for 'a final and successful effort to redress, according to the balance of justice, the wrongs of which Ireland has still just cause to complain', notably 'without more delay', considering that the work had been ongoing for 700 years.[34] The full context of Gladstone's invocation of the maxim is as follows:

> If we be chivalrous men, I trust we shall endeavour to wipe away the stains which the civilized world has for ages seen, or seemed to see, upon the shield of England in her treatment of Ireland. If we are compassionate men, I hope we shall now once, and once for all, listen to that tale of sorrow which comes from her, and the reality of which, if not its justice, is testified by the continuous migration of her people; that we shall endeavour to – Raze out the written troubles from her brain, Pluck from her memory rooted sorrow. But, above all, if we be just men we shall go forward in the name of truth and right, bearing this in mind – that, when the case is proved and the hour is come, *justice delayed is justice denied.*[35]

Nearly a century later, Martin Luther King Jr famously declared in a letter from Birmingham Jail that '[w]e must come to see, with one of our distinguished jurists, that "justice too long delayed is justice denied"'.[36] His declaration was made amidst the ongoing denial of human rights, oppression and segregation on the basis of race, and the futility of waiting for justice that would never be afforded.[37] *Justice*, therefore, meant the too long-awaited recognition of the applicability of human rights to all on an equal basis, shifting the 'quicksand of racial injustice to the solid rock of human dignity'.[38]

33 William Penn, *Fruits of Solitude, in Reflections and Maxims Relating to the Conduct of Human Life* (Philadelphia, M.DCC.XCII 1792), Maxim 393. University of Michigan Library Digital Collections <https://quod.lib.umich.edu/cgi/t/text/text-idx?c=evans;cc=evans;rgn=main;view=text;idno=N18963.0001.001> accessed 2 September 2024. Penn was also of the view that '[d]elays have been more injurious than direct injustice'. Penn (n 33) Maxim 390. The idea had already found its way into popular culture, with Shakespeare's *Hamlet* lamenting in the same breath the oppression of those in power and 'the law's delay'.

34 Adjourned Debate, HC Deb 16 March 1868, vol 190, cols 1688–792, 1742 <https://api.parliament.uk/historic-hansard/commons/1868/mar/16/adjourned-debate> accessed 2 September 2024.

35 Adjourned Debate, HC Deb 16 March 1868, vol 190, cols 1770–1771 (emphasis added).

36 Letter from a Birmingham Jail [King, Jr.] (16 April 1963) <www.africa.upenn.edu/Articles_Gen/Letter_Birmingham.html> accessed 2 September 2024.

37 Letter from a Birmingham Jail [King, Jr.] (n 36).

38 Letter from a Birmingham Jail [King, Jr.] (n 36).

The historical development and the use of the maxim suggest its invocation to convey a sense of urgency in righting past wrongs that may have become entrenched in society and the source of conflict. Indeed, Gladstone's references to wiping away the stains of the past, listening to the tales of sorrow, acknowledging the plight of refugees, erasing bad memories, and finding the truth correspond to modern-day concepts of transitional justice. Yet Gladstone is not saying that justice in the case of Ireland should necessarily have been achieved 700 years previously; rather, he identifies a proper time for justice that cannot, at that point, be further delayed. The process of digging justice out of the quicksand of injustice, as referred to by Martin Luther King, takes time, however, and the boundaries both of 'justice delayed' and 'justice denied' remain indistinct despite efforts by jurists such as Godolphin and Molloy to provide clarity.

Today, human rights treaties and national legislation incorporate the essence of the maxim as it relates to fair trial standards. For example, Article 6 of the European Convention on Human Rights (ECHR) provides that 'everyone is entitled to a fair and public hearing within a reasonable time by an independent and impartial tribunal established by law'.[39] Similarly, the statutes of international criminal tribunals, such as the International Criminal Tribunal for Rwanda (ICTR), protect the right of the accused to be tried without undue delay,[40] as does the statute of the ICC.[41]

The maxim 'justice delayed is justice denied', therefore, presents itself as a masterplot in international criminal justice for three reasons. First, it is not a rule with precise contours but highlights the central yet enigmatic role of temporality in this field. Second, just as it has become grounded in legal and political culture over centuries, it has a specific resonance in the culture of post-conflict justice which ties in with its historical origins, connecting injustice and war. Third, it has a dual operation in terms of the procedural guarantee – now recognised under human rights law – of trial without undue delay and in terms of the more fluid process of redress following pervasive human rights abuses.

Within the framework of a masterplot, narrative as a literary device involves time in two main aspects: first, the time it takes to tell the story and,

39 Council of Europe, European Convention for the Protection of Human Rights and Fundamental Freedoms, as amended by Protocols Nos. 11 and 14, ETS 5 (4 November 1950). See also, International Covenant on Civil and Political Rights, GA res 2200A (XXI), 16 December 1966, Article 9(3): 'Anyone arrested or detained on a criminal charge shall be brought promptly before a judge or other officer authorized by law to exercise judicial power and shall be entitled to trial within a reasonable time or to release.'

40 UN Security Council, UN Doc S/RES/955(1994), Statute of the International Criminal Tribunal for Rwanda (as amended) (8 November 1994), Article 20(4)(c).

41 ICC Statute (n. 10), Article 67(1)(c).

second, the time within the story.[42] Applied to the dual operation of the maxim 'justice delayed is justice denied', the first aspect can be said to relate to the length of the trial process and is therefore linked to procedure. Accordingly, the time taken to reach a verdict is an important factor in determining whether the process of justice is fair.[43] Fairness, in turn, underlies credibility. The second aspect relates to the question of the 'right time to prosecute war crimes',[44] considering the circumstances of a particular situation or sequence of international crimes encompassing the temporality of the events as they occurred and the temporality of the retelling of those events in court. Straddling these two aspects of narrative time is the gap that frequently occurs between the issuing of an indictment against a suspect, marking the formal initiation of a criminal process against a particular individual, and the arrest and commencement of proceedings.

The narrative layers may be broken down further by employing *aetia*, or 'stories of origin',[45] which provide a more textured way of construing temporality in this context. *Aetia* challenge the linearity of time by propelling the origins or causes of an event into the present telling of a story, demonstrating the ongoing effect of the past on the present, since 'the present is regarded as the result of the past events'.[46] *Aetia* have a 'ring-shaped structure' where 'the end circles back to the beginning'.[47] Thus, *aetia* 'function as flashbacks or flashforwards, often with an enormous temporal reach'.[48] This mimics both the judicial reconstruction of the causative background to the commission of atrocities and the piecing together of fragments of memory shared by witnesses, who must return to the origins of traumatic events to tell their version in the present, captured in a time-stamped courtroom transcript.

The masterplot of 'justice delayed is justice denied' is undergirded by these multi-layered aspects of narrative time that are uniquely complex in the context of mass atrocities, which are often accompanied by a breakdown of the rule of law and societal and institutional structures and grounded in historic enmity. The next sections examine whether the asserted masterplot has, in fact, earned credibility within the culture surrounding international criminal justice according to the time it takes to deliver justice, the time between the initiation and activation of justice, and the time within the justice eventually delivered.

42 Abbott, *Cambridge Introduction to Narrative* (n 13) 5.
43 Sourdin and Burstyner, 'Justice Delayed Is Justice Denied' (n 9) 49.
44 Robert Goldman, 'War Crimes Trial of Russian Soldier Was Perfectly Legal – But That Doesn't Make It Wise' *The Conversation* (23 May 2022).
45 Anke Walter, *Time in Ancient Stories of Origin* (OUP 2020) 3.
46 Annette Harder, 'The Invention of Past, Present and Future in Callimachus' "Aetia"' (2003) 131(3) *Hermes* 290.
47 Walter, *Time in Ancient Stories of Origin* (n 45) 16.
48 Walter, *Time in Ancient Stories of Origin* (n 45) 18.

The time it takes to tell the story

International criminal justice is peppered with examples of pre-trial, trial, and appeal processes that, to any objective observer, simply took too long. Commentators, whether academics, practitioners, policymakers, or the media, have consistently criticised both the delay in getting proceedings started once an ad hoc institution, or even the permanent ICC, is seized of a situation and the slow pace of international proceedings once underway. As Ralph Zacklin noted:

> The delays in bringing detainees to trial – and the trials themselves – have generally been so lengthy that questions have been raised as to the violation by the tribunals of the basic human rights guarantees set out in the International Covenant on Civil and Political Rights. . . . Justice delayed is justice denied, which also raises the question of whether justice has been done to the victims.[49]

The case against Mugenzi and Mugiraneza, who were both ministers in the Interim Government of Rwanda during the genocide, provides a prominent example. Both suspects were arrested in Cameroon in 1994 and transferred to the ICTR in 1999, whereupon indictments were issued and confirmed against them.[50] The evidentiary phase of the trial began in 2003 and lasted until 2008. In 2010, while awaiting the delivery of the judgment, Mugiraneza filed an '11th Anniversary Motion to Dismiss Indictment for Violation of Right to Trial without Undue Delay'.[51] He pointed to the 11 years that had passed since his arrest, during which time he had been incarcerated. Consequently, he argued that the length of time between his arrest and the anticipated delivery of the judgment was unacceptable under both the ICTR's statutory regime and the ICCPR. Further, he submitted that, given the length of the delay, prejudice should be assumed.[52] The Trial Chamber rendered its judgment in 2011 – more than 12 years after Mugenzi and Mugiraneza had been arrested – and sentenced them each to a term of 30 years' imprisonment for conspiracy and direct and public incitement to commit genocide.[53]

49 Ralph Zacklin, 'The Failings of Ad Hoc Tribunals' (2004) 2 *Journal of International Criminal Justice* 541, 543–4. For similar comments, see references in Whiting, 'International Criminal Prosecutions' (n 14) 324, footnote 1.

50 *Prosecutor v Bizimungu, Mugenzi, Bikamumpaka, Mugiraneza*, ICTR-99–5-I, Confirmation of the Indictment (12 May 1999).

51 *Prosecutor v Bizimungu, Mugenzi, Bikamumpaka, Mugiraneza*, ICTR-99–50-T, Prosper Mugiraneza's 11th Anniversary Motion to Dismiss Indictment for Violation of Right to Trial without Undue Delay (6 April 2010).

52 *Prosecutor v Bizimungu, Mugenzi, Bikamumpaka, Mugiraneza* (n 51) paras 2 and 9.

53 *Prosecutor v Bizimungu, Mugenzi, Bikamumpaka, Mugiraneza*, ICTR-99–50-T, Judgment and Sentence (*Mugenzi* Trial Judgment), (30 September 2011, pronouncement), (19 October 2011, written reasons).

Despite acknowledging that 12 years was 'lengthy',[54] the Trial Chamber rejected the contention of undue delay given the 'size and complexity of the case'.[55] The Appeals Chamber, rendering its judgment in 2013, gave careful consideration to the issue, emphasising that an accused is only protected against '*undue* delay'.[56] In view of the size and complexity of the case against four jointly charged senior government officials – 'one of the largest ever heard by the Tribunal'[57] – the Appeals Chamber did not consider that any delay had been *undue*, although Mugenzi and Mugiraneza were ultimately acquitted on other grounds.

The Appeals Chamber placed primary emphasis on the size and complexity of the case in determining the question of undue delay in *Mugenzi and Mugiraneza*, by which it meant the number of counts, accused, and witnesses, as well as the quantity of evidence and intricacy of the facts and law. However, it included other factors in its assessment, such as the length of the delay, the conduct of the parties, the conduct of the authorities involved, and any prejudice to the accused.[58] In different proceedings, the ICTR Appeals Chamber noted that 'because of the Tribunal's mandate and of the inherent complexity of the cases before the Tribunal, it is not unreasonable to expect that the judicial process will not always be as expeditious as before domestic courts'.[59] This view was echoed by an informal working group established to discuss measures available to the ICC to reduce the length of its proceedings, which found that there was no 'objective yardstick' to assess whether international trials are 'adequately expeditious'.[60] Well-rehearsed reasons and

54 *Mugenzi* Trial Judgment (n 53) para. 74.

55 *Mugenzi* Trial Judgment (n 53) para. 79.

56 *Justin Mugenzi and Prosper Mugiraneza v The Prosecutor*, ICTR-99–50-A, Judgement (*Mugenzi* Appeals Judgment) (4 February 2013), para. 30.

57 *Mugenzi* Appeals Judgment (n 56) para. 32.

58 *Mugenzi* Appeals Judgment (n 56) para. 30. These factors were recalled in the tumultuous proceedings against Vojislav Šešelj, a Serbian far-right politician, before the International Criminal Tribunal for the former Yugoslavia (ICTY). See *Prosecutor v Vojislav Šešelj*, Decision on Appeal against Decision on Continuation of Proceedings, IT-03–67-AR15bis (6 June 2014), para. 63. Šešelj's first appearance took place in 2003, after which proceedings were hampered by his assertion of the right to self-representation and disruptive conduct, followed by the disqualification of Judge Harhoff for alleged bias when the case had already entered the deliberations stage after all the evidence had been heard. Šešelj remained in custody, in part serving a sentence for contempt of court. He was eventually acquitted by the Trial Chamber in 2016, but this acquittal was reversed in part by the Appeals Chamber in 2018, resulting in a ten-year sentence, which was, at that point, declared served, warranting his release.

59 *Prosecutor v Nahimana, Barayagwiza and Ngeze*, ICTR-99–52-A, Judgement (Appeals Chamber) (28 November 2007), para. 1076.

60 Informal Expert Paper: Measures Available to the International Criminal Court to Reduce the Length of Proceedings, ICC-OTP (2003), para. 7, adding: 'We have not attempted to establish any specific yardstick over and above a general conclusion that international criminal trials can reasonably be expected to last longer than most national trials.'

justifications for the time it takes to try international cases, especially those concerning senior political and miliary leaders, include the challenges of investigating in war zones, the need for state cooperation, functioning in multiple languages, bringing together judges from different legal traditions, limited availability of courtrooms and support staff, and budgetary constraints.[61] To this list may be added the participation of victims in the process,[62] reparation proceedings, and investigating and securing witness attendance long after the events, including the impact of the time that has elapsed since the events on memory. In the context of the ICC, often unwieldy proceedings relating to admissibility under the complementarity principle, whereby national criminal jurisdictions have priority, and hearings on the confirmation of charges, for example, contribute to the time it takes to tell the story.[63] As it concerns financing, it should be noted that international criminal justice is relatively expensive, hence the creation of models such as the Special Court for Sierra Leone (SCSL), designed as a 'shoestring' court and funded via voluntary contributions by states.[64] This funding structure was arguably the SCSL's biggest structural defect, and there is a clear link between adequate financial support and efficiency.[65]

As international or specialised tribunals, applying the relevant factors on a case-by-case basis, have not so far found any delay to be so undue as to bring the case to a halt, precisely when lengthy proceedings will spill into the realm of the disproportionate is uncertain. In fact, Judge Robinson dissented on this issue in *Mugenzi and Mugiraneza*, finding in particular that two years and ten months to prepare the trial judgment was excessive, and that greater weight should have been given to the length of the judgment-drafting phase in determining undue delay.[66] He would have awarded moral damages of US$5,000.00 to each appellant. In the Trial Chamber, Judge Short also con-

61 See also Guillou, 'Time and International Criminal Justice' (n 11) 288.

62 See, for example, ICC Statute, (n 10) Article 68(3).

63 Informal Expert Paper: Measures Available to the International Criminal Court to Reduce the Length of Proceedings, ICC-OTP (2003), para. 9.

64 See, for example, Avril McDonald, 'Sierra Leone's Shoestring Special Court' (2002) 84(845) *International Review of the Red Cross* 121.

65 Report on the Special Court for Sierra Leone, submitted by the Independent Expert Antonio Cassese (12 December 2006), para. 293.

66 *Mugenzi* Appeals Judgment (n 56), Partially Dissenting Opinion of Judge Patrick Robinson, paras 1–2 and 12. The ICTR and ICTY, which were established by the UN Security Council, lacked authority to award compensation following an acquittal, although both tribunals had requested an amendment to their statutes to provide for such a remedy. See *Rwamakuba v Prosecutor*, ICTR-98–44C-A, Decision on Appeal against Decision on Appropriate Remedy (13 September 2007), paras 10 and 13–15. Rwamakuba had, however, been offered financial compensation of US$2,000.00 for a violation of his right to legal assistance and to an initial appearance without delay, and this decision was upheld by the Appeals Chamber. See *Mugenzi* Appeals Judgment (n 56) para. 31.

sidered that the right to trial without undue delay had been violated, and that the majority had not considered sufficiently the reasonableness of the time taken to prepare the judgment. He deemed the appropriate remedy to be a reduction of sentence rather than a dismissal of the indictment as requested by the accused.[67]

The case against the former Liberian president Charles Taylor before the Special Court for Sierra Leone (SCSL) is also informative. In that case, the Trial Chamber, balancing 'the right of the Accused to have adequate time for preparation of his case and his right to be tried without undue delay', refused in 2007 to set a trial date that would permit more than 14 months' pre-trial detention of Taylor, even though a request for a longer period was made by the defence.[68] Closing arguments in the case were heard in 2011, and the voluminous trial judgment was delivered a year later.[69] While the pre-trial and trial proceedings were relatively long, any proportionality assessment in this instance would need to take account of the particular circumstances. These included moving the proceedings from Freetown, Sierra Leone, where the SCSL was established, to temporary facilities in The Hague for security reasons, boycotts, postponements, changes to the panel of judges hearing the case, and institutional budgetary crises, coupled with the inevitable complexity of the case.[70] The trial had encompassed 'four hundred and twenty trial days, during which one hundred and fifteen witnesses were heard, one thousand five hundred and twenty-one exhibits were admitted and forty-nine thousand pages of transcript were produced'.[71] Still, the 11 counts were relatively narrow, addressing Taylor's role in Sierra Leone's civil war in accordance with the SCSL's limited jurisdiction, rather than his alleged involvement in war crimes in Liberia.

67 *Mugenzi* Trial Judgment (n 53), Partially Dissenting Opinion of Emile Francis Short, para. 7.

68 *Prosecutor v Charles Ghankay Taylor*, SCSL-03–1-PT, Joint Decision on Defence Motions on Adequate Facilities and adequate time for the preparation of Mr Taylor's defence (23 January 2007), para. 21.

69 *Prosecutor v Charles Ghankay Taylor*, SCSL-03–1-T, Judgment (Trial Chamber) (18 May 2012).

70 Addressing the question of 'justice delayed is justice denied', Mark Kersten describes the trial as 'an arduous and drama-filled affair' in 'Charles Taylor Verdict: Some Thoughts and Controversies' *Justice in Conflict Blog* (28 April 2012) <https://justiceinconflict.org/2012/04/28/charles-taylor-verdict-some-thoughts-and-controversies/> accessed 2 September 2024. Despite some unjustifiable delay, however, he suggests that the length of the trial might even have 'contributed to ensuring that the verdict was not a source of renewed violence and instability in Liberia and Sierra Leone'. Cf. Phil Clark, 'Do War Crimes Trials Really Help Victims?' *CNN* (30 May 2012) <https://edition.cnn.com/2012/04/26/opinion/charles-taylor-victims/index.html> accessed 2 September 2024, arguing that 'the length of the Taylor trial is unjustifiable, delaying justice for his victims, dulling the societal impact of the case and increasing the financial costs'.

71 *Prosecutor v Charles Ghankay Taylor*, SCSL-03–1-A, Decision on Prosecution and Defence Motions for Extension of Time and Page Limits for Written Submissions pursuant to Rules 111, 112 and 113 (7 August 2012), para. 26.

Acknowledging the problem of delay, tribunals have consistently examined the efficiency of their processes and taken action to expedite proceedings.[72] Procedural rules tend to contain time limits for all major stages of criminal proceedings, including sometimes the delivery of judgments.[73] According to a study, ICTR proceedings measured from the time of arrest to final judgment took, on average, almost 7.7 years, while the duration of proceedings at the International Criminal Tribunal for the former Yugoslavia (ICTY) was, on average, slightly less at 6.6 years.[74] The study defined 'disproportionately long proceedings' as 'unreasonably long proceedings and as proceedings in which there has been undue delay' based on the jurisprudence of human rights courts, international criminal tribunals, and national legal systems.[75] The length of proceedings has been a preoccupation of the ICC from its earliest stages.[76] It is perhaps reassuring to note that the same study examining seven trials conducted to date found that 'while trials at the ICC are long, they are not disproportionately long'.[77] It can be concluded on this basis that expedition is a fixation of international courts and tribunals. Moreover, fair trial rights of the accused as well as the rights of victims afford the maxim 'justice delayed is justice denied' credibility in this context. However, a finding of disproportionately long proceedings in violation of rights will be rare, provided procedures that are fine-tuned to the complexities of international trials are observed.

72 See, for example, Report on the completion of the mandate of the International Criminal Tribunal for Rwanda as at 15 November 2015, S/2015/884 (17 November 2015), para. 43: 'To improve efficiency at both the trial and appeals levels, amendments to the Rules of the Tribunal were continually made with a view to expediting and shortening trials.' ICTY Manual on Developed Practices, Prepared in conjunction with UNICRI as part of a project to preserve the legacy of the ICTY (2009). ICC ASP, Independent Expert Review of the International Criminal Court and the Rome Statute System: Final Report (30 September 2020), containing sections on both 'efficiency' (internal performance) and 'effectiveness' (impact), recommended use of data to 'enable benchmarking and determining "normality" in international justice, i.e. recognised standards of what can be expected from an international court' (para. 366). ICC Chambers Practice Manual (7th edn, 13 July 2023), para. 87: 'With due regard to the need for efficiency, the judges have agreed that certain time frames need to be introduced for trial judgments.'

73 See, for example, Rule 159(1), Rules of Procedure and Evidence before the Kosovo Specialist Chambers, adopted on 17 March 2017, revised on 29 May 2017, amended on 29 and 30 April 2020: 'The Trial Judgment shall be pronounced within ninety (90) days of the closing of the case.'

74 Nuremberg Report (n 14) 26.

75 Nuremberg Report (n 14) xviii and 51.

76 See ICC-OTP Informal Expert Paper (n 63).

77 Nuremberg Report (n 14) xviii.

The time between the stories

It is not always straightforward to secure the arrest of the world's most wanted war criminals, even if there is a court available with the necessary jurisdiction and a trial-ready case file. Félicien Kabuga was wanted by the ICTR for his involvement in the Rwandan genocide due to his roles as a founder of the radio station *Radio Télévision Libre des Mille Collines* (RTLM) and the president of a National Defence Fund committee between April and July 1994. He evaded capture until 2020, when he was eventually arrested in France.[78] By this time, his case had been transferred from the ICTR to the International Residual Mechanism for Criminal Tribunals (MICT).[79] Pre-trial proceedings centred on Kabuga's fitness to be transferred to the branch of the MICT in Arusha, Tanzania, where the ICTR had been based, and increasingly his fitness to stand trial at all. Being aware that Kabuga's health situation 'may change with the passage of time',[80] the Trial Chamber determined that he should be tried in The Hague, as dictated by his 'fundamental rights to fair and expeditious proceedings without undue delay'.[81] The trial commenced in late 2022 and proceeded on a reduced hearing schedule to accommodate Kabuga's deteriorating health condition. However, a year later, proceedings were ordered by the Appeals Chamber to be stayed indefinitely on the basis of Kabuga's medical unfitness.[82] This decision was made despite an attempt by a majority of the Trial Chamber to implement a novel 'alternative finding procedure' following its own conclusion that Kabuga was no longer fit to stand trial.[83] The Appeals Chamber was cognisant of the length of time victims and survivors had waited to 'see justice delivered' and their consequent disappointment.[84] However, 'justice delivered' meant holding fair trials, which was 'vital to the credibility' of the process, and 'endurance of [the] legacy' of ad hoc tribunals.[85] In fact, the Chamber invoked the axiom that 'justice must be done and must be seen to be done'[86] almost as if it were

78 The original indictment was confirmed in 1997. See *Prosecutor v Kabuga*, MICT-13–38, Warrant of Arrest and Order for Transfer addressed to all States (29 April 2013).

79 See operative indictment: *Prosecutor v Kabuga*, MICT-13–38-PT, Prosecution's Second Amended Indictment (1 March 2021).

80 *Prosecutor v Kabuga*, MICT-13–38-PT, Decision on Félicien Kabuga's Fitness to Stand Trial and to be Transferred to and Detained in Arusha (13 June 2022), para. 57.

81 *Prosecutor v Kabuga* (n 80) para. 61.

82 *Prosecutor v Kabuga*, MICT-13–38-AR80.3, Decision on Appeals of Further Decision on Félicien Kabuga's Fitness to Stand Trial (*Kabuga* Appeal Decision) (7 August 2023).

83 *Prosecutor v Félicien Kabuga*, Case No. MICT-13–38-T, Further Decision on Félicien Kabuga's Fitness to Stand Trial (6 June 2023).

84 *Kabuga* Appeal Decision (n 82), para. 78.

85 *Kabuga* Appeal Decision (n 82), para. 78.

86 *Kabuga* Appeal Decision (n 82), para. 78.

searching for a counterweight to the criticism that, in this instance, justice had, indeed, been delayed and consequently denied.

A long period between the filing of an indictment and an arrest increases the risk that a case will end prematurely, and '[t]he mantra of "justice delayed is justice denied" can ring very true, particularly when elderly defendants die before final verdicts are rendered'.[87] Several high-profile accused have died before the conclusion of proceedings, including Slobodan Milošević, former president of the Federal Republic of Yugoslavia, and Samuel Hinga Norman, a former internal affairs minister who led a civil defence forces militia during Sierra Leone's civil war.[88] The practice of international tribunals is to terminate proceedings upon the death of the accused on the basis that 'responsibility in a criminal matter is, in law, individual and personalised', irrespective of the stage at which the death occurs.[89] The death of victims and witnesses can be equally detrimental to proceedings, aside from those individuals and their communities never seeing justice done.

The time between the stories is influenced by several factors, including political will, pressure from groups representing victims, state cooperation in securing arrests, and not least, a suspect's determination to escape apprehension. Radovan Karadžić, charged in an indictment issued in 1995 with genocide in Srebrenica, among other crimes, was arrested and transferred to the ICTY in 2008 after 13 years in hiding.[90] As Whiting notes, the delay 'was an insult to victims and international criminal justice'.[91] However, Whiting also points to a positive consideration that the case against Karadžić strengthened in each year that passed.[92] The ICC's temporal jurisdiction extends backwards to crimes committed after the entry into force of its statute on 1 July 2002.[93] In late 2003, Uganda referred the situation concerning the Lord's Resistance Army (LRA) to the ICC, making it the court's first investigation. Warrants for the arrest of Dominic Ongwen, a brigade commander of the LRA, and Joseph Kony, allegedly the LRA's commander-in-chief, were issued in 2005. Ongwen surrendered to the court in 2015, and his conviction and sentence became final in late 2022, while Kony remains at large.[94] The

87 David Scheffer, 'The Fate of Justice in Russia-Ukraine Peace Talks' *Just Security* (25 September 2023) <www.justsecurity.org/88757/the-fate-of-justice-in-russia-ukraine-peace-talks/> accessed 2 September 2024.

88 See *Prosecutor v Norman*, SCSL-04–14-T, Decision on Registrar's Submission of Evidence of Death Accused Samuel Hinga Norman and Consequential Issues (21 May 2007), para. 14.

89 *Prosecutor v Norman* (n 88).

90 Proceedings concluded more than ten years later. See *Prosecutor v Karadžić*, MICT-13–55-A, Judgment (Appeals Chamber) (20 March 2019).

91 Whiting 'International Criminal Prosecutions' (n 14) 326.

92 Whiting 'International Criminal Prosecutions' (n 14) 326.

93 ICC Statute (n 10), Article 11.

94 *Prosecutor v Dominic Ongwen*, ICC-02/04–01/15–2022-Red, Judgment on the appeal of Mr Ongwen against the decision of Trial Chamber IX of 4 February 2021 titled 'Trial

ICC has an outstanding arrest warrant against now former Sudanese president Al Bashir concerning allegations of genocide, crimes against humanity, and war crimes committed in Darfur between 2003 and 2008.[95] By contrast, Ali Kushayb, a Janjaweed militia leader who was also wanted by the ICC in connection with crimes in Darfur, surrendered himself voluntarily following the change of regime in Sudan, and his trial commenced in 2022, albeit 15 years after the warrant seeking his arrest.[96] Arguably, this sequence of events could be beneficial for the discovery of the truth if the evidence heard in Ali Kushayb's case bolsters a future case against Al Bashir.

Irrespective of the factors that weigh in the balance and help explain why justice may be delayed, often in the most high-profile cases, today's conflicts and the volume of documented atrocities are clearly creating a backlog. Considered as a masterplot, the maxim 'justice delayed is justice denied' helps keep the juridical and political pressure on and gives hope that justice delivered will be more than a fantasy. The immediate surrender of President Vladmir Putin to the ICC to face war crimes charges relating to his full-scale invasion of Ukraine may not be feasible or even desirable, but there is a suggestion that the suspect, who happens to be a serving president, is on borrowed time. Justice may still be delivered after a long wait in Al Bashir's case. By contrast, in view of the temporal jurisdiction of the SCSL and the goal of embedding the judicial process in the transition to a sustainable peace in Sierra Leone, justice could perhaps not have waited any longer than it did in Taylor's case. At this juncture, the time between the stories overlaps with the more circuitous time within the story.

The time within the story

It is widely accepted that international crimes are timeless and that statutes of limitation do not apply in the context of their commission.[97] This view emerged 'because these crimes complicated and thus extended the duration of investigations [and] constituted such an affront to humanity that

Judgment' (15 December 2022); *Prosecutor v Joseph Kony*, ICC-02/04–01/05–52, Decision on the Prosecutor's application for unsealing of the warrants of arrest (14 October 2005).

95 Warrant of Arrest for Omar Hassan Ahmad Al Bashir, ICC-02/05–01/09–1 (4 March 2009); Second Decision on the Prosecution's Application for a Warrant of Arrest, ICC-02/05–01/09–94 (12 July 2010).

96 *Prosecutor v Ali Muhammad Ali Abd-Al-Rahman ('Ali Kushayb')*, ICC-02/05–01/20.

97 See, for example, ICC Statute, Article 29: 'The crimes within the jurisdiction of the Court shall not be subject to any statute of limitations.' Note, however, that the Convention on the Non-Applicability of Statutory Limitations to War Crimes and Crimes Against Humanity, GA res. 2391 (XXIII) (26 November 1968), which entered into force on 11 November 1970, has not been widely ratified. See also Jan A. Hessbruegge, 'Justice Delayed, Not Denied: Statutory Limitations and Human Rights Crimes' (2012) 43 *Georgetown Journal of International Law* 335.

taking responsibility for them was inescapable, however long after the fact'.[98] In this sense, '*in theory*, neither space nor time will provide escape from responsibility'.[99] An additional consideration is the time of the crime itself with many categories of offence, such as enforced disappearances or use of children to participate actively in hostilities, not to mention sustained aggression against the territory of another state, being of a continuing nature. Against this background, which may include chronic civil unrest, various factors coalesce to determine the right time to initiate prosecutions. These range from the legal to the purely political and include multiple, often competing interests of victims, civil society, the United Nations and other international organisations, government officials, and finally, alleged perpetrators, who may themselves be existing, former, or future government officials. The German concept of *Tatferne* provides a procedural measure of the length of time between the offence and the final judgment,[100] which assists in elucidating the operation of the maxim 'justice delayed is justice denied' in terms of the time within the story. The procedural right to be tried without undue delay does not directly incorporate a right to be brought to justice within a reasonable time following the alleged offence, although this time lag, viewed from the perspective of victims and communities affected by the criminal conduct, is still captured by the maxim. The lifespan of the suspects and witnesses is an important factor in determining whether criminal justice may be pursued at all.

The Extraordinary Chambers in the Courts of Cambodia (ECCC), mandated to try 'senior leaders of Democratic Kampuchea and those who were most responsible for the crimes and serious violations of Cambodian [and international law] committed during the period from 17 April 1975 to 6 January 1979', commenced its work a generation after the crimes in 2006, in accordance with an agreement between the UN and the government of Cambodia.[101] The ECCC's public website has a section titled 'How long will the trials take?'[102] The answer is vague. It 'depends on the time required' to try cases in accordance with international standards, given that '[l]egal processes take time'. Indeed, the ECCC did not complete its judicial caseload until 2022, by which point only one of the original five accused, which had included four surviving senior Khmer Rouge leaders and the head of the

98 De Baets, 'The View of the Past in International Humanitarian Law' (n 10) 1595.

99 Report of the Special Rapporteur on the promotion of truth, justice, reparation and guarantees of non-recurrence, Pablo de Greif, UN Doc. A/HRC/30/42 (7 September 2015), para. 48 (emphasis added).

100 Nuremberg Report (n 14) 9.

101 Law on the Establishment of the Extraordinary Chambers, with inclusion of amendments as promulgated on 27 October 2004 (NS/RKM/1004/006), Article 1.

102 <www.eccc.gov.kh/en/faq/how-long-will-trials-take> accessed 2 September 2024.

notorious Tuol Sleng prison, remained alive, raising the question of whether this amounted overall to a denial of justice.

Nonetheless, if the focus shifts from linear time represented by *Tatferne* towards the narrative of the Khmer Rouge period examined and re-examined in the courtroom, a different temporal perspective emerges. Arguably, however delayed, and however imperfect, the ECCC was justice just in time. The story of suffering from the 1970s was transported to the present, where surviving victims could confront the living ghosts of genocidal policymakers, history could be re-examined and re-defined as dynamic truth, and domestic and international society could reckon with causes and consequences, regrets and resolutions. While the ECCC may be at the limit of chronologically delayed justice that is not substantially denied justice, most international or hybrid tribunals that focus on the architects of the atrocities have been established years, if not decades, after the events. An agreement to establish the Extraordinary African Chambers within the courts of Senegal to prosecute international crimes committed in Chad between 7 June 1982 and 1 December 1990 was signed in 2012. This followed complex negotiations as to how to try the former president of Chad Hissène Habré, who had been residing in Senegal since his fall from power. Proceedings against Habré concluded in 2017, with his sentence of life imprisonment for war crimes, crimes against humanity, and torture being affirmed on appeal.[103]

As these examples suggest, sometimes justice according to the time within the story can only be achieved because of delay, or despite delay. There is no '"Goldilocks zone", no perfect moment when prosecutions should start'.[104] However, various factors help sketch the temporal boundaries of the zone in which justice may be deemed delivered in spite of delay. It is useful to frame these factors as *aetia*, as they serve to connect the past, present, and future, always circling back to original causes. In this sense, the past provides the backdrop for an evaluation of delay in the present.[105]

The first factor concerns the context of the armed conflict or situation of serious human rights violations. It may be termed the story of origin of the crime. Indeed, *aetia* have frequently been employed to explain the causes of war in historiography.[106] The word itself 'has the active meaning of "accusation" "complaint" "grievance" and the corresponding passive meaning "guilt" "blame" "responsibility"; and by logical development it also means "that which

103 *Ministère Public c. Hissein Habrè*, Jugement (30 May 2016) (Chambre Africaine Extraordinaire d'Assises); *Le Procureur Général c. Hissein Habrè*, Arrêt (27 April 2017) (Chambre Africaine Extraordinaire d'Assises d'Appel).

104 Kersten, 'Justice for War Crimes in Ukraine Must Not Be Delayed' (n 4).

105 Harder, 'The Invention of Past, Present and Future in Callimachus' "Aetia"' (n 46) 290.

106 See Walter, *Time in Ancient Stories of Origin* (n 45) 6–7, referring to the work of Herodotus and Thucydides.

is responsible" – the "cause"'.[107] The 'sword' may return where conflicts remain unresolved and impunity reigns.[108] The question of who shot down Rwandan president Habyarimana's plane in 1994, triggering the genocide, remained disturbingly present throughout proceedings before the ICTR. Similarly, the question whether genocide occurred in Rwanda remained open to litigation until, in 2006, judicial notice was taken of the fact that '[b]etween 6 April 1994 and 17 July 1994, there was a genocide in Rwanda against the Tutsi ethnic group'.[109] Notably, the ICTR Appeals Chamber commented that the basic facts were known at the time of the tribunal's establishment, but that it had nonetheless been 'valuable for the purpose of the historical record' to document the course of the genocide according to the evidence in the trials.[110] This repeated return to the original context of the atrocities had not been time wasted, even if the fact of the Rwandan genocide was only judicially labelled 'a part of world history' in 2006.[111]

The second factor relates to what is often presented as the peace-versus-justice conundrum, in other words, the sometimes-conflicting schedules of ending a conflict and ensuring accountability. This could be described as the story of origin of peace and stability. In principle, an ongoing conflict should not preclude justice. According to the UN Secretary-General, '[j]ustice, peace and democracy are not mutually exclusive objectives, but rather mutually reinforcing imperatives'.[112] The ICC 'was created on the premise that justice is an essential component of a stable peace'.[113] Instability may, however, impact on the gathering of evidence, and while this occurs, criminal regimes often endure. If there has been a transition to a new regime, delayed prosecutions may enable 'perpetrators to outlast the political cycle that discredited them and permitted their indictment'[114] and even to become more popular than

107 Lionel Pearson, 'Prophasis and Aitia' (1952) 83 *Transactions and Proceedings of the American Philological Association* 205.

108 See also De Baets, 'The View of the Past in International Humanitarian Law' (n 10) 1587: 'Memories of past wars linger on. They constitute a major factor to reckon with for anyone engaged in conflict resolution'.

109 *Prosecutor v Karemera*, ICTR-98–44-AR73(C), Decision on Prosecutor's Interlocutory Appeal of Decision on Judicial Notice (16 June 2006), para. 35.

110 *Prosecutor v Karemera* (n 109).

111 *Prosecutor v Karemera* (n 109).

112 Report of the Secretary general on the Rule of Law and Transitional Justice, S/2004/616 (23 August 2004), 1. See also Christine Bell, 'The "New Law" of Transitional Justice' in Kai Ambos, Judith Large and Marieke Wierda (eds), *Building a Future on Peace and Justice: Studies on Transitional Justice, Conflict Resolution and Development: The Nuremberg Declaration on Peace and Justice* (Springer 2009) 120: 'the choice is increasingly seen as "how much accountability when" rather than a choice between some and none.'

113 Office of the Prosecutor, Policy Paper on the Interests of Justice (September 2007), 8.

114 Mark Osiel, 'The Banality of Good: Aligning Incentives against Mass Atrocity' (2005) 105 *Columbia Law Review* 1751, 1807.

their accusers.[115] McAuliffe, however, points to examples of 'post-transitional justice'[116] in Latin America that belie the 'article of faith that justice delayed is justice denied',[117] arguing that it may be appropriate to move justice further down the temporal track to account for other relevant interests, such as stability and re-establishment of the rule of law.

An important aspect is the preference of local populations, which may or may not be matched with the preference of governments and may shift over time.[118] Two examples from the ICC illustrate the point. There was apparently widespread domestic support for the investigation into post-election violence in Kenya in 2010 opened on a proprio motu basis by the ICC Prosecutor. Yet two of the alleged perpetrators, Kenyatta and Ruto, were subsequently voted into the Kenyan government.[119] It may be difficult for international prosecutorial bodies to keep up with these changing perspectives without engaging in a potentially controversial re-prioritisation of investigations that itself denies justice to a subset of victims. The return to Taliban rule in Afghanistan in 2021, 20 years after the previous Taliban regime had been ousted in a US-led invasion, led to a re-prioritisation of the ICC's investigation and an amendment to its scope.[120] The passage of time may make it more difficult to justify 'reopening' an investigation, especially if the case has been 'settled' at a political level. It may be precisely in those instances where 'public interest and support shifts to other priorities, and indicted fugitives burrow ever deeper into safe havens to avoid arrest',[121] that delayed justice becomes necessary to counter an earlier denial of justice.

A third, related factor is the gathering of sufficient evidence to justify the issuing of an arrest warrant or indictment and to make a fair trial possible. This could be termed the story of origin of the charges. Ukraine is grappling with tens of thousands of case files alleging war crimes during Russia's full-scale invasion commencing in February 2022 and dating back to its annexation of Crimea in 2014.[122] Domestic trials have taken place, often

115 Osiel (n 114).

116 Paloma Aguiler, 'Transitional or Post-Transitional Justice? Recent Developments in the Spanish Case' (2008) 13(4) *South European Society and Politics* 417.

117 McAuliffe, 'Justice Delayed Is Justice Developed' (n 5) 323.

118 Jaya Ramji-Nogales, 'Bespoke Transitional Justice at the International Criminal Court' in Christian De Vos, Sara Kendall and Carsten Stahn (eds), *Contested Justice: The Politics and Practice of International Criminal Court Interventions* (CUP 2015) 111–12.

119 Ramji-Nogales (n 118).

120 See Judgment on the Prosecutor's appeal against the decision of Pre-Trial Chamber II titled 'Decision pursuant to article 18(2) of the Statute authorising the Prosecution to resume investigation', Situation in the Islamic Republic of Afghanistan, ICC-02/17–218 (4 April 2023).

121 Scheffer, 'The Fate of Justice in Russia-Ukraine Peace Talks' (n 87).

122 'Ukraine Probing over 122,000 Suspected War Crimes, Says Prosecutor' *Reuters* (23 February 2024).

in absentia, while the ICC, which also has jurisdiction, has so far issued arrest warrants against six high-ranking suspects.[123] There is clearly a sense of urgency in this situation, driven by Western support for Ukraine. If sufficient evidence is available and domestic institutions remain strong and functioning, it may be advantageous to conduct trials during a protracted conflict to bring timely justice to victims while crime scenes are undisturbed and eyewitnesses are available. Additionally, it may be important to signal to those in a leadership position that they are not above the law.[124] It may, however, be disadvantageous if potential witnesses are concerned for their own survival and a fair trial cannot be guaranteed for accused persons, some of whom may be prisoners of war.

Until recently, Syria was engulfed in conflict after the authority of President Bashar al-Assad was threatened in 2011. In the absence of ICC jurisdiction,[125] the International, Impartial and Independent Mechanism (IIIM) was established by the UN General Assembly in 2016 'to assist in the investigation and prosecution of persons responsible for the most serious crimes under International Law committed in the Syrian Arab Republic since March 2011'.[126] In this respect, the importance of timely documentation and cooperation with the directly affected states as well as interested states who may choose to exercise universal jurisdiction is well-recognised, even if trials only become possible much later.[127] Some cases against Syrian officials have been conducted

123 See Andrew S. Bowen and Matthew C. Weed, 'War Crimes in Ukraine' *Congressional Research Service* (16 October 2023); Sergey Vasiliev, 'The Reckoning for War Crimes in Ukraine Has Begun' *Foreign Policy Analysis* (17 June 2022). See also Human Rights Council, Conference room paper of the Independent International Commission of Inquiry on Ukraine, A/HRC/52/CRP.4 (29 August 2023), para. 844: 'One of the main challenges for the Office of the Prosecutor General is addressing the large number of registered cases relating to the armed conflict. . . . For any prosecution office anywhere in the world, this number of registered crimes would be a challenge to investigate and, if sufficient evidence exists, to prepare cases for trial and subsequent legal proceedings.'

124 McAuliffe, 'Justice Delayed Is Justice Developed' (n 5) 296–7, summarises some of the arguments in favour of expeditious prosecution, such as minimising reprisals, responding to the outrage of victims when it is at its most intense, and restoring the rule of law.

125 A draft resolution to refer the situation in Syria to the ICC was brought before the Security Council in 2014 but failed due to negative votes cast by Russia and China. See UN Press Release SC/11407 (22 May 2014).

126 Resolution adopted by the General Assembly on 21 December 2016, A/RES/71/248 (11 January 2017).

127 See also Resolution adopted by the Human Rights Council on 27 September 2018, A/HRC/RES/39/2 (3 October 2018), para. 22, establishing 'an ongoing independent mechanism to collect, consolidate, preserve and analyse evidence of the most serious international crimes and violations of international law committed in Myanmar since 2011, and to prepare files in order to facilitate and expedite fair and independent criminal proceedings, in accordance with international law standards, in national, regional or international courts or tribunals that have or may in the future have jurisdiction over these crimes, in accordance with international law'. Ben Kiernan, 'Documentation Delayed, Justice Denied: The Historiography

in domestic courts under the principle of universal jurisdiction,[128] and France has issued an arrest warrant against Assad himself.[129] Meanwhile, Syria was re-admitted to the Arab League in May 2023.[130] It has been suggested in relation to Ukraine that it may be necessary to 'play the long game' as it concerns bringing the Russian political and military leadership to justice before the ICC.[131] However, the situation in Syria is a reminder that waiting too long carries the risk of it being game over.

Conclusion

In J. G. Ballard's short story *Chronopolis*, the protagonist, Conrad, questions why clocks have been outlawed. He says to his teacher, 'It's against the law to have a gun because you might shoot someone. But how can you hurt anybody with a clock?' His teacher responds that you can time a person with a clock and know exactly how long it takes to do something. Conrad is still confused, and his teacher continues: 'Then you can make him do it faster.'[132] On the occasion of the 25th anniversary of the establishment of the ICC, Japan's permanent representative to the UN invoked the maxim 'justice delayed is justice denied', emphasising the need to expedite the court's work in the interests of victims because '[i]n any fight against impunity, the clock is always ticking'.[133] Steps have been taken to accelerate international justice,

of the Cambodian Genocide' in Dan Stone (ed), *The Historiography of Genocide* (Palgrave Macmillan 2008) 468.

128 The Higher Regional Court of Koblenz – Eyad A. case, (unofficial translation available at the website of the IIIM: <https://iiim.un.org/wp-content/uploads/2023/02/1StE3_21-Judgment_Unofficial-IIIM-Translation_EN.pdf> accessed 2 September 2024); Hannah El-Hitami, 'Anwar Raslan's Conviction: "The Beginning of a Wider Struggle"' *JusticeInfo.net* (20 January 2022) <www.justiceinfo.net/en/86775-anwar-raslan-conviction-beginning-wider-struggle.html> accessed 2 September 2024.

129 Kim Willsher, 'French Court Issues Arrest Warrant for Bashar al-Assad for Complicity in War Crimes' *The Guardian* (15 November 2023) <www.theguardian.com/world/2023/nov/15/french-court-arrest-warrant-bashar-al-assad-crimes-against-humanity-syria> accessed 2 September 2024; David Gritten, 'French Court Confirms Bashar al-Assad Arrest Warrant Over Syria Chemical Attack' *BBC News* (26 June 2024) <www.bbc.co.uk/news/articles/cn0090vrxgwo> accessed 2 September 2024.

130 Philip Loft, 'Syria's Civil War in 2023: Assad Back in the Arab League' *House of Commons Library Research Briefing* (9 June 2023).

131 Christopher Hale and Leila Nadya Sadat, 'How International Justice Can Succeed in Ukraine and Beyond' *Just Security* (14 April 2022) <www.justsecurity.org/81086/how-international-justice-can-succeed-in-ukraine-and-beyond/>.

132 J. G. Ballard, *The Complete Short Stories* (vol 1, Fourth Estate 2001) 207.

133 Statement by H.E. Ambassador Ishikane Kimihiro, Permanent Representative of Japan to the United Nations, at the United Nations Security Council Arria Formula Meeting '25th Anniversary of the Rome Statute: The Contribution of the International Criminal Court to the Maintenance of International Peace and Security' (18 July 2023) <www.un.emb-japan.go.jp/itpr_en/ishikane071823.html> accessed 2 September 2024.

without reducing the quality of the justice delivered, by introducing procedural rules aimed at efficiency.[134] Yet however much international criminal justice tries to move faster, there is a growing acceptance that delays may be proportionate and necessary.[135]

The ticking clock can hurt the conception of justice in this sphere if the interplay between the time it takes to tell the story of extraordinary crimes and the time within the story is ignored. As Conrad's teacher implies, making people and processes move faster can lead to negative outcomes. Different conceptions of temporality apply to the reading or hearing of the evidence in court, where the 'narrated action moves forward in a linear way'[136] and the identification of the right time to initiate a process or opportune moment to carry out an arrest. Kersten states that 'the dilemmas involved in the duration and timing of justice require more critical attention beyond the fancy rhetoric of "justice delayed is justice denied"'.[137] In a similar vein, Guillou highlights the need to 'standardize our conception of time, our measurement of time and our appreciation of time'[138] in the field of international criminal justice. While 'standardization' and 'measurement' convey the clinical undertones of 'clock time', 'appreciation' may be facilitated by a greater emphasis on the time within a story of injustice.

The right time to redress past injustice may or may not be during a period of present injustice, as no two situations are identical 'in the realm of peace and justice'.[139] Protracted conflicts tend to lead to protracted processes of justice, while incomplete justice may lead to renewed, often delayed attempts at achieving justice.[140] Viewed as a masterplot, the maxim 'justice delayed is justice denied' ensures that the ticking clock remains audible in the corridors of international criminal courts and tribunals while leaving the definition of 'undue delay' open to interpretation, depending on the circumstances. Al-

134 Guillou, 'Time and International Criminal Justice' (n 11) 287: '[S]trengthening efficiency without jeopardizing the quality of justice is perhaps the main challenge of judicial globalization.'

135 'A crime extraordinaire, temporalité extraordinaire, quitte à ce que les coûts soient considérables.' ('Extraordinary crimes mean extraordinary temporality even if the costs are considerable.') Guillou, 'Time and International Criminal Justice' (n 11) 291. See also James Meernik and Rosa Aloisi, 'Is Justice Delayed at the International Criminal Tribunals?' (2008) 91(6) *Judicature* 276, 277.

136 Walter, *Time in Ancient Stories of Origin* (n 45) 18.

137 Kersten, 'Charles Taylor Verdict: Some Thoughts and Controversies' (n 70).

138 Guillou, 'Time and International Criminal Justice' (n 11) 287.

139 Scheffer, 'The Fate of Justice in Russia-Ukraine Peace Talks' (n 87).

140 For example, human rights organisations called for a reopening of an investigation into the killings of six Kosovo Albanian civilians by Yugoslav Army troops in the Montenegrin village of Kaludjerski Laz in 1999. S. Kajosevic, 'Montenegro Urged to Reinvestigate 1999 Killings of Kosovo Albanians' *Balkan Insight* (18 April 2023) <https://balkaninsight.com/2023/04/18/montenegro-urged-to-reinvestigate-1999-killings-of-kosovo-albanians/> accessed 2 September 2024.

though the maxim is considered to capture both 'the time of the reading or hearing of a narrative and the temporal configuration within it',[141] it has limitations as a masterplot in the latter aspect as it fails to accommodate all the characteristics of international justice that make 'delay' integral to it. This is not to exclude the operation of the maxim as a masterplot altogether with respect to the timing of justice, since it incentivises stakeholders to overcome the forces and vulnerabilities that risk tipping delayed justice into no justice at all. Just as a narrative becomes spatialised when it 'looks backwards or forwards . . . or . . . is structured not so much by sequence and causality, but by repetition, gradation, or juxtaposition',[142] so might delay be regarded as a spatialised notion as it concerns the timing of justice. Such an appreciation makes the maxim 'justice delayed is justice denied' less about time than about the story, a story that resounds now as if it had been told then.

141 Walter, *Time in Ancient Stories of Origin* (n 45) 18.
142 Walter, *Time in Ancient Stories of Origin* (n 45) 18.

Part 5

Law, peace, and order

Chapter 9

The masterplot of 'Hoffmann's Bargain' in protest trials

Steven Cammiss and Graeme Hayes

Introduction

In February 2006, the House of Lords heard an appeal by 20 nonviolent direct action and disobedience (NVDAD[1]) activists.[2] The activists had been convicted and conditionally discharged for various offences of aggravated trespass or criminal damage at Marchwood military port facility and RAF Fairford in February and March 2003, immediately prior to the start of the US/UK invasion of Iraq. The appellants argued that their convictions were unsound, on the basis that the invasion of Iraq was illegal under international law,[3] thereby meaning that (1) they had a lawful excuse,[4] (2) they used reasonable force to prevent crime,[5] and (3) their actions were justified under the common law defence of necessity. The Lords dismissed the appeal, finding the public international law crime of aggression not to be a crime under domestic law, and thus, there was no crime that the activists were seeking to prevent.

This ruling is perhaps most interesting, and certainly most influential, for how the courts have subsequently dealt with NVDAD protest, given the comments by Hoffmann LJ on the place of civil disobedience. Examining 'the limits of self-help'[6] in the context of s3 of the 1967 Act (the use of 'reasonable

1 While terminology is important, in that it reflects different conceptions of protest and its place in democratic society, this is something we do not seek to address in detail here. Our work largely concerns the trials of activists and how the courts respond to protest. The distinctions between protest, civil disobedience, and NVDAD matter less, as the courts do not draw these distinctions. But for a recent exploration of 'disruptive protest' and its relationship to different conceptions of action, see Oscar Berglund, 'Disruptive Protest, Civil Disobedience and Direct Action' (2023) 45(2) *Politics* 239.
2 *R v Jones* [2006] UKHL 16.
3 As a 'crime of aggression' under Article 5 of the Rome Statute of the International Criminal Court.
4 Criminal Damage Act 1971, s1.
5 Criminal Law Act 1967, s3.
6 *Jones* (n 2) [70]–[94].

DOI: 10.4324/9781003404668-14

force'), Hoffmann LJ stated that the convictions would have been safe even if aggression had been a crime in domestic law,[7] as in a democratic state, 'the citizen is not entitled to take the law into his own hands'.[8] He stated:

> [C]ivil disobedience on conscientious grounds has a long and honourable history in this country. People who break the law to affirm their belief in the injustice of a law or government action are sometimes vindicated by history. The suffragettes are an example which comes immediately to mind. It is the mark of a civilised community that it can accommodate protests and demonstrations of this kind. But there are conventions which are generally accepted by the law-breakers on one side and the law-enforcers on the other. The protesters behave with a sense of proportion and do not cause excessive damage or inconvenience. And they vouch the sincerity of their beliefs by accepting the penalties imposed by the law. The police and prosecutors, on the other hand, behave with restraint and the magistrates impose sentences which take the conscientious motives of the protesters into account.[9]

Initially considered *obiter*, Hoffmann LJ's reasoning nonetheless proved influential, providing the courts with a means of resolving the tension between upholding the criminal law and protecting the Articles 10 and 11 ECHR rights of NVDAD protesters. We have termed this balancing act 'Hoffman's Bargain',[10] the Bargain being that NVDAD protesters, where they act with restraint, can expect to be treated with leniency at sentencing, thus avoiding the imposition of custodial sentences. But the Bargain is not just leniency in exchange for restraint; its central premise involves the acceptance of conviction by defendants and the systemic removal of defences that might otherwise be available to justify their actions. Consequently, a defence of necessity or the prevention of crime will not be available to protest defendants; 'the issue of justification should be withdrawn from the jury'.[11]

This is problematic, in that NVDAD activists are unlikely to accept sanctions, at least a priori.[12] For example, Howard Zinn, writing in the context of the US civil rights movement, states:

> If the social function of protest is to change the unjust conditions of society, then that protest cannot stop with a court decision or a jail sentence. If

7 *Jones* (n 2) [88].
8 *Jones* (n 2) [84].
9 *Jones* (n 2) [89].
10 Steven Cammiss, Graeme Hayes and Brian Doherty, 'Necessity, Non-Violent Direct Activism, and the Stansted 15: Reasserting "Hoffmann's Bargain"' (2022) 85(6) *Modern Law Review* 1515.
11 *Jones* (n 2) [94].
12 We will return to this; see n 74 and following text.

> the protest is morally justified (whether it breaks a law or not) it is morally justified to the very end, even past the point where a court has imposed a penalty. If it stops at that point, with everyone saying cheerfully, as at a football match, 'Well, we played a good game, we lost, and we will accept the verdict like sports' – then we are treating social protest as a game. It becomes a token, a gesture. . . . The sportsmanlike acceptance of jail as the terminus of civil disobedience is fine for a football game, or for a society determined to limit reform to tokens. It does not suit a society which wants to eliminate long-festering wrongs.[13]

Following the case of NVDAD defendants known as the Stansted 15, which we discuss later, the Court of Appeal held that Hoffmann LJ's observations were not *obiter* but part of the *ratio* of *Jones*.[14] This post-*Thacker* logic is neatly articulated in a pre-trial ruling against NVDAD defendants from the climate disobedience group Insulate Britain, handed down by HHJ Reid at Inner London Crown Court in November 2022. HHJ Reid, quoting Hoffmann LJ, summarised the position thus: defendants 'are not permitted to break the criminal law . . . and avoid conviction due to their motivations in acting the way they did';[15] '[i]t is for politics to decide the merits of deeply held beliefs not the Courts'.[16] When Insulate Britain defendants chose not to heed this ruling and attempted to explain their motivations to the jury, HHJ Reid imposed custodial sentences for contempt of court.[17]

Hoffmann's Bargain as masterplot

In this chapter, we consider the ideological function of Hoffmann's Bargain, developing the idea of this Bargain as an organising frame, or plot device, which has a strategic purpose. 'Plot is the knowing of destination', as

13 Howard Zinn, *Disobedience and Democracy: Nine Fallacies on Law and Order* (South End Press 1968/2002) 30 and 31.

14 *Thacker and ORS* [2021] EWCA Crim 97. For our commentary see, Graeme Hayes, Brian Doherty and Steven Cammiss, 'The Stansted 15 Appeal: A Hollow Victory for the Right to Protest?' *The Conversation* (10 February 2021) <https://theconversation.com/the-stansted-15-appeal-a-hollow-victory-for-the-right-to-protest-154694> last accessed 11 September 2024; and Cammiss, Hayes and Doherty (n 10).

15 We obtained the unpublished trial judge's ruling in the case, *Adams and ORS*, 'Ruling on Defences/Abuse/ETC' 31 October 2022 [79].

16 *Adams and ORS* (n 15) [88].

17 'Insulate Britain Activist Jailed for Eight Weeks for Contempt of Court' *The Guardian* (7 February 2023) <www.theguardian.com/environment/2023/feb/07/insulate-britain-activist-david-nixon-jailed-for-eight-weeks-for-contempt-of-court> last accessed 11 September 2024; 'Insulate Britain Protesters Jailed for Seven Weeks for Mentioning Climate Change in Defence' *itv.com* (3 March 2023) <www.itv.com/news/london/2023-03-03/insulate-britain-protesters-jailed-after-flouting-court-order-at-trial> last accessed 11 September 2024.

Elizabeth Bowen puts it,[18] serving to provide a repeating resolution structure from the combination of four broad elements: origins, characters, action, and destiny.[19] Plots are dialogic; they enable us to make sense of experience, identify causal chains, and make events meaningful.[20] They do so in response to the various situational, ideological, or aesthetic imperatives that guide their organisation and structure.[21] Emplotment may therefore have a collective identity-building function: abbott defines these plots as *masterplots*, or recurrent skeletal stories which are 'narrativized over and over again because they engage conflicts that seem to be a permanent part of our circumstances as human beings'.[22] Masterplots, in other words, are cultural structures which powerfully explain *who we are*. Moreover, they 'are fictions that privilege specialised ways of thinking, particularized ways of feelings and normalized ways of being, establishing nothing more than an artificially imposed order'.[23] But even as fictions, retellings 'in turn strengthen and recreate the narrative from which they are spawned'.[24]

Plots are differentiated from narratives and discourses as they provide causal structures linking characters and events; masterplots are skeletal, or abstracted, as they transcend their specific storytelling instantiations to situate and reproduce a particular shared cultural identity. Masterplots, therefore, function ideologically to create collective (imagined) communities, held together by the 'cultural glue' of stories with shared values, beliefs, and fates.[25] We can say that as plots are to story, masterplots are to myth; myth 'supplies models for human behavior and, by that very fact, gives meaning and value to life' through the sacralisation of culturally significant, exemplary stories;[26] 'myth not only authorizes or validates customs, rites, institutions, beliefs, and so forth, but frequently is directly responsible for creating them'.[27] As such, they are a 'means of acting upon the present'.[28] We can

18 Cited in Kieran Egan, 'What Is a Plot?' (1978) 9(3) *New Literary History* 455.

19 Eliade notes that fairy tales, one form of myth, proceed as an initiatory scenario, through three stages: initiatory ordeals, the descent to Hades or the ascent to Heaven, marrying the princess: Mircea Eliade, *Myth and Reality* (Harper & Row 1963) 201.

20 Egan (n 18) 470.

21 Hayden V. White, *Tropics of Discourse: Essays in Cultural Criticism* (Johns Hopkins University Press 1978).

22 H. Porter Abbott, *The Cambridge Introduction to Narrative* (2nd edn, CUP 2008) 195.

23 Bruce A. Arrigo, 'Identity, International Terrorism and Negotiating Peace: Hamas and Ethics-Based Considerations from Critical Restorative Justice' (2010) 50(4) *British Journal of Criminology* 772, 776.

24 Matthew J. Fraidin, 'Stories Told and Untold: Confidentiality Law and the Master Narrative of Child Welfare' (2010) 63(1) *Maine Law Review* 1.

25 Porter Abbott (n 22) 47.

26 Eliade (n 19) 2.

27 Raphale Patai, *Myth and Modern Man* (Prentice-Hall 1972) 2.

28 Patai (n 27) 2–3.

therefore understand the centrality of masterplots to mythmaking, in that they organise the forward motion of generative character types, drawn along identifiable lines of good and evil, legitimate and illegitimate, whose actions have broad cultural resonance and moral force.[29]

Here, we argue that Hoffmann's Bargain is such a masterplot, carrying a specific social purpose, on two levels. First, it – at least superficially – propagates a national myth of the importance of collective action for social and democratic progress. We can see from the passage cited earlier that Hoffmann's Bargain is organised, or plotted, in three parts: an origin story ('civil disobedience . . . of this kind'), a set of character types and action templates ('But there are conventions . . . damage or inconvenience', and again, 'The police . . . with restraint'), and a resolution structure which satisfies the preceding conditions ('And they vouch . . . imposed by the law', and again, 'and the magistrates . . . into account').[30] This myth is structured around the democratic legitimacy of judicial institutions, which can accommodate popular demands, notably through their own community representative composition.

There is, however, a further level to this emplotment. Though Hoffmann's Bargain seems to recognise and support the importance of militant unruliness for social progress, it instead imposes an artificial and arbitrary separation between the legal and the political, recognising the 'good', or deserving, protester as one accepting legal sanction. Second, therefore, the Bargain operates with the ideological imperative of *forestalling* political challenge, evacuating context and meaning from the courtroom, which becomes a hostile space for defendants seeking to justify their actions. The Bargain's emplotment achieves this through a series of oversights, misrecognitions, and silences, where 'civil disobedience', as Hoffmann LJ constructs it, is an invented tradition[31] whose original story establishes specific system-conforming features. On top of this origin story, Hoffmann LJ transposes the liberal assumptions of John Rawls's political theory[32] to privilege an abstract and restrictive model of legal accountability over a fluid, open, and dialogic model vested in actually available judicial processes. To show how this works, let us start at the beginnings.

Beginnings: the primordial event

In *Myth and Reality*, Eliade emphasises that *myth* is considered to be a 'true history' because it tells of things which have come to be, with actually existing

29 For an example of a masterplot being central to the framing of social problems, here the masterplot of environmental degradation, see Jedediah Purdy, 'The Politics of Nature: Climate Change, Environmental Law, and Democracy' (2010) 119(6) *Yale Law Journal* 1122.

30 *Jones* (n 2) 89.

31 Eric Hobsbawm and Terence Ranger (eds), *The Invention of Tradition* (CUP 2012).

32 John Rawls, *A Theory of Justice* (Harvard University Press 1971).

realities.[33] Myths are, in this sense, origin stories. Indeed, origins are central to the definition of myth; for Eliade, a *myth*

> narrates a sacred history, it relates an event that took place in primordial Time, the fabled time of the 'beginnings'. In other words, myth tells how, through the deeds of Supernatural Beings, a reality came into existence, be it the whole of reality, the Cosmos, or only a fragment of reality – an island, a species of plant, a particular kind of human behavior, an institution. Myth then is always an account of a 'creation'; it relates how something was produced, began to *be*.[34]

Myth's function is thus to identify and relate generative events as true and sacred: true in that they create observable realities, sacred in that these realities were formed by forces or beings which – at least in modern secular society, rather than by what Eliade identifies as 'supernatural beings' in what he terms 'primitive cultures' – enjoy popular and institutional legitimacy. For Eliade, 'every origin myth narrates and justifies a "new situation". . . . [T]hey tell us how the world has changed'.[35] For Patai:

> To know how the present world order came into being, what or who caused it, and what is its meaning is of primary significance, because only a correct understanding of those long past events can enable man to take his proper place and fulfil his proper role in the circumstances brought about by those primordial events.[36]

Origin stories, then, 'connect past and present, clarify the meanings of important events, reaffirm core norms and values, and assert particular understandings of social order and individual identity'.[37]

It is instructive to turn to the origin story that Hoffmann LJ selects to establish the 'new situation', concerning the importance of NVDAD to social progress, the suffragettes:

> [C]ivil disobedience on conscientious grounds has a long and honourable history in this country. People who break the law to affirm their belief in the injustice of a law or government action are sometimes vindicated by history. The suffragettes are an example which comes immediately to mind.[38]

33 Elide (n 19) 6.
34 Elide (n 19) 5–6.
35 Elide (n 19) 21.
36 Patai (n 27) 71.
37 David M. Engel, 'Origin Myths: Narratives of Authority, Resistance, Disability, and Law' (1993) 27(4) *Law & Society Review* 785.
38 *Jones* (n 2) [89].

This is a curious choice of primordial event, even if we restrict the 'long and honourable history' of disobedient social challenge within the development of modern parliamentary democracy. Not curious because the women's suffrage movement has not been vindicated by history; that is certainly true. Rather, it is curious that Hoffmann LJ should situate the relationship between social challenge and democratic progress as a story of self-limiting action, and that he should associate this development with the militancy of the Women's Social and Political Union (WSPU). There are two broad reasons for this. First, it downplays the significance of key movements of the nineteenth century, particularly abolitionism and Chartism. Chartism, indeed, was 'the last working-class movement in Britain in which economic and political issues were inseparable'[39] and arguably has a stronger claim for the importance of extra-parliamentary radicalism to the extension of democratic rights. Second, it erases the importance of social violence to the claiming and securing of moral and material rights in Britain (again, here we could cite many instances from the Chartist movement: for example, Monmouth's Shire Hall is now dedicated to telling the story of its role as the courthouse for the last mass treason trial held in mainland Britain, in 1839–40[40]). These factors are sufficiently well-known, and there is not space or need to go into them. What is worth further discussion here is the characterisation of the WSPU as an exemplar of self-restraining civil disobedience.

Civil disobedience: Hoffmann via Rawls

In his classic work of liberal political philosophy, *A Theory of Justice*, John Rawls defines *civil disobedience* as 'a public, nonviolent, conscientious yet political act contrary to law usually done with the aim of bringing about a change in the law or policies of the government'.[41] Civil disobedience is a public act, concerned with and guided by principles of collective justice; it is 'addressed to public principles, it is done in public', openly and with fair notice, and it is neither covert nor secretive.[42] Nor is it violent: to be civil, disobedience cannot interfere with the civil liberties of others; to be sincere and concerned with justice, it must display a fidelity to law. Further, Rawls argues that civil disobedience 'may require a certain restraint',[43] to avoid the escalation of unlawful action which would cumulatively destabilise a constitutionally

39 Ellen M. Wood, *The Pristine Culture of Capitalism: A Historical Essay on Old Regimes and Modern States* (Verso 1991) 73.
40 See Ruth Waycott, Les James and Elin Hwyel, *Voices for the Vote: Shire Hall and the Story of Chartism in Wales* (Monmouthshire County Council 2011).
41 Rawls (n 32) 364.
42 Rawls (n 32) 364.
43 Rawls (n 32) 373.

democratic regime ('if they were all to act in this way, serious disorder would follow', there would be a 'danger of anarchy').[44]

This sense of restraint applies to the judicial process. Civil disobedience involves a series of moral obligations, including the acceptance of legal consequences:

> The law is broken, but fidelity to law is expressed by the public and nonviolent nature of the act, by the willingness to accept the legal consequences of one's own conduct. This fidelity to law helps to establish to the majority that the act is indeed politically conscientious and sincere, and that it is intended to address the public's sense of justice. . . . We must pay a certain price to convince others that our actions have, in our carefully considered view, a sufficient moral basis in the political convictions of the community.[45]

This, in turn, places obligations on public authorities:

> Courts should take into account the civilly disobedient nature of the protester's act, and the fact that it is justifiable (or may seem so) by the political principles underlying the constitution, and on these grounds reduce and in some cases suspend the legal sanction.[46]

Though Hoffmann LJ does not in *Jones* mention Rawls, Rawls's definition is highly consonant with Hoffmann LJ's position: central to the notion of civility, in Rawls's articulation, and the hallmark of the 'civilised community', as Hoffmann LJ has it, are the adoption of restraint in action and the acceptance of sanction following action, and the accommodation of the judicial process to these features.

The suffragettes

The suffragettes are, then, an odd choice for this framework. The movement's militant phase is generally accepted to have started in 1905, when Christabel Pankhurst spat on and struck two police officers in the face after disrupting a Liberal Party election rally at the Free Trade Hall in Manchester.[47] The subsequent period up to the outbreak of the First World War featured an escalating series of attacks on property: from late 1910, window-breaking

44 Rawls (n 32) 374 and 390.
45 Rawls (n 32) 366–7.
46 Rawls (n 32) 387.
47 Andrew Rosen, *Rise Up, Women! The Militant Campaign of the Women's Social and Political Union, 1903–1914* (3rd edn, Routledge 1974/2013) 49ff.

was a 'systematically organized' tactic,[48] the initial concentration on Whitehall and the homes of cabinet ministers giving way in November 1911 and March 1912 to mass 'smashing rampages' in West End shopping districts;[49] in November 1912, WSPU activists started a campaign of letter-burning, pouring acid and other substances into pillar boxes, in a move that Rosen identifies as a strategic switch from attempting to gain public sympathy to producing coercion through sabotage,[50] culminating in what Bearman identifies as a 'continuous campaign' of 337 acts of bombings or arson between the end of January 1913 and August 2014, at what he estimates to be a cost to the British economy of £1–2 million at that time.[51] During this final phase in particular, WSPU activists carried out their actions covertly and without warning.

Far from accepting conviction as the legitimate outcome of their actions, members of the WSPU used their trials as platforms for political advocacy. Between 1906 and 1912, the suffragettes developed two primary strategies: '[T]hey refused to acknowledge the authority of the courts in trying them for offenses related to their political agitation, and they used the courtroom as a site for narrating militancy's defense.'[52] This culminated in the May 1912 Conspiracy Trial at the Old Bailey, when Frederick Pethick Lawrence, Emmeline Pethick Lawrence, Emmeline Pankhurst, and Christabel Pankhurst (who escaped to Paris to avoid prosecution) were charged with conspiring to organise the West End 'smashing rampages'. Making their case to the jury, the defendants repeatedly argued their trial was political, securing widespread national and international support.[53] Typically, once tried, suffragettes refused payment of fines or giving sureties for good conduct, choosing prison instead; in prison, their disruptive campaign continued, challenging prison order, demanding the status of political prisoners, and after mid-1909, adopting a generalised campaign of hunger striking.[54] Following the introduction

48 Wendy Parkins, 'Taking Liberty's, Breaking Windows: Fashion, Protest and the Suffragette Public' (1997) 11(3) *Continuum: Journal of Media & Cultural Studies* 37, 39.

49 Jane Chapman, 'The Argument of the Broken Pane' (2015) 21(3) *Media History* 238, 244.

50 Rosen (n 47) 183–6.

51 Christopher J. Bearman, 'An Examination of Suffragette Violence' (2005) 120(486) *The English Historical Review* 365, 369–74.

52 Laura E. Nym Mayhall, *The Militant Suffrage Movement: Citizenship and Resistance in Britain, 1860–1930* (OUP 2003) 72.

53 Nym Mayhall (n 52) 78–82.

54 Kevin C. Smith, 'The Militant Suffragettes as a Police Problem: London, 1906–1914' (1978) 51(3) *Police Journal* 274; Leon Radzinowicz and Roger Hood, *A History of English Criminal Law and Its Administration from 1750: Volume 5: The Emergence of Penal Policy* (Stevens and Sons 1986) 439–61; June Purvis, 'The Prison Experiences of the Suffragettes in Edwardian Britain' (1995) 4(1) *Women's History Review* 103; Elizabeth Crawford, 'Police, Prisons and Prisoners: The View from the Home Office' (2005) 14(3–4) *Women's History Review* 487, 498–502.

in April 1913 of the Prisoner's (Temporary Discharge for Ill Health) Act, or Cat and Mouse Act, as it was known, released suffragettes frequently evaded recapture by changing identities, going into hiding, or fleeing abroad.

The suffragettes, then, do not fit into the template of restraint and acceptance of sanction advocated by Hoffmann LJ. Neither, importantly, do public authorities who responded through a series of tactical and legal innovations, including the development of surveillance technologies, such as fingerprinting and photography. Perhaps the most well-known aspect of this is not just the introduction of brutal force-feeding of hunger-striking prisoners in September 1909 but the Cat and Mouse Act itself, which allowed for the early release of prisoners who were weak or at risk of death but who could be recalled to prison upon recovery. For this to work, the police required new and expanded covert surveillance resources.[55] The release of severely ill prisoners on condition of their future compliance was not simply an act of clemency but introduced a regime of surveillance and 'threatened coercion', adding 'a potentially sinister weapon to the control of political dissidents'.[56] Again, this is hard to square with the claim that social progress was achieved through self-limiting protest accompanied by an accommodatory state response.

A more obvious reading of the suffragette movement as foundation story is that gaining social progress – even (or perhaps especially) the type of ultimately limited progress which, from the vantage point of the early twenty-first century, appears *perfectly compatible* with the prevailing political and economic power structure – can *only be achieved* through the sort of sustained militant action campaign undertaken by the WSPU, where disruption and challenge do not stop at the point of intervention by the criminal justice process. We can be reasonably confident that Hoffmann LJ was familiar with at least the broad details of the suffragette campaign, as well as Rawls's widely accepted definition of *civil disobedience*. We can perhaps assume, therefore, that what makes it attractive to Hoffmann LJ as an exemplar of action is not the actual disruptive power of the campaign itself but, rather, what have proven to be the consensual, system-strengthening effects associated with the constrained political reform it achieved.

Character and action

So far, three things should be readily apparent: (1) Hoffmann LJ's commentary is strongly located in a Rawlsian normative framework; (2) this Rawlsian

55 Crawford (n 54) 492–5; Linda Mulcahy, 'Docile Suffragettes? Resistance to Police Photography and the Possibility of Object – Subject Transformation' (2015) 23 *Feminist Legal Studies* 79.

56 Radzinowicz and Hood (n 54) 460.

framework is culturally translated by Hoffmann LJ through a series of misrecognitions of how social change takes place and collective actors act; (3) the combination of these two elements works together with an overarching purpose, plotting a specific course for the regulation of protest in the English and Welsh courts and, in so doing, foreclosing alternative emplotments of the relationship between NVDAD protest and social change. In the next two sections, we will focus in greater depth on how Hoffmann's Bargain moves from the misdirection of its origin story towards its knowledge of destination, first by focusing on character and action, and in the next section, on resolution.

Porter Abbott argues that criminal trials are open to being read as structured around cultural masterplots, as the prosecution attempts to establish the accused's motivation, and situate their character within a framework that can be understood by a jury as that required to commit a given criminal act. To do this, characters are rendered as types: recurrent, familiar, and prejudicial, transcending a given instance, whose identity is already known.[57] Hoffmann's Bargain is explicitly and distinctly structured around this question of character:

> [T]here are conventions which are generally accepted by the law-breakers on one side and the law-enforcers on the other. The protesters behave with a sense of proportion and do not cause excessive damage or inconvenience. . . . The police and prosecutors, on the other hand, behave with restraint.[58]

This sense of character has two evaluative components. The first focuses specifically on self-limitation: to qualify for the Bargain, the action must not be adjudged violent, and any disruption must not be deemed excessive. But the sense of proportion, at least as far as this concerns the protest defendants, is not simply a question of the character of action; it is, in its second evaluative component, also a question of the character of the defendants.

Character and the Stansted 15

We can illustrate this by turning to the case of the Stansted 15, briefly outlined earlier, and in which the Court of Appeal[59] ruled that Hoffmann LJ's observations on protest formed part of the *ratio* of *Jones*. In this case, a group of NVDAD protesters were found guilty by a jury at Chelmsford Crown Court in December 2018 of the terrorism-related offence of the 'intentional disruption of services at an aerodrome' so as to 'endanger the safe operation

57 Porter Abbott (n 22) 185–9.
58 *Jones* (n 2) 89.
59 *Thacker* (n 14).

of the aerodrome or the safety of persons';[60] they had, in March 2017, cut through the perimeter fence of Stansted airport and locked on around the wheels and wings of a parked Home Office–chartered Boeing 767, scheduled to deport 60 detainees from an immigration removal centre. At the end of their ten-week trial, the judge ruled, citing *Jones*, that there was no evidential basis for the defence of necessity, despite allowing the defendants to give testimony as to their motives. Consequently deprived of a defence and having accepted that they had participated in the action (if not the offence) for which they were being prosecuted, the defendants were found guilty. The maximum penalty for this offence is life imprisonment; at sentencing, defendants with previous convictions for aggravated trespass arrived with suitcases, expecting to be taken directly to prison. Yet HHJ Morgan, sentencing, imposed no custodial terms, instead handing down a range of community service orders and (for three) suspended prison sentences of nine months.

We might consider this, therefore, to be a textbook example of the emplotment of Hoffmann's Bargain: defendants who had staged their action in such a way as to ensure they would be arrested (by locking themselves together under the aircraft), accepting their participation in the action, were unable to put forward a defence in law for their action and received lenient sentences. Of course, we could – and should – argue that the bringing of a terrorism-related offence for this type of action breaks the terms of the Bargain and is an act of prosecutorial, judicial, and governmental bad faith (or to put it another way, highly repressive and anti-democratic overreach). But this also serves to underline the power of the Bargain, as the sentences handed down bore no relation to the formal gravity of the offence.

In order to understand this outcome, we need to focus not just on action but on motivation and, therefore, *character*, on what it means to 'behave with a sense of proportion'.[61] The first element of this concerns the open nature of the action itself: arrest (and therefore public evaluation) was factored in from the start. But further elements became particularly clear at trial. As we argue in detail elsewhere, under the pressure of potential life sentences, the defendants sought to justify their actions by arguing that the disruption they had caused was proportionate to the harms they had sought to avoid, and they contrasted their humanitarian objectives with the cruelty and irrationality of the UK detention and deportation system, and the dangers into which this system was knowingly placing deportees.[62] In court, they presented their action as an act of necessity motivated by an apolitical ethics of care.[63] They

60 Aviation and Maritime Security Act 1990, s1(2)(b).

61 *Jones* (n 2) [89].

62 Graeme Hayes, Steven Cammiss and Brian Doherty, 'Disciplinary Power and Impression Management in the Trials of the Stansted 15' (2021) 55(3) *Sociology* 561.

63 Hayes, Cammiss and Doherty (n 62) 561.

presented themselves through acts of self-regulation, complying with the spatial and expressive orders of the court, or what we call in Foucauldian terms the disciplinary regime of the courtroom: 'dedramatising, suppressing their emotional expressivity: speaking sincerely, with moderation, responding to the leads given by counsel, they did not seek to disrupt or challenge the reproduction of authority in court.'[64] They denied their motivations were political, whilst those who had previous convictions – 8 of the 15 – did not testify in court, in case their prior direct action histories pointed towards political continuities rather than an exceptional intervention and become, in legal terms, a point of 'bad character'.[65]

Character is thus central and produced as reasonableness and conscientiousness. In other words, for the Bargain to be available, the defendants must act with integrity throughout: it is the qualifying threshold for consideration. Yet this integrity is not available as *political* consistency: it must be primarily moral, organised around the fates of individuals rather than policy choices or social structures, and must be available only exceptionally, axiomatically associated with good character. Neither is integrity available within the scope of a legal defence to the charge: it cannot constitute a lawful justification for action, only mitigation of it. The trial did not afford, therefore, a space for political challenge; indeed, the potentially political content of the act was a disqualifying feature, forming the basis of prosecutorial cross-examination, repeatedly denied by the defendants, but ultimately cited by the trial judge as the reason for withdrawing the defence of necessity from the jury.[66] The Court of Appeal ultimately agreed that the appellants' activities 'had to be considered in the context of a functioning state governed by the rule of law';[67] in this context, rather than rely upon direct action, the appellants could only rely upon lawful and proper channels in order to achieve their goals.

Resolution

This relationship between conscientiousness, compliance, and leniency is made explicit where Hoffmann LJ turns to the final destination of the Bargain's emplotment:

> And they vouch the sincerity of their beliefs by accepting the penalties imposed by the law . . . and the magistrates impose sentences which take the conscientious motives of the protesters into account.[68]

64 Hayes, Cammiss and Doherty (n 62) 574.
65 Hayes, Cammiss and Doherty (n 62) 574.
66 Cammiss, Hayes and Doherty (n 10).
67 *Thacker* (n 14) [101].
68 *Jones* (n 2) [89].

The emphasis that Hoffmann LJ places on accepting sanction is, as noted earlier, thoroughly inconsistent with its origin story: militant suffragettes evaded arrest, fled abroad, demanded to be classified as political prisoners, went on hunger strike, evaded recapture, and even where arrested and incarcerated, continued to engage in a series of everyday resistances against state power. We may consider this inconsistency in itself to be revealing: the narrative arc that Hoffmann LJ sets out is implicitly transformative, producing a pacification (at least in its discursive treatment) of the unruly subject, taking what is threatening to the social order (militant refusal) and turning it into foundational system compliance (the long course of social amelioration through uncontested standards of reasonableness).

Here, Hoffmann LJ's emphasis is once again consistent with the definition of *civil disobedience* as set out by Rawls, particularly the requirement that protesters display a fidelity to law and the mechanisms of democratic governance. As noted earlier, the acceptance of guilt is central to this equation. Rawls, for his part, recognises and warns against the 'anarchy' of individual citizens doing 'as they please'; the decision to engage in civil disobedience must therefore be a careful one, which sets aside personal interest and starts from a strong presumption of duty to comply with the law.[69] Only where the potential disobedient is satisfied that their action is compatible with constitutional principles should they act:

> If he [sic] comes to the conclusion after due consideration that civil disobedience is justified and conducts himself accordingly, he acts conscientiously. And though he may be mistaken, he has not done as he pleased. The theory of political duty and obligation enables us to draw these distinctions.[70]

This leaves an unanswered question: what is the mechanism for deciding whether an act of disobedience is justified? Rawls, earlier, allows for the disobedient to be conscientious but mistaken, yet there is no collective mechanism for deciding whether they are, or are not, mistaken; rather, there is an abstract set of first principles governing the decision to commit to action, to be taken by each in conscience, associated with an appeal to the electorate as a whole as final arbiter.[71] Further, Rawls argues that 'we must pay a certain price' to show that our actions have 'a sufficient moral basis in the political convictions of the community'.[72]

This view is, as befits its location in political theory, an abstracted one: it does not exist in the realm of empirical behaviours, or in the material

69 Rawls (n 32).
70 Rawls (n 32) 389.
71 Rawls (n 32) 389–90.
72 Rawls (n 32) 367.

processes of legal arbitration, or in the concrete circumstances of the political community. The law is represented as standing outside the political fray, whereas in reality, legal actors, be they police officers, prosecutors, or judges, are actors in a wider political process. Yet even within political theory, it is an approach that is contested.[73] Unsurprisingly, therefore, the view that 'we' must pay the price of accepting sanction is rarely shared by NVDAD activists themselves.[74]

For Zinn,[75] accepting sanction as an automatic and unchallenged outcome and as an end point of struggle is to reduce protest to a symbolic gesture, rather than the kind of sustained protest that is necessary to produce social change; without belabouring the point further, we may readily see how the refusal to play the game underscores, for example, the history of suffragette action. Yet Hoffmann LJ does more than simply transpose Rawls. Rawls, as noted, is concerned with abstract principles; Hoffmann LJ, in his translation of Rawls, is concerned with actually existing social histories and actually available means of legal adjudication. Hoffmann LJ's retelling of Rawls is thus faithful, but its emplotment also involves the subtraction of the jury as democratic arbiter, dissociating NVDAD from its potential legal justification and expressly separating legal and political spheres. Its logical resolution is that NVDAD defendants are left with no defence in law and must either accept guilt or present their action in court in the hope of securing a 'not guilty' verdict through the means of jury nullification.[76] Leniency at outcome does not just have formal conditions, concerning non-violence, or self-limitation of action, therefore; it is, rather, dependent upon the exclusion of the political from the legal process, an exclusion that supports a view of the legal as transcending the political. The law, therefore, is represented as being outside of politics, even when the operation of the law is political; politics, as the contestation of values (in this case through law), denies and effaces its true existence.

This resolution structure, therefore, points us towards a third evaluative component concerning character and self-limitation, which we can see more easily when we turn back again to Rawls. For Rawls, 'civil disobedience used with due restraint and sound judgment helps to maintain and strengthen just institutions'.[77] In this reading, direct action protest is not valuable because it

73 See, for instance: Kimberley Brownlee, *Conscience and Conviction: The Case for Civil Disobedience* (OUP 2012); Candice Delmas, *A Duty to Resist: When Disobedience Should Be Uncivil* (OUP 2018).

74 See Zinn (n 13).

75 Zinn (n 13).

76 For a treatment of whether defendants can lawfully call for nullification, see Kay Crosby 'When the Parties Call for Jury Nullification' in Nicola Monahan (ed), *Contemporary Challenges in the Jury System: A Comparative Perspective* (Routledge 2024).

77 Rawls (n 32) 383.

can effectively challenge power, bring about social change, or reorder social relations; rather, it is valuable insofar as it is able to contain collective resistance within the scope of existing institutional arrangements. The conduct of protest must, in other words, be compatible with the maintenance of public order and can be tolerated only so far as it is compatible with this order, not just in its action, but in its sensibility as expressed through character. For Illan Wall, public order is constructed through affective relations, where it is 'an everyday experience of sovereignty, where the sovereign order claims the peace and calm atmosphere of public space as an iteration of its glory and good government'.[78] In the masterplot of Hoffmann's Bargain, proportion and restraint, in deed and in self-presentation, are the affective regime of the constituted order. Here, the courthouse functions as a site of disciplinary power, enforcing the character of protest so that it cannot produce radical reconfigurations of the public order.

Discussion

The emplotment we saw earlier in Hoffmann's Bargain is one means of understanding the place of protest within liberal democratic states. Other alternatives are possible. These could recognise that democratic institutions are the result of successive waves of direct action, that protest self-limitation is not necessarily central to the historical development of these institutions or to progressive social change, and that moral adjudication is central to the operation of judicial institutions, which, as such, are always political.

But before we sketch out these alternatives, two things should detain us. The first is that the notion of restraint applies asymmetrically. The penalties for defendants for not behaving with restraint are clear, but there are no penalties if the police, prosecution, or courts do not keep their side of the Bargain. The second is that the game itself is asymmetrical. One could, following the previous logic, argue that recent charging and court decisions are only illiberal in that they are contingent; they are less determined by Hoffmann's Bargain than they are by the rise of a new majoritarian conservatism. Yet this would be to miss the structuring implications of Hoffmann's Bargain. By imposing conditions of action and specified outcomes of criminal trials, Hoffmann's Bargain serves to structurally deprive both defendants (through the removal of the availability of defences) and juries (through the consequent removal of their legal capacity to evaluate the facts in their full context, and thus act as a collective community counterweight to state overreach) of their democratic capacity. Elsewhere, we map what we describe as the integrity principle, which calls for trials to operate in a manner that allows protest defendants to speak in ways that are consistent with their political aims and

78 Illan Rua Wall, *Law and Disorder: Sovereignty, Protest, Atmosphere* (Routledge 2021) 9.

philosophical beliefs, and to do so within the terms of legal justification.[79] But for this to happen, Hoffmann's Bargain, as a masterplot, needs to be reconfigured in ways that value the place of protest in democratic states, so as to recognise that protest is inherent in democratic processes, rather than outside them.[80]

This all presupposes a shadow question: well, what are these alternatives?[81] As noted previously, there is perhaps no need to propose an alternative foundation myth to the suffragettes: the problem is not with the origins myth itself but with the misdirection central to Hoffmann LJ's plotting of the myth. Nevertheless, we may also consider that other masterplots are available, founded in the 'long and honourable history' of conscientious objection in Britain which Hoffmann LJ claims to celebrate and which have had direct and highly significant consequences for the way the courts deal with social challenge. We have sketched out some of these alternatives earlier, for instance, noting how Chartism has a particular claim on our imagination due to its importance in the extension of democratic rights through a mass movement, and the importance of social violence in the gaining of rights.

But the emplotment in Hoffmann's Bargain is also doubly curious in that other well-known foundational myths are available, ones that are far more closely aligned to the role of the courts in protecting civil liberties. One possible grounding of Britain's long and honourable history of protecting conscientious actors concerns the trial at the Old Bailey in 1670, where Quakers William Penn and William Mead were tried on the charge of seditious libel, for preaching nonconformist religious views. As is well-known, the jury refused to convict and, as a consequence, were fined, imprisoned for refusing to pay the fine, and released after a writ of habeas corpus; the case has, therefore, become a landmark decision for jury nullification.[82] 'Bushel's case' establishes juries as the embodiment of popular liberties in the face of authoritarian control. This masterplot produces a very different organisation of character and outcome: character is formed from a steadfast maintenance of collective principles, rather than their abnegation in restraint; the outcome is not the pre-ordained acceptance of judicial sanction but, rather, the presentation of contextualised evidence to the community as embodied by the jury. This mythos does not depend on restraint but on expression. As noted earlier,

79 Steven Cammiss, Graeme Hayes and Brian Doherty, 'Defending the Integrity Principle: Necessity, Remorse, and Moral Consistency in the Protest Trial' (2025)*Oxford Journal of Legal Studies* (online first).

80 Tabatha Abu El-Haj, 'Defining Nonviolence as a Matter of Law and Politics' in Melissa Schwartzberg (ed), *Protest and Dissent: Nomos LXII* (New York University Press 2020).

81 As we are mapping Hoffmann's Bargain as a masterplot, we can only provide a sketch of an answer here.

82 Kay Crosby, 'Bushell's Case and the Juror's Soul' (2012) 33(3) *The Journal of Legal History* 251.

we argue that the defendant's political integrity as well as their moral consistency should be at the heart of the protest trial, so that defendants should not have only to rely upon jury nullification but also be able to call upon defences which allow for their philosophical beliefs to be legally relevant to the proceedings as a prospective justification.[83] The emplotment central to Hoffmann's Bargain does not allow for this to happen.

Conclusion

In this chapter, we have examined Hoffmann's Bargain as a masterplot for the criminal trials of protesters. We have shown how this Bargain is structured to include four basic interlinked moves: a misrecognition of past struggle, an 'invented tradition' of Britishness, a narrative of a deserving protester, and the application of leniency to ensure 'script compliance'. We will summarise each of these moves next.

First, Hoffmann's Bargain misrepresents the nature of past struggle in Britain; in particular, through the selection of what we have shown to be a curious example on which to base the 'honourable history' of civil disobedience, the suffragette campaign, it evacuates this campaign of both its radical action repertoire and its refusal of institutional adjudication. As we noted, Hoffmann's Bargain omits reference to the WSPU; there is a strategic forgetting of the violence inherent in the WSPU's campaign methods, such as letter-burning, 'smashing rampages', and sabotage. There was, in short, an absence of 'proportionality' on the part of the WSPU. But there was also an absence of 'restraint' on the part of public authorities, through the actions of force-feeding and the enactment and operation of the Cat and Mouse Act.

Second, Hoffmann's Bargain develops an 'invented tradition' of Britishness, where social change is produced through restraint and mutual understanding, depriving the British history of protest of its radical, conflictual, social revolutionary, and system-challenging traditions. We have noted how this framing silences other possibilities that would highlight the place of mass popular working-class movements (Chartism, the trades union movement), which sought to radically reconfigure the state. This silencing produces a particular masterplot of how social progress is created; it is not the result of mass mobilisation and struggle (sometimes violent) but is instead through the extension of the franchise in response to middle-class militancy.

Third, Hoffmann's Bargain creates a narrative of the good and deserving protester, who may be dealt with leniently by the public authorities, and thus

83 Cammiss, Hayes and Doherty (n 79). We recognise that this goes against the default position in criminal law which seeks to restrict the availability of necessity-based defences. We do not here, however, have the space to expand on our argument as to why defences should be more widely available in NVDAD cases.

implicitly creates the binary opposite of the bad and undeserving protester, who is not rooted in historical processes of British state and identity formation, and who will not be treated leniently, and must face penalties because of their character and beliefs, rather than for the actions for which they are being prosecuted. We are currently seeing the culmination of this in the increasing use of custodial sentences for NVDAD protest.[84]

Fourth, the final move in Hoffmann's Bargain, the application of leniency at sentencing, is not, we consequently argue, a move designed to uphold freedom of expression; rather, it is an integral and *path-determining* step in a series of decisions designed to silence unruly actors, limiting their capacity to justify their own disruptive action and effectively enforcing 'script compliance' at trial as the central element of the Bargain.

The consequences of Hoffmann's Bargain as a masterplot for the treatment of NVDAD cases are clear. It operates in a manner that provides a scaffolding for the non-availability of the defences to social movement actors, leaving defendants without a justification in law for their actions. Defendants are only able to rely on jury nullification, with some trial judges drawing upon contempt proceedings to ensure that defendants are not able to explain their motives and philosophical beliefs.[85] This masterplot, therefore, serves ideologically to reduce and contain the rights and freedoms of expression and assembly, under cover of an invented tradition of collective national identity. As a consequence, its strategic social purpose is to disarm the very form of collective action that it claims to protect.

84 For instance, see the long prison sentences handed down in the case of the JSO 5, who were told they crossed the line from campaigners to 'fanatics': 'Five Just Stop Oil Activists Receive Record Sentences for Planning to Block M25' *The Guardian* (18 July 2024) <www.theguardian.com/environment/article/2024/jul/18/five-just-stop-oil-supporters-jailed-over-protest-that-blocked-m25> last accessed 11 September 2024. For our commentary, see Graeme Hayes and Steven Cammiss, 'Just Stop Oil's Harsh Sentences are the Logical Outcome of Britain's Authoritarian Turn Against Protest' *The Conversation* (19 July 2024) <https://theconversation.com/just-stop-oils-harsh-sentences-are-the-logical-outcome-of-britains-authoritarian-turn-against-protest-235148> last accessed 11 September 2024. While the Court of Appeal subsequently reduced their sentences, they remained substantial and in the range from 30 months to 4 years. See, *Hallam and ORS* [2025] EWCA Crim 199.

85 See (n 17) and associated text.

Chapter 10

International law's narrative of order, peace, and justice in light of the concept of masterplot and Franz Kafka's *The Castle*

Ekaterina Yahyaoui Krivenko

Introduction

International law, from its inception, is propelled by the grand narrative of the promotion and maintenance of order, peace, and justice. The cornerstone document of modern international law, the Charter of the United Nations, explicitly combines these three objectives into an apparently coherent narrative.[1] The Charter was drafted at the end of the Second World War, by 50 states that met at the San Francisco conference from 25 April to 26 June 1945, in the desire to ensure lasting peace and to prevent the atrocities of the war from re-occurring.[2] Thus, the preamble of the UN Charter affirms the determination 'to promote social progress and better standards of life in larger freedom', thus also marking the future-oriented nature of its purposes. The purposes formulated in Article 1 of the UN Charter emphasise such elements of progress towards order, peace, and justice as 'solving international problems of an economic, social, cultural, or humanitarian character',[3] 'development of friendly relations',[4] and promotion of human rights and fundamental freedoms.[5] The establishment of order as a function of international law dominates the landscape of the UN purposes, since the main function of the UN as an organisation is the prevention of war. The drafting history of the Charter demonstrates the extent to which this function, at times, even triumphed over progress- and justice-oriented goals, especially as they relate to human rights.[6] By bringing together order, peace, and justice in one sin-

1 Charter of the United Nations, adopted 26 June 1945, XV UNCIO 335, amendments in 557 UNTS 143, 638 UNTS 308 and 892 UNTS 119.

2 Some key structural elements of the future Charter were put in place before the conference through a series of agreements reached between Allied powers from 1941 onwards. See United Nations Documents, 1941–1945 (Royal Institute on International Affairs, 1947).

3 UN Charter, Art 1(3).

4 UN Charter, Art 1(2).

5 UN Charter, Art 1(3).

6 Katarina Mansson, 'Reviving "the Spirit of San Francisco": The Lost Proposals on Human Rights, Justice and International Law to the UN Charter' (2007) 76(2–3) *Nordic Journal of International Law* 217. See also discussion of the divide between justice (especially human

DOI: 10.4324/9781003404668-15

gle future-oriented narrative, international law creates a strong mechanism that prevents or at least complicates, critiques, neutralises the revolutionary potential of contestations and limits their ability to introduce change in the international law system as a whole.[7]

These three interrelated functions of international law, presented as a unified narrative, are easily accepted as a truthful reflection of international law's goals and functions in the mainstream representations of international law, for example, in manuals of international law intended for students: future international lawyers.[8] Thus, one of the widely used manuals intended for international law students opens with the statement: 'In the long march of mankind from the cave to the computer a central role has always been played by the idea of law – the idea that order is necessary and chaos inimical to a just and stable existence.' It then highlights that international law fulfils the same function in interstate relations, thus setting the tone and the general approach for the entire study of international law by future international lawyers.[9] Critical strands of international legal scholarship have demonstrated from various perspectives that international law is unable to live up to any of the promises of this narrative.[10] They have demonstrated, for example, either incoherence or indeterminacy of international law as a project.[11] However, even the most fervent critics of international law often find themselves, perhaps inadvertently, rephrasing this narrative in alternative ways. For example, in one of his writings, Martti Koskenniemi, one among the two most preeminent critical legal scholars in the field of international law,[12] after persuasively

rights) on the one hand and order and avoidance of war on the other, discussed from international relations perspective, in Hedley Bull, *The Anarchical Society: A Study of Order in World Politics* (Red Globe Press 1977) 74–94.

7 Within the framework of this chapter, it is impossible to provide a detailed justification of this statement and bring in practical examples. In the remainder of this section, the justification of this statement is approached through the prism of selected scholarly assessments of international law.

8 See, for example, Malcolm N. Shaw, *International Law* (9th edn, CUP 2021) 1–2; James Crawford, *Brownlie's Principles of Public International Law* (9th edn, OUP 2019) 18–19. Another interesting example is Jan Klabbers, *International Law* (3rd edn, CUP 2020), where the author affirms that the book proposes 'a more or less critical angle' (22) to international law but concludes with the same reaffirmation of the international law's narrative (356).

9 Malcolm N. Shaw, *International Law* (7th edn, CUP 2014) 1.

10 The range of critical approaches to international law is quite broad today and encompasses without being limited to feminist, queer, third-world approaches to international law. For a recent overview of the most popular, see part III in Jeffrey L. Dunoff and Mark A. Pollack (eds), *International Legal Theory: Foundations and Frontiers* (CUP 2022).

11 See, for example, Andrea Bianchi's interpretation of critical international legal theory, according to which David Kennedy represents the former strand, while Martti Koskenniemi the latter: Andrea Bianchi, *International Law Theories: An Inquiry into Different Ways of Thinking* (OUP 2016) 151–2.

12 The second is David Kennedy. See, for example, Bhupinder S. Chimni, *International Law and World Order: A Critique of Contemporary Approaches* (2nd edn, CUP 2017) 246. See also similarly Bianchi (n 7) 145.

demonstrating the emptiness of the UN purposes of achieving peace and justice and describing international law as a simple argumentative practice, still finds space to save the unity of its narrative. This occurs in the context of his answer to the question 'What is international law for?', which is the title of the chapter. In providing an answer, Koskenniemi affirms that international law has four specific purposes. Two of them are particularly notable for the present discussion. First is that

> international law's value and its misery lie in its being the fragile surface of political community among social agents . . . who disagree about their preferences but do this within a structure that invites them to argue in terms of an assumed universality.[13]

In the next sentence, which also forms the beginning of the next paragraph, he states: '[I]nternational law exists as a promise of justice.'[14] It is one thing to say that international law is an argumentative practice, another to go a step further and postulate that this argumentative practice has an underlying structure and value, a value that coincides with its postulated functions and goals of order, peace, and justice: a 'promise of justice', in Koskenniemi's words. In this context, the question arises: what makes the narrative of international law's purposes and goals so persuasive that even its most stringent critics have difficulty rejecting this narrative entirely? The answer can, of course, relate to many factors, including human psychological needs.[15] This chapter provides an answer to the question by deploying the concept of masterplot as an explanatory device. It will be argued that international law's narrative is based on a particularly skilful deployment of the form of masterplot, not one of the widely known literary masterplots.[16] This form of masterplot operates at a meta-level and could be called the masterplot of masterplots. It is revealed with exemplary lucidity in Kafka's novel *The Castle*. Therefore, to demonstrate how masterplot is mobilised by international law to secure the persuasiveness of its narrative, the chapter resorts to an analysis of Franz Kafka's novel *The Castle*.

Franz Kafka (1883–1924), writing in German but residing in Prague, was a lawyer and is considered today as one of the most illustrious writers of the twentieth century.[17] His novel *The Castle* was written between January and

13 Martti Koskenniemi, 'What is International Law For?' in Malcolm Evans (ed), *International Law* (5th edn, OUP 2018) 32, 52.

14 Koskenniemi (n 13).

15 Anja Van den Broeck, 'A Review of Self-Determination Theory's Basic Psychological Needs at Work' (2016) 42(5) *Journal of Management* 1195–229.

16 As described, for example, in Ronald B. Tobias, *20 Master Plots and How to Build Them* (3rd edn, Penguin 2012).

17 There are many biographical works on Franz Kafka's life. See, for example, Jeremy Adler, *Franz Kafka* (Overlook Press 2004).

July 1922 but never finished.[18] It remained in unfinished manuscript form until his death and was first published posthumously by his friend Max Brod in 1926.[19] Brod made some decisions about how to organise the manuscript, what to include: decisions which were questioned by subsequent researchers.[20] Therefore, later editions of the novel vary somewhat, and translations of the novel into English are also quite diverse, adding to this multiplicity of versions.

The remainder of the chapter first introduces the concept of masterplot and the way it is understood for present purposes. The use of Kafka's work, and especially of his novel *The Castle* as a bridging device enabling the connection between the idea of masterplot and the field of international law as a discipline, is also justified on this occasion. The next section discusses the approach to the concept of masterplot in *The Castle*, further justifying the use of that novel as a lens through which to analyse the key question of this chapter about the endurance of international law's narrative. The chapter then proceeds to the analysis per se, discussing how Kafka's approach to writing in *The Castle* reveals the power of international law's narrative emerging from a specific deployment of masterplot. This analysis proceeds in two steps. In the first step, the focus is on the substance or subject matter of *The Castle*. In the second step, more formal, style-related aspects of the approach to writing in *The Castle* are discussed. Final reflections on the possibility of avoiding masterplot as an instrument of power are offered.

On the concept of masterplot

If we recognise narrative as an instrument of power which leads us to see life from a particular angle that normalises some behaviours, events, and perspectives while condemning others – as extensively discussed by such thinkers as Althusser, Bakhtin, or Foucault,[21] to name just a few – then we must ask the question about the reasons for the power of narratives. One

18 The start of the writing coincides with Kafka's travel to Spindlermühle, which occurs on 27 January 1922 (see on this Roland Reuß, 'Das Schloss. Zur Einführung' in *Franz Kafka Das Schloss. Historisch-kritische Edition sämtlicher Handschriften, Drucke und Typoskripte*, Franz Kafka-Heft 9 (Stroemfeld Verlag 2018) 3). The specific date when Kafka stopped writing *The Castle* is more difficult to determine. There is a hypothesis that this was somewhere in July, but a later date in August or September 1922 is more probable according to Reuß. For details, see Reuß (n 18) 5–7.

19 Franz Kafka, *Das Schloss* (Kurt Wolff Verlag 1926).

20 Two most controversial decisions were the exclusion of the first four pages of the manuscript as well as the division in chapters and tiles of chapters. Both are discussed in Reuß (n 18) 8–18.

21 Instead of many, see an informative summary in Gregory Castle, *The Literary Theory Handbook* (Wiley Blackwell 2013) 75–84, where these thinkers are situated within the historical development of the theory of the novel, highlighting Bakhtin's dialogical and, thus, social view of the narrative; Foucault's insights on discourse and, thus, narrative as a disciplinary

of the widely accepted explanations for the power of narratives centres on the role of masterplots. At a very basic level, Abbott defines masterplots as 'recurrent skeletal stories, belonging to cultures and individuals that play a powerful role in questions of identity, values, and the understanding of life'.[22] A key element of masterplots as explanatory devices for the power of narrative relates to the meaning of 'master' in 'masterplot'. This meaning has three connotations which are not separate but sustain and support one another. The first and most obvious meaning is that of 'dominant', 'governing', or 'prevailing'. This meaning is supported by the second, which relates 'master' in 'masterplot' to the idea of the original in the sense of establishing or pointing out to origins, emergence, or genesis of something, thus also fundamentality or the foundationalist claim of masterplots. These two meanings together position any masterplot as a matrix with a high capacity to be reproduced. The positioning of a particular narrative as a masterplot remains dependent on the frequency of this reproduction,[23] which refers to the third meaning of 'master' in 'masterplot'. These three aspects lend any masterplot a superior power of persuasiveness in specific cultural contexts and add credibility to narratives structured according to masterplots.[24] It has been successfully demonstrated that masterplots work even at a more unconscious level, satisfying our desires for stability, knowledge, and ending.[25] In this regard, Ricœur highlights an important aspect of masterplots. According to Ricœur, any masterplot (he refers to received paradigms) does not only operate in one direction but also affects the reader through a process that structures their expectations and furnishes guidelines for an encounter between the reader and the text, thus governing the story's capacity to be followed. In order to acquire all its power, the masterplot requires actualisation. This actualisation of the masterplot occurs through the reader, who actualises the story's capacity to be followed and, thus, all the powers of the masterplot.[26]

Kafka's work intervenes into this vision of narrative and the role of masterplot in an unconventional way. In general, Kafka's writings, whether literary (short stories, novels), personal (letters, diaries), or professional (submissions, speeches, and other documents produced in his capacity as a lawyer),

power; and Althusser's discussion of narratives as a vehicle of the political unconscious, with references to their key works.

22 H. Porter Abbott, *Cambridge Introduction to Narrative* (2nd edn, CUP 2008) 236.

23 Nicoló Crisafe, *Dante's Masterplot and Alternative Narratives in the Commedia* (OUP 2022) 10; Porter Abbott (n 22) 52–3.

24 Abbott (n 22) 52.

25 Peter Brooks, *Reading for the Plot: Design and Intention in Narrative* (Alfred A. Knopf 1984) for a general psychoanalytical approach to narrative and Frank Kermode, *The Sense of an Ending: Studies in the Theory of Fiction* (OUP 1967) where the need for ending and closure is emphasised.

26 Paul Ricœur, *Time and Narrative* (vol 1, Kathleen McLoughlin and David Pellauer tr, The University of Chicago Press 1984) 76.

continue soliciting numerous and often contradictory interpretations. The fact that his work attracted the attention of some of the most prominent postmodern and post-structuralist philosophers is also a testimony to the profound multivalence of his writing.[27] The multivalence and profundity of Kafka's work emerge not only from the content or meaning of his writing but also from Kafka's narrative style and form. Beicken straightforwardly affirms: 'Kafka's narrative rhetoric entails a radical critique of the traditional modes of storytelling and storytelling.'[28] Deleuze and Guattari famously oppose Kafka's writings as minor literature, as revolutionary conditions of any literature, to the mainstream tendencies within a great (or established) literature focusing on expression and non-representative use of language by Kafka.[29] I argue that, in this subversive, ambivalent, and critical writing style, Kafka offers a powerful tool to lay bare or dismantle the grandiose tendencies of masterplot. Using *The Castle* as the primary reference point, this chapter demonstrates that Kafka's achievement consists in revealing the absurdity of the claim to authority that underlies the 'master' in the masterplot. Some of the tools which enable Kafka to achieve this deconstruction of the masterplot are further explored in this chapter as a means to reveal the reasons for the persuasiveness of international law's narrative of order, peace, and justice.

The first reason for focusing on Kafka's *The Castle* resides in its exemplary unconventional narrative style, characterised as a 'strange loop' comparable to a Möbius strip.[30] *The Castle* is also a novel without ending, which creates an additional layer of complexity in interpreting its narrative, explains its power of fascination, but also sheds new light on the concept of masterplot itself. Kafka's unconventional approach to narrative in *The Castle* thus creates a particularly fertile ground for analysing the operation of conventional narratives and masterplots. Just as Kafka's work provides critical insights into the nature and operation of law and normativity,[31] it also offers new perspectives on the traditional construction of narratives according to the

27 Derrida's reflection on Kafka's parable *Before the Law* is perhaps among the best-known in this category (Jacques Derrida, 'Before the Law' in Derek Attridge (ed), *Acts of Literature* (Routledge 1992) 183). Other examples include, without being limited to, Giorgio Agamben, 'K.' in Giorgio Agamben (ed), *Nudities* (David Kishil and Stefan Pedatella tr, Stanford University Press 2011) 20; Theodor W. Adorno, 'Notes on Kafka' in Theodor W. Adorno (ed), *Prisms* (Sam and Shierry Weber tr, Spearman 1967); Gilles Deleuze and Felix Guattari, *Kafka: Towards a Minor Literature* (Dana Polan tr, University of Minnesota Press 1986).

28 Peter U. Beicken, 'Kafka's Narrative Rhetoric' in Angel Flores (ed), *The Kafka Debate: New Perspectives for Our Time* (Gordian Press 1977) 178.

29 Deleuze and Guattari (n 27) in general.

30 Jacob Burnett, 'Strange Loops and the Absent Centre in the Castle' in Stanley Corngold and Ruth V. Gross (eds), *Kafka for the Twenty-First Century* (Camden House 2011) 105, 107.

31 The literature analysing Kafka's work as providing powerful insights into law and normativity is quite extensive so cannot be fully covered here. For examples, see Robert P. Burns, *Kafka's Law – 'The Trial' and American Criminal Justice* (University of Chicago Press 2014)

masterplots of Western civilisation. The second reason for selecting *The Castle* resides in the affinity that this novel has with international law, as I have demonstrated elsewhere.[32] Both aspects of this affinity – those highlighted in my previous work and the novel aspects relevant to the discussion of masterplot in international law – are addressed later in this chapter. Applying critical insights emerging from *The Castle* in relation to the concept of the masterplot to international law's narrative – which, in turn, is critically reflected in the narrative of *The Castle* – enables an answer to the key question of the endurance of international law's narrative of order, peace, and justice.

About the 'masterplot' of *The Castle*

Before offering an interpretation of the masterplot in *The Castle*, a brief summary of the story is presented to better contextualise the discussion. The main protagonist of the story, a man named K., arrives at a village inn. The village itself belongs to a nearby castle, so that anybody staying in the village requires approval from the castle.[33] When questioned about his reasons for arriving at the inn and at the village, K. claims to have been summoned by the castle as a land surveyor. When one of the persons present (son of a castle warden) challenges K. and seeks confirmation through a phone call with the castle about the summoning of a land surveyor, he is first told that no record of such a summon exists. However, very quickly, a second call comes which confirms the summoning of the land surveyor. From this point on, the entire story revolves around K.'s efforts to acquire some form of access to the castle or its officials. The purpose of these efforts remains ambiguous. In English translations, it is variously referred to as a fight, a struggle, a combat, or even a challenge.[34] Sometimes a need to explain something or to acquire confirmation of something comes to the forefront. In both cases – whether we focus on the combat or on the need for a communicative exchange of some sort – it remains unclear what is the ultimate purpose either of the fight or of the communicative exchange. Given the opening of the story, at the

or Douglas E. Litowitz, *Kafka's Indictment of Modern Law* (The University Press of Kansas 2017).

32 Ekaterina Yahyaoui Krivenko, 'International Law, Literature and Interdisciplinarity' (2015) 9(1) *Law and Humanities* 103, 112, 115, 116, 118.

33 Franz Kafka, *The Castle* (Anthea Bell tr, OUP 2009) 5.

34 In the German text, the recurrent term is 'Kampf', and the diversity of translators' choices leads to the erosion of this lexical choice by Kafka. The closest English translation of 'Kampf' is either 'combat' or 'fight'. It is notable that when the phone call comes to the village inn confirming K.'s position as a land surveyor, K. regards this as a confirmation that the castle accepts 'den Kampf'. However, in the translation used here, this becomes acceptance of 'a challenge' (Kafka (n 33) 8), which has weaker connotations. When K. reflects on the first letter he received from the castle, in the German text again, he expresses the need to face 'den Kampf', which in the English translation becomes 'the danger' (Kafka (n 33) 25).

formal surface level, K.'s desire to acquire access to the castle could be understood as a search for official confirmation of his status as a land surveyor who can stay and live in the village. However, as the story evolves, even this interpretation becomes problematic. Therefore, K.'s attempts have been variously interpreted as a search for the self,[35] for God's blessing, salvation, or redemption,[36] or even as a 'subversive power aimed at the abolishment of the structures of sovereign power and the virtual state of exception',[37] to name some recurrent themes. Since the novel remains unfinished, we do not know whether K. was ever successful in his efforts. However, a report from Kafka's friend Max Brod informs us that Kafka shared with him his plans for the ending of *The Castle*:

> The alleged land-surveyor gains at least partial satisfaction. He does not slacken in his struggle, but dies of exhaustion. The community gathers round his death-bed, and just then the decision comes down from the Castle that although he has no legal claim to live in the village, nevertheless, in the light of certain circumstances, he is allowed to live and work there.[38]

Against this background of a multitude of interpretations, an answer to the question of what the plot or, indeed, the masterplot in *The Castle* is is not straightforward but multidirectional. The approach adopted here insists primarily on the political dimension of Kafka's writing and, more specifically, on reading Kafka's work as a critique of authority.[39] Fundamentally, the interpretation adopted here sides with those authors who see in Kafka's work a staunch denouncer of any authority, and thus an anarchist.[40] Given the preceding discussion of the concept of masterplot, this denunciation of authority by Kafka necessarily includes a deconstruction of masterplots and the very idea and concept of a masterplot itself. As I demonstrate using *The Castle* as an example, Kafka's literary work is, to a significant degree,

35 See, for example, form a psychoanalytical perspective, Peter Dow Webster, 'A Critical Examination of Fran Kafka's "The Castle"' (1951) 8(1) *American Imago* 35.
36 The most widely known promoter of the theological interpretations was Max Brod. For another example, see John Winkelman, 'An Interpretation of Kafka's "Das Schloss"' (1972) 64(2) *Monatshefte* 115.
37 Boštjan Nedoh, 'Kafka's Land Surveyor K. Agamben's anti-*muselmann*' (2011) 16(3) *Angelaki: Journal of the Theoretical Humanities* 149.
38 Max Brod, 'Nachwort' in Franz Kafka (ed), *Das Schloss* (Kurt Wolf 1926) 493. English translation is from Kafka (n 33) xxiv.
39 Most prominently, see Costas Despiniadis, *Anatomist of Power: Franz Kafka and the Critique of Authority* (Black Rose Books 2019). See also Walter Corbella, 'Panopticism and the Construction of Power in Franz Kafka's The Castle' (2007) 43(1) *Papers on Language and Literature* 68.
40 See, on this, Micheal Löwy, 'Franz Kafka et l'anarchisme' (2017) 21 *Raison Publique* 63.

an unveiling of the operation of authority where most already accepted this authority as a natural part of life and a depiction of the seamlessness, often invisibility, of that operation. As a writer, as a producer of narratives, Kafka is able to denounce authority in such a way as not to replace it with another authority, or one masterplot with another: it is a paradoxical revelation of a narrative without a masterplot. *The Castle* is not a standard narrative with a clear beginning and an end with a clear teleology or even a clear resolution of an enigma. This is not due exclusively to the unfinished nature of *The Castle*. Even if we consider the projected ending of *The Castle* as reported by Kafka to Brod, we still face an 'unfinished' storyline at the formal level (K.'s arrival and his quest for an admission to and an authorisation to stay in the village). In the reported ending, it is not possible to say that K. was entirely unsuccessful, because he does receive a special authorisation to stay in the village. However, it is impossible to say that he truly achieved what he aimed for, because this authorisation comes last minute, at his deathbed, when he really does not need it anymore; furthermore, it is only a provisional authorisation taking into account some special circumstance, not a recognition of a legal claim. Such special authorisations are volatile, as they can be retracted faster and easier than they were given. Depending on one's deeper interpretation of the story in theological or existential terms, one can even see the projected ending as an utter failure. This is the first element that enables Kafka to identify a line of escape from the 'master' in the masterplot.

Subversiveness in Kafka's works operates at least at two levels. First is the level of content of his literary works, including the storyline, and the possible interpretations of its meaning. This is the level with which many legal scholars who use literature in some way to illuminate their analysis of law are most familiar. For the purposes of this chapter, this will be referred to as the 'matter'. At the level of 'matter', the operation of the 'master' in the masterplot is most forcefully laid bare. The second level is less widely popularised among legal scholars and concerns Kafka's overall approach to writing, such as his style, expressions, use of language (or its formal side, therefore 'form' for short). The 'form' of Kafka's *The Castle* represents a true key entry point into the deconstruction of the concept of masterplot. By focusing on devices that enable Kafka to start a deconstruction of the very concept of masterplot, it is possible to formulate an explanation for the endurance of the dominant narrative of international law. Therefore, the discussion that follows first focuses on analysing the substance or 'matter' of *The Castle*'s narrative especially as it illuminates and reveals the operation of international law's narrative of order, peace, and justice. Thereafter, the analysis delves into the 'form'-related aspects, which offer insights into the possibility of a narrative without a masterplot, thus leading to an answer to the key question of this chapter about the endurance of international law's narrative.

The 'matter' of *The Castle* and of international law

Interpreted as a critique of authority, *The Castle* is particularly relevant to understanding international law because of the nature of authority depicted in it. International law is a peculiar branch of law inasmuch as it lacks some of the standard characteristics of law. For example, many who espouse John Austin's definition of *law* as a command backed by sanction, which is also a dominant everyday understanding of law, would deny that international law is truly law, due to lack of enforcement mechanisms in some areas and insufficiency of such mechanisms in others.[41] International law as a law agreed between equals (states) also lacks a clear centre of authority, unlike domestic legal systems; even in most democratic states, parliaments as lawmaking bodies, for example, constitute an explicit locus of legislative authority. The UN remains an inadequate attempt at creating something like such a locus of authority. This is often revealed when states, particularly powerful states, successfully challenge UN decisions and actions.[42] These ambiguities around the nature of authority in international law are perfectly reflected in the castle's structure and operation: 'If you hadn't known it was a castle, you might have taken it for a small town.'[43] The only tower which was visible also has an ambiguous status: one 'could not make out whether it was a dwelling or belonged to a church.'[44] Thus, already at first approach, the spatial arrangement of the castle creates uncertainty about its authority similarly to international law. This is further deepened and confirmed through an examination of the operation of the castle's authority through its clerks, its wardens, and numerous other officials with various competences.

K.'s conversation with Bürgel[45] contains an illustrative example of the way the responsibility is shared or distributed in the castle, mirroring international law's approach to many questions of responsibility.[46] In *The Castle*,

41 For a brief overview of this point, see Crawford (n 8) 9–11. For a more extensive overview of the debate, see contributions collected in Part II of Gerry Simpson (ed), *The Nature of International Law* (Routledge 2019).

42 This is also visible in the discussions on global or international constitutionalism, especially when the UN Charter is analysed as a constitutional document and such an analysis provides difficult and parallels strained. See, for example, Bardo Fassbender, *The United Nations Charter as the Constitution of the International Community* (Martinus Nijhoff 2009) and Michael W. Doyle, 'Dialectics of a Global Constitution: A Struggle of the UN Charter' (2012) 18(4) *European Journal of International Relations* 601. The former work is more optimistic, and the overall complexity of the argument illustrates the point, while the latter, while still arguing for the UN Charter as a constitution, expressly discusses difficulties related to the absence of a centralised authority.

43 Kafka (n 33) 11.

44 Kafka (n 33).

45 Kafka (n 33) 225–36.

46 It is impossible to provide here even a cursory overview of these issues. However, the concept of shared responsibility which was developed in response to impossibility to always attribute

Bürgel is a secretary of a castle official, about whom no further information is given but that his name is Friedrich. K. meets Bürgel during the night when he is summoned for questioning by another castle official in the village inn. When looking for the room of this other official, by error, he enters Bürgel's room. Bürgel starts a conversation with K., indirectly suggesting a possibility of help in K.'s affair, but K. is too tired to listen and seize the opportunity. In his talk, Bürgel reveals important details about the functioning of the castle and various responsibilities of different castle officials.

In his explanation to K. about the responsibilities of various castle officials, Bürgel starts by affirming that each matter has a secretary who is mainly responsible for this matter. However, things immediately get muddy because Bürgel emphasises that other secretaries will have responsibility for other parts of the same matter, and then even goes on to affirm: 'Even what I have said about the main responsibility is going too far. Is not the whole thing also contained in the smallest responsibility?'[47] This lays bare the operation of the castle's authority through a variety of channels, none of which guarantee the outcome but all of which promise some form of partial resolution; this, too, is uncertain, however, because 'the organization and its particular needs at the time influence the decision'.[48] In international law, depending on the subject matter, one could identify something like an institution holding the main responsibility. For example, the UN Security Council is responsible for matters pertaining to peace and security.[49] However, history has demonstrated that the specific arrangements of the Security Council's operation (the 'organisation', in Kafka's words)[50] can lead to the matter being unresolvable by this 'primarily' responsible institution, and the substitute solution or partial response can come from a different organ. For example, oftentimes, when the Security Council is not able or willing to act due, for instance, to the veto power of its permanent members, the General Assembly will step in and adopt a resolution which, while not entirely resolving the matter (since General Assembly resolutions are non-binding), gives an impression of some partial satisfaction.[51] In other instances, when states are dissatisfied with the

responsibility clearly to one single state is perhaps the best illustration of the point. On the concept of shared responsibility, see, for example, André Nollkaemper, Ilias Plakokefalor and Jessica Schechinger (eds) *The Practice of Shared Responsibility in International Law* (CUP 2017).

47 Kafka (n 33) 233.

48 Kafka (n 33) 234.

49 See UN Charter Art 24(1): 'In order to ensure prompt and effective action by the United Nations, its Members confer on the Security Council *primary* responsibility for the maintenance of international peace and security' (emphasis added).

50 In German, the term is 'die Organisation'. It appears several times in the conversation with Bürgel when he describes the functioning of the castle and its bureaucracy. The English translation is straightforward here: 'an organisation'. See Kafka (n 33) 232, 233, 234.

51 Examples are numerous, but the most iconic historical example is the so-called 'Uniting for Peace' resolution of the UN General Assembly that was adopted as a consequence of a flagrant absence of action from the Security Council: UN GA Res 377(V) 3 November 1950.

actions of the Security Council, the General Assembly, or other UN organs, they can also take matters into their own hands, as the actions of NATO in Kosovo or of the USA in Iraq demonstrate. As widely discussed by scholars, such actions of states assuming the role of the law enforcers are often selective and motivated not by legal rules but by their political or economic goals.[52] This resonates with another aspect of Bürgel's description of the way castle officials deal with matters within their purview, namely, ardour: 'Is not the ardour with which one approaches the case the crucial point?'[53] Thus, personal motivation and interest in the case override objective need for law enforcement or fulfilment of responsibilities – the latter typically postulated as the principal of official motives for action. International law is a structure that makes it difficult to locate responsibility and find a mechanism able to provide a solution to a concrete problem despite its claim to a worldwide application and supposed ability to resolve world problems.

The nature of the castle's authority is closely tied to its relationship to the village and its inhabitants. Very early in the novel, it becomes obvious to K. and to the reader that there is no clear line separating the castle from the village or castle officials from villagers: 'There's no distinction between the local people and the castle', announces the teacher to K. when K. first walks into the village.[54] K. and the reader gradually realise the profound truthfulness of this statement, despite apparent inaccessibility of the castle to K., by observing close intertwining between what is usually considered private with what is usually considered an official or public matter. Not only relationships between the village's women and castle officials (of which Frieda's relationship to Klamm and Amalia's relationship to Sortini are two central examples) but also the way in which summons and other interactions with castle officials occur illustrate the same point. While these elements of *The Castle*'s narrative can shed light on various aspects of international law's narrative, only one is highlighted here. This particular aspect is selected because it not only establishes similarities between international law and the meaning of the narrative in *The Castle* but also provides a first explanation as to the endurance of international law's narrative. This aspect emerges from quite an obvious and widely accepted interpretation of the relationship between the village and the castle. According to this interpretation, the authority of the castle, while being perceived as external to the village and the villagers, especially through the spatial arrangements, reveals itself as dependent upon

52 For an analysis of international lawyers' opinions on Kosovo, see, for example, Hilary Charlesworth, 'International Law: A Discipline of Crisis' (2002) 65(3) *The Modern Law Review* 317 or Michael J. Glennon, *Limits of Law, Prerogatives of Power: Interventionism after Kosovo* (Palgrave 2001). For a detailed economic argument on US actions in Iraq, see Christopher Doran, *Making the World Safe for Capitalism: How Iraq Threatened the US Economic Empire and Had to Be Destroyed* (Pluto Press 2012).

53 Kafka (n 33) 233.

54 Kafka (n 33) 12.

and emerging from the village and the villagers. The village and its inhabitants imbue the authority of the castle with meaning and create the 'insurmountable net of power'[55] of the castle. While none of them is primary, one is impossible without the other.

Similarly to the co-dependency between the village and the castle, between authority and its users, international law's narrative and its force are unsustainable without those who use this narrative the most, even when criticising it, namely, international lawyers. International lawyers as users of international law give it meaning, authority, and strength that it exercises upon them. K. and the villagers turn to the castle in the hope of acquiring or achieving something. In doing so, they not only legitimise and sustain but also create the authority of the castle. This is particularly visible in villagers' voluntary compliance with alleged but nowhere-to-be-found rules.[56] Some authors advanced an interpretation of K.'s quest as a form of defiance of the castle and its authority.[57] Even if one accepts such interpretations, the very fact of the belief in the capacity and power of the castle and the ensuing behaviour adopted to defy some perceived rules allegedly coming from the castle unwittingly leads to the submission to and legitimation of the castle's authority.[58] In international law, a similar tendency is visible in the attitude of critical international law scholars, as illustrated earlier in the example of Koskenniemi. This tendency is even stronger and more pervasive in the attitude of more mainstream commentators and scholars who appeal to international law as an authority for solving pressing problems, such as appeals to the institutions of the UN to address the crisis in Ukraine or Gaza, despite these very situations having been enabled by previous (in)actions of those institutions.

55 Despiniadis (n 39) 16.

56 This is particularly remarkable in the events that develop around Barnabas's family after Amalia's refusal to accept the sexual invitation of the castle official Sortini. Although no official condemnation comes from the castle, both the family and the villagers act as if the family were condemned and requires pardon from the castle.

57 This interpretation is perhaps most famously advanced by Agamben: see Agamben (n 27), but also Nedoh's interpretation of Agamben's view (n 37). Whether such an interpretation is tenable or not does not affect the argument advanced in this chapter. However, it is worth noting that if one bases an argument that K. is a sort of hero or somebody who challenges and defies authority on his status as land surveyor, as Agamben does, problems arise given the uncertainties surrounding K.'s professional standing. On this latter aspect, see, for example, Steinberg, who suggests that K. is seeking something to which he has no right : Erwin R. Steinberg, 'K. of the Castle: Ostensible Land Surveyor' (1965) 27(3) *College English* 185.

58 The attitude of defiance of the castle's authority in K.'s behaviour can be most obviously interpreted from his occasional references to his task vis-à-vis the castle as 'Kampf' (see n 34), but also the way he attempts to establish more direct and immediate connection to the castle officials, even in breach of existing rules and customs.

Thus, the storyline of *The Castle* demonstrates that we, ourselves, create authority, which we imbue with power and capacity to move progressively in a certain direction, where rescue from our current ills lies. That there might be no such authority and no castle is immaterial to the seeker unable to recognise this reality, where the narrative of order, peace, and justice is simply a mirage. International law, as reflected in the UN Charter, was constructed out of the despair in which Europe found itself during the Second World War, but with a belief in the possibility of order, peace, and justice, and a belief in the possibility of a centre and of coordinated action driven by reason. Just as international law's narrative was created by a group of politicians and lawyers who then became the readers and users of this narrative, so does its force remain dependent on the readers, most important of whom are international lawyers. This finding, however, does not explain all the reasons for the persuasiveness of international law's narrative. Especially, it remains unclear why, beyond the need for hope, structure, and meaning, international law exerts such a force of persuasion despite its numerous failings. Some additional reasons are revealed through an analysis of the formal aspects of *The Castle* in the next section.

The form of *The Castle* and international law's masterplot

The storyline and characters of *The Castle* demonstrate dependency of the persuasiveness of the authority's power, and the very existence of authority, on those who are submitted to this authority. Masterplot is also a form of authority exercised by certain stories upon our minds, imagination, and as a consequence, actions. Thus, the power and authority of any masterplot are not simply given but are interactively created, as already mentioned in the section introducing the concept of the masterplot with reference to Ricœur. However, not only, and perhaps not primarily, the substance of the narrative but also the way we use language and construct a written or an oral account contribute to the creation and sustenance of masterplots' authority. Kafka's unconventional writing style lays bare some of the formal mechanisms which create and sustain masterplots in their authority and power. The centrality of form as opposed to content in Kafka's writings is a hypothesis expressed by Kafka's interpreters and translators in light of the fact that many of his writings, including *The Castle,* were not intended for publication, at least not in the form in which they were published.[59] The depiction of these mecha-

59 Anna Jell, *Die französischen Übersetzungen von Kafkas Prozeß* (Innsbruck University Press 2012) 77–80. The fact that *The Castle* in particular was not intended for publication is confirmed by his statements to Brod that he has to abandon ' the Castle story' ('Schlossgeschichte' in German) and will have to let it stay unfinished (see Reuß (n 18) 7). Reuß also

nisms is a useful tool for further explaining the power of any masterplot, and thus also of the persuasiveness of international law's narratives about its functions.

The role of language in communication is generally a central theme in Kafka's work. To some extent, one could even affirm that Kafka's fascination with writing is determined by his complex view of language and communication. With regard to *The Castle*, a good entry point to this topic is the opening passage, which Max Brod considered not to belong to the body of the novel and which therefore was not included in the published text, except in more detailed editions, as an annex. In this passage, which extends to almost four handwritten pages, a guest arrives at a guesthouse, is received by the innkeeper, and then interacts with the innkeeper, with the chambermaid also present.[60] This passage is persuasively interpreted by Reuß as dealing with the topics of trust and communication, which are, according to him, intrinsically connected to the concepts of power and will to power.[61] Reuß also highlights the importance of these omitted pages as a programmatic prologue which sharpens all the central questions of *The Castle in abstracto*.[62] Thus, according to Reuß, *The Castle* itself has as the main theme the topic of trust and communication in their relation to power and authority, which, according to the interpretation adopted here, is the essence of any masterplot. Kafka's position on language and its communicative capacity is expressly stated in his 57th Zürau aphorism:

> For everything outside the phenomenal world, language can only be used allusively, but never even approximately in a comparative way, since, corresponding as it does to the phenomenal world, it is concerned only with property and its relations.[63]

Thus, language is, for Kafka, fundamentally an instrument of power, since it is concerned with property and its relations. In this quotation, 'property'

concludes that like the previous two attempts at writing a novel, this third attempt had to be brought to a standstill (Reuß (n 18) 7).

60 The analysis in this section relies heavily on Kafka's manuscript of *The Castle*. The manuscript was consulted in the facsimile edition by Reuß: Roland Reuß, *Franz Kafka Das Schloss. Historisch-kritische Edition sämtlicher Handschriften, Drucke und Typoskripte* (Stroemfeld Verlag 2018). The opening passage is contained in Heft (notebook) 1, 5–11.

61 Reuß (n 18) 18–20.

62 Reuß (n 18) 18.

63 Zürau aphorisms are a collection of Kafka's brief reflections on various metaphysical topics. The preceding English text is from Franz Kafka, *The Blue Octavo Notebooks* (Max Brod ed, Ernst Kaiser and Eithne Wilkins tr, Exact Change 1991) 79; German: 'Die Sprache kann für alles außerhalb der sinnlichen Welt nur andeutungsweise, aber niemals auch nur annähernd vergleichsweise gebraucht werden, da sie, entsprechend der sinnlichen Welt, nur vom Besitz und seinen Beziehungen handelt.'

translates to German 'Besitz', which is one of the standard translations in any German–English dictionary. However, in this standard translation, an important layer of meaning is lost due to different origins of the German and the corresponding English terms. German noun 'Besitz' is derived from the verb 'besitzen', which literally means 'to sit', 'to besiege'. Therefore, although it is mostly used today to denote property or possession more correctly, it also directly refers to the relationship of subjugation and exercise of violent force over something regarded as an object. In this sense, there can be no Besitz/property as a rightful possession, only one that is justified *ex post facto* by the exercise of power and violence. Therefore, 'Besitz', and with it, language, is 'might that makes right'. From this follows that, for Kafka, language is always an extremely violent tool that not only does violence to everything outside the phenomenal world, including one's feelings, as the quick reading of this aphorism might suggest, but also affects the phenomenal world, which itself is concerned with property (Besitz) and its relations. Even if the phenomenal world is not reducible to violence, language mirrors it by mirroring its violence, not its other characteristics. However, not all uses of language are an exercise of violence. What Kafka attempts through his writing is to find for language as the medium of communication an escape from this violence. Kafka highlighted many negative emotions associated with writing, but he was nonetheless inescapably attracted to it. This is perhaps best illustrated by his famous diary entry after he finished his story 'The Judgment':

> This story, wrote at one sitting during the night of the 22nd-23rd, from ten o'clock at night to six o'clock in the morning. . . . The fearful strain and joy, how the story developed before me, as if I were advancing over water. . . . How everything can be said, how for everything, for the strangest fancies, there waits a great fire in which they perish and rise up again. . . . *Only in this way* can writing be done, only with such coherence, with such a complete opening out of the body and the soul.[64]

In this account of writing, Kafka expresses the possibility of a certain type of writing producing something of value through an 'opening' of both 'the body and the soul'. However, he also alludes to the associated negative side of the experience, especially when he describes his strain and joy as 'fürchterlich' (translated here as 'fearful'). This term expresses the greatness and immensity of the feelings of both joy and strain, but also their dreadful

64 Franz Kafka and Max Brod (ed), *The Diaries of Franz Kafka 1910–1913* (Jozef Kresh tr, Secker & Warburg 1948) 275–6. A very insightful, detailed analysis of the ambiguous relationship Kafka entertained with language and writing based on Kafka's diaries is provided in Florence Bancaud, *Le Journal de Franz Kafka ou l'écriture en procès* (CNRS éditions 2001) 72–88.

nature. It is important to note that Kafka discusses here not so much the creation of a particular work as a completed entity but the very process of writing as such. Thus, the escape from the violence of language does not reside in a specific work (story or novel) but in the particular form of the process of writing that enables such an escape. This form of writing, the process, cannot rely exclusively, and perhaps even not primarily, on the meaning of words. Words and their meaning were recognised by Kafka as inadequate. Thus, he remarks already in 1902, '[f]or words are miserable mountain climbers and miserable miners of meaning. They do not retrieve the hidden treasures from the heights or dredge them from the depths!'[65] A full analysis of the elements of the form of writing utilised by Kafka to suspend some of the violent mechanisms of language cannot be performed in the framework of this chapter. Only some elements emerging from *The Castle* and enabling an answer to the question of the persistence of international law's narrative are discussed here.

The narration in *The Castle* is set in the third person. This is an important choice for Kafka, because the manuscript shows that, initially, Kafka started writing *The Castle* as a first-person account.[66] This change to the third-person account allowed Kafka to make the world of *The Castle* more open to interpretations, but also less easily subsumable into standard masterplots. *The Castle*'s narration contains many statements which, taken on their own, are simply impossible to reconcile. Examples include such key elements of the story as whether K. is a land surveyor or whether Jeremias and Artur are really K.'s assistants, whom he worked with prior to his arrival to the village.[67] This impossibility of reconciliation or 'right' interpretation is the key element that does not allow a traditional masterplot to emerge from the narrative of *The Castle*. Multiple interpretations and the absence of a definitive conclusion about the meaning of *The Castle* are the best evidence of Kafka's success. Therefore, it is important to understand in some more detail how exactly he achieves this irreconcilability to be fully embedded into the narration while, at the same time, not allowing his narrative to fall apart and be regarded as an incoherent collection of statements.

65 In German: 'Denn Worte sind schlechte Bergsteiger und schlechte Bergmänner. Sie holen nicht Schätze von den Bergeshöhn und nicht die von den Bergestiefen!' Franz Kafka, *Briefe 1902–1924* (Max Brod ed, Fischer Verlag 1958) 9. English translation from Franz Kafka, *Konundrum: Selected Prose of Franz Kafka* (Peter Wortsman tr, Archipelago Books 2016) 11.

66 This can be observed by consulting the manuscript (n 60), where in notebook 1 of the manuscript up to the page 102, the first-person singular pronoun is used, which then is crossed over and changed to the third-person singular, and all the subsequent narration in this and other notebooks occurs in the third-person singular.

67 For a detailed discussion of these irreconcilable elements, see Frieder Krauß, *Kafka und das Kafkaeske: Lektüren aus rezeptionstheoretischer Sicht (Die Sorge des Hausvaters, Der Prozeß, Das Schloß, Der Verschollene)* (FAU University Press 2022) 159–74.

The first important element which emerges from the examination of Kafka's manuscript of *The Castle* is an intentional preference for a less personal, more distanced type of account. In many instances in the manuscript, Kafka removes passages where the feelings and intentions of K. could become more obvious or where they are unambiguously stated. However, the narrative does not thereby become completely depersonalised, which would make it too artificial and, thus, less credible. Of course, the recourse to the third-person account also helps achieve this effect, since the storyteller in *The Castle*, who is not K., cannot know all his intentions or feelings. However, this is not the only way Kafka achieves the desired effect, namely, a less obvious, more mysterious account which pushes the reader towards a search for the masterplot, if the reader is inclined, like the villagers, to create and sustain authority. For example, in one passage of the manuscript, Kafka removes the direct words of K., which the third-person account does not require him to remove since the storyteller could have heard these words. In the first version of the passage, K.[68] sounds assertive and openly confrontational, thus revealing his opinions and positionality towards the castle very clearly. The relevant words constitute K.'s response to the village mayor's interpretation of the letter K. received from Klamm, a castle official. In the final published text, K.'s reaction reads as follows:

> You interpret the letter so well, Mr Mayor . . . that in the end there's nothing left of it but the signature on a blank sheet of paper. Don't you think that in doing so you are belittling Klamm's name, which you claim to respect?[69]

In the manuscript, the first version of this passage reads as follows:

> You interpret the letter so well, Mr Mayor . . . that in the end there's nothing left of it but the signature on a blank sheet of paper. My interpretation is different, and I hold to it, and will ensure its recognition when I also have other weapons. Don't you think that in doing so you are belittling Klamm's name, which you claim to respect?[70]

68 Reuß (n 60) Heft 2, 14.

69 Kafka (n 33) 66.

70 The English translation is my own. The sentence starting with 'My interpretation is different . . .' is somewhat convoluted in German but has very assertive and combative undertones: 'Meine Meinung is anders, ich bleibe bei ihr, und werde ihre wenn ich auch noch ganz andere Kampfmittel habe, und werde ihre Anerkennung durchsetzen suchen.' In the German version, the term I translated as *weapons* is 'Kampfmittel' (means of combat) and uses the root 'Kampf', which means 'struggle', 'fight, or 'combat' and is central to understand K.'s positionality towards the castle (see n 34 earlier).

Initially, Kafka removed only one portion of this statement:

> You interpret the letter so well, Mr Mayor . . . that in the end there's nothing left of it but the signature on a blank sheet of paper. My interpretation is different, and I hold to it. Don't you think that in doing so you are belittling Klamm's name, which you claim to respect?[71]

In this version, the combative intention to fight and actively oppose authority is removed. However, K.'s situatedness in opposition to the authoritative opinion, and thus an unambiguous stance, is still visible. When, in the second revision, Kafka removes 'My interpretation is different, and I hold to it', K.'s statement acquires precisely this mysterious, open-to-interpretation form, which accommodates opposing perspectives without the story falling apart. Despite the apparent existence of a unique storyteller, instead of constructing a unidirectional storyline, Kafka is able to open the space to multiple voices. This is also reinforced by the fact that many of the apparently contradictory statements from characters in the novel are not reconciled (either confirmed or denied) through the voice of the storyteller.[72]

Such a technique enables Kafka to immerse readers in the story, forcing them to interpret it for themselves and to construct their own masterplots, should they wish to. As a result, Kafka reveals that just as the authority of the castle is non-existent without the village, and that authority is being sustained by its users, so does the masterplot not exist but for its readers who need it. Thus, while *The Castle* itself contains no masterplot, it is able to reveal the entirely constructed nature of the masterplot. A masterplot is constructed by those who need it: by readers for a novel, by users for international law. It should be noted that Kafka's revelation of the construction of any masterplot by readers goes a step further than Ricœur's insight on the role of readers in the actualisation of any masterplot. Kafka's form of writing demonstrates that readers desirous of authority will construct such a masterplot even where the oeuvre itself has no masterplot. This is best visible in the variety of interpretations of *The Castle*, many of which correspond to dominant Western masterplots, such as search for God or salvation, self-discovery or contestation of power and authority. At this stage, it becomes possible to draw some conclusions on the reasons for the persistence of international law's narrative.

Just like *The Castle*, international law contains contradictory pointers that are not all reconciled, since it lacks a clear centre of authority which could occupy the place of the storyteller. It could be possible to suggest that the

71 See n 34 above. Reuß's edition clearly traces all corrections and establishes their temporal order.

72 For a demonstration of these instances with examples, see Krauß (n 67) 159–63.

polyphony of voices, interpretations, opinions, and perspectives is just part of our human condition, that it is in the nature of life, not only of international law. Thus, the problem is not the polyphony but how we deal with it. The masterplot and authority come into play when, instead of facing this polyphony, as Kafka attempted through his lifelong dealings with writing, we endeavour to reduce this polyphony to a simplistic, single, unified voice. In *The Castle*, Kafka skilfully reveals some of the devices utilised to this end. While not all of them could be discussed in this chapter, some of the most obvious elements which also appear as explanations of the power of international law's narrative are the following. First, international law depersonalises any storytelling, which is a general feature of any legal system but is particularly strong within the field of international law, where the main actors are states. This depersonalisation occurs in several ways, including through a peculiar construction of discourse which, in order to be accepted as legitimate, in order to be heard by international law, has to present a clear, non-contradictory linear narrative, thus inevitably silencing some parts of the polyphony.[73] The general legal requirement of objectivity resonates with the avoidance of subjective internal feelings, impressions, and even opinions in *The Castle*. However, in *The Castle*, the use of the third-person narrative, which has no clearly fixed point of reference, combined with minimal reference to subjective internal feelings, impressions, and opinions, enables Kafka to reveal and coherently present the polyphony as an integral part of the story, of life. Moreover, this also reveals the role of the reader as the agency which constructs and sustains the force of the masterplot, just as the villagers construct and sustain the authority of the castle. The outcome in international law is different because it allows disagreement only to a limited extent within the confines of established argumentative rules, as Martti Koskenniemi so persuasively demonstrated. These rules can be deployed to formulate contradictory and conflicting positions. For example, it is a common recurrence that both the aggressor and the international institutions counteracting this aggressor appeal to the same or neighbouring norms and rules. Thus, to justify its war in Ukraine, Russia appealed to the rules contained in the UN Charter, citing previous similar practices, for example, by the USA when justifying their intervention in Iraq.[74] These rules constrain the

73 This is clearly visible in how case accounts in the International Court of Justice (ICJ) are construed where the complexity of political and historical interactions between various parts of the world are often reduced to a dry chronology of selected events which count as politically significant. For an example, see the analysis of ICJ's approach to territorial questions in Sookyeon Huh, 'Title to Territory in Postcolonial Era: Original Title and Terra Nullius in the ICJ Judgments on Cases Concerning Ligitan/Sipadan (2002) and Pedra Branka (2008)' (2015) 26(3) *European Journal of International Law* 709.

74 For an analysis of Russia's argument justifying its aggression on Ukraine, see, for example, René Värk, *Russia's Legal Arguments to Justify Its Aggression against Ukraine* (International

possibility of contestation and limit the diversity of possible differences while simultaneously enabling the maintenance of international law's narrative about its function. The fact that these rules are sustained and constructed as a meta-masterplot by international lawyers themselves is evident at various levels: how some arguments in scholarly discourses are devalued as political[75] or, even more so, emotional.[76] Thus, the silencing of the polyphony in international law occurs not at the substance or 'matter' level but at a meta level of form. The form is always less visible and less obvious to the users of either literary texts or of international law. However, as analysis of form-related devices deployed by Kafka in *The Castle* has hopefully demonstrated, for this very reason, the form contributes to and enables the propelling of the narratives and their positing as masterplots with more power.

By accepting the form of the argument as a legitimate constraining device, the attempt is constantly made by those who construct the discourse of international law to make it sound as if it comes from one single clearly situated storyteller. So instead of revealing the polyphony, in international law it is silenced. Such a streamlining of the range of acceptable forms of arguments also results in a purposeful infliction of violence through language, which limits communicative range. This represents precisely the type of language use that Kafka denounced in his writing. Until the majority of international lawyers, as both readers and storytellers of international law, are able, like Kafka, to face the polyphony, international law's narrative of order, peace, and justice will continue to operate as a legitimating device for a limited but diverse range of actions, including those that resort to violence in various forms. These actions, in turn, being embedded in the acceptable range of international law's argumentative forms, will continue to lend persuasive force to its narrative of peace, order, and justice. Kafka's life and struggle with writing demonstrate that it is extremely difficult, painful, and even fearful (fürchterlich) to write a story which (like those of Kafka) are without a masterplot, without an end: a story fully open to *all* the diversity of communication without violence. Just as the villagers are afraid to see the authority of the castle (and thus their way of life) fall apart, and so sustain this authority through their everyday practices, so international lawyers maintain their identity by constantly reinstating and

Centre for Defence and Security 2022). Focusing only on Russia's arguments, the authors do not make connections to similar uses of the same arguments by other states in the past or to UN's silence in the face of similar arguments in the past.

75 See for example, Jed Odermatt, 'Patterns of Avoidance: Political Questions before International Courts' (2018) 14(2) *International Journal of Law in Context* 221.

76 For an example, see Jean d'Aspremont, 'Affect, Emotions and the Cartesian Epistemology of International Law' (2023) 14(3) *Journal of International Dispute Settlement* 281 or Vasselin Popovski, 'Emotions and International Law' in Yohan Ariffin et al. (eds) *Emotions in International Politics: Beyond Mainstream International Relations* (CUP 2016) 184.

recreating the purposefulness and univocity of international law's narrative of order, peace, and justice, even as they criticise it. Polyphony, instead of being accepted as part of life and its richness, is relegated to the status of chaos, which needs ordering.

Final reflections

Kafka forcefully reveals that there is no masterplot (authority) but the one we, as readers (or users of authority), create. The persistence of the narrative of order, peace, and justice in international law is also explicable by the work of international lawyers who, through their use of international law, constantly reinstate its authority and the strength of its narrative. Whether there is a way out of this vicious circle has been an open question in this chapter. Kafka certainly believed that this is possible and tried to find a way out through his writing. One of the ways Kafka attempted to escape the grip of the masterplot, or authority, was by enabling polyphony to take place without imposing on it a unifying interpretation, notably in *The Castle*, but also in his entire oeuvre and life.[77] Such an attitude does not lead to a loss of meaning and structure but to a discovery of different nuances of meaning and of alternative, more complex structures which are able to produce life in common without relying on the unifying force of a single authority. To organise our life, including relationships at the global level, accounting for all the complexity of the polyphony, is a tremendously difficult and tremendously fearful task. However, without attempting it, as Kafka did, we will never discover the tremendous joy Kafka experienced.

77 Given the constraints of this chapter, it is impossible to discuss in detail many strategies Kafka employed to this end. Some of the analyses of Kafka's work which discuss some of the elements of Kafka's strategy are Malte Kleinwort, '*Das Schloss* zwischen Buch und Handschrift' in Malte Kleinwort and Joseph Vogl (eds), *'Schloss'-Topographien: Lektüren zu Kafka's Romanfragment* (Transcript Verlag 2013) 85; Dimitris Vardoulakis, *Freedom from the Free Will: On Kafka's Laughter* (SUNY Press 2017).

Chapter 11

The never-ending story

Unpicking the masterplot justifying UK military intervention

Lynsey Mitchell

The operation of the masterplot begins with the government seeking to convince Parliament and the public that military action is necessary and time-critical, and that the UK only uses military means as a last resort. Military intervention is then framed as a noble and virtuous operation that the UK is duty-bound to participate in, in order to maintain global peace and security.[1] The success of this masterplot is that it characterises the UK as a reluctant participant in military matters overseas and as a state doing its duty to uphold international law.[2] This impresses on the public the appropriateness of the use of military force and silences criticism that UK military force is aggressive or imperialistic.[3] If invoking these time-honoured tropes about altruism and adherence to duty is not enough to generate support for war, the addition of legalistic language can further bolster the idea that military action is appropriate, by trading on the assumption that law provides a determinative mechanism for sanctioning military action. Having established the necessity of any action in contemporary political discussions, legal language is then invoked to position the intervention in compliance with international law, and the UK as a nation that respects the rule of law. This invocation of legality embeds law as a character within this familiar masterplot to sell war to the public. This chapter therefore unpicks the role of law in selling war to the UK public.

This chapter begins by defining what is meant by the term 'masterplot' and explains why this literary device is such an effective way of communicating the need to go to war. It sets out why it is so important for governments to sell the use of a state's military force to the public. It then focuses on the evolution of the masterplot from the Blair-era interventions (1999–2004) to

1 Jack Holland, *Selling the War on Terror: Foreign Policy Discourses after 9/11* (Routledge 2013).

2 Jack Holland, 'Blair's War on Terror: Selling Intervention to Middle England' (2012) 14(1) *The British Journal of Politics & International Relations* 74, 7.

3 Vasuki Nesiah, 'From Berlin to Bonn to Baghdad: A Space for Infinite Justice' (2004) 17 *Harvard Human Rights Journal* 75.

DOI: 10.4324/9781003404668-16

more recent ones in Syria and Yemen (2015–24).[4] It highlights that, while imagery of UK militarism as benevolent and the UK as a reluctant leader, is present throughout, the importance of compliance with the law has become more prominent since 2003 due to the backlash over the UK's role in Iraq. Having established how this masterplot operates, this chapter then turns its attention to the pivotal role that law and legal language play in the continued facilitation of the masterplot, arguing that law now plays a central role through its ability to sanction the use of force and thereby legitimate the narrative that war is necessary. The chapter then outlines how legal mythmaking allows law to be understood as being imbued with objective power to declare the use of military force as legal and, thereby, justified. In this way, law plays an important, but somewhat overlooked, role in this familiar masterplot, as the invocation of legal language has powerful persuasive properties. Thus, while the traditional narrative of duty and obligation is no longer enough to sell war to the public, the invocation of law repairs any fracture in this narrative and allows it to endure.

Masterplots as a way of making sense of the world around us

Despite much attention being paid to law and narrative in law and literature scholarship, such literature either focuses on the storytelling arenas (such as courtrooms), where law utilises storytelling, or seeks to uncover stories about law itself.[5] Since law is rarely considered a character purposely wielded by others in a wider political masterplot, its power as such is rarely discussed.[6] As Baron highlights, '[l]aw-and-literature scholarship has not questioned what the category "law" consists of and has thus tended inadvertently to reinforce the notion of law as autonomous'.[7] It is this lack of interdisciplinary exploration of the narratology of law and its power to grant legitimacy that is the focus of this chapter. Specifically, it highlights the persuasive power of law and legal language, and how this is deliberately invoked to gain approval

4 This chapter focuses on UK military interventions from the late 90s onward. This is because the period at the end of the Cold War was considered the beginning of a new world order in which the stalemate in the UN would be overcome and so herald an era of intervention.

5 Peter Brooks, 'Narrative Transactions-Does the Law Need a Narratology' (2006) 18 *Yale Journal of Law and the Humanities* 1.

6 Tait and Norris highlight the dearth of material exploring the genesis of law from a narrative standpoint. Similarly, Posner called for the separation of law and literature, highlighting law's hermeticism and arguing that literature has little to add to the study of law. See Allison Tait and Luke Norris, 'Narrative and the Origins of Law' (2011) 5 *Law and Humanities* 11 and Richard Posner, 'Law and Literature: A Relation Reargued' in Lenara Ledwen (ed), *Law and Literature* (Routledge 2015).

7 Jane B. Baron, 'Law, Literature, and the Problems of Interdisciplinarity' (1999) 108 (5) *The Yale Law Journal* 1059, 1061.

for military action. However, despite compliance with domestic and international law being a prominent theme of discussion in debates about whether to authorise military force, the reality is that legal language is invoked to suggest an objective determination of legality even though the actual arbiters of legality – the courts – are never actually utilised for this purpose.

The operation of this masterplot in positioning the turn to war as rational, necessary, and time-critical is neither new nor unique to the UK. Its existence can be traced to ancient times, when folk tales, mythology, and epic literature aimed to generate support for war, as well as telling the origin stories of peoples and states. Homer's *Iliad* is perhaps one of the best examples of this within the European tradition.[8] It tells of a just cause, patriotic and noble warriors, and a fierce enemy.[9] Glorification of war is achieved by arousing national pride and mythologising the fighters as heroes, all while positioning war as necessary and just. The same themes have consistently and successfully been invoked through the ages, the aim being to create a sense of national unity and culture worth protecting.[10] The contemporary narratives which underpin the UK's decision to go to war reimagine these familiar tales in a way that resonates with a modern British audience but, at the same time, invokes the nostalgia of a glorious British past.

The appeal of constructing elaborate narratives to position the nation's military as a force for good is that such narratives can tell powerful stories that affect people and, more importantly, can sway opinion in a subtle way. Humans have shared ideas and values through storytelling since the dawn of time.[11] Stories are a way of rationalising events and helping people to make sense of the world that they live in, especially historically, when the majority of a population could not read or write. Storytelling is particularly prominent in times of crisis, as it provides a simple way of communicating cohesive ideas and motivating and empowering people. Because it is so intrinsic to how people rationalise and understand the world, literary scholars have identified certain key archetypical stories that are familiar to people.[12] These archetypes form the basis of familiar childhood stories and can also be found in popular film, television, and literature, which utilise these tropes in more complex or abstract ways to tell modern versions of these childhood stories.

8 Philip Taylor, *Munitions of the Mind: A History of Propaganda* (Manchester University Press 2003), 31.

9 Homer, *The Iliad* (Penguin Classics Penguin 2003 (Rev. Ed.)).

10 Oliver Thomson, *Easily Led: A History of Propaganda* (Sutton Publishing Ltd 1999).

11 Alan Farmer points out that the word 'story' draws from the same root as the word 'history' in many languages. He states that history is a form of storytelling. Alan Farmer, 'Story-Telling in History' (1990) 58 *Teaching History* 17. Early human history was mostly conveyed orally, and myths told of the origins of a civilisation or people. See Francesca Polletta and others, 'The Sociology of Storytelling' (2011) 37 *Annual Review of Sociology* 109.

12 Carl Gustav Jung, *The Archetypes and the Collective Unconscious* (Routledge 2014).

These archetypical stories can be adapted to feature different events, different characters, and different moments in time, but the overarching skeleton plot of each remains the same. As such, they are referred to as masterplots.

In this way, masterplots serve as fundamental frameworks that shape how people understand and interpret the world around them. According to Ritivoi they provide a sense of order and meaning to those that share and believe in them.[13] As such, they are a source of normativity, exercising 'a certain authority over our moral imaginations and play[ing] a role in informing our moral intuitions'.[14] Iversen and Pers-Højholt state that 'the term masterplot aims at getting at a subset of culturally shaped and culturally shaping stories that exists on a transindividual level but has effect on the individual level'.[15] However, they acknowledge that among those researching narrative theory, there is a lack of common ground in terminology, and there is an abundance of terms used to describe ideas similar to the masterplot: 'metanarratives', 'schematic narrative templates', 'good reasons', 'master narratives', and 'story skeleton', as well as 'masterplot'.[16]

The term 'masterplot' was coined by Porter Abbott[17] and is often used to refer to the use of stories within strategic public discourse. Porter Abbott defines *masterplots* as 'recurrent skeletal stories, belonging to cultures and individuals that play a powerful role in questions of identity, values, and the understanding of life'.[18] He favours 'plot' over 'narrative' because he claims that such stories exist as a template for individual narratives that might tell different versions of the same story. While there are multiple renditions or narratives that tell the story of the American dream, the fundamentals of the American dream storyline can be said to exist as a masterplot because of its 'skeletal quality, a quality that enables it to exist above or below the many individual incarnations one might encounter it in'.[19] Similarly, the term 'master' is used to purposely convey the idea that such stories exert resonance and influence. People in a specific cultural group tend to 'give credibility to narratives that are structured by' the masterplots shared by the group.[20] This is

13 Andreea Deciu Ritivoi, 'Explaining People: Narrative and the Study of Identity' (2009) 1 *StoryWorlds: A Journal of Narrative Studies* 25, 35.
14 Hilde Lindemann, *Damaged Identities, Narrative Repair* (Cornell University Press 2001) 6.
15 Stefan Iversen and Mikka Lene Pers-Højholt, 'Interlocking Narratives: The Personal Story and the Masterplot in Political Rhetoric' in Cindie Aaen Maagaard, Daniel Schäbler and Marianne Wolff Lundholt (eds), *Exploring Fictionality: Conceptions, Test Cases, Discussions* (Syddansk Universitetsforlag 2020) 183.
16 Iversen and Mikka Pers-Højholt (n 15).
17 H. Porter Abbott, *The Cambridge Introduction to Narrative* (3rd edn, Cambridge University Press 2020).
18 Michael L. Kent, 'The Power of Storytelling in Public Relations: Introducing the 20 Master Plots' (2015) 41(4) *Public Relations Review* 480, 192.
19 Iversen and Pers-Højholt (n 15) 10.
20 Porter Abbott (n 17) 42.

why masterplots have been described as providing a 'cultural glue' that binds communities together.[21] This is also why masterplots that sell war are often specific to a particular state's culture and history, and why such a simplistic framing has endured.

The masterplot to sell war

War is one of the biggest crises that a state can face, and even if that state is not immediately facing threat, the decision to resort to war has serious consequences, and governments who pursue unpopular wars often face hostility from the public.[22] How a particular conflict is presented to the public is almost as important as how it is fought. Gaining public support is key to being able to deploy military force in democratic nations.[23] For this reason, communications scholars explain that a multitude of rhetorical devices or tropes exist to facilitate public understanding of government policy, particularly when that policy is war.[24] Such devices include using the memory of past events to shape contemporary understandings, employing vague but idealistic language, and framing conflicts in simplistic good-versus-evil discourse.[25] Together, these allow politicians to position recourse to war as not just a natural response but the *only* response, even though force is positioned as a last resort within the UN pacific settlement scheme.

The language and individual narratives employed to facilitate war are then tailored to specific global crises or an individual state's mythology. The tropes used to generate support for war in America are particular to American mythology about itself and invoke Western or frontier mythology, in which America is positioned as the tough sheriff in a lawless land.[26] The stories the

21 Porter Abbott (n 17) 44.

22 There is longstanding friction in American consciousness over the anti-war protests that took place during the American war in Vietnam, and how this was latterly constructed as hostility towards the US military as well as the politicians who orchestrated this action. See Bruce Jentleson, 'The Pretty Prudent Public: Post-Vietnam American Opinion on the Use of Military Force' (1992) 36 (1) *International Studies Quarterly* 49; and Thomas D. Beamish, Harvey Molotch and Richard Flacks, 'Who Supports the Troops? Vietnam, the Gulf War, and the Making of Collective Memory' (1995) 42(3) *Social Problems* 344, 344–6.

23 Edward Herman and Noam Chomsky, *Manufacturing Consent: The Political Economy of the Mass Media* (Vintage Books 1994).

24 Andrew Frank and Kenneth Osgood, *Selling War in a Media Age: The Presidency and Public Opinion in the American Century* (University Press of Florida 2010) 3.

25 Frank and Kenneth Osgood (n 24).

26 Stacy Takacs, 'The Contemporary Politics of the Western Form: Bush, Saving Jessica Lynch and Deadwood' in Jeff Birkenstein, Anna Froula and Karen Randell (eds), *Reframing 9/11: Film, Popular Culture and the 'War on Terror'* (Continuum 2010); Ruth Buchanan and Rebecca Johnson, 'The Unforgiven Sources of International Law: Nation-Building, Violence, and Gender in the West(ern)' in Doris Buss and Ambreena Manji (eds), *International Law: Modern Feminist Approaches* (Hart 2005).

UK tells about itself are rooted in memory of the empire and of WWII. Noon refers to this as 'historical analogy'.[27] These stories tend to characterise the UK as a powerful saviour figure who is obligated to act and are replete with themes of humanitarianism, democracy, and duty, all of which position the UK as a force for good, and its enemies as evil. In justifying intervention in Kosovo in 1999, Tony Blair described Milosevic's 'brutal suppression of the civilian population' and stated that '[w]e have no alternative but to act and act we will'.[28] In justifying the deployment to Iraq in 2003, he described the urgent need to tackle the threat of Sadam Hussein and reminded the House that Hussain was a 'cruel and sadistic dictator' who was a threat to his own people.[29]

Similarly, in announcing military action in Afghanistan in 2001, Tony Blair explained that the military operation had three prongs: diplomatic, humanitarian, and military.[30] He referred to the 'appalling suffering of the people of Afghanistan'.[31] In later discussions in Parliament, and in wider discourse, there was a focus on the treatment of Afghan women, and the specific need to liberate Afghan women became a focal point when explaining the necessity of UK military action. This framed the UK military as heroic figures rescuing oppressed women.[32] In the House of Commons, MPs specifically invoked the media reports about the mistreatment of Afghan women, using this to highlight the barbarism of the Taliban regime and to further justify that the UK had no option but to resort to war:

> How can we reason with a regime that, as we saw on 'Panorama' last night, revels in the public execution of its women?[33]
>
> The Taliban have burnt all the books in the libraries and destroyed all the schools. They do not allow any of their people to go to school. They do not allow Afghani women to set foot outside the house unless they are fully covered and accompanied by their husband. Women are certainly

27 David Hoogland Noon, 'Operation Enduting Analogy: World War II, the War on Terror, and the Uses of Historical Memory' (2004) 7(3) *Rhetoric and Public Affairs* 339; Stuart Croft, *Culture, Crisis and America's War on Terror* (Cambridge University Press 2006), 55 and Richard Jackson, *Writing the War on Terrorism: Language, Politics and Counter-Terrorism* (Manchester University Press 2005) 41–4.

28 Tony Blair, 'Statement to Parliament' HC Deb, 23 March 1999, vol 328, col 162.

29 Tony Blair, HC Deb, 24 September, vol 390, col 1.

30 Statement by Prime Minister Tony Blair, Downing Street (7 October 2001) <https://edition.cnn.com/2001/WORLD/europe/10/07/gen.blair.speech/> last accessed 27 June 2024.

31 Statement by Prime Minister Tony Blair, Downing Street (n 30).

32 Sonali Kolhatkar, '"Saving" Afghan Women' *RAWA Website* <www.rawa.org/znet.htm> accessed 27 June 2024; Christine Delphy, 'A War for Afghan Women?' in Susan Hawthorne and Bronwyn Winter (eds), *After Shock: September 11, 2001 Global Feminist Perspectives* (Raincoast Books 2003).

33 Jim Knight MP Debates 8 October 2001, vol 372, Col 876.

never allowed into someone else's house. The poor people of Afghanistan are living under that type of regime.[34]

This framing reinforces the UK in the role of the righteous hero defending innocent people from an evil villain[35] and ultimately positions UK military intervention in foreign states as an altruistic act reminiscent of the UK's decision to enter WWII to defend Poland and stand against Hitler.[36] The power and attraction of this framing make it exceptionally difficult to reject. In the run-up to the commencement of miliary action in Afghanistan following the 9/11 attacks, humanitarian agencies warned that rather than liberate Afghans, the military campaign would, in fact, kill tens of thousands and likely lead to famine.[37] Their warnings were not only disregarded, but those who opposed military action on the basis that it would halt humanitarian aid were also labelled as being soft.[38]

This characterisation of the UK as a heroic actor resonates with the public because the plot and story arc are enduringly familiar, both from the actual fairy tales we are told as children, where the prince rescues the princess, and also because this characterisation evokes cultural nostalgia about the UK's role in WWII as a heroic nation liberating oppressed people. Together, these stories, and the imagery they evoke, work to cement the UK as a protector of innocent victims and as a reluctant world leader that will stand against tyranny. They operate not simply to justify war but also to reinforce the public's image of the UK.[39] Whether the military action does, in fact, liberate or save oppressed people is less important than the imagery it conjures of the UK. Writing about how the military intervention in Afghanistan was sold to the British public, Holland notes that the 'reluctant leader' trope 'helped to sell a moral foreign policy to "Middle England" through appeals to romanticised images of a glorious imperial past, to which Britons could now return guilt free'.[40] In this way, the masterplot which is used to sell the UK's wars relies heavily on retelling stories about the UK's military prowess and its altruism.

34 Geoffrey Clifton-Brown MP, HC Debates 8 October 2001, vol 372, Col 884.

35 Judith H. Stiehm, 'The Protected, the Protector, the Defender' (1982) 5(3–4) *Women's Studies International Forum* 367.

36 Anne Orford, *Reading Humanitarian Intervention: Human Rights and the Use of Force in International Law* (Cambridge University Press 2003) 180. See also Sherene Razack, *Dark Threats and White Knights: The Somalia Affair, Peacekeeping, and the New Imperialism* (University of Toronto Press 2004) and David Chandler, *From Kosovo to Kabul and Beyond: Human Rights and International Intervention* (Pluto 2006).

37 <www.afghanwomensmission.org/2001/10/afghan-womens-mission-to-u-s-government-halt-bombing-immediately/> accessed 27 June 2024.

38 Charles Hirschkind and Saba Mahmood, 'Feminism, the Taliban, and Politics of Counter-Insurgency' (2002) 75 *Anthropological Quarterly* 339, 346.

39 Holland (n 1) 118.

40 Holland (n 2) 7.

This masterplot was perfected throughout the New Labour years and was deployed repeatedly.[41] However, since 2003, politicians have been reluctant to automatically endorse UK force used abroad due to the backlash against the Iraq war.

In addition to giving meaning to public discourse, masterplots are said to 'create an image of the world in which good and evil is clearly identifiable'.[42] This ability to simplify complex geo-political decisions to familiar stories makes the masterplot to sell war attractive. Yet the attraction of simplistic moral tales for communicating complex geo-political situations means that more nuanced or complicated narratives are rejected even when they are more appropriate. Writing about how Western militarism is often packaged within a simplistic fairy-tale saviour narrative, Anne Orford notes that the saviour masterplot allows Western states to mythologise about their motivations for using military force to gain public support and detract from the unpleasant realities of war.[43] Similarly, Makua Mutua argues that the power of the rescue narrative is such that Western states not only frame military force as benevolent but also that the wider human rights project is organised around states in the Global North rescuing states in the Global South through the exportation of Western liberal values.[44] This results in a blurring between human rights and humanitarian objectives and military objectives, which further allows military action to be presented as a welcome and benevolent intervention in a foreign states.[45]

Law's role in the masterplot that sells war

Since international law prohibits the use of military force in another state except in very limited circumstances,[46] states are often at pains to demonstrate that any use of military force complies with international law.[47] White

41 As a variety of critical scholarship has pointed out, 'crises' in international law are often discursively manufactured and the means by which certain geo-political situations become understood as 'crises' and others do not is not random. See further Dianne Otto, 'Remapping Crisis through a Feminist Lens' in Sari Kouvo and Zoe Pearson (eds), *Feminist Perspectives on Contemporary International Law: Between Resistance and Compliance* (Hart 2011), 83.

42 Porter Abbott (n 17).

43 Orford (n 36).

44 Makau Mutua, 'Savages, Victims, and Saviors: The Metaphor of Human Rights' (2001) 42 *Harvard International Law Journal* 201.

45 Gina Heathcote, 'Article 51 Self-Defense as a Narrative: Spectators and Heroes in International Law' (2005) 12 *Texas Wesleyan Law Review* 131.

46 Article 2(4) of the UN Charter prohibits the threat or use of force unless authorised by the UN Security Council under Article 39 and in accordance with Article 42, or as an act of self-defence under Article 51.

47 The prohibition of the use of force is said to be the cornerstone of international law but is often criticised for failing to prevent states from resorting to force. Thomas Franck famously declared in 1974 that Article 2(4) was dead. In response to this, Louis Henkin argued that

highlights that since the Iraq War, 'states have taken much greater care to ensure their actions [are] underpinned by legality'.[48] This can be seen in the UK, where, since 2003, discussions in Parliament and in wider political discourse about deploying the UK's armed forces have been explicit and have hinged on establishing the deployment's compliance with international law.[49]

This section sets out how law plays a central role in further legitimating military action by providing an objective metric to gauge appropriateness. It is well established that political rhetoric for selling war invokes various familiar narratives to impart the idea that war is necessary or that the UK must act due to its international obligations. This section focuses on how law and legal language are utilised to bolster these narratives by implying that any such use of force is sanctioned and thereby appropriate.[50] In this way, the operation of the masterplot benefits from the prestige and power of law to unemotionally declare a use of force as legal. The importance of law in legitimating the use of force within the wider masterplot underpinning such action has grown since the political fallout from the decision to send UK troops to Iraq in 2003, where it was subsequently acknowledged that even cabinet ministers were not given full access to government legal advice and that claims of weapons of mass destruction were much exaggerated.[51] Given the public's rejection of the Iraq War and eventual discontent over continued military engagement in Afghanistan, it stands to reason that

while Article 2(4) has been regularly breached, it was not dead. Instead, he argues that state practice has developed whereby states attempt to mitigate conflict or downplay it, but that even when force is used, states are keen to argue that it is force that is permitted by international law. In this way, he argues that Article 2(4) is taken seriously by states and that they are aware of the stigma around appearing to ignore international law. See Thomas Franck, 'Who Killed Article 2 (4)? Or: Changing Norms Governing the Use of Force by States' (1970) 64(5) *The American Journal of International Law* 809 and Louis Henkin, 'The Reports of the Death of Article 2 (4) Are Greaty Exaggerated' (1971) 65(3) *American Journal of International Law* 544.

48 Nigel D. White, 'Libya and Lessons from Iraq: International Law and the Use of Force by the United Kingdom' (2011) 42 *Netherlands Yearbook of International Law* 215.

49 Veronika Fikfak, 'The Legacy of Iraq: Bringing Parliament into a Debate on War' Cambridge University Legal Studies Research Paper Series (No 55/2017) (November 2017) 1–3.

50 Lynsey Mitchell, 'International Law as Shibboleth: The Continued Appeal of Heroic Narratives in Support of Military Intervention' (2023) 11(3) *London Review of International Law* 481, 500.

51 The author acknowledges that the legality of the military action in Iraq was a key feature of the discourse in 2003, and there were mass public protests against the decision to send troops, and many people spoke out in public against the war. However, public analysis over the merits of the government's legal advice has become much more pressing since then, after it emerged that advice that deploying troops to Iraq without a UN Security Council resolution might be illegal had been supressed. See 'The Report of the Iraq Inquiry' (Report of a Committee of Privy Counsellors) *The Iraq Inquiry* (6 July 2016), Volume V, paras. 671–8, 121 <https://assets.publishing.service.gov.uk/media/5a80f42ced915d74e6231626/The_Report_of_the_Iraq_Inquiry_-_Executive_Summary.pdf> accessed 27 June 2024.

subsequent deployments would be treated more cautiously by the public, and as such, the narrative framing of military intervention as heroic and virtuous is not enough on its own to generate support.[52] Since then, compliance with international law has become a mainstay of public scrutiny of UK decisions to go to war.[53] While this might appear to be a welcome alternative to political hyperbole and emotive media framing, law has a long history of lending itself to the justification and legitimation of war.[54] Therefore, this section explores how a legalistic framing underpins narratives about the UK's military deployments and how this lends credence to the overarching masterplot and further entrenches it. The effect of this legal packaging is to silence criticism of the UK's decision to deploy the military abroad, because if the decision to go to war can be declared legal, then there can be no accusation that the UK is acting self-interestedly or from an imperialist standpoint.[55] The incorporation of legality works to silence criticism of the rescue narrative and repels any suggestion that the UK is not acting in a benevolent way, or that war is problematic. Where war is sanctioned by law, it is understood as legitimate and appropriate, even if the military action in question does not demonstrably comply with the law.[56] In this way, the masterplot gains more credence and so becomes further cemented as the go-to explainer for governments justifying war.

Compliance with domestic and international law as a metric for justifying military intervention

The incorporation of law within the generic masterplot for selling war ticks several boxes. As well as needing to present military deployment as complying with international law, individual states generally have their own constitutional laws that determine when and how their military can be deployed abroad.[57] Making sure to comply with domestic rules on when to deploy force bears the hallmarks of democracy and, in the European tradition, can

52 Colin Murray and Aoife O'Donoghue, 'Towards Unilateralism? House of Commons Oversight of the Use of Force' (2016) 65(2) *International and Comparative Law Quarterly* 305 and Fikfak (n 49) 1–3.

53 White (n 48) 215.

54 Jack Landman Goldsmith and Eric A. Posner, 'Moral and Legal Rhetoric in International Relations: A Rational Choice Perspective' (2000) *University of Chicago Law & Economics, Olin Working Paper* 4.

55 Murray and O'Donoghue (n 52).

56 Anthea Roberts, 'Legality vs Legitimacy: Can Uses of Force Be Illegal But Justified?' in Philip Alston and Euan MacDonald (eds), *Human Rights, Intervention, and the Use of Force* (Oxford University Press 2008).

57 Lori Fisler Damrosch, 'Trends in Executive and Legislative Powers' in Charllote Ku and Harold K. Jacobson (eds), *Democratic Accountability and the Use of Force in International Law* (Cambridge University Press 2003) 39.

be traced back to the Romans, who developed and codified just war theory as a way to measure or declare the legitimacy of war.[58] The use of such checks and balances also served to evince that war was not being undertaken on a whim. However, just war theory is a problematic doctrine that was ultimately abandoned as a valid legal principle during the Enlightenment, because the notion of a 'just war' was seen as being entirely subjective.[59] The use of just war theory can be understood as an exercise in co-opting legal frameworks to sanction and reify the decision to go to war. Despite this being viewed as a flawed doctrine, the appropriation of legal language within the masterplot can be understood as a modern incantation of just war theory. As such, there is a need to be cautious about the turn to law within discussions about war and the reliance on pronouncements that war is legal. Current incarnations rely on the same historic claims to morality and the notion of war being appropriate but similarly offers little in the way of objective determinism of whether force is appropriate.

In the UK, the authorisation of military force has historically been understood as falling within the prime minister's parliamentary prerogative.[60] Power over the armed forces rested with the monarch, but over time, as the UK emerged as a democracy, the power to wage war transferred to the government, which, in turn, is accountable to Parliament.[61] This traditionally meant that the UK military could be deployed abroad without parliamentary approval. Not only was Parliament not asked to vote or approve the deployment of troops, but also, on many occasions, it was only informed after the military mission had commenced.[62] The deployment of troops to Kosovo in 1999, Sierra Leonne in 2000, Afghanistan in 2001, and Iraq in 2003 was

58 Arthur Nussbaum, 'Just War: A Legal Concept?' (1943) 42 *Michigan Law Review* 453.

59 The inability of just war theory to offer an objective framework to determine the legality of law led, in part, to its abandonment. See Joachim Von Elbe, 'The Evolution of the Concept of the Just War in International Law' (1939) 33(4) *The American Journal of International Law* 665 and Simon Chesterman and Ian Brownlie, *Just War or Just Peace? Humanitarian Intervention and International Law* (Oxford University Press 2001).

60 For a helpful analysis on the historical role of Parliament in authorising military interventions, see Nigel D. White, *Democracy Goes to War: British Military Deployments under International Law* (Oxford University Press 2009); Emily Young, 'Britain Goes to War: An Analysis of the Developing Role of the House of Commons in Determining Whether HM Forces Should be Deployed on Military Operations' (December 2015) 6 *ASLR* 57; House of Lords Select Committee on the Constitution, *Waging War Parliament's Role and Responsibility Session 2005–06*, 15th Report, Volume I (HL Paper 236-I, 27 July 2006) 7; The House of Commons Political and Constitutional Reform Committee, *Parliament's Role in Conflict Decisions: A Way Forward* (HC 892, 20 March 2014) 6.

61 White (n 60) 12.

62 In response to the leader of the opposition Neil Kinnock's claim that decisions on the deployment of UK troops to the Falklands was a decision for Parliament, the prime minister, Margaret Thatcher, replied that 'it is an inherent jurisdiction of the government to negotiate and reach decisions. Afterwards the House of Commons can pass judgment on the government'.

announced by Prime Minister Tony Blair in the House of Commons after the decision to deploy had already been taken. MPs were free to speak on the matter in debates, and on the deployment to Iraq, there was later a vote in the House of Commons, but there was no way for Parliament to curtail these deployments.[63] Instead, the majority of MPs acquiesced that it was 'necessary' to deploy the military and generally endorsed these actions publicly to demonstrate political support and unity.

Criticism of the Iraq War led to increasing public awareness and critical discourse on the legality of the UK's military actions abroad. While, at that time, the government had claimed it was acting in accordance with international law, there was high-profile criticism that such action was illegal.[64] The Iraq War Inquiry subsequently found problems with the government's decision-making and highlighted that legal advice that military action without a further UN SC resolution might not be in accordance with international law should have been made available to cabinet ministers.[65] However, the view that the Iraq deployment was illegal soon became a mainstay of public discourse where this particular war was concerned.[66] The public became much more interested in the decision-making around military deployment, and compliance with international obligations was given more prominence in the media. Mindful of this, and distancing themselves from their predecessor, both Gordon Brown and David Cameron stated publicly that they would

HC Debates vol 23 cols 597–598, 11 May 1982. For a discussion on the evolution of parliamentary involvement in military deployment, see White (n 60) 19–25.

63 There were two debates in the House of Commons following the 9/11 attacks, and the prime minister and the foreign secretary announced the involvement of the UK military as part of the NATO operation in Afghanistan. Parliament was told that the UK was acting in self-defence in accordance with Article 51 of the UN Charter, but there was no formal vote for MPs: HC Deb vol 372, col 690, 4 October 2001.

64 Criticism of the Iraq War is well documented. In the run-up to the deployment, an estimated 2 million people protested in London in what was described as the UK's biggest ever demonstration. See <www.theguardian.com/uk/2003/feb/15/politics.politicalnews> accessed 26 June 2024. Blair's decision was criticised in Parliament by then Liberal Democrat leader Charles Kennedy. See HC Debates 18 March 2003 vol 401 col 781. The decision to intervene militarily in Iraq in the absence of a UN Security Council resolution was the subject of fierce academic critique. See, for example: Christopher Greenwood, 'International Law and the Pre-Emptive Use of Force: Afghanistan, Al-Qaida, and Iraq' (2003) 4 *San Diego International Law Journal* 7; Christine Gray, 'From Unity to Polarization: International Law and the Use of Force against Iraq' (2002) 13(1) *European Journal of International Law* 1.

65 'The Report of the Iraq Inquiry' (Report of a Committee of Privy Counsellors) *The Iraq Inquiry* (6 July 2016), Executive Summary, para. 811, 120 <https://assets.publishing.service.gov.uk/media/5a80f42ced915d74e6231626/The_Report_of_the_Iraq_Inquiry_-_Executive_Summary.pdf> accessed 13 September 2024.

66 The mother of a soldier who was killed in Iraq was supported by high-profile figures to bring judicial review proceedings against the prime minister's decision to deploy the military. *R (Gentle) v Prime Minister* [2008] UKHL 20.

legislate to give Parliament a more formal role in decisions to go to war.[67] Since 2010, a convention has emerged that the UK Parliament will have a vote on whether to authorise military force abroad.[68] This increased parliamentary authority has meant more debate and scrutiny over questions of military intervention. One of the key barometers employed in these debates is whether such action would be legal under international law.[69]

Seeking parliamentary support for intervention in Libya in 2011 and Syria in 2013, David Cameron told the House of Commons that he was mindful of the failings in 2003 and that he was seeking endorsement from Parliament before authorising force.[70] This led to the government famously losing a vote in Parliament on whether to authorise force in Syria in 2013.[71] Yet while there has been a trend towards increasing involvement of Parliament rather than simply using prerogative powers, constitutionally, there has been no actual change to the legal powers of the prime minister to deploy the military. When the UK military engaged in strikes against the Houthis in Yemen in 2024, Rishi Sunak only informed Parliament after the action had commenced and members were not offered a vote. Instead, he made clear that the action was necessary, proportionate, and in self-defence.[72] Thus, there is a narrative that current governments respect Parliament and democracy and that decisions to go to war are now subject to a parliamentary veto, all of which suggest an ever more legalistic approach, and with that the assumption that this will operate to determine when military deployment is appropriate.

67 Gordon Brown, 'Speech to the Fabian New Year Conference' (14 January 2006) <www.britishpoliticalspeech.org/speech-archive.htm?speech=316> accessed 13 September 2024; David Cameron, 'A New Approach to Foreign Affairs—Liberal Conservatism' *Speech to the British-American Project* (11 September 2006) <www.theguardian.com/politics/2006/sep/11/conservatives.speeches> accessed 13 September 2024.

68 While this commitment to a parliamentary vote was lauded as a constitutional innovation and Parliament celebrated this newfound oversight, there has not yet been an actual constitutional amendment, and the power to deploy the armed forces remains with the prime minister using their prerogative powers. The government has committed to making it a legal requirement that Parliament must be consulted. See the House of Commons Political and Constitutional Reform Committee, *Parliament's Role in Conflict Decisions: A Way Forward* (HC 892, 20 March 2014); Aileen McHarg, 'Reforming the United Kingdom Constitution: Law, Convention, Soft Law' (2008) 71(6) *Modern Law Review* 853; Alexander Bolt, 'The "Convention" to Consult Parliament on Decisions to Deploy the Military: A Political Mirage?' in Michel Bedard and Philippe Lagasse (eds), *The Crown and Parliament* (Yvon Blais 2015).

69 Mitchell (n 50).

70 Nicholas Watt and Patrick Wintour, 'David Cameron Praised for Decisive Action Over Libya' *The Guardian* (18 March 2011) <www.theguardian.com/politics/2011/mar/18/david-cameron-praised-action-libya> accessed 26 June 2024.

71 Nicholas Watt, Rowena Mason and Nick Hopkins, 'Blow to Cameron's Authority as MPs Rule Out British Assault on Syria' *The Guardian* (30 August 2013) <www.theguardian.com/politics/2013/aug/30/cameron-mps-syria> accessed 26 June 2024.

72 HC Deb 15 January 2024, vol 743 col 577.

However, this is not a move away from the heroic masterplot framing but an additional layer that works to facilitate the existing masterplot and does not necessarily ensure any greater accountability.

Compliance with international law as a metric for justifying intervention

Post-WWII international law is clear that resorting to force to solve disputes is prohibited. Instead, states are mandated to use peaceful means and to refrain from using force.[73] The only exceptions to this are force used in self-defence, which is permitted under Article 51 of the United Nations (UN) Charter, and force that is authorised by the UN Security Council (SC) under Article 39 of the UN Charter in accordance with Article 42.[74] The Cold War stalemate in the UN SC meant that initial assumptions that the maintenance of international peace and security, and the administration of force, would be overseen by the UN did not come to pass, and there was relatively few situations where the SC was able to oversee international peace and security.[75]

However, the end of the Cold War heralded an optimistic era where the SC passed an ever-increasing number of resolutions authorising force.[76] The SC's understanding of what constitutes a threat to international peace and security has also evolved, and so has its justification for force. Heathcote highlights how the rescue narrative has come to infuse the SC's language when it passes resolutions justifying force. 'Security Council initiatives to authorise the use of force have expanded alongside the protection of civilians agenda while actively referencing the protection of civilians to underscore the use of force and ensure widespread support for these decisions.'[77] It is easy to see

73 Article 2(4) of the United Nations Charter states that '[a]ll Members shall refrain in their international relations from the threat or use of force against the territorial integrity or political independence of any state, or in any other manner inconsistent with the Purposes of the United Nations'. This is often considered the 'cornerstone' of the UN Charter and is also considered a norm in customary law. See James Leslie Brierly, 'An Introduction to the International Law of Peace' in Sir Humphrey Waldock (ed), *The Law of Nations* (Clarendon Press 1963).

74 Article 42 provides that '[s]hould the Security Council consider that measures provided for in Article 41 would be inadequate or have proved to be inadequate, it may take such action by air, sea, or land forces as may be necessary to maintain or restore international peace and security. Such action may include demonstrations, blockade, and other operations by air, sea, or land forces of Members of the United Nations'.

75 Due to political differences during the Cold War, the UN Security Council was effectively 'paralysed' due to the use of the veto by the permanent members. See Nigel D. White, *Keeping the Peace: the United Nations and the Maintenance of International Peace and Security* (Manchester University Press 1997).

76 Sean D. Murphy, 'Security Council, Legitimacy, and the Concept of Collective Security after the Cold War' (1994) 32 *Columbia Journal of Transnational Law* 201.

77 Gina Heathcote, 'Women and Children and Elephants as Justification for Force' (2017) 4(1) *Journal on the Use of Force and International Law* 66, 79.

how the language of protection that has become ubiquitous within the UN is then appropriated and replicated within domestic arenas, further legitimising military force that is ostensibly for the protection of civilians.

The power of law to sell war

In addition to positioning the turn to militarisation as rational by offering an objective metric, the invocation of law also allows for the framing of war as humanitarian and in service of human rights.

However, it is argued that this benchmark is less about wishing to restrict military deployment or engage in a robust analysis using objective measures. Instead, the invocation of law merely reinforces the narrative of the overarching masterplot in which the decision to go to war can be positioned as rational and not self-interested. Additionally, presenting military action as something that can be measured and adjudicated by law renders war as bureaucratic and legalistic and has the effect of sanitising it.[78] The result is that the invocation of law renders war clinical but, at the same time, differentiates it from the usual day-to-day decisions that politicians make. In the same way that the Romans were able to justify their wars by drawing on the legalistic construct of just war theory, states such as the UK can justify their decision to go to war by declaring that military action is legal as well as necessary.

The intrinsic power of law to authorise or sanction war means that legal adjudication can be wielded as a trump card. What this emphasises is that international law is a clear marker of legitimacy and order and a source of obligation. If military intervention is permissible under international law, then this reduces the opportunity to call for restraint. This is because law serves as a powerful marker of what is 'appropriate'. It is important for states to attempt to position their behaviour in compliance with international law, even when it is not, because respect for international law is seen as a hallmark of civilised nations. However, international legal scholarship has long grappled with accusations that the international legal system is weakened by states routinely flouting the law despite claiming compliance.[79] States, therefore,

78 It is also acknowledged that war is sanitised in various other ways. The 24-hour news cycle and the use of embedded reporters attached to the military have been criticised for presenting war as entertainment. See Richard Keeble, 'Operation Moshtarak and the Manufacture of Credible "Heroic Warfare"' in Richard Keeble and John Mair (eds), *Afghanistan, War and the Media: Deadlines and Frontlines* (Arima, 2010) and Daya Thussu, 'Live TV and Bloodless Deaths: War, Infotainment and 24/7 News' in Daya Thussu and Des Freedman (eds), *War and the Media: Reporting Conflict 24/7* (Sage Publications, 2005).

79 On the question of how and why states comply or do not comply with international law, see Louis Henkin, *How Nations Behave: Law and Foreign Policy* (Columbia University Press 1979) and Abram Chayes and Antonia Handler Chayes, 'On Compliance' (1993) 47(2) *International Organization* 175.

go to such extremes to present their behaviour in compliance with the law to suggest that their behaviour is acceptable.

As well as providing a benchmark for delineating appropriate behaviour, law also provides an attractive lexicon, in the form of human rights and humanitarian language, through which to frame war as liberation. The euphoria that followed the end of the Cold War and the anticipation of a fully realised international security model led to an expectation that militarism could solve the world's problems. Anne Orford refers to this as 'muscular humanitarianism' – the idea that military force could be wielded for every and any humanitarian purpose, thus rendering military force as benign and making war appear manageable and bureaucratic.[80] So attractive was this vision of early twenty-first-century militarism that it began to supplant the historical understanding that war inevitably wrought chaos and devastation and should be avoided at all costs. The interventions of the Blair era represent the apotheosis of this, which somewhat explains why this particular masterplot has had such enduring success in the UK, even though public support shifted away from supporting military deployment after the Iraq War.

David Kennedy wrestles with how law has increasingly provided an alternative lexicon for discussing war and military force and criticises law's role in normalising military solutions to humanitarian crises.

> What does it mean, however, to find the humanist vocabulary of international law mobilized by the military as a strategic asset? How should we feel when the military 'legally condition the battlefield' by informing the public that they are *entitled to* kill civilians, or when our political leadership justifies warfare in the language of human rights? We need to remember what it means to say that compliance with international law 'legitimates'. It means of course that killing, maiming, humiliating, wounding people is legally privileged, authorized, permitted, and justified.[81]

Kennedy is correct to be wary. Law's facilitation of war is rarely questioned in wider political discourse.[82] Indeed, an analysis of the role of law in legitimating war is noticeably absent from many of the wider multi-disciplinary critiques of selling war. Instead, the acceptance of law as a neutral arbiter of appropriateness inevitably allows militarism to be sanctioned by the power of law and, thus, can render military intervention by states in the Global

80 Anne Orford, 'Muscular Humanitarianism: Reading the Narratives of the New Interventionism' (1999) 10(4) *European Journal of International Law* 679. See also Karen Engle, 'Calling in the Troops: The Uneasy Relationship among Women's Rights, Human Rights, and Humanitarian Intervention' (2007) 20 *Harvard Humam Rights Journal* 189.

81 David Kennedy, *Of War and Law* (Princeton University Press 2009) 8.

82 Ulf Linderfalk, 'The Post-9/11 Discourse Revisited-the Self-Image of the International Legal Scientific Discipline' (2010) 2 *Goettingen Journal of International Law* 893.

North as sensible and natural in the fight against disorder and chaos, and those states as heroic liberators and protectors. In this way, the same masterplot found in the just war narratives and valiant tales of ancient times and the Middle Ages operates today under the guise of legalistic oversight and the language of humanitarianism. The effect of such narratives is to perpetuate a vicious circle in which military action is positioned as legal because it is just, and then positioned as just and appropriate because it is understood to be legal.[83] However, as Linderfalk concludes, there is often an unwillingness on the part of international law scholarship to contend with whether pronouncements about legality are valid,[84] and in the UK domestic arenas, where deployment of troops is discussed, there is no meaningful objective assessment of legality.[85] Instead, law is simply invoked as an incantation and to answer any public criticism of illegal wars.

Conclusion

This chapter has set out how political discussions around the deployment of UK military force subscribe to a familiar masterplot that positions military intervention as urgent, necessary. and humanitarian. This positions the UK as a reluctant hero which is duty-bound to intervene to protect innocent civilians and promote global peace.[86] This masterplot also involves mythmaking about the UK's role in the world, by reifying interventions and depicting UK military deployment as benign and altruistic. The effect of this is to position the British military as a force for good[87] and as a tool that can be wielded to protect people from tyranny.[88] This then allows the British public to understand that the UK is a global leader who uses its military for good and trades on collective cultural memory of WWII. The success of this masterplot makes it difficult to criticise the use of military force, as to do so is seen as abandoning civilians in need and asking the UK to shirk its international duties.[89]

83 It is outwith the scope of this chapter to engage with the detailed debates on the intersection of legality and legitimacy of deployments of military force.

84 Linderfalk (n 82).

85 Fikfak (n 49) 13.

86 Mitchell (n 50).

87 Victoria M. Basham, 'Gender, Race, Militarism and Remembrance: The Everyday Geopolitics of the Poppy' (2016) 23(6) *Gender, Place & Culture* 883; John Kelly, 'Popular Culture, Sport and the "Hero"-Fication of British Militarism' (2013) 47(4) *Sociology* 722.

88 Lynsey Mitchell, 'Re-Affirming and Rejecting the Rescue Narrative as an Impetus for War: to War for a Woman in a Song of Ice and Fire' (2018) 12(2) *Law and Humanities* 229.

89 In 2013, after the UK government lost a vote in the House of Commons to authorise the use of force in Syria, the late Paddy Ashdown commented that the failure to authorise force had 'diminished' the UK, and that those MPs who had failed to back the motion made him ashamed. See Claire Carter, 'Syria Crisis: Paddy Ashdown "Ashamed" of Britain Over Commons Vote' *The Telegraph* (30 August 2013) <www.telegraph.co.uk/news/

Despite the UK public's ambivilence toward military intervention abroad in the wake of Iraq, the masterplot has continued to endure by evolving to incorporate compliance with law as a key theme. This makes clear that the UK respects and adheres to its international obligations and respects the rule of law, thus allowing the masterplot to drive the narrative. Having loosely established that military force is sanctioned by law, the UK government is then free to narrativise how necessary war is and how it is acting out of altruism. This works to continue to sell war to the public. In this way, the story about the UK's benevolence toward other states, often those in the Global South, is further cemented by the legitimacy lent to it by law. Military action sanctioned by law is understood to be inherently good. Establishing compliance with the law ostensibly distinguishes the UK from those states that use force needlessly.

politics/10275565/Syria-crisis-Paddy-Ashdown-ashamed-of-Britain-over-Commons-vote.html> accessed 2 September 2024.

Part 6

Personal choice and state intervention

Chapter 12

Cohabitation and the masterplot of choice

Andy Hayward

Introduction

Family law abounds with myths and narratives. The familiar stories of love, betrayal, and loss are routinely played out in the courts and then chronicled in case reports. This human dimension adds a richness and vibrancy to the study of family law and, unlike other areas of law, allows us as individuals to connect with these stories.[1] Masterplots, or super-narratives, exist too. In the field of adult relationships, one striking masterplot is readily identifiable: the firm belief that couples should marry if they desire the protection of the law. This masterplot is so entrenched that the very concept of family and even the discipline of family law have been built upon the foundation of marriage. For centuries, marriage was the only source of legal entitlement and societal acceptability. The promotion of marriage by successive governments and its longstanding glamorisation in art and literature also meant that other equally meaningful relationships were either expressly excluded from the law's protection or viewed with indifference or apathy.

This chapter asks whether another masterplot exists in relation to relationships outside of marriage. It identifies what will be termed the masterplot of choice, whereby cohabitants are assumed by the public, politicians, and policymakers to have made an active, informed, and deliberate decision not to marry. Drawing upon the related concept of 'legal rationality',[2] it will be argued that underpinning this masterplot is a further assumption that couples purposefully choose the consequences of their interpersonal relationship based on, or guided by, knowledge of the law. Thus, in the cohabitation context, it is assumed that couples do not want the legal consequences of marriage to attach to their relationship.

1 See Victoria Chase and Ann E. Freedman, 'Reframing Family Law: Using Narratively-Informed Lawyering to Build an Inclusive Curriculum' (2022) 60(4) *Family Court Review* 669.
2 See, for example, Anne Barlow, 'Legal Rationality and Family Property: What Has Love Got to Do With It?' in Joanna Miles and Rebecca Probert (eds), *Sharing Lives, Dividing Assets: An Interdisciplinary Study* (Hart 2009).

DOI: 10.4324/9781003404668-18

Referencing the literature on masterplots, legal storytelling, and legal narrative, the first part of this chapter untangles the masterplot of marriage from that relating to choice to reveal their distinct qualities. The second part draws upon recent reform efforts in the field of cohabitation to delineate the masterplot of choice more precisely and determine how it finds expression in government policy and wider public discourse. It will draw heavily upon written and oral evidence submitted to the Women and Equalities Committee of the UK Parliament as part of their Rights of Cohabiting Partners Inquiry undertaken in 2021.[3] The third and final part identifies the implications of the masterplot of choice and its potential to frustrate reform efforts. Choice has been discussed extensively in the academic scholarship relating to cohabitation. However, it is argued in this chapter that by elevating choice and the associated assumption of legal rationality to the status of a masterplot, we can identify how they interconnect with broader trends prevailing in family law policy, especially neoliberalism and privatisation. More importantly, by exposing that link, greater potential is created to correct the narrative and combat the use of the masterplot of choice in the political sphere as a barrier to cohabitation reform.

Family law and legal storytelling

Relationship status has never been neutral. In the past, the decision as to whether we formalised our relationships, and with whom, spoke to important questions of status, class, and acceptability in society. The institution of marriage, imbued with its religious origins, was strongly influenced by a public morality, with the community having as much interest in the union as the parties themselves. Eekelaar argued that this conception of marriage was underpinned by duty and corresponding obligations, with the state promoting the institution of marriage with a view to 'securing adherence, as far as possible, to a particular social order'.[4] Given the benefits to the couple, entry and exit from marriage were tightly regulated. Douglas provided further evidence of this duty-based conception of marriage by emphasising the strong allegiance in the past to fault-based divorce alongside the underpinning doctrines of unity of person (conceptualising husband and wife as one) and consortium (the enforceable duty of husband and wife to live together).[5]

Over the past century, this conception of marriage has given way to a different one that attaches greater weight to the choices and individual happiness

3 Women and Equalities Committee, *The Rights of Cohabiting Partners* (2022–23 HC 92). Written and Oral Evidence submitted to the inquiry is available at <https://committees.parliament.uk/work/1196/the-rights-of-cohabiting-partners/publications/> accessed 22 August 2024.

4 John Eekelaar, 'Family Law and Love' (2016) 28(4) *Child and Family Law Quarterly* 289, 290.

5 Benedict Douglas, 'Love and Human Rights' (2023) 43(2) *Oxford Journal of Legal Studies* 273, 284.

of the parties themselves. The influence of public morality has declined, and restrictions on the availability of divorce have been lifted to the point where a negative stigma no longer exists, and it is now freely available without any reasons needing to be given.[6] But despite it becoming more individualised, marriage cannot be fully disconnected from its public aspects or its place within wider societal structures. Indeed, the relatively recent extension of marriage to same-sex couples in 2014 illustrated how the ability of couples to formalise was much more than a private expression of love but touched upon important questions of citizenship, public acceptance, and dignity.[7] This more modern choice-based vision of marriage also raises questions of the allocation of legal responsibility both between the parties themselves and the state. For example, who determines its consequences, and how far does the state's interest extend? But even when marriage is seen as a more individualised union and most of its inner workings deemed 'none of our business',[8] there remains, from a legal perspective, an irreducible minimum of marriage that cannot be modified or contracted away by the parties themselves.[9]

The emphasis placed on choice today aligns with prevailing themes in family law, such as respect for individual autonomy, equality, and individualism.[10] But by focusing so closely on the ability to choose, do we run the risk of overlooking how those choices were made? Love plays a complicating role here, and the pursuit of happiness, as opposed to legal entitlements, is often the main driver into why we enter interpersonal relationships. Much has been written on love, but for present purposes, when motivated by love, sometimes the choices we make about interpersonal relationships prove to be mistakes.[11] Resultantly, by acting against one's own self-interest, economic vulnerability can arise.

For centuries, the straightforward promotion of the masterplot of marriage has been an easy way of tackling this particular issue.[12] Put simply, marriage protected individuals against bad choices. Questions as to the inner

6 See the Divorce, Dissolution and Separation Act 2020 creating comprehensive no-fault divorce.

7 See, for example, *Minister of Home Affairs v Fourie*, Case 60/04, Constitutional Court of South Africa [47] (Sachs J) and *R (On the Application of Baiai and Others) v Secretary of State for the Home Department* [2008] UKHL 53 [44] (Baroness Hale).

8 *X (A Child: foreign surrogacy)* [2018] EWFC 15 [7] (Munby P).

9 *Radmacher v Granatino* [2010] UKSC 42 [132] (Lady Hale).

10 See Alison Diduck, 'What Is Family Law For?' (2011) 64(1) *Current Legal Problems* 287 and Anne Barlow, 'Solidarity, Autonomy and Equality: Mixed Messages for the Family?' (2015) 27(3) *Child and Family Law Quarterly* 223.

11 See Ulrich Beck and Elisabeth Beck-Gernsheim, *The Normal Chaos of Love* (Polity 1995).

12 See Nitya Duclos, 'Some Complicating Thoughts on Same-Sex Marriage' (1991) 1(1) *Law & Sexuality: A Review of Lesbian and Gay Legal Issues* 31, 44 cited in Lisa Glennon, 'The Limitations of Equality Discourses on the Contours of Intimate Obligations' in Julie Wallbank, Shazia Choudhry and Jonathan Herring (eds), *Rights, Gender and Family Law*

workings of the relationship or whether it was loving and committed were simply avoided because we assumed the presence of certain qualities merely by virtue of the couple's choice to be married. The very act of formalisation enabled us to assume an expression of choice by the parties. On the practical side, we satisfied the state's understandable concern for legal certainty through a clear start date and potential end date if there was a divorce, thereby allowing us to calculate legal entitlements. It even did not matter if marriage was ultimately a bad choice for the parties, because if the relationship were to end, the weaker party would get, at the very minimum, a safety net of protections and, more recently, entitlement to share the fruits of the marriage partnership. Entry into marriage, operating as its 'own little social security system', allowed us to assume the presence of valuable qualities about the relationship by reference to a prevailing image or ideology of marriage.[13] Whether the couple understood the law was largely irrelevant, given that any negative consequences could be remedied through the courts.

But today, the landscape of families has changed. With cohabitation on the rise and marriage statistically on the decline, we must ask more difficult questions about the reality of choice and how far it is expressed in all interpersonal relationships.[14] This is particularly important, as in England and Wales, no safety net exists for cohabitants, nor is there an irreducible minimum of obligations. So if individual choice is now central to modern relationships, can it be said that cohabitation, like marriage, is always a choice of both parties, and by choosing *not* to marry, couples have purposefully rejected legal protections? Moreover, can we expect cohabiting couples to make choices that are considered informed and rational when we know, as Barlow reminds us, that love is the 'very antithesis of rational behaviour and thought'?[15] This raises the question of whether the influence of the masterplot of marriage that has been so dominant for centuries has dwindled and a new masterplot has emerged.

Narratives of choice in the cohabitation context

After cohabitation became a 'statistically significant family form' in the 1970s onwards, policymakers had to confront the issue of regulation.[16] Extolling the virtues of formalisation through the masterplot of marriage and

(Taylor & Francis Group 2009), noting how society has been socialized to believe marriage is 'monolithic' when, in reality, we know that it is not.

13 Lady Hale, 'What Is a 21st Century Family?' *Lecture Given at the International Centre for Family Law, Policy and Practice 2019* <www.supremecourt.uk/docs/speech-190701.pdf> accessed 17 July 2024.

14 Office for National Statistics, *Marriages in England and Wales: 2021 and 2022* (20 June 2024).

15 Barlow (n 2) 305.

16 Rebecca Probert, *The Changing Legal Regulation of Cohabitation: From Fornicators to Family, 1600–2010* (Cambridge University Press 2012) 14.

ignoring the cohabiting family, a position that Cretney argued characterised much of the twentieth century, was no longer tenable.[17] Some meaningful, albeit context-specific, protections were introduced in England and Wales;[18] however, they fell short of the more comprehensive legal remedies provided to cohabitants in other jurisdictions, such as Australia and New Zealand.[19] Instead, the approach to legal regulation adopted here drew heavily upon narrative, legal storytelling and, arguably, choice.

Massaro reminds us of the power of legal storytelling that cuts across legal disciplines. They note that the practice encompasses telling

> stories that bridge, providing connections between people of different experience, stories that explode (like grenades) certain ways of thinking, stories that mask, devalue, or suppress other stories, stories that consolidate, validate, heal, and fortify (like therapy), and even stories that maim or 'spirit murder' and so should not be told at all.[20]

Massaro notes that these stories are often told to different audiences too. Stories could, for example, include lawyers drawing upon narrative when pleading to judges, or the judiciary using their reported judgments, and perhaps anticipated media coverage, as a means of speaking to the public. This legal storytelling might occur outside the courtroom, with campaigners using 'hard' cases as a way of showcasing a need for reform or the personal accounts of litigants to expose a pressing social issue. Stories serve different purposes too; they may merely chronicle facts or, more powerfully, raise awareness to shock the public into activism.

Against this backdrop, it is argued that legal narrative has played an unusually prominent role in the context of cohabitation, especially when compared to other areas of family law. A well-known source of this narrative here is the Court of Appeal decision in *Burns v Burns* that illustrates clearly the masterplot of choice.[21] That case saw Valerie Burns, known in the literature as 'Mrs Burns', unable to establish an interest in the family home owned by Patrick Burns, despite their living together for 19 years and her caring for their two children. Mrs Burns wanted to marry Mr Burns but could not do so as Mr Burns's wife was a Catholic and refused to grant him a divorce. Even though the relationship was marital in all but name, Mrs Burns was unsuccessful in her claim because she

17 Stephen Cretney, *Family Law in the Twentieth Century* (Oxford University Press 2005) 517.

18 In relation to, for example, tenancy succession and domestic abuse.

19 See, for example, Patrick Parkinson, 'Reforming the Law of Family Property' (1999) 13(2) *Australian Journal of Family Law* 117 and Bill Atkin, 'The Rights of Married and Unmarried Couples in New Zealand – Radical New Laws on Property and Succession' (2003) 15(2) *Child and Family Law Quarterly* 173.

20 Toni M. Massaro, 'Empathy, Legal Storytelling, and the Rule of Law: New Words, Old Wounds?' (1989) 87(8) *Michigan Law Review* 2099, 2104.

21 [1984] Ch 317.

could not adduce evidence that ownership of the home was to be shared or financial contributions upon which such a finding could be inferred. Quite unusually, we know a lot about Mrs Burns owing to the legal archaeology work of Watkins, who traced Mrs Burns after the litigation in a bid to tell her story.[22] Similarly, Mrs Burns featured in a BBC Panorama documentary called *The Cost of Living in Sin* that aired in 2002 and was aimed at raising awareness of the risks of cohabitation.[23] These elements have allowed *Burns* to capture the imagination and ensured that the case is discussed widely, albeit for a variety of different reasons, purposes, and agendas.

For some, *Burns* can be characterised as the 'classic'[24] or 'most infamous' instance of injustice, thereby justifying cohabitation reform.[25] Indeed, May LJ even concluded his judgment in that case with the striking remark that Mrs Burns 'can justifiably say that fate has not been kind to her'.[26] Others conceptualise *Burns* very differently, noting that it has been peddled subsequently as an 'atrocity tale' and is an exaggerated example of the perceived plight of unmarried cohabitants.[27] Such is the influence of this case that Probert noted that it was 'rare to find a critic that does not mention *Burns*'.[28] Whether *Burns* should assume such a canonical place in the discourse or be used as a rallying cry for reform today is very much contested.[29] Those questions, however, are not the focus of this chapter; rather, this chapter seeks to connect *Burns* to the broader literature on masterplots. It is arguable that, when viewed from this new perspective and through the lens of choice, the reason *Burns* has such an enduring role in this area becomes clearer.

Masterplots have been conceptualised by Grouse and Johnson as 'stories that we tell over and over in myriad forms and that connect vitally with our deepest values, wishes, and fears'.[30] The reference to fear is interesting, and it is arguable

22 Dawn Watkins, 'Recovering the Lost Human Stories of Law: Finding Mrs. Burns' (2013) 7(1) *Law and Humanities* 68.

23 See <http://news.bbc.co.uk/1/hi/programmes/panorama/2489373.stm> accessed 17 July 2024. A full transcript of the programme is available.

24 Law Commission, *Cohabitation: The Financial Consequences of Relationship Breakdown* (Law Com No 307 2007) 21 FN 27.

25 Sarah Beresford, 'It's Not Me, It's You: Law's Performance Anxiety Over Gender Identity and Cohabitation' (2012) 63(2) *Northern Ireland Legal Quarterly* 187, 190.

26 Beresford (n 25) 345.

27 See Helen Reece, 'Leaping without Looking' in Robert Leckey (ed), *After Legal Equality: Family, Sex, Kinship* (Routledge 2015); and Rosemary Auchmuty, 'The Limits of Marriage Protection in Property Allocation When a Relationship Ends' (2016) 28(4) *Child and Family Law Quarterly* 303.

28 Rebecca Probert, 'Cohabitation: Current Legal Solutions' (2009) 62(1) *Current Legal Problems* 316, 317.

29 See, for example, Rebecca Probert, 'Trusts and the Modern Woman' (2001) 13(3) *Child and Family Law Quarterly* 275 and Andy Hayward, 'Burns v Burns: The Fable Forty Years On' in Margaret Briggs and Andy Hayward (eds), *Research Handbook on Family Property and the Law* (Edward Elgar 2024) 441.

30 H. Porter Abbott, *The Cambridge Introduction to Narrative* (2nd edn, Cambridge University Press 2008) 46.

that that dimension fuels the persuasive effect or impactful nature of the masterplot. Indeed, they note that '[f]or a masterplot to be effective . . . it *must* be based on a specific community's particular values, wishes, and concerns'.[31] Viewed from this perspective, masterplots have clear scope to be weaponised. Indeed, Porter Abbott argued that when telling a story, the closer it is to a masterplot and its underlying values, the more credibility is assigned to it. Writing in the context of litigation, Porter Abbott believed that the lawyer who can 'activate [a] cherished masterplot' can often gain 'rhetorical leverage'.[32]

Transposing this understanding onto *Burns*, it is easy to see how the case speaks to broader truths and fears about marriage, cohabitation, and gender roles. Arguably, one of the reasons that many view *Burns* as a 'hard case' is that Mrs Burns wanted to comply with the dominant narrative of marriage by marrying Mr Burns but that 'choice' could not be realised owing to his refusal. This perhaps explains why *Burns* has been later deployed as a cautionary tale about the risks to women of cohabiting without marriage,[33] especially for so-called 'uneven couples', where one wishes to marry but the other does not.[34] Interestingly, Mrs Burns's 'choice' to continue the relationship rather than leave it can be seen as a justification for the unfavourable outcome. This sentiment is expressed by Fox LJ, where, after dismissing her claim in *Burns*, he remarked:

> I only add this. The plaintiff entered upon her relationship with the defendant knowing that there was no prospect of him marrying her. And it is evident that in a number of respects he treated her very well. He was generous to her, in terms of money, while the relationship continued.[35]

Here, we see a move away from the simplistic retort used in the past that the parties should have married. Instead, choice, whether exercisable or not, is foregrounded much to the detriment of Mrs Burns.

Like a masterplot, the saga of *Burns* has been continuously repeated in legal discourse. This process has seen Mrs Burns's story distorted over time and, as Watkin argues, her individuality stolen,[36] so much so that no longer is she a litigant in a particular case but instead has been elevated to the apocryphal 'figure of Mrs Burns'.[37] As Mee remarks, the power of the case is not

31 Carolyn Grose and Margaret E. Johnson, 'Braiding the Strands of Narrative and Critical Reflection with Critical Theory and Lawyering Practice' (2019) 26(2) *Clinical Law Review* 203, 211.

32 Porter Abbott (n 30) 46.

33 Anne Bottomley, 'From Mrs. Burns to Mrs. Oxley: Do Co-Habiting Women (Still) Need Marriage Law?' (2006) 14(2) *Feminist Legal Studies* 181.

34 See Anne Barlow and Janet Smithson, 'Legal Assumptions, Cohabitants' Talk and the Rocky Road to Reform' (2010) 22(3) *Child and Family Law Quarterly* 328.

35 *Burns v Burns* [1984] Ch 317, 332.

36 See Watkins (n 22).

37 See Bottomley (n 33) 184.

necessarily the actual unfavourable outcome but, rather, the 'perceived injustice which *Burns* has come to symbolise'.[38] The fact *Burns* is still discussed today, 40 years after it was decided, is testament to how a particular legal story and narrative influence and can shape reform conversations concerning cohabitation.[39]

Tracing the masterplot of choice today

Since *Burns*, there has been a dramatic increase in the number of cohabiting couples in England and Wales. There have been reform proposals to improve the legal position, but to date, none have been successful.[40] Marriage and its recent counterpart of civil partnership remain privileged statuses in law, and what remains for cohabitants is a framework of context-specific protections and rights that fail to tackle relationship-generated disadvantage upon separation and death. Navigating this framework is difficult, given the prevalence of an erroneous belief that living together creates a 'common-law marriage'. Further issues arise in relation to religious-only marriages that are not currently legally recognised, and thus, couples believing themselves to be married may end up treated in law as cohabitants.[41] This context sees the emergence of the masterplot of choice. We have moved on from the simplicity of branding such couples as 'living in sin' or overtly encouraging all couples to marry; instead, as will be argued, we are now imputing intentions to cohabitants and emphasising their autonomy, with a view to justifying why they are not marrying.

Evidence for the recent emergence of this masterplot comes from the Women and Equalities Committee of the UK Parliament that launched an inquiry, *The Rights of Cohabiting Partners*, in April 2021.[42] The terms of reference for that inquiry were broad, focusing on claims upon separation and death. After noting the exponential rise in cohabitation, the inferior pro-

38 John Mee, 'Burns v Burns: The Villain of the Piece' in Stephen Gilmore, Jonathan Herring and Rebecca Probert (eds), *Landmark Cases in Family Law* (Hart 2010) 186.

39 See the Oral Evidence given by Mike Horton KC to the Women and Equalities Committee (n 3), HC 130 – Q101 where he notes '[i]t was Mrs Burns who was left in the lurch, not Mr Burns, and I think in the generality of cases it will be [women].'

40 See, for example, Law Commission, *Sharing Homes* (Law Com No 278, 2002) and Law Commission (n 24).

41 See Anne Barlow, 'Modern Marriage Myths – The Dichotomy between Expectations of Legal Rationality and Lived Law' in Rajnaara Akhtar, Patrick Nash and Rebecca Probert (eds), *Cohabitation and Religious Marriage: Status, Similarities and Solutions* (Bristol University Press 2020) 39 and Rebecca Probert, Rajnaara Akhtar, Sharon Blake, Tania Barton and Vishal Vora, *When Is a Wedding Not a Marriage? Exploring Non-Legally Binding Ceremonies* (Nuffield Foundation 2022).

42 See Women and Equalities Committee (n 3).

tections available today, and the widespread misunderstandings as to the law, the inquiry sought evidence covering a range of issues affecting cohabitants. Of the 215 published responses (out of 380 received), it is interesting to note that academics and practitioners were virtually unanimously in favour of cohabitation reform but divided as to how generous it should be. In contrast, responses from members of the public and religious organisations were unanimously against reform. The evidence also revealed orchestrated submissions from certain religious organisations, such as the Christian Institute encouraging their members to oppose reform. Many of these written responses cited the same statistics and, at times, were identically worded. There were often political undertones and explicit references to religion,[43] with calls for the Conservative government in power at that time to support the institution of marriage and adhere to true Conservative values.[44] Given this demographic, the written evidence must be approached with a degree of caution when extrapolating trends. Nevertheless, it does still give a sense of modern viewpoints on cohabitation from certain sections of society.

Clear evidence of the masterplot of choice is present, whereby cohabitants are assumed to have made a deliberate decision not to marry based on an understanding of the law. Responses frequently questioned why rights should be given to cohabitants that have 'freely chosen not to be committed to one another' and have made 'a clear choice NOT to avail themselves of the benefits of marriage or a civil partnership'.[45] Formalisation is a 'choice that the couple has expressly rejected',[46] with one respondent going further, believing that cohabitation is a 'refusal' to marry.[47] A fuller written response noted:

> It should be remembered that people who are cohabiting have made a deliberate and conscious decision not to get married (as is their right). If we offer the same financial rights to cohabiting couples as we do to married couples, this is essentially going to have the same effect as imposing marriage terms on them. This is despite the fact that they have chosen to not make any public declaration to each other.[48]

Interestingly, the meaning ascribed to 'choice' in this context is multifaceted. It relates not only to a choice to cohabit in the first place but also to a choice as to the consequences flowing from that decision. The evidence emphasises the

43 See, for example, Written Evidence submitted to the Women and Equalities Committee (n 3), Rev Oliver Bayley [HAB0025] and Heidi Acland [HAB0108].
44 See Rev James Pennington [HAB0127] (n 3).
45 Mr Philip Mear [HAB0066] (capitalisation in original) (n 3).
46 Brian Clarke [HAB0356] (n 3).
47 David Rodda [HAB0298] (n 3).
48 Mr Christopher Langdown [HAB0013] (n 3).

implications of choice, especially in relation to the jettisoning of legal rights. Responses noted how cohabitants 'choose to have no rights'[49] and choose not to put their relationship 'on a legal footing'.[50] These comments reveal a factually incorrect belief that cohabitants are provided 'no rights'. While remedies on separation are not available and there is widespread misunderstanding by cohabitants as to the extent of their rights, limited context-specific protections do exist. Similarly, these comments also evidence an assumption that all or most cohabitants seek to be outside of the law, which again lacks nuance, as further explored later.

Other responses stated that while cohabitants might not know the full extent of the risk posed by cohabitation, it was not the role of the state to correct the 'bad' choices made or to rescue couples when they had 'neglected to choose'.[51] One respondent remarked that 'good publicity might encourage people to make a better choice',[52] and another stated that '[w]e do not make everyone a member of a tennis club because we think it would be good for them'.[53] The consequences associated with exercising choice or when failing to do so were expressed in a negative manner. In particular, individuals that cohabited were cast in a negative light. One respondent observed:

> If people choose not to marry but only to live together, should they not consider the consequences for a surviving partner after a death? Is the state required always to make up for people's lack of foresight and planning? Death comes commonly to all.[54]

These observations, repeated throughout the written evidence from members of the public, suggest the presence of the masterplot of choice and resonate strongly with the view of Barlow and Smithson relating to assumptions of 'legal rationality'. They have argued that:

> In the cohabitation context, law assumes people are making an active choice to cohabit rather than marry and that they will act in a legally rational way to order their legal affairs within the confines of property and succession law, should they wish to. This places the onus for action on the couple.[55]

This idea of 'doing something' accompanies most of the comments regarding choice in the written evidence submitted to the inquiry. However, a slight

49 Mr John Ward [HAB0129] (n 3).
50 Mrs C Blackman [HAB0313] (n 3).
51 Sir Paul Coleridge and Harry Benson of the Marriage Foundation [HAB0007] (n 3).
52 Mr Roger Kendall [HAB0030] (n 3).
53 Mr John Ward [HAB0129] (n 3).
54 Anthony Ford [HAB0020] (n 3).
55 Barlow and Smithson (n 34) 333.

contradiction is noticeable between cohabitants being conceptualised as having a worked-out intention to avoid marriage but then lacking the same decisiveness when it came to their own self-regulation. One respondent thought that cohabitants 'can't be bothered',[56] and as '[i]t is their choice; they made their bed and should lie in it!'[57] Another used the perceived ease of regulation as a criticism of cohabitant behaviour, stating:

> People do not think twice about the cost of a TV licence, and one can get married for less than the cost of a TV licence. If people are serious about their relationship, there is no reason that they cannot legalise it very cheaply.[58]

As will be explored later, viewing this as a masterplot helps us appreciate that these comments go further than merely highlighting that individuals can choose their particular relationship status. Choice is bound up in a network of other values and assumptions that, in turn, reveal a perceived hierarchy of relationships. This enables the masterplot of choice to engage with broader societal values and concerns about interpersonal relationships and how far they should be valued by the state. Marriage becomes synonymous with forethought, respectability, and commitment, while cohabitants, despite possessing the autonomy to choose, are painted as the reverse: disorganised, unworthy, and uncommitted.

Despite the strong opposition expressed in the public responses to the inquiry, the Committee made several recommendations for reform.[59] These included, *inter alia*, better public awareness of the distinctions between marriage, civil partnership, and cohabitation, and targeted information campaigns aimed at dispelling the common-law marriage myth. The Committee sought a commitment from the then Conservative government to introduce opt-out cohabitation reform along the lines of the Law Commission's recommendations from 2007[60] and the immediate introduction of their subsequent recommendations in relation to intestacy and claims upon death.[61]

Unfortunately, the government at that time largely rejected all the recommendations using rather unpersuasive reasoning.[62] The logic behind rejecting

56 Paul Quayle [HAB0064] (n 3).
57 Mr Philip Mear [HAB0066] (n 3).
58 David Rodda [HAB0298] (n 3). While marrying for less than the cost of a TV licence is technically possible, it is difficult to do in practice: see Rebecca Probert, Rajnaara Akhtar, Sharon Blake, Tania Barton and Vishal Vora, 'Trying to Get a Piece of Paper from City Hall? The Availability, Accessibility, and Administration of the Register Office Wedding' (2022) 44(2) *Journal of Social Welfare and Family Law* 226.
59 Women and Equalities Committee (n 3).
60 Law Commission (n 24).
61 Law Commission, *Intestacy and Family Provision Claims on Death* (Law Com No 331 2011).
62 Women and Equalities Committee, *The Rights of Cohabiting Partners: Government Response to the Committee's Second Report* (2022–23 HC 766).

these proposals is not the focus of this chapter,[63] but what is of note is that embedded within the government's reasoning is both the masterplot of marriage and also the masterplot articulated in this chapter regarding choice. As striking evidence of the former, the government emphasised the need for pupils in schools to be made

> aware of what marriage is, including its legal status . . . that marriage carries legal rights and protections not available to couples who are cohabiting or who have married in an unregistered religious ceremony) . . . [and] . . . why marriage is an important relationship choice for many couples.[64]

While the government response does call for education in schools, referencing the 'characteristics and legal status of other types of long-term relationships',[65] it is implicit from their response that a hierarchy is present with such relationships not necessarily sharing the same importance or 'unique' nature as marriage and civil partnership.[66] This sentiment is echoed in oral evidence to the Committee given by former Member of Parliament Tom Pursglove, then Minister for Justice, who expressed clear favour for any type of relationship formalisation, remarking, 'I think civil partnerships are a good thing; I think marriage is a good thing'.[67]

As for the masterplot of choice, the government's position is harder to discern, particularly as their reform 'solution' was to await the findings of an ongoing Law Commission project looking at reform of the law relating to financial remedies upon divorce. The government response did not directly engage with cohabitants choosing to reject marriage canvassed in the written evidence but did emphasise the importance of autonomy and choice. In particular, the government response noted the need for future review to acknowledge that both same- and mixed-sex couples possessing reservations as to marriage can now register civil partnerships. In the oral evidence session, Tom Pursglove MP said that this was 'one area that resolves quite a lot of the challenges in this space',[68] again shifting the onus onto couples to formalise or, in default, engage in self-ordering. This comment is rather reminiscent of an extra-judicial observation made by Baroness Hale when discussing couples choosing between

63 See, for example, Andy Hayward, 'Evaluating the Government's Response to the Women and Equalities Committee Rights of Cohabiting Partners Inquiry' *Financial Remedies Journal Blog* (7 November 2022) <https://financialremediesjournal.com/content/evaluating-the-governments-response-to-the-women-and-equalities-committee-rights-of-cohabiting-partners-inquiry.e25d1e771c464ab88f3f2e8c160da6d4.htm> accessed 4 March 2025.

64 Women and Equalities Committee (n 62) iii.

65 Women and Equalities Committee (n 62).

66 Women and Equalities Committee (n 62) vi.

67 Oral evidence submitted to the Women and Equalities Committee (n 3) HC 130 – Q153.

68 Oral evidence submitted to the Women and Equalities Committee (n 3) HC 130 – Q139.

marriage, civil partnership, and cohabitation: '[W]hy should we mind which they do, as long as they do something?'[69] More importantly, for this chapter, a focus on couples 'doing something' raises questions of whether, and if so, how, the masterplot of choice influences cohabiting couple behaviour.

The implications of the masterplot of choice

Identifying the existence of this masterplot of choice is an important academic exercise, but understanding its influence offers particularly useful insights. Its presence has direct consequences both for couples themselves and, like masterplots in general, shapes conversations happening at the political level in relation to reform. Indeed, its influence may become more noticeable, given the current Labour government's commitment to 'strengthen the rights and protections available to women in co-habiting couples', as expressed in their manifesto.[70] It is therefore important to ask how far the masterplot aligns with the practice and perceptions of cohabiting couples and how it finds expression at a political level.

Alignment of the masterplot with the lived experience of couples

A key feature of any masterplot is that it has a degree of universality. There must be evidence upon which it is based; otherwise, it would not be believed. In the written evidence to the inquiry, that element is present as cohabitants are constructed in a particular manner, sharing specific qualities. However, a starting point in the endeavour to disrupt or dispel a masterplot must be to challenge that generalised scope. There is potential to do this as empirical studies emphasise repeatedly that cohabitants vary tremendously in terms of their perceptions of commitment and understanding of the law.[71] It must, therefore, be questioned whether the masterplot of choice actually maps onto how cohabiting couples live their lives.

69 Brenda Hale, 'Private Family Law Reform' (2018) *Family Law* 810, 814.

70 See Change: Labour Party Manifesto <https://labour.org.uk/wp-content/uploads/2024/06/Labour-Party-manifesto-2024.pdf> accessed 23 August 2024. See also Andy Hayward, 'Cohabitation and Labour's Commitment to Changing the Law: What Reform Might Look Like' (2023) *Financial Remedies Journal Blog* (23 November 2023) <https://financialremediesjournal.com/content/cohabitation-and-labours-commitment-to-changing-the-law-what-reform-might-look-like.683ae4cfd6cf4342b9e20f62c0cb8fe1.htm> accessed 4 March 2025.

71 See, for example, Carol Smart and Pippa Stevens, *Cohabitation Breakdown* (Family Policy Studies Centre 2000), Anne Barlow and Grace James, 'Regulating Marriage and Cohabitation in 21st Century Britain' (2004) 67(2) *Modern Law Review* 143 and Simon Duncan, Anne Barlow and Grace James, 'Why Don't They Marry? Cohabitation, Commitment, and DIY Marriage' (2005) 17(3) *Child and Family Law Quarterly* 383.

First, as we have seen, the masterplot places the concept of choice at its centre. It is undoubtedly the case that some couples will cohabit after making a clear and informed choice. The most common example would be the so-called 'ideologue' couples identified by Barlow and Smithson in their study.[72] These couples are defined as being in 'long-term, committed relationships, but one or both partners will have an ideological objection to marriage'.[73] Choice was found to be central to their decision to cohabit, and despite being considered legally rational, that decision was so strong that couples even knowingly exposed themselves to 'financial disaster'.[74] Ideologue couples in their study knew, for example, about the adverse consequences of inheritance tax liability if one partner died.

But it is a truism that just as there is a diverse range of cohabiting couples, there is also an infinite variety of explanations as to why couples might cohabit. Understanding these reasons allows us to see that the language of choice embedded within this masterplot is overly simplistic. It must be understood in a contextualised manner to recognise that, for some couples, 'choices were not made in the first place'.[75] Barlow and Smithson's typology of couples identifies some cohabitants where that is readily apparent. These are so-called 'uneven couples', where 'one wants to marry, and one does not or where one is more committed to the relationship than the other'.[76] Such couples are exposed to what they term 'relationship-generated disadvantage' because of the potential power imbalance between the parties. Of course, one party may choose to leave the relationship in these circumstances, but that expectation or perceived 'solution' defies how interpersonal relationships generally operate in practice. Moreover, understanding this diversity of relationships allows us to question whether cohabitation, in this particular scenario, was a genuinely collective decision and the choice of both parties.

Second, the masterplot presupposes that by making a choice to cohabit, couples are also choosing to reject legal protection or are making decisions informed by an understanding of the law. This connects choice with legal remedies and, in a related manner, explains why policymakers push the idea that the law can influence or incentivise certain behaviour in relationships. We know that there will be some couples that actively choose cohabitation, and that choice is informed by knowing what they would receive in terms of rights or obligations. The aforementioned ideologue couples in Barlow and Smithson's study exemplify this behaviour. They are legally rational because they will make wills, declarations of trust regarding ownership of their real property, and, consistent with their desire not to marry, may even register

72 See Barlow and Smithson (n 34).
73 Barlow and Smithson (n 34) 335.
74 Barlow and Smithson (n 34) 337.
75 Dr Sharon Thompson, Cardiff University [HAB0342] (n 3).
76 Barlow and Smithson (n 34) 335.

civil partnerships as an alternative to marriage. In a sense, these couples conform with and, in turn, reinforce the masterplot of choice.

But empirically, the connection between choice and legal rights can be disputed. Couples are generally not driven to marry or cohabit because of the availability of legal rights. That has been largely established in several studies.[77] Unlike in the past, where marriage was expected of couples owing to the societal opprobrium associated with cohabitation and concerns over illegitimacy relating to any children, such context does not exist today. Similarly, attempts to exploit that connection between marrying in order to obtain rights have proved futile. Government intervention to stimulate the marriage rate through tax incentives has had limited success, again revealing the difficulty of using the law to steer behaviour and influence the choice of couples.[78] Indeed, legal interventions rarely have this effect. It is interesting to note that the introduction of cohabitation law in other countries has neither resulted in an increased uptake in couples cohabiting nor a correlating reduction in the marriage rate.[79]

Put simply, it is non-legal factors that tend to drive decision-making regarding interpersonal relationships.[80] While legal rights are certainly a welcome benefit of formalisation, couples tend to choose a relationship type for a range of different, potentially unquantifiable reasons that are unrelated to law. Cohabitation can be explained by convenience, perceptions of commitment,[81] or even financial resources. The latter point may be attributable to the increasing cost of weddings today and that, as a group, cohabitants are statistically in a weaker economic position when compared to spouses.[82] Similarly, in the context of same-sex relationship recognition, these more ephemeral, symbolic, or ideological qualities have been identified as important drivers behind formalisation. For example, the European Court of Human Rights, in *Oliari v Italy*, noted that there was an intrinsic value of civil partnerships that exists 'irrespective of the legal effects, however narrow or extensive, that they would produce'.[83]

77 See John Eekelaar and Mavis Maclean, 'Marriage and the Moral Bases of Personal Relationships' (2004) 31(4) *Journal of Law and Society* 510 and Mary Hibbs, Chris Barton and Joanne Beswick, 'Why Marry? Perceptions of the Affianced' (2001) *Family Law* 197.

78 Elizabeth van Acker, 'Disconnected Relationship Values and Marriage Policies in England' (2016) 38(1) *Journal of Social Welfare and Family Law* 36. See also Rebecca Probert, 'Cohabitation and Marriage in England and Wales' (2015) 4(1) *Families, Relationships and Societies* 157.

79 Kathleen Kiernan, Anne Barlow and Roseangela Merlo, 'Cohabitation Law Reform and Its Impact on Marriage' (2006) *Family Law* 1074.

80 See, for example, Eekelaar and Maclean (n 77).

81 See Smart and Stevens (n 71).

82 See Joanna Miles, Pascoe Pleasence and Nigel Balmer, 'The Experience of Relationship Breakdown and Civil Law Problems by People in Different Forms of Relationship' (2009) 21(1) *Child and Family Law Quarterly* 47.

83 [2015] ECHR 716 [174] citing *Vallianatos v Greece* (2013) 59 EHRR 519 [81].

However, despite this evidence, the presence and promotion of the masterplot of choice align very much with the assumption suggested in the Conservative government's own approach that there exists a 'rational economic man' or 'rational economic subject' making 'individualistic, cost–benefit type decisions about how to maximize their own personal gain'.[84] Proceeding on this basis, it would follow that if the government changes financial structures or legal frameworks, then 'people will modify their social behaviour in the desired direction'.[85] This perhaps explains why mixed-sex civil partnerships were advocated for so strongly by the previous Conservative government ministers in the Women and Equalities Committee inquiry as a recent purposive modification of the law aimed at steering couple behaviour towards formalising their relationship.

This whole endeavour has been termed the 'rationality mistake' by Barlow and Duncan.[86] The approach overlooks how decision-making in interpersonal relationships is frequently borne out of a complex and sophisticated process of negotiation that is highly context-specific. In addition, choice is heavily conditioned by 'hidden psychological inhibiters'[87] that prevent couples from behaving rationally. For example, one feature cutting across all interpersonal relationships is 'optimism bias', which is the belief that a relationship will not break down. Similarly, this belief may prevent couples from having potentially difficult conversations about regulation that might result in separation. Other barriers to legal rationality are unspoken social expectations, especially in relation to childcare, that can influence decision-making. These often have gendered impacts, too, as seen in written evidence submitted to the inquiry.[88] Realising legal rationality also requires an opportunity to arise for couples to regulate their relationship and the parties possessing the financial resources to do so. As relationships tend to develop organically over time, that opportunity may never present itself, and the financial position of many cohabitants might inhibit couples from regulating. The masterplot of choice is thus misguided: it simply does not follow that a free choice to cohabit (if that even exists in all circumstances) also encompasses a free choice to reject legal protections.

Third, if couples have actively chosen to reject legal rights, as the masterplot of choice suggests, then it surely follows that they must know what they are rejecting. This viewpoint finds expression in the academic scholarship.

84 Anne Barlow and Simon Duncan, 'Supporting Families? New Labour's Communitarianism and the "Rationality Mistake": Part I' (2000) 22(1) *Journal of Social Welfare and Family Law* 23, 24.

85 Barlow and Duncan (n 84).

86 Anne Barlow and Simon Duncan, 'New Labour's Communitarianism, Supporting Families and the "Rationality Mistake: Part II"' (2000) 22(2) *Journal of Social Welfare and Family Law* 129.

87 Barlow and Smithson (n 34) 346.

88 See Dr Anna Heenan, Cardiff University [HAB0286] (n 3).

Writing in 1980, Deech stated that *cohabitants* are 'people who are well aware of the situation they have placed themselves in'.[89] More recently, Auchmuty attacked the exaggerated perception of a lack of understanding of the law, noting that the law of property on co-ownership is relatively clear.[90] They further argue that complex constructive trust litigation over real property, like that seen in *Burns v Burns*, only arises in the statistical minority of cases, given the prevalence of purchases of the family home in joint names. However, the difficulty with both of these arguments is that studies still show a considerable and enduring degree of misunderstanding among cohabitants as to legal protections.[91] This lack of understanding clearly does not apply to all cohabiting couples but to some.

A well-known contributing factor is the common-law marriage myth, which is the erroneous belief that living together for a period of time gives couples legal protection. Recent research has revealed just how entrenched this myth still is.[92] In 2019, 47% of the population believed in common-law marriage giving cohabitants the same legal rights as if they were married, with that belief increasing to 55% when couples had children. This picture is further complicated by the complexities of the legal framework itself. A simple binary presented in the written evidence of formalisation equating to bountiful protection and cohabitation conferring nothing does not exist. Cohabitants may receive identical protection to spouses and civil partnerships in some contexts and, in others, may receive lesser or no protection at all. While there will be cohabitants that can navigate this landscape, perhaps with the help of legal advice, practitioner organisations attest to recent examples where couples have been mistaken or such advice has come only too late.[93]

Understanding this aspect, again, reveals the fallacy of legal rationality embedded within the masterplot of choice. That argument becomes more convincing when it is appreciated that even when couples are made aware of their legal rights (or the lack thereof), many are not prompted into action. They neither conform to the foundational masterplot by marrying nor do they use private ordering mechanisms by entering a cohabitation contract or making a will.[94] It is apparent that the promotion of the masterplot of choice views cohabitation in a particular manner that is very much at odds with

89 Ruth L. Deech, 'The Case against Legal Recognition of Cohabitation' (1980) 29(2–3) *International and Comparative Law Quarterly* 480, 483.

90 See Auchmuty (n 27).

91 See, for example, Gillian Douglas, Julia Pearce and Hilary Woodward, *A Failure of Trust: Resolving Property Disputes on Cohabitation Breakdown* (Cardiff University and Bristol University 2007).

92 Muslihah Albakri, Suzanne Hill, Nancy Kelley and Nilufer Rahim, 'Relationships and Gender Identity' in *British Social Attitudes 36* (The National Centre for Social Research 2019).

93 See Written Evidence to Women and Equalities Committee (n 3) by Resolution [HAB0238].

94 See Barlow and Smithson (n 34) 331. See also Anne Barlow, Simon Duncan, Grace James and Alison Park, *Cohabitation, Marriage and the Law* (Hart 2005) 97.

couples' lived experiences. Moreover, this dissonance between perception and actual practice suggests that the masterplot of choice is operating within a highly politicised context, which, in turn, forces us to question whether other policy aims, imperatives, and agendas are at play.

Politicising the masterplot

If masterplots speak to prevailing beliefs and concerns in society, it is unsurprising that their influence might affect not just the couples themselves but broader family law policies as well. The emphasis placed on choice within this masterplot connects it with certain political ideologies. Several of the written submissions to the recent Women and Equalities Committee inquiry stated that the choice to cohabit rather than marry is a manifestation of autonomy and, relatedly, the loftier notion of freedom. That connection has been analysed in the academic scholarship for some time. Fuelling the masterplot of choice, Deech has argued extensively for the preservation of a 'corner of freedom' for couples to escape the reach of family law and, more recently, grounded such freedom to the right to privacy recognised in human rights law.[95] Deech argues that legislating for increased legal protections for cohabitants would infringe Article 8 of the European Convention on Human Rights protecting the right to respect for private and family life. In short, Deech believes '[p]rivate adult choices should be respected'.[96] Members of the public expressed similar viewpoints in the written evidence submitted to the inquiry. One response remarked that freedom was their 'first concern'[97] and that regulating cohabitation was 'an assault on freedom'.[98] Another respondent stated that 'the government should not trespass into the personal life of individuals', and that '[t]o legislate would be like putting a permanent CCTV on their lives'.[99]

Concern as to autonomy in this context is certainly understandable, especially when it is appreciated that a key role of family law is to balance protection for a weaker party against respect for autonomy. But this bold and romanticised conception of autonomy expressed in the written evidence overlooks the fact that autonomy is never absolute and is frequently curtailed by the state. As Scherpe noted, 'almost all legal rules are – and are meant to be – infringements on autonomy', and that is often done to 'address an imbalance of power and/or pursue an important social policy aim'.[100] Thus, the presentation of autonomy, freedom, and choice for cohabitants is somewhat

95 Deech (n 89) 483.
96 HL Deb [HL] Cohabitation Rights Bill vol 796, col 1265 (15 March 2019).
97 Mr Roger Kendall [HAB0030] (n 3).
98 Mr Paul Nicholas [HAB0071] (n 3).
99 Patrick Pullicino [HAB0058] (n 3).
100 Women and Equalities Committee (n 3) 19.

idealised, open-textured, and nostalgic, which perhaps might explain why many are drawn into believing it.

There is also a duality to autonomy that requires nuanced understanding because it effectively 'cuts both ways'. Expressed differently, autonomy can be viewed both positively and negatively. Written responses to the inquiry speak of respecting the autonomy of couples to positively do something, such as assuming rights voluntarily by marrying or registering civil partnerships or self-regulating via contract or a will. At the same time, they recognise respect for autonomy in a negative manner, requiring protection for couples from state-imposed obligations, which is consistent with the prevailing political climate adopting a 'policy of general retreat from legal interference with the individual and with family life'.[101] This rather inconsistent use of autonomy suggests that choice is being used as a shorthand to oppose reform while, at the same time, framing that opposition as (perhaps disingenuous) benevolence to cohabitants. Thus, by standing up for freedom and defending the choice to avoid marriage, cohabitants and their decision-making capacity are being respected and protected.

Intentions may be honourable here, but it should be noted that virtually all responses from members of the public evince clear support for marriage as the preferred union. Indeed, the metaphor of being a member of a club is used in several of the responses, indicating 'gatekeeping' or a concern that any reform would, in some way, diminish or devalue their own relationships. One respondent was concerned that the very concept of rights was being 'abused to give people outside the "club" of marriage the same benefits', and remarked: 'I may be an excellent professional golfer but unless I pay the subscription and join the club, I can't play on their course and enjoy the membership perks'.[102]

Another consequence of the masterplot of choice is that we can discern clear evidence of neoliberalism. This is to be expected, as Thompson's research in the field of prenuptial agreements has shown how promulgating the 'mantra that "autonomy is good for you"' fuels the neoliberal tendency to drive family law regulation and dispute resolution into the private sphere.[103] It becomes a matter for the parties themselves to do something, and unless and until the parties act, any intervention by the state is seen as intrusive or unwarranted. Aligning with the shift from duty-based conceptions of relationships to ones premised on individual choice articulated earlier, this theme is picked up in the written evidence, with one respondent stating the approach of the government should be 'Responsibility, Responsibility, Responsibility, not Give, Give, Give'.[104] Doing otherwise would pander to the

101 Rebecca Bailey-Harris, 'Law and the Unmarried Couple – Oppression or Liberation?' (1996) 8(2) *Child and Family Law Quarterly* 137, 138.

102 Mr Granville Routledge [HAB0024] and Mr John Ward [HAB0129] (n 3).

103 Sharon Thompson, 'Feminist Relational Contract Theory: A New Model for Family Property Agreements' (2018) 45(4) *Journal of Law and Society* 617, 622.

104 Mr Martin Brunning [HAB0214] (n 3).

'me-first' culture[105] or the belief that cohabitants 'want [to have] their cake and eat it'.[106] Put simply, it should be on the parties themselves to regulate, or better still, regularise, their relationship.

The masterplot of choice also benefits politicians too, especially those reluctant to change the law. The reason for this is that a dominant focus on choice influences not only whether the law should be reformed in the first place but also what model to adopt. The preferred reform strategy would be to deconstruct the meaning of choice used in this context and show that it is highly contested and draw attention to the fact that whether it is always 'free' is questionable in interpersonal relationships. Thus, as Barlow and Duncan have argued, reform should involve showing that a belief in legal rationality is misguided, which then might persuade politicians to engage with more interventionist strategies to combat relationship-generated disadvantage. This could pave the way for the introduction of a presumptive 'opt-out' scheme of legal remedies that would apply to qualifying cohabitants after they satisfy certain eligibility criteria. Given their response to the recent inquiry, this approach was not favoured by the Conservative government at that time.

Instead, the seductive appeal of choice is being used to enhance and encourage greater legal rationality at the expense of intervention.[107] The masterplot of choice reinforces the belief in the existence of deliberate regulatory avoidance on the part of all cohabitants. This can be seen in the government response to reform and the written evidence. Rather than committing to creating a legislative framework, or even at least contemplating that as a possibility, the approach favoured was to provide *more* information to help couples make *better and more* informed choices. This is discernible in the observation of former MP Tom Pursglove in oral evidence to the Committee:

> It is an awareness point, is it not . . . ? The more that we can do to educate and inform, clearly, the better it is. We want people to have security. We want people to be protected from adverse outcomes. Anything that we can do to improve awareness, to make sure that people have all the information that they can possibly have to make the best-informed decisions that they can make, clearly, that is a good thing.[108]

The written evidence adopts a similar and strangely uniform position. One respondent noted that '[i]t makes no sense to change a law merely to avoid

105 Mr Alex Stewart, ACA Research [HAB0022] (n 3).

106 Mr Roy White [HAB0158] (n 3).

107 See, for example, Antony Dnes, 'Rational Decision-Making and Intimate Cohabitation' in Joanna Miles and Rebecca Probert (eds), *Sharing Lives, Dividing Assets: An Interdisciplinary Study* (Hart 2009).

108 Oral evidence submitted to Women and Equalities Committee (n 3) HC 130 – Q154.

explaining it properly'.[109] Another remarked that '[t]he right solution . . . is publicity and education – in the same way that the solution to the dangers of cliff-top paths in areas of outstanding natural beauty is signage, not the destruction of the cliff'.[110]

While providing more information is never a bad thing, there are deficiencies to this as a potential solution for cohabitants. We know that pushing greater autonomy in the domestic sphere can often be at the expense of other values, such as protection of a weaker party.[111] Public awareness campaigns have had mixed results in terms of steering behaviour.[112] Also, the idea of enhancing autonomy or empowering cohabitants to make 'the best-informed decisions that they can make' is unlikely to be neutral.[113] This belief is neatly encapsulated by the following response to the inquiry:

> The government is constantly encouraging people to take the best action. They teach children to look both ways before crossing the road. They encourage people to wear face masks to prevent infection. So why not promote the best form of relationship. Why help people to take a more risky route through life.[114]

This resonates with Barlow and Duncan's 'rationality mistake', a dimension of which proceeds on the basis that if people 'make suboptimal decisions where they lack information about this cost–benefit structure . . . providing better information, or educating people so that they can access it and act upon it more effectively, will have the desired social effects'.[115] But by seeking to influence people's choices and promote the inherent value of choice itself rather than combatting the adverse consequences of them, the government would arguably entrench pre-existing relationship hierarchies and norms. The approach feeds the overly simplistic belief that formalisation gives couples rights whereas non-formalisation is seen as a decision to be corrected. More importantly, it goes to the pathologising of cohabitation because that relationship is seen as the problem or a predicament from which couples need to escape through exercising (better) choices.[116]

109 Rev James Pennington [HAB0127] (n 3).
110 Simon Watson [HAB0278] (n 3).
111 Jonathan Herring, 'Relational Autonomy in Family Law' in Julie Wallbank, Shazia Choudhry and Jonathan Herring (eds), *Gender Rights and Family Law* (Routledge 2009) 275.
112 See Anne Barlow, Carole Burgoyne and Janet Smithson, 'The Living Together Campaign – The Impact on Cohabitants' (2007) *Family Law* 165.
113 Oral evidence submitted to Women and Equalities Committee (n 3) HC 130 – Q154 (Tom Pursglove MP).
114 Stephen Lally [HAB0059] (n 3).
115 Barlow and Duncan (n 84) 24.
116 Auchmuty (n 27) 322.

Negative and pejorative language runs through the written evidence. Cohabitation is viewed as bad for couples as it is unstable, lacking in commitment, and transient. Indeed, one respondent saw marriage as a 'critical life choice', whereas cohabiting couples 'just shack up, perhaps have children by accident and drift on'.[117] As for the broader impact of cohabitation on the wider community, many respondents saw the promotion of marriage as a solution to 'restore our society'.[118] The positive contribution that marriage gave society was then juxtaposed against that stemming from cohabitation: 'Stability, good health, less drug addiction, less crime – all are associated with marriage; the reverse is associated with cohabiting couples.'[119] The implication is, if cohabiting couples realised this, then their actions would change. This has echoes of the caricatures of divorcing couples created around the time of the proposed no-fault divorce reforms contained in Part II of the Family Law Act 1996. With that law's focus on mandatory mediation and procedures aimed at couple reconciliation, Dewar saw it as constructing individuals going through divorce as 'reasonable, self-denying, conciliatory, and fully conscious of the implications of their actions for themselves and for others'.[120] Given the negative perceptions of cohabitants, is it not the case the masterplot of choice is doing the same?

Lastly, the masterplot of choice affects broader policy too. It can be questioned whether the masterplot of choice, and even masterplots more generally, is used to resist change or ensure the status quo is maintained. Perhaps they also can be used to distract and shift reform conversations away from the more pertinent issues. Parallels may be drawn from a recent reform relating to civil partnerships and same-sex marriage. When exploring reform in that field, Glennon identified a strategy of policymakers maintaining a focus on 'accessibility' to a status rather than legal 'content'.[121] More specifically, the accessibility of same-sex marriage or civil partnership was centred as the key goal rather than the more complicated question of the content of both regimes and, in particular, the appropriateness of the marital norms underpinning them. This was arguably because if we focused on content, we would prompt much more difficult discussions about why regimes treated couples in factually analogous positions differently. Although the legal differences between marriage and civil partnership have subsequently been removed, this argument resonates with cohabitation reform and the emphasis placed on choice. Conversations about whether cohabiting couples *should* access a regime in the first place prevent government engagement with the more difficult and disruptive conversations as to legal content or the normative justification

117 Stephen Lally [HAB0059] (n 3).
118 Richard Worthington [HAB0039] (n 3).
119 Brian Clarke [HAB0356] (n 3).
120 John Dewar, 'The Normal Chaos of Family Law' (1998) 61(4) *Modern Law Review* 467, 483.
121 See Glennon (n 12).

for treating arguably functionally similar relationships differently. Even if the Conservative government at that time engaged in reform beyond public awareness campaigns, by emphasising concern as to 'choice', it would have been likely that any reform would be relatively weak. Low-level or the least intrusive type of reform would be considered more acceptable for fear of overriding those choices and the country becoming, as one respondent noted, a 'nanny state'.[122] This suggests, perhaps, an incidental benefit to governments of the masterplot of choice – its use can be expedient through supporting and justifying government inertia. That position, however, may now change, given the Labour government's commitment to reform this area, but at present, the shape that future reform might take is unknown.

Conclusions

Choice and legal rationality, especially the acceptance that cohabiting couples may act in a legally irrational manner, have long been acknowledged and analysed in academic scholarship. This chapter has drawn upon submissions to the recent Women and Equalities Committee inquiry to provide further and more contemporary evidence pointing to the centrality of choice in the way members of the public think about cohabitation. However, where this chapter departs from the existing literature is through conceptualising choice not as a dimension, explanation, or driver for why couples cohabit but as a foundational masterplot.

It is argued that multiple benefits arise when choice is characterised as a masterplot. First, it allows for a much richer understanding of opposition arguments to cohabitation reform and their constituent elements. Put differently, we can identify those arguments and then, as Sadler notes, 'set them into relationships with each other and interpret their significance in terms of their positions within larger narrative units'.[123] For example, the discourse surrounding choice is not focusing on a simple decision of couples to cohabit; rather, overlaid onto the concept of choice is a network of connected or follow-on assumptions and values stemming from the exercise of that choice. We believe that choosing to cohabit is, at the same time, choosing to reject any form of legal protection. As a result, we impute to the parties a 'deliberate intention of regulatory avoidance' that may not exist in the circumstances.[124] This misconstrues couple behaviour because, as Barlow notes, 'there is no evidence that the majority of cohabitants are seeking to avoid the legal implications of marriage'.[125]

122 Mr John Lazenby [HAB0055] (n 3).
123 Neil Sadler, 'Myths, Masterplots and Sexual Harassment in Egypt' (2019) 24(2) *The Journal of North African Studies* 247, 254.
124 Glennon (n 12) 174.
125 Anne Barlow, 'Cohabitation Law Reform – Messages from Research' (2006) 14(2) *Feminist Legal Studies* 167, 173.

Secondly, viewing this area through the lens of a masterplot allows us to see how choice is weaponised by politicians opposed to reform. By emphasising choice, we shift responsibility away from the state onto the parties themselves. We relinquish the responsibility to fix the negative consequences of 'bad' choices as we do in marriage, believing instead that it is for the cohabiting parties to resolve. After all, to fix these consequences could be seen as paternalistic, patronising, and undermining of party autonomy. Rejecting statutory intervention because of choice also militates towards a less intrusive or 'light touch' option if the state ever were to regulate in the future. As we have seen following the Women and Equalities Committee inquiry, the preferred approach chosen by the government at that time was greater public awareness. This would, it is believed, make couples better informed and, as a result, more capable of exhibiting greater legal rationality. Yet noting how masterplots draw upon and weaponise concerns and fears of the community, it is readily apparent how such awareness can absorb political ideology.

It is without doubt that some cohabitants deliberately avoid marriage and do so in full appreciation of the law. As a result, they squarely align with the masterplot of choice, which is to be expected, because without some connection to reality, such a masterplot would lose its universality and power. But as this chapter has argued, by both discerning and then dissecting the implications of the masterplot of choice, we can better understand how it fails to recognise the diversity and reality of all cohabiting relationships. Once that is understood, we can then combat its influence in the enduring quest for cohabitation reform.

Chapter 13

Family autonomy and child protection

The stories we tell ourselves

Julie Doughty

This chapter considers the contradiction between, on the one hand, law and policy based on the ideal of family autonomy, with children being best brought up by their birth parents, and, on the other, the seemingly inexorable rise in the number of children being removed from their parents into state care in England and Wales.[1] The flaws in the narrative of child removal as a last resort will be highlighted through four different values perspectives on childcare policy that were identified by Lorraine Fox Harding in the 1990s.[2] The legislative basis for family support will first be set out, followed by the legal framework for child removal. Discussion of these four themes as 'masterplots' brings to light the influence of successive stories about child protection, often in the form of scandals that capture the public imagination and can lead to changes in policy or practice. Other stories that reflect the lived experiences of families and practitioners are also emerging and shifting the narrative.

The Children Act 1989: powers and duties to support children and their families

Child welfare systems in Europe and the USA, since the second half of the twentieth century, have been categorised as either risk-oriented or service-oriented, with the latter description commonly applied to Scandinavian countries. The USA is an example of a risk-oriented approach, with a high threshold to be reached before state intervention. The UK and Ireland have also been seen as tending more toward a high threshold, despite the Children Act 1989 in England and Wales ('the 1989 Act') placing a duty on local authorities to provide family support services before using compulsory

1 This chapter focuses on policy in England. For recent analysis of the position in Wales, see Helen Hodges and Jonathan Scourfield, 'Why Are There Higher Rates of Children Looked after in Wales?' (2023) 18(3) *Journal of Children's Services* 165–79.
2 Lorraine Fox Harding, *Perspectives in Child Care Policy* (2nd edn, Pearson 1997).

DOI: 10.4324/9781003404668-19

powers of removal.[3] As discussed later, the 1989 Act introduced principles of parental responsibility and working in partnership with parents.[4]

The Children Act 1989, s17, sits centrally in Part III of the Act, headed 'Support for children and families provided by local authorities in England'. The section imposes a general duty on local authorities to provide a range of services to children who need support to achieve and maintain a reasonable standard of health or development, or because their health or development is likely to be significantly impaired without services. Children 'in need' and their families are therefore entitled to provision of support services, but there are often tensions between parents' perceptions of their children's well-being and the benefits that additional services will bring and local authority decisions on what constitutes a reasonable standard or significant impairment.[5] Whether a particular service is offered to a child or not will depend on professional judgment and local protocols rather than on universally agreed expectations.

Rather than ensuring families are entitled to assistance, the general s17 duty has been traced back to Poor Law principles as a legal device to legitimise public spending on children's welfare. There is an inherent tension between encouraging expenditure on children and spending public money only where necessary, from the standpoint of the taxpayer.[6] This has played out as the interpretation of s17 as a general duty to children who live in the locality, not to any individual child's entitlement to services. The duty does not oblige a local authority to meet every assessed need; an assessment of an individual child's needs does not crystallise the general duty to become a specific duty to a child.[7] Although s17 places a duty on a local authority to assess the need for services, there is no duty to subsequently provide a service.[8] As Piper argues, s17 became an instrument for rationing and is essentially a mechanism to ensure a local authority is not unlawfully spending money.[9] Although the welfare of the child is the court's paramount consideration, as set out in Part I and applicable to most of Parts II and IV, s17 appears in Part III, where welfare is cited only as a general duty to be safeguarded and promoted for children in care. Local authority decision-makers are therefore

3 Kenneth Burns, Tarja Poso, and Marit Skivenes, *Child Welfare Removals by the State: A Cross-Country Analysis of Decision-Making Systems* (OUP 2017).

4 *Parental responsibility* is defined in the Children Act 1989, s3. 'Partnership' does not appear in the Act itself but in Department of Health and Social Security, *Review of Child Care Law: Report to Ministers of an Interdepartmental Working Party* (HMSO 1985).

5 Joanne Westwood, *Children in Need of Support* (Palgrave Macmillan 2014).

6 Christine Piper, *Investing in Children: Policy, Law and Practice in Context* (Willan 2008).

7 *R (G) v Barnet LBC* [2003] UKHL 57.

8 Although disabled children may be entitled to receive services under the Chronically Sick and Disabled Persons Act 1970.

9 Piper (n 6).

not required to place a child's welfare above all other considerations when providing family support. This lack of enforceability in the drafting of Part III was predicted as problematic by a number of social policy academics, for example, Hendrick stating that the emphasis on children 'in need' was a new ideology of residualism allowing resource pressures to restrict the concept of 'need' to those children 'at risk'.[10]

By 1997, Parton was asking whether it was even possible to combine family help and support with child protection in children's services.[11] He acknowledged that the drafters of the Act had emphasised partnership and support, minimising policing and coercive intervention: 'In effect policy and practice would be driven by Part III and Section 17 of the Act.'[12] However, already, he argued, child protection concerns were beginning to dominate.

It should be noted that the Act states that local authorities shall take reasonable steps designed to reduce the need for children to be taken into care.[13] Even these specific duties are discretionary and subject to budgetary constraints.[14] However, government 'austerity' policies of reducing public expenditure since 2010 have led to gradual abandonment of most services that had developed to (in Piper's description) 'invest in children'. The swift rebranding by the incoming administration of the Labour government's Department for Children, Schools, and Families (the secretary of state being Ed Balls) to the Department for Education (under Michael Gove) symbolised the narrowing ideology from holistic investment in childhood to producing the future economically active adult.

Taking reasonable steps to avoid children going into care requires public investment in early help for families who are facing difficulties. A recent report from children's charities found that local authority expenditure in England on early intervention services had halved in the last 12 years; although by 2021 expenditure on children's services overall had increased, 80% of that increase was spent on late crisis intervention.[15] This snapshot suggests that it has become politically acceptable to ignore children 'in need' until compulsory intervention is essential – far from the stated aims of the 1989 legislation. This is dangerous not only socially but also economically. The authors of that report conclude that children's services are in a 'doom spiral',

10 Harry Hendrick, *Child Welfare: England 1872–1989* (Routledge 1994) 277.

11 Nigel Parton, 'Child Protection and Family Support: Current Debates and Future Prospects' in Nigel Parton (ed), *Child Protection and Family Support: Tensions, Contradictions and Future Possibilities* (Routledge 1997) 1–24.

12 Parton (n 11) 3.

13 Children Act 1989 Sch 2 Part 1 Para 7(a).

14 *R (G) v Barnet LBC* [2003] UKHL 57.

15 Jon Franklin, Jack Larkham and Mariam Mansoor, *The Well-Worn Path: Children's Services Spending 2010–11 to 2021–22* (Children's Services Funding Alliance and Pro-Bono Economics 2023).

with 'local authorities trapped providing high-cost, late interventions, with demand for services for children in care growing, and the cost of providing them increasing too'. Specifically, there was disproportionate expenditure on resource-intensive residential care placements in the private sector.[16]

Alongside Part III of the 1989 Act, Parts IV (Care and Supervision) and V (Protection of Children) were anticipated to reduce the number of children in care by significant reform in the criteria and process for entry into the care system through court proceedings.

The Children Act 1989: threshold for child removal

Prior to the 1989 Act, the removal of children by the state was rarely subject to judicial scrutiny.[17] Under the existing legislation of the 1970s and 80s, children could be taken into care by local authorities on grounds of abuse and neglect, being generally troublesome, or criminally offending. Care applications were usually preceded by a period during which a child was subject to a 'place of safety order' granted by a juvenile court, where only the local authority and the child were parties. Proceedings were held in private before lay magistrates; parents had no right to legal representation. There was a parallel purely administrative mechanism whereby children were taken into care simply through councillors passing a resolution of assumption of parental rights. A third possibility was the local authority applying for wardship in the High Court, which was the only means of obtaining judicial oversight. However, the 1989 Act effectively closed off routes for the local authority other than applying for a care order under Section 31, which must be based on evidence of the risk of significant harm.[18]

The wording of Section 31 largely followed a report to government ministers in 1985 that actual or likely harm to the child was grounds for a care order.[19] The interdepartmental working party rejected suggestions that the child's welfare on its own could justify compulsory intervention. Such a test would be too subjective and insufficient protection of the family from disproportionate interference with their rights to respect for family life.[20] As expressed by Lady Hale in a House of Lords judgment in 2008:

> Taking a child away from her family is a momentous step, not only for her, but for her whole family, and for the local authority which does so.

16 Franklin, Larkham and Mansoor (n 15) 22.

17 Mary Hayes, 'Removing Children from Their Families before the Children Act 1989' in Nigel Lowe and Gillian Douglas (eds), *The Continuing Evolution of Family Law* (Jordans 2009).

18 Joan Hunt, Alison McLeod and Caroline Thomas, *The Last Resort* (TSO 1999) 3.

19 Department of Health and Social Security, *Review of Child Care Law: Report to Ministers of an Interdepartmental Working Party* (HMSO 1985).

20 Nick Allen, *Making Sense of the Children Act 1989* (4th edn, John Wiley & Sons Ltd 2005).

> In a totalitarian society, uniformity and conformity are valued. Hence the totalitarian state tries to separate the child from her family and mould her to its own design. Families in all their subversive variety are the breeding ground of diversity and individuality. In a free and democratic society we value diversity and individuality. Hence the family is given special protection in all the modern human rights instruments including the European Convention on Human Rights (article 8), the International Covenant on Civil and Political Rights (article 23) and throughout the United Nations Convention on the Rights of the Child. As McReynolds J famously said in Pierce v Society of Sisters (1925) 268 US 510, 535 'The child is not the mere creature of the state'.
>
> That is why the Review of Child Care Law (Department of Health and Social Security, 1985)) and the White Paper, The Law on Child Care and Family Services (1987) (Cm 62), which led up to the Children Act 1989, rejected the suggestion that a child could be taken from her family whenever it would be better for her than not doing so. As the Review put it, only where their children are put at unacceptable risk should it be possible compulsorily to intervene.[21]

At around the same time as this House of Lords judgment was being delivered, Mr Justice Hedley issued his oft-quoted warning in a High Court judgment about the proportionality of making a care order:

> It is the tradition of the United Kingdom, recognised in law, that children are best brought up within natural families. Lord Templeman, in Re: KD (a minor ward) (termination of access) [1988] 1 AC 806, at page 812 said this:
>
>> 'The best person to bring up a child is the natural parent. It matters not whether the parent is wise or foolish, rich or poor, educated or illiterate, provided the child's moral and physical health are not in danger. Public authorities cannot improve on nature.'
>
> There are those who may regard that last sentence as controversial but undoubtedly it represents the present state of the law in determining the starting point. It follows inexorably from that, that society must be willing to tolerate very diverse standards of parenting, including the eccentric, the barely adequate and the inconsistent. It follows too that children will

21 *Re B* [2008] UKHL 35 [20–21]. This phrase from the *Pierce* case might suggest an element of freedom for children, but the case itself was about parents' rights to exercise a choice of religious instead of state education. The Supreme Court held that 'liberty' under the 14th amendment included parents' rights to control their children's education.

> inevitably have both very different experiences of parenting and very unequal consequences flowing from it. It means that some children will experience disadvantage and harm, whilst others flourish in atmospheres of loving security and emotional stability. These are the consequences of our fallible humanity and it is not the provenance of the State to spare children all the consequences of defective parenting. In any event, it simply could not be done.
>
> That is not, however, to say that the State has no role, as the Children Act 1989 fully demonstrates. Nevertheless, that Act, wide ranging though the courts and social services' powers may be, is to be operated in the context of the policy I have sought to describe. Its essence, in Part III of the Act, is the concept of working in partnership with families who have children in need. Only exceptionally should the State intervene with compulsive powers and then only when a Court is satisfied that the significant harm criteria in Section 31(2) is made out. Such an approach is clearly consistent with Article 8.[22]

In the landmark case of *Re B* in 2013, where the Supreme Court examined the proportionality of removing a child for closed adoption on the basis of the likelihood of future risk of harm, Lady Hale cites these paragraphs from Hedley J as meaning that the court must identify what 'tips the case over the threshold' of a 'character or significance to justify the compulsory intervention by the state'.[23] This Supreme Court judgment famously coined the phrase that adoption against the will of birth parents is proportionate only 'when nothing else will do',[24] but Lady Hale was in a minority in suggesting that the applicant local authority might have taken a more collaborative approach with these particular birth parents. The majority decision accepted the evidence that the parents would continue to refuse any attempts at supportive protective services.[25]

These excerpts from judgments capture the spirit of the 1989 Act in bolstering the narrative of the state exercising compulsory intervention powers only when there was no other acceptable option. The principle that family life was independent and free from unjustified interference by the state was universally recognised as integral to the Act.[26] A great deal of consultation and multi-disciplinary training was put into implementing the new statute, and expectations were high.

22 *Re L* [2007] 1 FLR 2050 [50–51].

23 *Re B (A Child (Care Proceedings) (Appeal)* [2013] UKSC 33 [179–182].

24 *Re B (A Child (Care Proceedings) (Appeal)* [2013] UKSC 33 [198; 215].

25 Julie Doughty, 'Case Comment: Re B (A Child) (Care order) (2013) UKSC 33' (2013) 35(4) *Journal of Social Welfare and Family Law* 491–501.

26 Richard White, A. P. Carr and Nigel Lowe, *The Children Act in Practice* (4th edn, Lexis Nexis 2008).

The impact of the implementation of the 1989 Act on care proceedings

In a series of studies on the implementation of the Act, government-commissioned research on the impact of law reform focused on changes in criteria for care orders was published as 'The Last Resort'. This title reflected the new emphasis on working *with* families where there were child protection concerns. This comparative study found that most children who did become subject to care orders under the Act were in families who had lengthy involvement with children's services. It concluded that the Act had made it less likely that compulsion would be an early response to family difficulties than previously, and that the emphasis on exploring alternatives had had a real impact.[27] There was a range of quite complex reasons for this, not necessarily the Section 31 threshold criteria (referred to by Lady Hale and Hedley J earlier), but including practitioner awareness of the new ethos and the 'no order principle'[28] that was making social workers and local authority lawyers more hesitant about going to court.[29] Although the phrase 'last resort' does not literally appear in the report, apart from the title, it is implicit throughout.

Hunt et al.'s findings were further confirmed some ten years later by an extensive study on the profile of families going through care proceedings. Masson et al. found that most children and families had been known to social services departments for some time before a decision was made to apply to court. More than 80% had been known for more than a year, and almost half for five years or more. Even proceedings that were initiated by a 'crisis' rarely came out of the blue; again, the majority of families had been involved with social services for more than a year, with one-third having been involved for more than five years.[30] This would indicate that local authorities were, indeed, working *with* families in the spirit of the Act. However, this report expressed some concern about inequality in practice and standards applicable in cases according to whether or not there was court scrutiny. There was a risk that the demands of the minority of local authority cases that went to court meant those families' rights being prioritised over those of other families who were receiving less attention. The report notes that it was a key principle of the 1989 Act that proceedings should not be brought to provide access to services.[31]

27 Hunt et al. (n 18) 42.

28 Under Section 1(5), the court is not to make an order unless doing so will be better for the child than making no order at all. This section became known as 'the no order principle', although it was primarily designed to avoid unnecessary applications in private law family disputes than in deterring public law applications.

29 Hunt et al. (n 18) 37.

30 Judith Masson, Julia Pearce and Kay Bader, *Care Profiling Study* (Ministry of Justice 2008).

31 Masson, Pearce and Bader (n 30) 58.

Research for the period up to the mid-2000s therefore suggests that the 1989 Act was successful in preventing unnecessary court proceedings and complying with human rights proportionality principles. Unfortunately, court studies on that scale have not since been repeated, although a Family Justice Review panel, led by David Norgrove, reported in 2011 on widespread concerns across the system.[32] This Review briefly investigated options other than care orders, such as mediation, family group conferences, and specialist problem-solving courts.[33] However, the report was primarily focused on undue delay in court proceedings, and the actual volume of cases was seen as incidental to this dilemma rather than an issue in itself. Consequent legislative reform introduced mechanisms that aimed to avoid delay once cases had gotten into court, rather than limit the number of applications, although a pre-proceedings process that front-loaded work for local authorities did sometimes divert cases altogether.[34] At that time, policy concerns about children's welfare and the expense associated with care orders still centred on case duration – within court proceedings, not necessarily the period of interaction between families and services.

However, within a few years from that Review's report, the volume of care cases was being viewed by courts and local authorities as unsustainable. However, it was possible for those in the field to speculate as to the reasons – the reduction of public services, the increased awareness of the harm caused by child neglect, and 'the Baby P effect' (see later in this chapter) – the family justice system was overwhelmed, with no clear strategy for recovery.[35]

This widespread concern led to a Care Crisis Review which examined the evidence on contributing factors to record levels of children in care.[36] Statistics analysed in this Review indicated a pattern of sustained increase in numbers of looked-after children between 1994 and 2017.[37] There had been a decrease between 2004 and 2009, but numbers rose significantly from

32 Family Justice Review Panel, *Final Report* (Ministry of Justice, Department for Education, and Welsh Government 2011).

33 Julie Doughty, 'Care Proceedings: Is There a Better Way?' (2014) *Child and Family Law Quarterly* 113.

34 Judith Masson, 'Reforming Care Proceedings in England and Wales: Speeding Up Justice and Welfare?' in John Eekelaar (ed), *Family Law in Britain and America in the New Century: Essays in Honor of Sanford N. Katz* (Brill 2016) 187–206.

35 Sir James Munby, 'View from the President's Chambers' (September 2016) <www.judiciary.uk/wp-content/uploads/2014/08/pfd-view-15-care-cases-looming-crisis.pdf> accessed 20 December 2023.

36 Reports from the Care Crisis Review (2018) <https://frg.org.uk/policy-and-campaigns/the-care-crisis-review/> accessed 20 December 2023.

37 The term 'looked-after children' includes children in care under agreements with their parents and children subject to court orders.

2010.[38] Although it would appear on the face of this that the rise could be simply attributed to the change in government, with its austerity politics and reductions in public spending, there were other factors, which are discussed later.

The most recent statistics, for the year 2022–23, show that the number of children in care in England rose by 2% from the previous year to 83,840, a rate of 71 children looked after per 10,000 children, from 70 the previous year. The number of children entering care had increased by 6% to 33,000.[39] This steady increase suggests that the narrative of respect for family autonomy supported by legal safeguards on oppressive practice is being seriously undermined. We appear to have arrived at a place very distant from that inhabited by the senior judges quoted earlier.

The Care Crisis Review described the contributing factors to high numbers of children entering care as complex and difficult to disentangle. It will be argued here that they will remain entangled while the contradictions remain between the four values perspectives conceptualised by Lorraine Fox Harding in the 1990s, these having become embedded as masterplots.

The values perspectives as masterplots

The four values perspectives identified by Fox Harding as the most significant in classifying the diverse views in understanding childcare law and policy were:

1. *Laissez-faire and patriarchy*. The state's role is minimal and disturbs family autonomy only in exceptional circumstances.
2. *State paternalism and child protection*. State intervention to protect children is legitimate, and where substitute care is provided, it will meet children's needs.
3. *Defence of the birth family and parents' rights*. Poor and socially deprived families are victims of state actions. Intervention is legitimate but is supportive.
4. *Children's rights*. Recognising children's agency and respecting their human rights. This perspective emphasises children's participation in decision-making as well as their welfare rights.[40]

38 Caroline Thomas, *Care Crisis Review: Factors Contributing to National Increases in Number of Looked-after Children and Applications for Care Orders* (Family Rights Group 2018).

39 Department for Education, 'National Statistics' <https://explore-education-statistics.service.gov.uk/find-statistics/children-looked-after-in-england-including-adoptions> accessed 20 December 2023.

40 Fox Harding (n 2) 9 et seq.

Fox Harding did not draw up strict barriers between the four, acknowledging that there was some convergence around genuine concern for children's welfare, rather than just managing children as a social problem, and that at least some role for the state was accepted. As the following discussion will show, the relationship and conflicts between these four themes can be seen as different stories to support the narrative of the reification of family life.

Despite the judicial acknowledgement of diversity in parenting cited in court judgments earlier, the narrative in the twenty-first century has not shaken off the image of 'the cornflakes packet family', in which children's health and well-being are provided within the normative family unit, creating a binary of the 'ordinary' and the 'problematic other' or 'troubled' family.[41] When the pervasive narrative of the conventional family form is challenged, explanation is sought in terms of who and what went wrong, rather than reconceptualising the overarching narrative.

Masterplots create an image of the world in which good and evil (or right and wrong) are clearly identifiable and blame can fall squarely on one party or the other.[42] Fox Harding's four values perspectives cast differing lights on the archetypal 'good' and 'bad' parent and on the street-level bureaucracy of public bodies. Abbott wrote that skeletal narrative structures that encode abstract configurations of causal relationships between events can be used to structure accounts of specific happenings. Applying this to the values perspectives, the masterplots cast parents and social workers (as agents of the state) into certain roles:

1. *Laissez-faire.* Only 'bad' parents fail, and social workers fix high thresholds for intervention. Where needed, substitute parents will conform to the family ideal.
2. *State paternalism.* Some parents cannot be trusted to put their children's interests ahead of their own. Social workers' role is to rescue children.
3. *Defence of the birth family.* Parents want the best for their children, and social workers can support them in resisting state oppression.
4. *Children's rights.* Children's individual needs and aspirations are denied by parents and social workers who do not respect their agency.

In his theory of street-level bureaucracy, Lipsky argued that the work of police, social workers, health, and the lower courts cannot be performed to the highest possible standards of decision-making because workers lack the time, information, and resources to react to individual client needs. They develop

41 Janet Boddy, Fidelma Hanrahan, and Bella Wheeler, *Thinking Through Family* (Bristol University Press 2023) ch 1.

42 H. Porter Abbott, *The Cambridge Introduction to Narrative* (2nd edn, Cambridge University Press 2008) 48.

routines of practice that simplify their client groups. This mass processing downgrades the quality of treatment and services.[43] Addressing injustice in legal systems, Abbott suggested that stories of the disempowered can lead to cultural transformation. A question arises: would individual social workers, lawyers, parents, children, and their advocates (groups 'on the margins of cultural power'[44]) be treated more justly by the system if they could disseminate counternarratives that undermine and balance the dominant masterplots and weaken the power of prejudicial types? We can perhaps see this process beginning with the third and fourth themes challenging the first and second.

This chapter will now consider how Fox Harding's four values perspectives can be viewed as masterplots that try to explain our adherence to the narrative of state respect for family life.

Laissez-faire and patriarchy

Parents' and children's interests are seen as identical in this perspective, but just as the *laissez-faire* capitalism model can be criticised for embedding inequality and exploiting weaker members of society, so did Fox Harding point out that by choosing *not* to intervene directly in the family, the state enables power to remain in the hands of adults and, ultimately, with fathers and male cohabitants. She therefore linked non-interventionism in this context with gender issues. However, it should be acknowledged that this patriarchal aspect of childcare policy has been challenged by subsequent research on the marginalisation of fathers in child protection.[45] The exclusion or demonisation of fathers in child protection processes is now widely seen as yet another element in discrimination.[46] Another development since the early 1990s was the rise of the fathers' rights movement, initially as a response to the Child Support Act 1991, which was a more explicit expression of Thatcherite neoliberalism than the 1989 Act.[47] However, this patriarchal aspect of family justice remains confined to the private law jurisdiction.

Fox Harding applied the lens of a patriarchal society, but primarily in a historical context, tracing the Victorian concept that no court knew better than a child's father how to bring her up,[48] through to the Goldstein, Freud, and Solnit psychoanalytical approach, to the importance of continuity of

43 Michael Lipsky, *Street Level Bureaucracy: Dilemmas of the Individual in Public Services* (Russell Sage 2010).

44 Porter Abbott (n 42) 188.

45 Jonathan Scourfield, 'Improving Work with Fathers to Prevent Child Maltreatment' (2014) 38(6) *Child Abuse and Neglect* 974–81.

46 See Polly Curtis, 'Daniel's Story: Dad Is Not in the Picture' in Polly Curtis (ed), *Behind Closed Doors: Why We Break Up Families and How to Mend Them* (Virago 2022) 92–108.

47 Nick Wikeley, *Child Support: Law and Policy* (Hart 2006).

48 *Re Agar-Ellis* (1883) 24 Ch. D. 317.

care by the psychological parent (in fact, usually the mother as the primary caregiver).[49] It has also been noted that Goldstein et al. were highly influential in the early 1970s, not simply because of their belief in a policy of non-intervention, but more with an emphasis on continuity of a child's social parent and the development of 'permanency planning'.[50] In extreme cases of lack of parental care, state intervention is justified by moving the child to a new, permanent secure home, and then the state withdraws. The concept of permanence is discussed later in the context of the protectionist masterplot.

When the Fox Harding typology was reconsidered in a social work perspective by Roger Smith in 2017, Conservative-led UK government policies were again under scrutiny. Smith focused on adoption policy as the exemplar of the *laissez-faire* perspective, a notion that adoption was the gold standard of permanence having been zealously promoted by Michael Gove as secretary of state for education, supported by David Cameron as prime minister.[51] However, the adoption narrative has changed significantly since its origins of the normalisation of family life by giving babies of unmarried mothers to infertile married couples. The evolution into adoption for child protection purposes has been subject to considerable controversy, and the recognition that adoptive families need continuing support has effectively removed it as a simple solution within the *laissez-faire* perspective.[52] More children are now leaving care through special guardianship orders than adoption orders, as discussed in the section on the birth family later.

What, then, remains of the influence of the *laissez-faire* perspective? The 1989 Act received cross-party support, even though introduced by a Conservative administration. Although the scandal of the Cleveland enquiry was not the main factor in the drive for childcare law reform, this had damaged the reputation of social workers and paediatricians across ideological lines.[53] The government headed by Margaret Thatcher was ideologically distrustful of professionals and believed in family values and individual responsibil-

49 Joseph Goldstein, Anna Freud and Albert Solnit, *Beyond the Best Interests of the Child* (Free Press 1979) cited in Fox Harding (n 2) 13 and ch. 2.

50 Stephen Cretney, *Family Law in the Twentieth Century* (OUP 2003) 701–2.

51 Roger Smith, 'Reconsidering Value Perspectives in Child Welfare' (2018) 48(3) *British Journal of Social Work* 616–32. Michael Gove had been adopted when a few months old and often referred to this as relevant to his policies. There was also a high-profile media campaign promoting adoption – see Martin Narey, 'A Blueprint for the Nation's Lost Children' *Times* (5 July 2011).

52 See the Introduction to Nigel Lowe and Claire Fenton-Glynn (eds), *Research Handbook on Adoption Law* (Edward Elgar 2023) 2–13 and Julie Selwyn, 'Outcomes for Children Adopted in the UK' and June Thoburn, 'Understanding Adoption Breakdown: A Socio-Legal Perspective' in Nigel Lowe and Claire Fenton-Glynn (eds), *Research Handbook on Adoption Law* (Edward Elgar 2023) 228–47 and 269–85, respectively.

53 Beatrix Campbell, *Secrets and Silence: Uncovering the Legacy of the Cleveland Child Sexual Abuse Case* (Policy Press 2023).

ity. The new definition of parental responsibility rather than rights was said to be primarily based on children's welfare, but in effect, much of the Act shifted the balance more toward parental rights, especially with the introduction of threshold criteria for care orders. Cretney cited Lord Mackay. Unless it was evident that a child is or is likely to be positively harmed by a failure of the family, the state should not interfere: 'The integrity and the independence of the family is the basic building block of a free and democratic society.'[54] However, although one of the basic objectives of the 1989 Act was to keep compulsory intervention to a minimum, representing the *laissez-faire* viewpoint, the interventionist perspective also came in, as local authorities acquired increased powers to initiate a forensic process regarding the 'likelihood' of significant harm.

State paternalism and child rescue

This second perspective differs from *laissez-faire* in requiring surveillance of parents and identifying those who do not bring up their children well and cannot expect to keep them. Children's welfare is therefore paramount, but unlike the fourth children's rights perspective, children are given little agency and depend on adults, whose duty it is to protect them. Despite the appearance of these first two perspectives as polar opposites, there is some commonality in attributing problems to individual parents' own psychological profile and history. The paradox is that alongside the *laissez-faire* tendencies of government over most of the past 30 years, the rising number of children going into care indicates the domination of this child rescue theme. 'We have quietly become one of the most interventionist states in the world', wrote Polly Curtis in 2022.[55]

In this perspective, parents have been described as trustees of their children's interests who, like any trustees, if they fail in their duties, should be discharged from them.[56] The state can legitimately monitor and enforce these duties. In the early 1980s, Dingwall et al. conducted a large-scale ethnographic study in three diverse localities in England in which they followed cases of child abuse and neglect from identification through intervention toward outcomes. They mounted a powerful rejection of the autonomy perspective, finding that child protection agencies were structured in such a way as to prefer the least stigmatising assessment of the families and 'the least overtly coercive disposition'.[57] This work coined the phrase 'rule of optimism' in as-

54 Cretney (n 50) 726–7.
55 Curtis (n 46) 8.
56 Robert Dingwall, John Eekelaar and Topsy Murray, *The Protection of Children* (2nd edn, Avebury 1995) 224.
57 Dingwall et al. (n 56) 207.

sessing parental capacity – the institutionalised preference for positive evaluations of parents. This concept was interpreted in some quarters as criticism of an individual approach by naïve practitioners, but the authors emphasised in their second edition that they were describing an *organisational* culture of child protection services founded on the deep ambivalence in liberal society about state interference with families; individual workers were acting within those structures.[58] Their observed overdeference of individual workers towards parents was not so much failings of the agencies but in the limitations society had placed on them. An attempt to make child-rearing a matter of public interest without destroying the ideal of the autonomous family as a counterweight to state power was described as a liberal compromise.

Dingwall et al. described the parent–child relationship as an unequal one, but society had a vital interest in making that relationship work. They argued that because the state is accountable to the whole population, it is legitimate for the state to 'survey the whole population', and they decried 'Utopian libertarians'.[59] While Fox Harding described the moral panic of child abuse in the 1970s and 80s as the rationale for this second perspective, Dingwall et al. pointed out that this had not prevented the justification for rationing resources made available for families who were in difficulty.

The new definition of parental responsibility replacing concepts of parental rights in the 1989 Act had a number of purposes, across public and private law, but was generally thought to bolster the principle of non-intervention. Eekelaar pointed to a fallacy in an assumption that a reduction in state control of parents who were given responsibility would naturally exercise it responsibly. On the other hand, he predicted that weakening the state's supervisory role had potential unintentional consequences of pushing 'middle range' parenting issues from being managed safely into compulsory intervention through the courts.[60]

These views are magnified when we look at the public and political reactions to high-profile child protection stories, which never seem to result in empowering social workers but rather force them into yet more defensive practice. The Care Crisis Review noted the trend following the Baby P story of local authorities making more protective interventions than previously, resulting in more involuntary engagements where parents had not sought contact with services. Practice was dominated by risk assessment and monitoring.[61] Extensive and hyperbolic media coverage in 2008 of the murder of

58 Dingwall et al. (n 56). See also Robert Dingwall, 'The Rule of Optimism – Thirty Years On' *Social Science Space* (2013) <www.socialsciencespace.com/2013/09/the-rule-of-optimism-thirty-years-on/> accessed 20 December 2023.

59 Dingwall et al. (n 56) 220.

60 John Eekelaar, 'Parental Responsibility: State of Nature or Nature of the State?' (1991) 13(1) *Journal of Social Welfare and Family Law* 37–50.

61 Thomas (n 38) 51.

17-month-old Peter Connelly created a highly risk-averse culture amongst practitioners.[62] Fear of the consequences of non-removal of children whose homes had previously been deemed adequate went alongside fears of the consequences to practitioners and their employers, stirred up by vilification of social workers by the press.

Some commentators saw the impact on practice resonating with social anxieties beyond 'the terrible facts of Peter Connelly's individual story'.[63] Described as an exemplar of 'the politics of outrage', Parton has claimed that attitudes to social work with children and families are a proxy for feelings of inadequacy and frustration that much of the population harbour with regard to welfare and the state more generally. As Butler and Drakeford had observed some years earlier, landmark scandals in social welfare do not just happen in a policy vacuum but develop in particular contexts at particular times, whereby some individual tragedies achieve emblematic status.[64] It was social work that was labelled as the villain in the stories of Peter Connelly and of Victoria Climbie, although both children had suffered through the failings of several agencies, not just local authorities. The extraordinary media persecution of individuals working for the local authority involved almost ignored the culpability of the actual murderers of the children. Perhaps it is easier to accept the story of the lazy or incompetent employee than a different narrative of extreme cruelty that some adults in a caring role are capable of. Although by their nature extremely rare, and although subsequent enquiries and reviews invariably identify poor communications between agencies as a significant contributory factor, the usual outcome of these scandals is a renewed emphasis on highly centralised and risk-averse procedures.[65]

Another, and more nuanced story in the child rescue perspective is that of 'the baby brain' – increased professional knowledge of the harm caused to children's development by early neglect. There has been some debate about the extent to which the infant brain is vulnerable to irreparable neurological damage, subject to critique as 'parent-blaming'.[66] Less controversial is the gradual increased awareness since the 1980s of the risks of emotional harm to children being brought up in a domestic abuse environment, the statutory definition of 'harm' being extended to include harm experienced 'from seeing

62 Ray Jones, *The Story of Baby P* (Policy Press 2014).

63 Joanne Warner, 'Heads Must Roll? Emotional Politics, the Press and the Death of Baby P' (2014) 44(6) *The British Journal of Social Work* 1637–53.

64 Ian Butler and Mark Drakeford, *Scandal, Social Policy and Social Welfare* (Policy Press 2005).

65 Brid Featherstone, Kate Morris and Sue White, 'A Marriage Made in Hell: Early Intervention Meets Child Protection' (2013) 44(7) *British Journal of Social Work* 1–15.

66 Dave Wastell and Sue White, 'Blinded by Neuroscience: Social Policy, the Family, and the Infant Brain' (2012) 1(3) *Families, Relationships and Society* 397–414.

or hearing the ill-treatment of another'.[67] More recently, children who 'see, hear or otherwise experience the effects of abuse' are defined as victims in criminal law.[68] The story of a childhood blighted by adverse childhood experiences (ACEs) offers the tempting possibility of scientific certainty, diagnosis, and treatment as 'trauma-informed'.[69] However, whether the therapeutic services that may be identified as necessary will be made available is another matter.

There are a number of problems associated with the protectionist perspective, apart from that of the drain on resources, for which there seems little political appetite to fund. State-substituted care has been found to be potentially dangerous in itself, especially during the era of large-scale residential care.[70] It is widely accepted that plans for looked-after children must seek permanence, that is to say a sense of belonging: a secure base, through childhood and beyond. This work has to extend beyond the legal permanence envisaged in adoption (discussed earlier) to meet the varying needs of individual children to include kinship placement, long-term fostering, or safe return home.[71] Special guardianship orders, introduced in 2005, have gradually become the preferred permanence option for many children and now exceed the numbers adopted.[72]

Another feature of this perspective is the lack of trust between families and agencies. Relegating the child's bonds with their birth parents, however flawed the parenting, presents the child as an isolated individual, separated from their wider family and community.[73] Too often, families feel misunderstood, blamed, mistrusted, and threatened rather than helped; the children's social care system needs to engage much more effectively with children's and families' basic material needs as a key factor for child protection.[74]

The paternalism/child rescue masterplot will inevitably take strength from future child death tragedies and calls for greater social control of dangerous families. In contrast, the third perspective differs in attributing parenting problems more to factors such as external material circumstances, resources,

67 Children Act 1989, s31(9) amended in 2005.

68 Domestic Abuse Act 2021, s3.

69 For an up-to-date overview of theory and practice, see Centres for Disease Control and Prevention <www.cdc.gov/violenceprevention/aces/index.html> accessed 16 January 2024.

70 Butler and Drakeford (n 64).

71 Janet Boddy, *Understanding Permanence for Looked-after Children: A Review of Research for the Care Inquiry* (2013) <https://thecareinquiry.files.wordpress.com/2013/04/understanding-permanence-for-lac.pdf> accessed 16 January 2024.

72 Under Children Act 1989, s14, a special guardian exercises parental responsibility exclusively, although, unlike adoption, birth parents do not completely lose parental responsibility and parental status.

73 Featherstone et al. (n 65).

74 Paul Bywaters and Guy Skinner, *The Relationship between Poverty and Child Abuse and Neglect: New Evidence* (Nuffield Foundation 2022) 98.

opportunities, and life chances. The third perspective offers individual counternarratives to the prevailing mix of the first two perspectives.

Defence of the birth family and parents' rights

Curtis describes the decision-making systems on child removal as 'riddled' with class bias and prejudice against people from some ethnic groups, or of different abilities, focusing its power on marginalised women.[75] She presents a picture far removed from a legal system that respects diversity, as claimed by Lady Hale and Hedley J in the judgments quoted earlier. Curtis's investigations and recommendations explore the contemporary relevance of the third classification, which prioritises the value of the biological family but differs from the *laissez-faire* classification by promoting state intervention, and from the second classification by requiring supportive, not punitive, involvement. This third perspective originally saw families with parenting problems as victims of oppression, recognising the social context of their struggles.

Deprivation has been identified as the single biggest risk factor in a child going into care by the UK-wide Child Welfare Inequalities Project: a child is ten times more likely to go into care from the poorest 10% of the UK than the wealthiest 10%.[76] A more recent complementary review of international literature found that changes in income level alone had a significant impact on levels of child abuse and neglect, and poverty also increases risks of domestic abuse and mental illness.[77] This series of studies calls for national and local strategic responses to reduce family poverty and inequality to rebalance the current emphasis on investigating individual families. A research focus on the behaviour and circumstances of individuals and families had distracted from the state's responsibility to prevent child abuse and neglect through economic and social policies. Family support needs to provide an adequate level of resources for families to ensure their children's development and health and also focus on the psychological consequences of resources being inadequate, because shame and stigma can exacerbate stress.[78] Just the precarity of moving in and out of poverty has been shown to have a far more direct impact on children's awareness of family stresses than might be imagined.[79] Unsurprisingly, Bywaters et al. concluded in 2022 that some UK policies,

75 Curtis (n 46) xiii.

76 Paul Bywaters and the Child Welfare Inequalities Project, *Final Report* (University of Huddersfield 2020).

77 Bywaters and Skinner (n 74).

78 Kinship, 'Government Announces First Ever Kinship Strategy for England' (2023) <https://kinship.org.uk/news/government-publishes-first-ever-national-kinship-care-strategy-for-england/> accessed 16 January 2024.

79 Tess Ridge, 'We're All in This Together'? The Hidden Costs of Poverty, Recession and Austerity Policies on Britain's Poorest Children (2013) 27(5) *Children & Society* 406–17.

particularly those on benefits, housing, and immigration, conflicted with the principle that the welfare of children should be paramount.[80]

However, as noted earlier, there is no legal duty on any government to make children's welfare its paramount consideration – the welfare principle is only a requirement for court decisions. The narrowness of the application of the welfare principle to section 31 has been described by Piper as designed 'to constrain intervention and ration expenditure to a relatively narrow category of children'.[81]

How, then, do social workers square their professional ethics with potentially discriminatory practice? While the reports from the Child Welfare Inequalities Project are careful to explain that the links between poverty and child abuse are complex, a number of social work researchers have expressed concern about practice that attempts to ignore what might easily be described as the elephant in the room. One study found widespread attempts in practice to avoid as stigmatising any link between poverty and child protection, the rationale being that, of course, not all poor people abuse their children. Morris et al. concluded that a blinkered view means poverty can become invisible in practice, with a different story of an underclass that social work must regulate and persuade into respectability.[82] The defence of the birth family proponents associate this invisibility with the organisational systems and cultures that reinforce risk management, which chimes with Lipsky's street-level bureaucrat story. Such research findings have strengthened a movement toward 'relational social work', where practitioners are encouraged to engage holistically with families and communities.[83]

The Care Crisis Review referred to 'the untapped resources of children's wider families and communities'.[84] Previously viewed with some suspicion as an aspect of the *laissez-faire* perspective (with public authorities divesting themselves of the expense of foster care), this story has more recently been seized for themselves by activists in charities and pressure groups such as Family Rights Group and Kinship, as well as an increasing number of parents advocacy organisations.[85] The scope of permanence has extended beyond its being synonymous with adoption.[86]

80 Bywaters and Skinner (n 74) 18.
81 Piper (n 6) 146.
82 Kate Morris, Will Mason et al., 'Social Work, Poverty and Child Welfare Interventions' (2018) 23(3) *Child & Family Social Work* 364–72.
83 Brid Featherstone, Kate Morris and Sue White, *Reimagining Social Work: Towards Humane Social Work with Families* (Policy Press 2014).
84 Thomas (n 38) 63.
85 See Simon Haworth, Andy Bilson et al., 'Parental Partnership, Advocacy and Engagement: The Way Forward' (2022) 11(8) *Social Sciences* 353 and Richard Devine, Katy Benson et al., 'Peer Parental Advocacy: A Narrative Review of the Literature' (2023) 18(3) *Journal of Children's Services* 244–60.
86 June Thoburn, 'What Kind of Permanence?' (1985) 9(4) *Adoption & Fostering* 29–34.

Special guardianship orders are now commonly used to secure placements of children with their grandparents, and there is a range of other types of less-formal legal status in kinship care. Previously known as 'families and friends care' and largely reliant on extended family members' goodwill in taking responsibility for children who would otherwise have to be accommodated by local authorities, recognition that this is a realistic option for permanence only with financial and practical support led to the government announcing a national kinship strategy.[87] From 2019, the number of children leaving care under special guardianship orders began to exceed the number being adopted, and this trend has continued as at the date of writing.[88]

This third perspective presents clear examples of parents and professionals rejecting the first and second perspectives – they do not want to be 'left alone', nor do they want to be subject to too much control. It has much in common with the fourth perspective, children's rights. While the children's rights discourse was in its infancy when Fox Harding wrote on it, human rights law in general has since developed in the UK. The European Convention on Human Rights Article 8, the right to respect for private and family life, has been effectively, if narrowly, applied to situations where children were removed from parents solely on the grounds of poverty.[89] Discrimination against families in poverty has been described by Barker and Casla as 'povertyism' and in breach of human rights law, specifically the International Convention on Economic, Social, and Cultural Rights (ICESCR), Article 2.[90] They note that Article 10 of that Convention states that families, as the natural and fundamental group unit of society, should be given the widest possible rights to protection and assistance. While the ICESCR remains at a level of 'secondary rights' and unenforceable, these authors' co-productive work involving social workers, parents, and young people with experience of the care system illustrates the developing power of the counternarrative from people with lived experience.

Children's rights

The children's rights theme was described by Fox Harding as distinct from the other three, which emphasise children's vulnerability and dependence rather than their competence and strengths. She predicted, correctly, that children's

87 Kinship (n 78).

88 Bachar Alrouh and Judith Harwin, 'Keeping Children within the Family: Changing Patterns in the Use of Special Guardianship Orders' (2023) 8(2) *International Journal of Population Data Science* 2231.

89 For example, Soares de Melo v Portugal 72850/14 16 February 2016.

90 Lyle Barker and Koldo Cala, '"I Have Walked This Journey Alone: My Soul Is Tired": Poverty, Child Protection and the Right to Protection and Assistance to the Family in England' (University of Essex 2023).

rights would eventually come to be more strongly expressed in law, policy, and practice. However, the concept remains relatively weak and, arguably, not yet influential enough to gain the status of a masterplot. Children's rights remain largely theoretical, having been developed for hypothetical children as a class, and of seemingly little relevance to judges and social workers.[91] Although human rights law generally accepts that children have the same rights as adults, and this has been articulated in ECHR case law, especially applying ECHR Article 8, the right to respect for private and family life, children's rights contained in wider international treaties are not enforceable in UK courts.

Although children's rights were not articulated in the 1989 Act, their wishes and feelings are one of the factors to be taken into consideration in arriving at decisions about their welfare.[92] The lack of explicit expression of children's rights has been said to have been due to the ideas being too controversial and the risk of them delaying reform.[93] That may be an accurate observation, as children's rights were associated with an extreme child liberation movement in the 1980s, a concept that has become anachronistic.[94]

The 1989 Act came into force in 1991, the same year that the UK ratified the UN Convention on the Rights of the Child (UNCRC), which has subsequently influenced developments and progress towards taking children's rights seriously.[95] UNCRC Article 3 (that a child's best interests shall be a primary consideration in actions taken by the legislature, courts, and other institutions) has been held by the UK Supreme Court to be a binding obligation in international law, and its spirit, if not the precise language, translated into domestic law.[96] Article 3 is one of the general principles overarching the Convention, as is Article 12 (participation in decision-making). The welfare principle applied by courts aligns with UNCRC Article 3 and has been interpreted as compliant with ECHR Article 8. There are various mechanisms in the public and the third sector that aim to implement the scope of Article 12 in listening to children's views.

Although all four UK nations have a children's commissioner, whose role it is to promote the views and interests of children and young people, the remit of the English commissioner is more restricted than the other three and less independent of government. In England, a director of children's rights was

91 Jane Fortin, *Children's Rights and the Developing Law* (3rd edn, Cambridge University Press 2009) 29.
92 Children Act 1989, s1(3)(a).
93 Hendrick (n 10) 281.
94 Fox Harding (n 2) 112–18.
95 Michael D. A. Freeman 'Taking Children's Rights Seriously' (1987) 4(1) *Children & Society* 299–319 and Michael Freeman, 'Why It Remains Important to Take Children's Rights Seriously' (2007) 15 *International Journal of Children's Rights* 5–23.
96 *ZH (Tanzania) FC v Secretary of State for the Home Department* [2011] UKCS 4 [23].

appointed between 2001 and 2014, who actively championed the views of children and young people in care, reporting directly on their views and undertaking individual advice and casework with thousands of young people.[97] Removing this post and diluting its functions did not reflect well on any commitment to children's rights. Nevertheless, there have been positive developments in children's rights in parallel with the third perspective in recent years, suggesting that they have converged since the original Fox Harding typology. The activists and researchers cited in the birth parents' perspective earlier do not generally see parents' and children's interests as being indistinguishable, as in the *laissez-faire* perspective, but, rather, as being due equal entitlement to participation and consideration.

Challenges to the masterplots

The four values perspectives that inform law and policy about children's welfare have historical and current significance in their influence on the narrative of care orders as a last resort, as accepted and incorporated in the 1989 legislation. In subsequent years, more stories have been told that both reinforce and challenge these themes.

The stories of children who drifted through care in multiple placements or suffered institutional abuse told us about the need for permanence, whether replicating the normative family through adoption (*laissez-faire*) or prioritising kinship care placements (birth family). Stories of poor outcomes for children who grew up in state care or who suffered disrupted adoptions warned us against the protectionist perspective and highlighted the value of respecting children's rights. However, the scandals when children known to protective services were not removed and suffered serious harm became huge stories in the public consciousness, leading back to the stronger imposition of the protectionist approach.

Might the rise in numbers of children in care indicate the child rescue masterplot has fatally undermined the family autonomy masterplot? The growing power of the stories from parents, extended family members, children, and many legal and social work practitioners is changing the story again. Even those researchers identified by Fox Harding with the second perspective were not zealous advocates of child removal but sought a positive political commitment to children's welfare, with the powers in the 1989 Act used to offer parents resources, 'rather than to wait to react to the failures of overburdened families'.[98]

97 Roger Morgan, *The Children's Views Digest* (2014) <https://webarchive.nationalarchives.gov.uk/ukgwa/20141107024648/www.ofsted.gov.uk/resources/childrens-views-digest> accessed 16 January 2024.

98 Dingwall et al. (n 56) 255.

The fatal flaw in the *laissez-faire* perspective is that the impact of child poverty on wider society cannot be ignored. As Bywaters et al. explained, deep, persistent poverty is more harmful for children than a low income or temporary hardship. However, the problems of parenting on an inadequate income are compounded by insecurity of housing and employment, which are often caused by welfare benefits processes and/or a lack of rights.[99] Given the impact on child poverty caused by further years of public spending cuts, with several local authorities giving notice of insolvency, the economic damage caused by Brexit, and the economic and social harm endured by families during the Covid-19 pandemic, we are unlikely to see a drop in the demands on courts and the care system soon. A recent report suggests that it will take ten years for access to health and justice systems to recover to pre-pandemic levels.[100] Social care services are, of course, interdependent with these.

An even more disturbing story about the connection between poverty and the US child welfare system is starkly portrayed by Roberts as being so deeply embedded in history and the present-day foster 'industry' that the only solution is to dismantle the system by way of 'abolition of family policing'. She does not use 'policing' in Donzelot's sense of regulating families but literally as reflecting the carceral system by criminalising, pathologising, and stigmatising poor Black communities.[101]

The power of narrative is well illustrated in one of the sources referred to in this chapter, the book by Polly Curtis, which is formatted as a series of stories from individual family members and professionals in family justice, in the author's attempt to reconcile some of the contradictions she had found when previously undertaking straight news reporting on the topic. She noted that the 'real story' lay in the contradictions that she had originally been obliged to 'clean up' for mainstream news consumption.[102] While this chapter has relied on Fox Harding's typology as helpful in explaining the divergence between the narrative of state care as 'the last resort' and the challenges modern families face in bringing up their children, some inherent contradictions have also come to light.

Conclusion

This chapter has set out the statutory and judicial principles of non-intervention in family life – with compulsory removal of children into state care being the

99 Bywaters and Skinner (n 74).

100 Harry Quilter-Pinner and Halima Khan, *Great Government: Public Service Reform in the 2020s* (Institute for Public Policy Research, 2023) <www.ippr.org/research/publications/great-government> accessed 29 December 2023.

101 Dorothy E. Roberts, *Torn Apart: How the Child Welfare System Destroys Black Families and How Abolition Can Build a Safer World* (Basic Books, 2022).

102 Curtis (n 46) 282.

last resort – that forms the narrative of family justice. Legislative reform in the 1980s was premised on the provision of family support that would keep children and parents together unless a high threshold of significant harm was forensically scrutinised. However, the number of children being taken into care has increased at a rate that undermines that narrative. Different values perspectives were discussed as masterplots that take on greater and lesser influence when different stories capture more or less attention. While some stories have played into the dominant narrative, others have interrogated and challenged these. Although tensions between perceptions of children's welfare are inevitably going to persist to some extent, one constant message through these shifts in perspective is the failure of the family support provisions in the 1989 Act.

Chapter 14

Masterplots of demand and supply and the energy trilemma

Delaying the transition

Chris Hilson

Introduction

This chapter explores the competing masterplots around the role of fossil fuels in the energy transition to a decarbonised economy. The fossil fuel industry has typically emphasised the need for production to keep up with consumer demand for fossil fuels, arguing that it is irresponsible to cut supply independently of that demand. However, the climate movement has increasingly stressed the need to reduce the supply of fossil fuels, in part because targeting dirty fossil fuel production is seen as more likely to mobilise the public than more abstract technical legal measures like the Paris Agreement and its nationally determined contributions (NDCs) or emissions trading schemes.[1] These competing visions form the essence of the relevant masterplots here – the demand masterplot and the supply masterplot.

A *masterplot* is a deeply rooted, recurrent, but skeletal story which informs the way the public sees a policy issue.[2] Actors in that policy field will often draw upon this story when creating their own individual narrative statements on the issue. Where there is a dominant masterplot, it usually takes on a hegemonic form, appearing simply as the normal way of things. The fossil fuel industry's demand masterplot has, as we shall see, historically been the dominant one: extraction of fossil fuels has long been the taken-for-granted way of powering our economies and society, going back at least as far as the Industrial Revolution. The climate movement's supply masterplot is trying to displace this normalised way of seeing the matter.

1 Fergus Green, '"Keep It in the Ground": What We Can Learn from Anti-Fossil Fuel Campaigns' *The Conversation* (14 November 2018) <https://theconversation.com/keep-it-in-the-ground-what-we-can-learn-from-anti-fossil-fuel-campaigns-100005> accessed 13 July 2023.

2 H. Porter Abbott, 'The Rhetoric of Narrative' in *The Cambridge Introduction to Narrative* (CUP 2008) 47.

DOI: 10.4324/9781003404668-20

Law and society scholarship, like broader work on social movements,[3] has taken a cultural turn – with academics interested in how law both creates meaning and also reflects wider cultural understandings. This cultural turn is reflected in a growing literature exploring the role of meaning-making concepts such as framing[4] and narrative[5] in law and litigation. However, this literature has not yet explored masterplots as a form of deep-rooted public discourse bearing on law. And while the existing fossil fuel supply-side literature has touched on framing,[6] it has not looked at the wider narrative construction of fossil fuels in the transition. In this chapter, I aim to add to both literatures by examining the way the climate movement has set out to challenge the dominant demand masterplot with an alternative supply masterplot. As we shall see, these masterplots help shape the ways in which law is used to manage the climate crisis. Law has, thus far, tended to focus on fossil fuel demand and emissions rather than directly targeting the extraction and supply of fossil fuels and placing restrictions on those. In doing so, the law typically both reflects that accepted way of doing things[7] and also reinforces it.[8] The climate movement, via the supply masterplot, is seeking to turn this extractivist business-as-usual model around.

3 James Jasper, 'Cultural Approaches in the Sociology of Social Movements' in Bert Klandermans and Conny Roggeband (eds), *Handbook of Social Movements Across Disciplines* (Springer 2010).

4 For example, Nicholas Pedriana, 'From Protective to Equal Treatment: Legal Framing Processes and Transformation of the Women's Movement in the 1960s' (2006) 111(6) *American Journal of Sociology* 1718; Chris Hilson, 'UK Climate Change Litigation: Between Hard and Soft Framing' in Stephen Farrall, Tawhida Ahmed and Duncan French (eds), *Criminological and Legal Consequences of Climate Change* (Hart Publishing 2012); Chris Hilson, 'Framing Time in Climate Change Litigation' (2017) 9(3) *Oñati Socio-Legal Series* 361; Lisa Vanhala, 'Is Legal Mobilization for the Birds? Legal Opportunity Structures and Environmental Nongovernmental Organizations in the United Kingdom, France, Finland, and Italy' (2018) 51(3) *Comparative Political Studies* 380; Holly McCammon and Cathryn Beeson-Lynch, 'Fighting Words: Pro-Choice Cause Lawyering, Legal-Framing Innovations, and Hostile Political-Legal Contexts' (2021) 46(3) *Law & Social Inquiry* 599.

5 For example, Joshua Wilson, 'Sustaining the State: Legal Consciousness and the Construction of Legality in Competing Abortion Activists' Narratives' (2011) 36(2) *Law & Social Inquiry* 455; Grace Nosek, 'Climate Change Litigation and Narrative: How to Use Litigation to Tell Compelling Climate Stories' (2018) 42(3) *William & Mary Environmental Law & Policy Review* 733; Chris Hilson, 'Law, Courts and Populism: Climate Change Litigation and the Narrative Turn' in Susan Sterett and Lee Walker (eds), *Research Handbook on Law and Courts* (Edward Elgar 2019).

6 Georgia Piggot, 'The Influence of Social Movements on Policies that Constrain Fossil Fuel Supply' (2018) 18(7) *Climate Policy* 942.

7 In, for example, the EU, as will be seen, the EU emissions trading system, under Directive 2003/87/EC [2003] OJ L275/32, is at the heart of EU climate mitigation policy and focuses on reducing greenhouse gas emissions and curbing demand, not on cutting fossil fuel supply.

8 Because of the legitimacy law confers. Climate laws can confer legitimacy on emission removal technologies that are largely pipe dreams, as early UK laws did with carbon capture

My purpose in this chapter is therefore both to show the existence of the two masterplots and to reveal the way in which they shape individual narratives on the role of fossil fuels in the energy transition. I also discuss the way in which the energy trilemma has complicated those individual narratives. I argue that the demand masterplot is an example of climate delayism because it seeks to delay the transition to a decarbonised economy. It protects a space for ongoing fossil fuel use by placing the blame on individual consumer demand rather than government and industry taking responsibility for leading the necessary structural reduction in supply. As will be seen later, the consumer as a character here is also an important feature of the relevant masterplot.

The structure of the chapter is as follows. I start by examining the literature on masterplots before proceeding to set out my methodology. I then analyse law's role in the energy transition and the way in which it is directed mostly at demand and not the supply of fossil fuels. Next, I outline and discuss various examples of narratives which draw upon the relevant demand and supply masterplots. This includes legislation as a form of narrative, but the examples go beyond the purely legal to include wider statements by powerful actors. The latter help construct the way in which the policy issue is understood and, ultimately, therefore, how law should be responding to it. In the section after that, I turn to explore the energy trilemma, and I examine the way in which it has complicated the individual narratives (although not the original masterplots which those narratives draw upon). The conclusion provides a summary of the chapter and reconsiders its principal arguments.

Masterplots

Porter Abbott defines *masterplots* as 'stories that we tell over and over in myriad forms and that connect vitally with our deepest values, wishes, and fears'.[9] He then defines *narrative* as a 'particular rendering of a story'.[10] As Abbott notes, the concept of a masterplot is closely associated with the idea of a character type, and often even a stereotype. He puts these three together with the example of the O. J. Simpson trial, in which you saw lawyers on both sides offering different narrative renderings of the story of the events, drawing on different American cultural masterplots. One of these involved a type – the female victim of domestic abuse – suffering at the hands of male violence. Another masterplot involved a Black man stepping out of his

and storage: Elen Stokes, 'Beyond Evidence: Anticipatory Regimes in Law' (2021) 43(1) *Law & Policy* 73, 80; Chris Hilson, 'The Role of Narrative in Environmental Law: The Nature of Tales and Tales of Nature' (2022) 34(1) *JEL* 1, 11.

9 Porter Abbott (n 2) 46.

10 Porter Abbott (n 2) 47.

expected role as poor and powerless and being punished by the criminal justice system for this role transgression.[11] Of course, as Abbott notes, courts are not the only place where contesting narratives drawing on masterplots are to be found.[12] As we shall see, one finds them, too, in legislation, in media statements made by politicians and governments, in protest slogans, corporate reports, speeches, and interviews, and on NGO websites.

Sadler defines *masterplots* as 'skeletal narrative structures which do not relate specific events occurring in specific places, but encode abstract configurations of causal relationships between events that can be used to structure accounts of specific happenings'.[13] These overarching abstract narratives are an important aspect of meaning-making.[14] They do not simply reflect the world – they also shape public understanding of it: powerful masterplots that tap into key societal values can sway understandings of social phenomena in particular directions.[15] Sadler cites the example of sexual harassment in Egypt, where a common masterplot holds that women are harassed because of their provocative clothing or behaviour.[16] As will be seen, this trope shares much in common with the blame-shifting which the fossil fuel industry also engages in when emphasising the responsibility of the consumer. Sadler then advocates the promotion of alternative masterplots that help shape different causal interpretations of sexual violence against women.[17]

My use of 'masterplot' in this chapter broadly follows that of the two aforementioned authors. I see masterplots as abstract, overarching narratives or stories which are typically accompanied by archetypal characters and which also have a temporal dimension. These collective masterplots then get drawn on in individual 'narratives', which I understand as stories which apply or render masterplots in particular settings ('individual' here thus meaning individual or particular narrative statements by people or organisations, not statements made only by individuals). In practice, the two are co-constitutive: masterplots have to originate from somewhere; that 'somewhere' is a repeated set of narratives that, in time, become solidified into a recognisable masterplot, which then itself becomes a source for off-the-shelf narratives. The 'master' element need not mean there can only be one masterplot in play; rather, it connotes the power of their influence.[18] But the credibility that a masterplot

11 Porter Abbott (n 2) 48–9.
12 Porter Abbott (n 2) 50.
13 Neil Sadler, 'Myths, Masterplots and Sexual Harassment in Egypt' (2019) 24(2) *Journal of North African Studies* 247, 254.
14 Sadler (n 13).
15 Sadler (n 13).
16 Sadler (n 13) 254–5.
17 Sadler (n 13) 261–2.
18 Stefan Iversen and Mikka Pers, 'Interlocking Narratives: The Personal Story and the Masterplot in Political Rhetoric' in Cindie Aaen Maagaard, Daniel Schäbler and Marianne Wolff

gives to narratives that are structured by it is specific to particular groups.[19] Thus, the fossil fuel demand masterplot may be culturally dominant, but it is contested by climate groups and others, whose individual narratives draw instead on the supply masterplot. The latter, too, has emerged as a powerful story, trying to unseat its hegemonic demand counterpart.

Methodology

I identified the two energy transition masterplots from an inductive but unstructured process of reading media articles about fossil fuel supply and demand, and also academic articles looking at supply-side measures. For the purposes of the current chapter, I then set out to examine this more systematically, in a back-and-forth process which ended up both confirming the theory (the existence of the two masterplots) and analysing the way in which those two masterplots informed individual narratives in practice. In terms of narrative practice, I looked for illustrative examples of climate legislation that reflect both competing masterplots. However, my main focus was on looking for individual narratives in corporate, media, and other online sources which clearly drew on either the demand or the supply masterplot. I did this by looking at a number of key oil and gas company sustainability reports and senior management speeches or interviews from the past few years, searching for the terms *supply* and *demand*. I also used a standard search engine to look for these terms and others like 'leave it in the ground' in online newspaper articles and on environmental NGO websites. My aim in doing this was not to produce an exhaustive catalogue; it was simply to provide some illustrative examples of the way in which individual narrative statements made by companies, politicians, governments, protestors, litigants, and NGOs can be seen to be drawing on one of the relevant masterplots. However, my aim in the current chapter is also to explore whether, and if so, how, the Ukraine war and the energy trilemma, with its three energy policy frames of sustainability, security, and affordability, have affected these individual narratives. Time-wise, I therefore looked at sources before the Russian invasion in February 2022, and after to August 2023.

Law's role in the energy transition away from fossil fuels

How are we to understand the role of fossil fuel production in the energy transition, involving as it does a change from an economy based on fossil

Lundholt (eds), *Exploring Fictionality: Conceptions, Test Cases, Discussions* (University Press of Southern Denmark 2020) 183.
19 Iversen and Pers (n 18).

fuels to a decarbonised one running predominantly on renewable-powered electricity? And how does law feature in that? The understanding is contested and, I argue, rests on competing masterplots.

Law's role comes in two forms. First, in a dominant role, law acts to reinforce the existing fossil fuel status quo. Legal instruments of the transition, like the EU emissions trading system (ETS),[20] are typically directed only at reducing demand for fossil fuels and/or greenhouse gas emissions and not at cutting off the supply of fossil fuels.[21] Or law may give promise to future speculative technologies like carbon capture and storage (CCS).[22] By promising carbon emissions removal, CCS law becomes an instrument in enabling, not the cuts in supply necessary for transitioning to a fully decarbonised economy,[23] but rather, fossil fuel business as usual on the road to the less-stringent destination of net-zero emissions (where emissions can be balanced out by removals).

Secondly, law also features amongst the various mobilisation strategies deployed by the climate movement against supply by fossil fuel producers, ranging from climate change litigation brought against them to stop new extractive developments, and thus to keep fossil fuels in the ground,[24] to use of corporate and securities law to bring shareholder pressure to bear on fossil fuels through divestment campaigns and shareholder resolutions

20 n 7.

21 Piggot (n 6); Michael Lazarus and Harro van Asselt, 'Fossil Fuel Supply and Climate Policy: Exploring the Road Less Taken' (2018) 150 *Climatic Change* 1; Georgia Piggot and others (2020) 'Curbing Fossil Fuel Supply to Achieve Climate Goals' (2020) 20(8) *Climate Policy* 881; Harro van Asselt, 'Governing Fossil Fuel Production in the Age of Climate Disruption: Towards an International Law of 'Leaving It in the Ground' (2021) 9 *Earth System Governance* 100118.

22 See Stokes and Hilson (n 8).

23 Some view fossil fuels with CCS as 'decarbonised' (e.g. <www.gov.uk/guidance/uk-carbon-capture-and-storage-government-funding-and-support> accessed 15 August 2023; Tara Righetti and Matteo Fermeglia, 'Introduction – Decarbonizing Oil and Gas and Energy: Carbon Capture and Storage' (2023) 3 *OGEL*. However, given the likelihood of, for example, fugitive methane emissions in extraction, like the UK Climate Change Committee, I regard gas with CCS as 'low-carbon', not decarbonised (<www.theccc.org.uk/2023/03/09/a-reliable-secure-and-decarbonised-power-system-by-2035-is-possible-but-not-at-this-pace-of-delivery/> accessed 15 August 2023).

24 See, for example, *Greenpeace Nordic Association* v *Ministry of Petroleum and Energy* (2020) Case no 20–051052SIV-HRET, Supreme Court of Norway, *The People v Arctic Oil* <http://climatecasechart.com/non-us-case/greenpeace-nordic-assn-and-nature-youth-v-norway-ministry-of-petroleum-and-energy/> accessed 13 July 2023, where the applicants mounted a rights-based challenge to the Norwegian government's decision to grant production licences for a new oil and gas field in the Barents Sea. This was, in other words, supply-focused climate change litigation. The Norwegian Supreme Court ruled against the applicants, who then took their case to the European Court of Human Rights. On the Supreme Court ruling, see Christina Voigt, 'The First Climate Judgment before the Norwegian Supreme Court: Aligning Law with Politics' (2021) 33(3) *Journal of Environmental Law* 697.

or proposals.[25] These have been characterised in the academic literature as supply-side strategies or initiatives.[26] Other supply-side strategies include protest – for example, against fracking developments, against new oil and gas pipelines, or against other oil and gas infrastructure. Greenpeace's protest in relation to UK oil infrastructure is an example of the latter, with activists boarding a ship carrying Shell's floating production storage and offloading unit to the North Sea.[27] This, too, may have a strategic legal element because protestors, when arrested, have often raised defences like the necessity defence, which, where still available, enables their climate justifications to be communicated to the jury in the criminal trial.[28]

More recently, there has been backlash – notably in the United States – against environment, social, and governance (ESG) shareholder activism, which seeks divestment from fossil fuels or restrictive supply-side cuts by fossil fuel producers.[29] Large asset managers such as BlackRock have been targeted by a number of Republican states, including Texas, which have introduced legislation banning the state from doing business with companies said to be boycotting fossil fuel energy companies.[30] Whether or not this backlash was the cause, in 2022, BlackRock supported many fewer shareholder climate-related resolutions than in 2021. Its explanation for this was:

> [W]hereas last year [2021] climate-related shareholder proposals tended to address climate risk, often by requiring greater disclosure, in 2022, BlackRock observed a number of proposals considered to be 'more prescriptive' by asking companies to decommission fossil fuel assets, cease

25 Benjamin Richardson and Maziar Peihani, 'Universal Investors and Socially Responsible Finance: A Critique of a Premature Theory' (2015) 30(3) *Banking and Finance Law Review* 405; Stephen Park, 'Investors as Regulators: Green Bonds and the Governance Challenges of the Sustainable Finance Revolution' (2018) 54(1) *Stanford Journal of International Law* 1, 8–11.

26 Piggot (n 6); van Asselt (n 21); Nicolas Gaulin and Philippe Le Billon, 'Climate Change and Fossil Fuel Production Cuts: Assessing Global Supply-Side Constraints and Policy Implications' (2020) 20(8) *Climate Policy* 888.

27 Tom Wilson, 'Shell-Chartered Vessel Boarded by Greenpeace Activists' *FT* (31 January 2023) <www.ft.com/content/18e3a5b6-ae95-4ba8-bfd1-63080699c6c8> accessed 5 July 2023. Their banner read 'Stop Drilling. Start Paying'.

28 Hilson 2017 (n 4); Nicole Rogers, *Law, Fiction and Activism in a Time of Climate Change* (Routledge 2019).

29 Chris Hilson, 'Climate Change and the Politicization of ESG in the US' (2024) 6 *Frontiers in Political Science* 1332399; Amy Westervelt, 'The Right's Desperate Push to Tank ESG and Avoid Disclosing Climate Risks' *The Intercept* (2 July 2023) <https://theintercept.com/2023/07/02/esg-investing-sec-climate/> accessed 4 July 2023.

30 Hilson (n 29); Ryan McGlashan, 'The Rise of State Anti-ESG Legislation' *Fordham Journal of Corporate & Financial Law Blog* (11 November 2022) <https://news.law.fordham.edu/jcfl/2022/11/11/the-rise-of-state-anti-esg-legislation/> accessed 5 July 2023.

> fossil fuel exploration and development, and eliminate financing and insurance underwriting for fossil fuel projects.[31]

In other words, much more aggressive, strategic supply-side shareholder resolutions were not supported. In the end, what is important to note about this ESG backlash is that it, too, involves the law and the idea of supply; however, instead of pushing *for* restrictions on fossil fuel supply using the law, the relevant Republican states are using it to push back *against* those seeking such restrictions.

Law is therefore important both as a *potential* instrument for delivering the transition to a decarbonised economy and as a strategic means, among others, like protest, for pressuring a shift to supply-side measures, as well as for resisting that (as the Republican ESG backlash demonstrates). Of course, as we have seen, the word 'potential' is important here. In practice, law's potential is currently rather limited, at best because of its focus on the demand side and emissions reductions rather than seeking to phase out the supply of fossil fuels, and at worst because law's recognition of CCS maintains the fiction that some supply of fossil fuels can be maintained well into the future without causing harm. In the world where net-zero rather than a (fully) decarbonised economy is the target or destination, that fiction becomes allowable.[32] In masterplot terms, as will be explored further in the next section, the dominant energy masterplot, supported by the current law, is one of demand, with individual corporate narratives then drawing on and reinforcing this. The alternative, supply, masterplot is designed to counter this prevailing legal masterplot and is deployed in the narratives of climate NGOs, among others.

Energy masterplots and associated narratives

The demand masterplot and narratives based on it

The current, dominant energy masterplot is thus one of consumer demand. The demand masterplot states that 'extraction is inevitable' and that the emphasis of climate law and policy should be on reducing demand for fossil fuels and/or reducing emissions and not on restricting supply.[33] Two of the primary characteristics of this masterplot are character types and time.

31 Polly Bindman, 'World's Largest Asset Managers Block Climate Action Amid Anti-ESG Backlash' *Energy Monitor* (17 January 2023) <www.energymonitor.ai/finance/investment-management/worlds-largest-asset-managers-block-climate-action-amid-anti-esg-backlash/> accessed 5 July 2023.

32 On climate targets, see, for example, Chris Hilson, 'Hitting the Target? Analysing the Use of Targets in Climate Law' (2020) 32(2) *JEL* 195; on net zero, see, for example, Sam Fankhauser and others, 'The Meaning of Net Zero and How to Get It Right' (2022) 12 *Nature Climate Change* 15.

33 Piggot (n 6).

As seen earlier, stereotypes are a common feature of masterplots. In the demand masterplot, the individual consumer is the character that gets blamed and responsibilised for the energy transition, rather than it being seen as a structural supply issue to be addressed by governments and the oil and gas industry.[34] Fossil fuel companies, in contrast, are portrayed as benign characters who are merely being responsive to that consumer demand. The oil and gas supermajor bp actively spun such a story after employing the advertising and public relations agency Ogilvy & Mather, who developed a campaign for them popularising the idea of the 'carbon footprint' in order 'to promote the slant that climate change is not the fault of an oil giant, but that of individuals'.[35] As Emma Pattee puts it, this 'crucially shifted the narrative from corporate accountability to personal responsibility'.[36] However, as we will see later, bp is not alone here – other oil supermajors, like ExxonMobil, similarly emphasise consumer demand in their corporate reporting in order to individualise responsibility for climate change and the transition.[37]

Time is also important in masterplots – stories invariably involve an internal set of events unfolding over time. Here, the temporal trajectory is the transition towards a decarbonised economy or, in the demand story, net-zero.[38] In the demand masterplot, we must take our time and not rush the transition. CCS plays a heroic future role, enabling remaining demand for fossil fuels to be met unproblematically (and supply to continue), because the troublesome carbon emissions will be neatly removed.

34 Nosek (n 5).

35 Mark Kaufman, 'The Carbon Footprint Sham' *Mashable* <https://mashable.com/feature/carbon-footprint-pr-campaign-sham> accessed 12 July 2023. See also Julie Doyle, 'Where Has All the Oil Gone? BP Branding and the Discursive Elimination of Climate Change Risk' in Nick Heffernan and David Wragg (eds), *Culture, Environment and Ecopolitics* (Cambridge Scholars Publishing 2011); Rebecca Solnit, 'Big Oil Coined "Carbon Footprints" to Blame Us for Their Greed: Keep Them on the Hook' *The Guardian* (23 August 2021) <www.theguardian.com/commentisfree/2021/aug/23/big-oil-coined-carbon-footprints-to-blame-us-for-their-greed-keep-them-on-the-hook> accessed 17 July 2023. Although popularised by the bp campaign in 2004, the origins of the *carbon footprint* lie within the idea of an ecological footprint, conceived in 1990 (and which can be country- or corporate-focused rather than simply looking at the footprints of individuals): see <www.footprintnetwork.org/our-work/ecological-footprint/> accessed 17 July 2023.

36 Emma Pattee, 'Forget Your Carbon Footprint: Let's Talk about Your Climate Shadow' *Mic* (12 October 2021) <www.mic.com/impact/forget-your-carbon-footprint-lets-talk-about-your-climate-shadow> accessed 13 July 2023. Pattee's idea of the 'carbon shadow' includes the totality of one's climate choices and actions, including, for example, discussing climate at work, working on local renewable projects, and lobbying politicians.

37 Geoffrey Supran and Naomi Oreskes, 'Rhetoric and Frame Analysis of ExxonMobil's Climate Change Communications' (2021) 4(5) *One Earth* 696.

38 I am grateful to Graeme Hayes for reminding me about time.

We can then look for various individual or organisational narratives, put forward by corporate spokespeople and others, that draw upon or reflect this dominant, demand masterplot. If one looks at climate law's legislative or regulatory narrative – in other words, climate legislation as itself a form of narrative[39] – the EU ETS, for example, involves a (quiet) story about cutting demand and emissions. This centrepiece of EU climate law and policy is directed at reducing greenhouse gas emissions and demand for fossil fuel energy by setting a disincentive carbon price on its use.[40] As Lazarus and van Asselt note, it is possible for climate law to address the supply cutting side via, for example, government moratoriums on new oil and gas exploration[41] or new coal mines. However, such measures are much less common. What we often find more emphasis on is CCS, which conveniently enables supply not to be cut but to continue without harm. From a political economy perspective, the fact that the law and powerful fossil fuel business narratives are aligned is no surprise.

Most existing climate law, like the EU ETS and CCS, thus contains its own narrative that reflects the consumer demand masterplot, but its presence is often an implicit or quiet one – you may need to go looking for it because it is somewhat hidden as a taken-for-granted element of the business-as-usual approach. However, as will be seen later, other narratives that draw upon one of the two relevant masterplots explicitly use the language of supply and demand. These individual narrative statements may be ones made by politicians and governments, by companies and their senior management, and by international agencies, NGOs, protestors, and litigants. Some of these statements are made in a legal context (for example, in Paris Agreement COP statements, or in court proceedings), but many of them are not. However, they remain important for lawyers because they help create the wider public discourse on which law is premised. To change the law, you need to change understandings of what needs to be done, and masterplots are a key battleground for that. These statements therefore matter.

First, relevant statements drawing on the demand masterplot can be found in the form of pronouncements by political leaders of states that are large fossil fuel producers and rely on them for a significant part of their GDP. Thus, Justin Trudeau, the Canadian prime minister, stated that 'there isn't a country in the world that would find billions of barrels of oil and leave it in the ground while there is a market for it'.[42] Like Canada, Norway, as a major

39 On different types of narrative in environmental law, including this legislative one, see Hilson (n 8).

40 (n 7). The US story is even quieter. With no explicit federal climate law, emissions reductions fall within pollution law (the Clean Air Act): *Massachusetts v EPA* 549 US 497 (2007).

41 For example, the joint Obama/Trudeau decision to rule out offshore Arctic oil and gas activity – Lazarus and van Asselt (n 21) 7.

42 Piggot (n 6) 942–3.

petrostate, has likewise come out with a narrative that reflects the dominant demand masterplot. As the Norwegian climate and energy minister stated in 2016, 'as long as the world needs oil and gas, we will provide it'.[43]

Next, narratives based on the demand masterplot can be found in fossil fuel corporate sustainability reports and in CEO and senior officer speeches and interviews.[44] Reflecting in 2023 on bp's bumper profits from the previous year, then CEO Bernard Looney stated:

> We need continuing near-term investment into today's energy system – which depends on oil and gas – to meet today's demands and to make sure the transition is an orderly one. . . . At the end of the day, we're responding to what society wants.[45]

ExxonMobil's 2021 Sustainability Report similarly states that:

> Under most third-party scenarios that meet the objectives of the Paris Agreement, oil and natural gas continue to play a significant role for decades in meeting increasing energy demand of a growing and more prosperous global population. ExxonMobil will play an important role in meeting society's need for energy and at the same time is committed to supporting efforts to mitigate the risk of climate change.[46]

Shell's narratives also deploy the demand masterplot. In 2022, its director of strategy, sustainability, and corporate relations stated, '[W]e must match up our role as the supplier of energy . . . with the role of others as the consumers of energy. Supply and demand both have to change. Demand is fundamental'.[47]

43 Michelle Jonker-Argueta, 'Closing the Supply-Side Accountability Gap through Climate Litigation' *OpenGlobal Rights* (19 October 2020) <www.openglobalrights.org/closing-the-supply-side-accountability-gap-through-climate-litigation/?lang=English> accessed 5 July 2023.

44 For a discourse analytical study of environmental reporting by oil companies, including mention of demand, see Sylvia Jaworska, 'Change But No Climate Change: Discourses of Climate Change in Corporate Social Responsibility Reporting in the Oil Industry' (2018) 55(2) *International Journal of Business Communication* 194.

45 Oliver Milman, 'Monster Profits' for Energy Giants Reveal a Self-Destructive Fossil Fuel Resurgence' *The Guardian* (9 February 2023) <www.theguardian.com/environment/2023/feb/09/profits-energy-fossil-fuel-resurgence-climate-crisis-shell-exxon-bp-chevron-totalenergies> accessed 5 July 2023.

46 ExxonMobil, 'Sustainability Report Highlights' (9 January 2021) <https://corporate.exxonmobil.com/-/media/global/files/sustainability-report/publication/sustainability-report.pdf> accessed 6 July 2023.

47 Ed Daniels, 'Our Progress in the Energy Transition' (26 April 2022) <www.shell.com/media/speeches-and-articles/articles-by-date/our-progress-in-the-energy-transition.html> accessed 6 July 2023.

This narrative, which draws on the demand masterplot and the role of consumers, was also echoed by Shell's then CEO in 2022:

> In an interview at Shell's headquarters in London, van Beurden argued that governments had too often set emissions goals without a plan of how to achieve them and pushed for cuts in oil and gas production without taking measures to curb consumer demand. 'As long as society believes that by starving [fossil fuel] supply you will somehow force demand to come down as well, that is not a sustainable way of tackling the energy transition,' the 64-year-old said. 'Supply needs to adjust but it needs to adjust to less demand.'[48]

If we return to the earlier definition of a *masterplot* as a deeply rooted story which informs the way a policy issue is seen, then one can see from the preceding statements that they are all individual narratives which draw on this deep-seated view about the primary role of demand for fossil fuels in the energy transition. The role they envisage for climate law is one of curbing emissions and demand, not cutting off supply directly. The role for fossil fuel companies is to match supply to changing consumer demand: consumers are placed in the driving seat; companies cannot be expected to reduce supply independently of their demand.

The supply masterplot and narratives based on it

The alternative or competing energy masterplot – the supply one – seeks to challenge the idea that continued extraction is inevitable, stressing the idea that fossil fuels should be left in the ground. It emphasises the need for direct legal restrictions on supply and not just, as we tend to find at present, legal measures aimed at reducing demand and/or emissions. One of the supply masterplot's character types, designed to frighten off capital, is the out-of-pocket investor whose fossil fuel investment assets may become 'stranded' unless they divest away from them.[49] In temporal terms, the supply masterplot calls for rapid decarbonisation. It argues that we urgently need cuts to fossil fuel supply because we do not have time for the delay involved in waiting for demand to drop.

Narratives that reflect this alternative, supply masterplot can be found in a range of places, including the pronouncements of influential international

48 Tom Wilson, 'Shell Boss van Beurden: "Supply Needs to Adjust Butto Less Demand"' *FT* (21 July 2022) <www.ft.com/content/fe3247bf-8868-49fb-9b7d-5869f59e2bef> accessed 6 July 2023.

49 Assets likely to be held mostly by the very well-off: Gregor Semieniuk and others, 'Potential Pension Fund Losses Should Not Deter High-Income Countries from Bold Climate Action' (2023) 7(7) *Joule* 1383.

organisations like the International Energy Agency (IEA), summit agreement texts at climate COPs, and of course, in statements made and actions brought by the climate movement. The IEA, for example, has stated that '[b]eyond projects already committed as of 2021, there are no new oil and gas fields approved for development in our pathway, and no new coal mines or mine extensions are required'.[50] This sentiment has been echoed by Fatih Birol, the IEA executive director: 'If governments are serious about the climate crisis, there can be no new investments in oil, gas and coal, from now – from this year.'[51]

It is not only in official statements like this that the supply masterplot can be seen at work. As far back as 2008, protestors at the UK Drax coal-fired power station, who had hijacked a coal train serving the plant, raised a banner saying, 'Leave it in the ground'.[52] When prosecuted for obstruction of the railway, they unsuccessfully sought to rely on the necessity defence in what can be characterised as 'reactive' climate change litigation.[53] The supply masterplot has also informed the name of the Leave It in the Ground Initiative (LINGO), an NGO whose mission states that we need to '[l]eave fossil fuels in the ground and learn to live without them'.[54] It lists climate litigation in its recommended activist toolkit, including supply-focused litigation aimed at blocking fossil fuel projects.[55] The divestment movement similarly took on this 'leave it in the ground' narrative informed by the supply masterplot.[56] It started as a student movement campaigning for US university endowments to divest from coal and, with the involvement of the activist Bill McKibben

50 IEA, 'Net Zero by 2050: A Roadmap for the Global Energy Sector' (2021) 21.

51 Fiona Harvey, 'No New Oil, Gas or Coal Development If World Is to Reach Net Zero by 2050, Says World Energy Body' *The Guardian* (18 May 2021) <www.theguardian.com/environment/2021/may/18/no-new-investment-in-fossil-fuels-demands-top-energy-economist> accessed 10 July 2023.

52 Chris Hilson, 'Climate Change Litigation: An Explanatory Approach (Or Bringing Grievance Back In)' in Fabrizio Fracchia and Massimo Occhiena (eds), *Climate Change: La Riposta del Diritto* (Editoriale Scientifica 2010) 421.

53 Hilson (n 52).

54 <www.leave-it-in-the-ground.org/about/> accessed 10 July 2023.

55 <www.leave-it-in-the-ground.org/projects/climate-litigation/> accessed 10 July 2023. On various forms of supply-focused litigation of this kind (albeit not necessarily with submissions or judgments explicitly using supply language), see further Briony Eales and others, 'Climate Change, Coming Soon to a Court Near You: Climate Litigation in Asia and the Pacific and Beyond' (Report Two, Asian Development Bank, December 2020) 62–71.

56 Benjamin Franta, 'Litigation in the Fossil Fuel Divestment Movement' (2017) 39(4) *Law & Policy* 393, 396 notes the supply focus of divestment strategies: the 'fossil fuel divestment movement focus[es] explicitly on the supply side of the fossil fuel economy, in contrast to climate discourses that focus primarily on fossil fuel demand and consumption.' He also observes the infrequency of litigation as a means to try to force divestment.

and the organisation 350.org, broadened out to include other fossil fuels.[57] In due course, the movement targeted not only universities but also other institutional investors with significant fossil fuel holdings. In the UK, *The Guardian* newspaper helped support this movement, notably adopting the 'Keep It in the Ground' narrative informed by the supply masterplot as the byword of their campaign.[58]

However, where narratives that draw upon this alternative supply masterplot are put forward, they are often countered by a retelling of the dominant demand masterplot which attempts to see off the new pretender. Thus, in the context of the Glasgow COP26, where the UK presidency was seeking agreement on the 'phase-out' of coal, only for it to be watered down at the last minute to the language of 'phasing down', key coal-producing countries 'said the change of wording showed they had successfully defended the use of natural resources for which demand is still high and supply is tight'.[59] Here, the phasing out of coal wording attempted to tell a story about coal supply coming to a planned end but was successfully countered by a narrative informed by the standard demand masterplot, where coal supply would gradually come down in line with market demand. Similarly, at COP27 in Sharm el-Sheikh, where India and the EU were calling for the phasing down of all fossil fuels (not just coal), Saudi Arabia's foreign minister, Adel al-Jubeir, responded in interview that:

> tackling climate change was 'not about fossil fuels' production but about reducing emissions across sectors. Asked whether Riyadh believed a phase down or phase out of oil and gas would be necessary to limit global warming, he said 'not even phase down'.[60]

Here, the narrative is one of reducing the emissions associated with demand, but it still draws on the dominant demand masterplot.

One of the fossil fuel corporate responses to supply-focused climate change litigation has similarly involved emphasising demand – that the company is

57 Julie Ayling and Neil Gunningham, 'Non-State Governance and Climate Policy: The Fossil Fuel Divestment Movement' (2017) 17(2) *Climate Policy* 131; Noam Bergman, 'Impacts of the Fossil Fuel Divestment Movement: Effects on Finance, Policy and Public Discourse' (2018) 10(7) *Sustainability* 2529.

58 Emma Howard, 'Five Lessons from the Fossil Fuel Divestment Movement' *The Guardian* (16 July 2015) <www.theguardian.com/environment/2015/jul/16/five-lessons-from-the-fossil-fuel-divestment-movement> accessed 10 July 2023.

59 Shivani Singh and others, '"Down" and "Out"? COP26 Wording Clouds Way Ahead on Climate' *Reuters* (15 November 2021) <www.reuters.com/business/cop/business-usual-global-fossil-fuel-firms-now-after-un-climate-deal-2021-11-15/> accessed 10 July 2023.

60 Camilla Hodgson, 'COP27: India Draws Support for Wider Climate Target Than Coal Alone' *FT* (15 November 2022) <www.ft.com/content/eedc63fd-8f69-49f8-9a22-2dfe77d6a24a> accessed 10 July 2023.

merely supplying the fossil fuels that are being demanded out there in the market. The Australian *Waratah Coal* case,[61] for example, involved merits review by the Queensland Land Court of whether to grant licences for a new thermal coal mine in the Galilee Basin. Although, in the end, the judge recommended the relevant mining and environmental applications be rejected, the coal company had argued that if they did not supply the coal, given that the demand for coal would still be there, someone else would, and that it was unlikely that the other supplier would be producing coal that was as thermally efficient and, hence, as carbon friendly. Michelle Jonker-Argueta aptly describes this as the 'drug dealer' defence and rightly questions the basis of its economic assumptions.[62] However, for present purposes, it provides an illustration of a narrative drawing on the demand masterplot in response to a court challenge premised on the alternative, supply masterplot.

One also hears a similar narrative in some quarters of the financial services industry in response to divestment. Some leading figures in asset management, like Blackrock's Larry Fink, have opined that divestment or exit is inferior to staying invested and exerting voice[63] because, with divestment, either demand for ownership of fossil fuel companies will simply shift to other, less-dependable characters, such as private equity or state-owned national oil companies. Both sets of alternative owners may be less concerned about climate change and are not subject to stock market discipline and accountability in the same way:

> [s]trategies to choke off oil and gas supply from publicly traded companies only cause the assets to change hands, often into the control of less transparent actors that are not as committed to environmental improvement, Fink said. 'If a foundation, or an insurance company, or a pension fund says, "I'm not going to own any hydrocarbons," well, somebody else is. So you're not changing the world. My view is it is those pension funds, foundations and endowments actually should have a loud voice with companies to move forward,' he said.[64]

61 *Waratah Coal v Youth Verdict* (No 6) (2022) *QLC* 21 <www.sclqld.org.au/caselaw/QLC/2022/21> accessed 11 July 2023. See also *Gloucester Resources Limited v Minister for Planning* (2019) NSWLEC 7.

62 As she notes, reducing supply will tend to lead to an increase in price and thereby help lower demand: Michelle Jonker-Argueta, 'Closing the Supply-Side Accountability Gap through Climate Litigation' in César Rodríguez-Garavito (ed), *Litigating the Climate Emergency: How Human Rights, Courts, and Legal Mobilization Can Bolster Climate Action* (Cambridge University Press 2022) 319. See also Justice Brian Preston in *Gloucester Resources* (n 61).

63 On exit and voice in an investment context, see Park (n 25) 9–11.

64 Deborah Jaremko, 'Don't Divest from Oil and Gas, Says BlackRock CEO Larry Fink' *Canadian Energy Centre* (26 November 2021) <www.canadianenergycentre.ca/dont-divest-from-oil-and-gas-says-blackrock-ceo-larry-fink/> accessed 11 July 2023.

For commentators like Fink, the reason for this continuing demand for ownership of fossil fuel assets by other actors is, in the end, linked with the continuing demand by consumers for those fossil fuels and the ability of those actors to profit from this financially.[65]

The energy transition and the energy trilemma

The energy trilemma famously involves three elements which governments must deliver but which are often in tension in various ways at different times.[66] Those elements are environmental sustainability, affordability, and energy security. The energy trilemma is, I suggest, best seen as a contest between different 'frames' or ways in which the energy problem can be seen.[67] Some might see these as narratives or perhaps even masterplots around energy. However, they lack the temporal, causal element associated with plots.[68] And they are better seen as frames rather than narratives because they have the snapshot[69] quality of a frame within the climate/energy debate, as opposed to taking the narrative form of a story with characters. That is not to say that the three values cannot be deployed within energy stories (one can easily tell a story about consumers facing higher energy bills using the affordability element of the trilemma for example). However, they are not themselves narratives – they are frames or ways of selectively constructing the climate–energy policy problem. In other words, that problem can be seen through the lens of environmental sustainability, with carbon emissions at the centre of that. It can be viewed from the perspective of affordability for consumers. And it can be seen from a security frame, where domestic supplies are not easily threatened by exogenous forces.

65 Jaremko (n 64).

66 On the energy trilemma, see Neil Gunningham, 'Managing the Energy Trilemma: The Case of Indonesia' (2013) 54 *Energy Policy* 184; Raphael Heffron, Darren McCauley and Benjamin Sovacool, 'Resolving Society's Energy Trilemma through the Energy Justice Metric' (2015) 87 *Energy Policy* 168.

67 Piggot (n 6) also regards energy security as a frame. On policy frames/framing see, for example, Donald Schön and Martin Rein, *Frame Reflection: Toward the Resolution of Intractable Policy Controversies* (Basic Books 1994). On framing in environmental and climate law, see, for example, Hilson 2012 and 2017 (n 4); Craig Arnold, 'Framing Watersheds' in Keith Hirokawa (ed), *Environmental Law and Contrasting Ideas of Nature: A Constructivist Approach* (Cambridge University Press 2013); Elizabeth Fisher, 'Environmental Law as "Hot' Law"' (2013) 25(3) *JEL* 347; Chris Hilson, 'Framing Fracking: Which Frames Are Heard in English Planning and Environmental Policy and Practice?' (2015) 27(2) *JEL* 177; Carrie Bradshaw, 'England's Fresh Approach to Food Waste: Problem Frames in the Resources and Waste Strategy' (2020) 40(2) *Legal Studies* 321; Carolyn Abbot and Maria Lee, *Environmental Groups and Legal Expertise: Shaping the Brexit Process* (UCL Press 2021).

68 Iversen and Pers (n 18).

69 As Gitlin puts it, '[f]rames are principles of selection, emphasis and presentation composed of little tacit theories about what exists, what happens, and what matters': Todd Gitlin, *The Whole World Is Watching: Mass Media in the Making and Unmaking of the New Left* (University of California Press 1980) 6.

When talking about energy, government and corporate officials – particularly since the Ukraine war – are often telling a story or narrative involving these frames and how they see them intersecting. In what follows, I will be exploring how these narratives around fossil fuels relate to the two competing demand and supply masterplots examined earlier. The war – which led to a sizeable increase in global energy prices – certainly brought the intersecting frames of the energy trilemma into sharp focus. What we find is that while narratives that incorporated these frames drew on a relevant masterplot, the narratives no longer deliver the masterplot's message in a straightforward way. The trilemma complicates that message and, at first sight, even appears to invert the relevant masterplots. As we will see later, in the UK, for example, the short-lived Liz Truss government emphasised not demand, as might be expected from our earlier discussion, but rather supply.[70] However, instead of the climate activist strategic masterplot of *cutting* the new supply of fossil fuels, the government here was calling for the opposite – to double down on supply, especially from the North Sea. Similarly, the climate movement also shifted to arguing both for *increasing* energy supply (but of renewables rather than fossil fuels) and for addressing energy demand (but wanting to reduce it via demand management measures and energy efficiency improvements like home insulation rather than, as in the demand masterplot, accepting that demand for fossil fuels is there and needs to be met).[71] This reshaping of the supply and demand arguments came about principally because of the way the intersecting frames of the energy trilemma themselves interconnected with the relevant demand and supply masterplots. The masterplots did not change – these different supply and demand elements were always implicit in them – but narratives drawing on the two masterplots were having to move away from the earlier, simpler supply and demand messaging.

Changing narratives

In the period well before the Ukraine war, Shell's integrated gas and new energies director was confidently stating not only that fossil gas ticked all the energy trilemma boxes but gas from Russia no less:

> Governments typically have three major priorities when setting energy policies: security of supply, economic competitiveness and a reduction of

70 Maryam Zakir-Hussain and Namita Singh, 'Energy Crisis – Live: Liz Truss Issues Hundreds of New Oil and Gas Licences Despite Climate Change' *Independent* (7 October 2022) <www.independent.co.uk/news/uk/home-news/energy-uk-blackout-2022-truss-b2197790.html> accessed 12 July 2023.

71 For example, Friends of the Earth, 'Five Ways the New PM Must Tackle Climate and Energy Crises' (24 October 2022) <https://friendsoftheearth.uk/climate/five-ways-new-pm-must-tackle-climate-and-energy-crises> accessed 12 July 2023.

> greenhouse gas emissions. At present, only gas can meet all three priorities simultaneously. This puts Russia, home to the largest gas reserves in the world, at the heart of the debate. When it comes to energy security, Russia has demonstrated it is a reliable supplier. Looking at Europe, for example, Russia exported gas throughout the Cold War. In more than 17,500 days, there have only been 14 days when gas did not reach Europe. That's almost half a century of energy security. Russia is moving forward with several projects to increase gas supplies. Nordstream 2, the proposed expansion of the pipeline capacity from Russia to Germany, will bolster energy security in Europe.[72]

While (as the preceding quote makes clear) Russian gas was once the option to tick both the cheap, affordability trilemma box and the energy security box, after the Ukraine war, it clearly no longer ticks either of these boxes. Indeed, few statements look so misjudged with the benefit of hindsight. And although gas may win out against coal on the sustainability element of the trilemma, most in the climate movement question whether it can be counted as sustainable. Recent EU sustainable finance law – notably the EU taxonomy[73] on what counts as a sustainable investment – nevertheless controversially included it. A number of environmental NGOs requested an internal review of the relevant delegated act[74] in 2022[75] and, on rejection of this, brought proceedings before the Court of Justice.[76]

Turning to the post–Ukraine war oil and gas supermajor narratives, in February 2023, bp rowed back from its previous 2020 climate commitments to reduce oil and gas production by 40% by 2030 to a much lower 25% figure. In seeking to justify this ramping up of current supply, CEO Bernard Looney pointed not only to expected shareholder returns from this strategic shift (with oil and gas prices at near record post-invasion highs at that time, after their pandemic collapse) but also to the fact that governments had been

72 Maarten Wetselaar, 'Gas Is Critical to Meeting Global Energy Demand' (1 August 2016) <www.shell.com/media/speeches-and-articles/articles-by-date/gas-is-critical-to-meeting-global-energy-demand.html> accessed 12 July 2023.

73 Regulation (EU) 2020/852 on the establishment of a framework to facilitate sustainable investment [2020] OJ L198/13.

74 Delegated Regulation (EU) 2022/1214 [2022] OJ L188/1.

75 For the legal arguments made by one of these NGOs, see Greenpeace European Unit, 'Media Briefing: Greenpeace's Legal Arguments against Including Gas and Nuclear in the EU Taxonomy' (9 February 2023) <www.greenpeace.org/eu-unit/issues/climate-energy/46567/media-briefing-greenpeaces-legal-arguments-against-including-gas-and-nuclear-in-the-eu-taxonomy/> accessed 12 July 2023.

76 Case T-214/23 *Greenpeace v Commission* [2023] OJ C235/61; ClientEarth press release, 'EU Taxonomy: Environmental Groups Take EU to Court Over "Green" Gas Label' (18 April 2023) <www.clientearth.org/latest/press-office/press/eu-taxonomy-environmental-groups-take-eu-to-court-over-green-gas-label/> accessed 12 July 2023.

asking for increased production to combat the effects of the Russian invasion on energy security and energy prices:

> It's clearer than ever after the past three years that the world wants and needs energy that is secure and affordable as well as lower carbon – all three together, what's known as the energy trilemma. To tackle that, action is needed to accelerate the transition. And – at the same time – action is needed to make sure that the transition is orderly, so that affordable energy keeps flowing where it's needed today. As an integrated energy company, bp is very deliberately set up to help on both counts. . . And with today's announcement we are leaning further in. We are growing our investment into our transition and, at the same time, growing investment into today's energy system. In doing so – we see tremendous opportunity to create value. And it's what governments and customers are asking of companies like us.[77]

ExxonMobil's 2023 report likewise stressed energy supply security:

> As the world continues to face the challenge of securing adequate energy supply while ensuring the energy transition proceeds at pace – divergent views have emerged. There are some who believe that society's efforts should be solely directed toward the energy transition without considering the very real consequences of not ensuring energy security.[78]

The report proceeds to state that, instead of either transition or continuing supply of oil and gas, there is a need for both. While both of the quotes above mention energy security, like Looney, Wael Sawan, the new Shell CEO, has also stressed affordability, stating in July 2023 that '[w]hat would be dangerous and irresponsible is cutting oil and gas production so that the cost of living, as we saw last year, starts to shoot up again'.[79]

The key point here in relation to all three pronouncements is that their post–Ukraine war narratives involve a significant foregrounding of the energy trilemma frames, now including security of supply and affordability alongside demand from its standard masterplot. The latter masterplot has not gone away: in its report, Exxon describes oil and gas as continuing to play an

77 bp, 'Integrated Energy Company Strategy Update: Growing Investment, Growing Value, Growing Distributions' (7 February 2023) 2 <www.bp.com/en/global/corporate/news-and-insights/press-releases/4q-2022-update-on-strategic-progress.html> accessed 12 July 2023.

78 ExxonMobil, '2023 Advancing Climate Solutions Progress Report' 4 <https://corporate.exxonmobil.com/news/reporting-and-publications/advancing-climate-solutions-progress-report> accessed 12 July 2023.

79 Simon Jack, 'Oil Giant Shell Warns Cutting Production "Dangerous"' *BBC News* (6 July 2023) <www.bbc.co.uk/news/business-66108553> accessed 12 July 2023.

important role through to 2050, with 'sustained investment . . . needed to meet demand'.[80] And in bp's report, Bernard Looney similarly talks in the earlier quote about 'need', which is synonymous with *demand*, but also directly mentions *demand* when he states that '[w]e need continuing near-term investment into today's energy system – which depends on oil and gas – to meet today's demands and to make sure the transition is an orderly one'.[81] However, the demand narrative has been joined by affordability and security of supply from the energy trilemma, and the overall story has become more complicated. The simplicity of the demand narrative drawn from the dominant masterplot is no longer there.

What, then, of government narratives? Initial post–Ukraine war UK government energy security strategy under then prime minister Boris Johnson emphasised the need for new North Sea oil and gas but otherwise stressed a renewed emphasis on the speed of the transition to renewables and nuclear as a way of meeting the challenge of energy security while also delivering cheaper and cleaner power.[82]

With the next, Truss government, business and energy secretary Jacob Rees-Mogg argued that encouraging more domestic supply – now not only through new North Sea licensing rounds but also by ending the moratorium on fracking – would address energy security and sustainability (based on the argument that domestically produced energy is less carbon-intensive than relying on imported LNG).[83]

Opposition parties were not convinced. Nicola Sturgeon, then leader of the SNP, responded to Rees-Mogg's activation of a new North Sea licensing round by suggesting that the Westminster government's policy was more likely to undermine energy security than to protect it, commenting that energy security is 'difficult, it's challenging, but the route to energy security is to secure that transition away from fossil fuels to renewable'.[84]

Caroline Lucas, then a Green MP, also questioned the government's energy trilemma–based narrative from a price and environmental perspective as well as one based on energy security:

> Grotesque – now oil and gas licenses won't cut energy bills as fuel gets sold at global prices; it'll drive #climateemergency since it adds to total global

80 ExxonMobil (n 78) 7.

81 n 77.

82 HMG, *British Energy Security Strategy* (April 2022).

83 Jacob Rees-Mogg, 'Deluded Green Narratives around Oil and Gas Must Not Allow Us to Surrender Our Energy Security' *The Telegraph* (7 October 2022) <www.telegraph.co.uk/politics/2022/10/07/deluded-green-narratives-around-oil-gas-must-not-allow-us-surrender/> accessed 12 July 2023.

84 Alex Lawson, 'UK Offers New North Sea Oil and Gas Licences Despite Climate Concerns' *The Guardian* (7 October 2022) <www.theguardian.com/business/2022/oct/07/uk-offers-new-north-sea-oil-and-gas-licences-despite-climate-concerns> accessed 12 July 2023.

emissions; takes years to come on line & won't help energy security. Environmental & economic madness.[85]

In the summer of 2023, Prime Minister Rishi Sunak announced new North Sea oil and gas licences, underlining that even with net zero in 2050, a quarter of UK energy demand would be met from oil and gas. In doubling down on domestic supply to meet that demand, he drew on the trilemma frames, emphasising affordability and energy security as well as claiming an environmental, carbon intensity advantage over imported gas.[86] New CCS clusters were announced at the same time and described as the way in which the aforementioned demand would be met while realising the UK's net-zero target. Conservative strategy was also to paint the opposition under Keir Starmer as aligned with the protest group Just Stop Oil. Starmer's response to being portrayed as a supporter of supply-side cuts was to describe Just Stop Oil demands as 'contemptible', despite the fact that its policy, like Labour's, is for no *new* licences to be granted.[87] He nevertheless drew on the supply masterplot in arguing that the Conservatives had failed to deliver enough renewable energy or invest in energy efficiency. He stated that these failures were a 'gift to Putin' and that they had exacerbated the cost-of-living crisis – reflecting a security and affordability frame, respectively.[88]

The aforementioned industry and government and opposition narratives can then be compared with those of the climate movement. Friends of the Earth's narrative, like Starmer's, is about the need for increased supply (but of renewables, not fossil fuels) and of demand measures (but to decrease demand for fossil fuels, not meet it) and is quite representative of the movement as a whole:

> Friends of the Earth has long argued that soaring energy bills and the climate crisis are two sides of the same coin. Both are driven by our seemingly insatiable appetite for more gas, coal and oil, and both can be addressed with the same solutions – investment in homegrown renewables and energy efficiency.[89]

85 Lawson (n 84).

86 PM and DESNZ Press Release, 'Hundreds of New North Sea Oil and Gas Licences to Boost British Energy Independence and Grow the Economy' (31 July 2023).

87 Charlie Cooper, 'Just Stop Oil Approach "Contemptible" Says Starmer' *Politico* (7 August 2023) <www.politico.eu/article/just-stop-oil-approach-contemptible-says-starmer/> accessed 15 August 2023.

88 Keir Starmer, 'Rishi Sunak's Climate Failure Is a Gift to Putin' *The Times* (6 August 2023) <www.thetimes.co.uk/article/keir-starmer-rishi-sunaks-climate-failure-is-a-gift-to-putin-rfhhv6gxp> accessed 15 August 2023.

89 Mike Childs, 'The UK's New Department for Energy Security and Net Zero Must Be More Than a PR Exercise' *The Big Issue* (17 February 2023) <www.bigissue.com/news/environment/the-uks-new-department-for-energy-security-and-net-zero-must-be-more-than-a-pr-

In the end, then, there is a visible conflict of narratives between the UK government and corporates on the one hand and the opposition and the climate movement on the other. The former argued that a greater supply of (non-Russian, domestic) fossil fuels was needed in order to provide for energy security, to reduce energy prices faced by consumers (affordability), and to reduce emissions intensity (sustainability). The latter argued that any new supply of fossil fuels would come too late to address the energy security and affordability element and that a dramatic and rapid increase in the supply of cheap renewables was and remains the best option for tackling all three parts of the energy trilemma, including, of course, sustainability.

At this point, however, although the individual energy narratives can still be traced back to the dominant demand and alternative supply masterplots, the energy trilemma complicates those narratives. For the climate-ambitious side, cutting the supply of fossil fuels by keeping them in the ground is still key, but security of supply and affordability from the energy trilemma oblige them to also talk about increasing the supply of renewables in order to address those. For the business side, ensuring that they keep up with demand for fossil fuels during the transition remains an important part of their narrative. However, while it was one that was previously used as a somewhat-defensive counternarrative to the sustainability-driven one calling for rapid, stringent cuts in supply, the post–Ukraine war energy landscape emboldened them to be more on the front foot. It was no longer just them arguing for supply needing to keep up with existing demand, as that demand lowered during the transition; rather, as we saw with bp earlier, in 2023, a number of the oil and gas supermajors unapologetically reduced their previous targets to cut production of oil and gas[90] or, in Shell's case, committed to growth in its integrated gas business.[91] In doing so, the companies tended to emphasise shareholder returns and also energy security and affordability.

Former Shell CEO van Beurden's 2023 retirement interview perfectly captures the way in which the security and affordability elements of the trilemma have changed the focus away from purely sustainability-driven narratives:

> For a long time, the only discussion that people were prepared to entertain with us was that you need to be more sustainable, you need to invest more

exercise/> accessed 12 July 2023. Childs is Head of Science, Policy, and Research at Friends of the Earth.

90 Lottie Limb, 'Shell Joins BP and Total in U-Turning on Climate Pledges "To Reward Shareholders"' *euronews.green* (15 June 2023) <www.euronews.com/green/2023/06/15/shell-joins-bp-and-total-in-u-turning-on-climate-pledges-to-reward-shareholders> accessed 12 July 2023.

91 Shell Global, 'Shell to Deliver More Value with Less Emissions' (14 June 2023) <www.shell.com/media/news-and-media-releases/2023/shell-to-deliver-more-value-with-less-emissions.html> accessed 12 July 2023.

> in making clean and green, low-carbon products. And we get all of that and we are doing this. But that is not the full story. Energy is not just a matter of whether it can be cleaner. It also has to be available and affordable. Can all these things come together? Yes, but often one comes at the expense of the other. What we have seen over the last 10 years ignores that reality because of the almost exclusive focus on cleaner energy rather than also available and affordable energy.[92]

Conclusion

How should we understand the place of fossil fuels within the transition to a decarbonised economy and the role which law plays in that transition? I have argued that we are in a battle of competing understandings in which the masterplots of energy supply and demand feature strongly. The demand masterplot reflects business as usual and sees law's role primarily as one of reducing demand and reducing greenhouse gas emissions via legal means, such as emissions trading schemes. However, the story of the demand masterplot takes us to a different destination – not a fully decarbonised economy, but a net-zero one (where carbon removals from, for example, CCS can be used to net out remaining carbon emissions). Law's role there, in bringing the heroic CCS future into the present,[93] becomes one of ensuring fossil fuels remain to meet future demand, but with their troublesome emissions removed. The supply masterplot has a different understanding, arguing that the climate crisis necessitates law being much more focused on urgently cutting fossil fuel supply, for example, via moratoriums on new exploration. The first of these two masterplots is delayist. It seeks to slow down the transition, leaving it to consumers to lead a reduction in demand, when in reality the latter are often faced with structural barriers (for example, provision of EV charging infrastructure and training of heat pump fitters) that only government and industry can address. The pipe dream of CCS – an expensive technology yet to be deployed at the removal scale needed – then throws a delayist lifeline to fossil fuel producers, enabling a future for gas as a source of 'clean energy'[94] to be envisaged. The supply masterplot, in contrast, treats the climate crisis as the crisis that it is. It seeks to move the dial more quickly by tackling fossil fuel supply directly and proactively and not relying simply on matching supply to reducing demand or, even worse, increasing supply.

92 Chris Logan and Robert Stiphout, 'Ben van Beurden: Lead with Your Head and Your Heart' *Inside Energy* (12 December 2022) <www.shell.com/inside-energy/lead-with-your-head-and-your-heart.html> accessed 12 July 2023.

93 Stokes, and Hilson (n 8).

94 Lawson (n 86).

The current chapter set out not only to identify these two competing masterplots but also to show how individual narratives draw upon them. Some of those narrative examples were legislative; however, the majority I examined were statements made about the energy transition and fossil fuels that clearly drew upon the respective masterplots. Even where these narrative statements were not made in an explicitly legal context like the Paris Agreement COPs or in court proceedings, they are still important for law, because law typically reflects the dominant understanding of a particular policy issue. A battleground to try to change that understanding is therefore worth paying attention to.

The Ukraine war complicated the picture with the renewed salience of the energy trilemma and, in particular, the elements of energy security and affordability. The fossil fuel industry was previously always on the back foot on the environmental sustainability aspect of the trilemma, which was where its defensive demand arguments came in. However, these other two elements of the trilemma emboldened the Conservative government and industry, in their post–Ukraine war narratives, to make more excuses for continuing or even increasing production of fossil fuels and delaying the transition to a decarbonised economy. While the climate movement had to acknowledge both security of supply and affordability as important issues, it pointed instead to renewables and energy efficiency and other demand reduction measures as the way to address those issues. In any event, what we saw was that the three frames of the energy trilemma complicated the previously relatively straightforward narratives based on the two masterplots, albeit that the masterplots themselves remained unchanged.

Index